The Cognitive Neuroscience of Human Communication

The Cognitive Neuroscience of Human Communication

Vesna Mildner

Lawrence Erlbaum Associates
Taylor & Francis Group

New York   London

Lawrence Erlbaum Associates
Taylor & Francis Group
270 Madison Avenue
New York, NY 10016

Lawrence Erlbaum Associates
Taylor & Francis Group
2 Park Square
Milton Park, Abingdon
Oxon OX14 4RN

International Standard Book Number-13: 978-0-8058-5436-7 (Softcover) 978-0-8058-5435-0 (Hardcover)

Library of Congress Cataloging-in-Publication Data

Mildner, V (Vesna)
    The cognitive neuroscience of human communication / Vesna Mildner.
        p. cm.
    Includes bibliographical references and index.
    ISBN 0-8058-5435-5 (alk. paper) -- ISBN 0-8058-5436-3 (pbk.) 1.
    Cognitive neuroscience. 2. Communication--Psychological aspects. 3.
    Communication--Physiological aspects. I. Title.

QP360.5.M53 2006
612.8'233--dc22
                                          2005049529

Visit the Taylor & Francis Web site at
http://www.taylorandfrancis.com

*For Boris,
without whom none of this would
be possible or even matter.*

Contents

Foreword

Raymond D. Kent

As humans try to understand themselves, one of the greatest fascinations—and most challenging problems—is to know how our brains create and use language. After decades of earnest study in a variety of disciplines (e.g., neurology, psychology, psycholinguistics, neurolinguistics, to name a few), the problem of the brain and language is now addressed especially by the vigorous interdisciplinary specialty of cognitive neuroscience. This specialty seeks to understand the neural systems that underlie cognitive processes, thereby taking into its intellectual grasp the dual complexities of neuroscience and cognition. In her extraordinary book, Vesna Mildner gives the reader a panoramic view of the progress that cognitive neuroscience has made in solving the brain–language problem.

Mildner covers her topic in eight chapters that can be read in any order. Each chapter is a tightly organized universe of knowledge; taken together, the chapters are complementary in their contribution to the overall goal of the book. The first chapter addresses basic aspects of the development, structure, and functioning of the human central nervous system (CNS), arguably the most complexly organized system humans have ever tried to fathom. The author systematically identifies and describes the tissues and connections of the CNS, thereby laying the foundation for the succeeding chapters that consider the topics of sex differences, the history of neurolinguistics, research methods, models and theories of the central nervous system, lateralization and localization of functions, learning and memory, and—the culminating chapter—speech and language. The sweep of information is vast, but Mildner succeeds in locking the pieces together to give a unified view of the brain mechanisms of language.

Science is a procession of technology, experiment, and theory. Mildner's comprehensive review shows how these three facets of scientific progress have shaped the way we comprehend the neurological and cognitive bases of language. From early work that relied on "accidents of nature" (brain damage resulting in language disorders) to modern investigations using sophisticated imaging methods, the path to knowledge has been diligently pursued. The unveiling of the brain through methods such as functional magnetic resonance imaging and positron emission tomography has satisfied a scientific quest to depict the neural activity associated with specific types of language processing. Today we stand at a remarkable confluence of information, including behavioral experiments on normal language functioning, clinical descriptions of neurogenic speech and language disorders, and neuroimaging of language processes in the intact living brain. But the profound potential of this synthesis is difficult to realize because the knowledge is spread across a huge number of journals and books. Vesna Mildner offers us a precious gift of scholarship, as she distills the information from more than 600 references to capture the science of brain and language.

Preface

This book is intended for those interested in speech and its neurophysiological basis: phoneticians, linguists, educators, speech therapists, psychologists, and any combination of *cognitive* and/or *neuro-* descriptions added. In order to get a comprehensive picture of speech production and perception, or representation of speech and language functions in the brain, it is usually necessary to go through page after page, actual and virtual, of texts on linguistics, psychology, anatomy, physiology, neuroscience, information theory, and other related areas. In most of them language is covered in one or at best a few very general chapters, with speech as a specific, but the most uniquely human means of communication, receiving even less attention and space. On the other hand, the books that focus on language do not have enough information on the neurophysiological bases of speech and language either with respect to production or perception. My intention was to make speech the central topic, and yet provide sufficient up-to-date information about the cortical representation of speech and language, and related topics (e.g., research methods, theories and models of speech production and perception, learning and memory). Data on clinical populations are given in parallel to studies of healthy subjects, because such comparisons can give a better understanding of intact and disordered speech and language functions.

The book is organized into eight chapters. They do not have to be read in the order they are written. Each of them is independent and may be read at any time or skipped entirely if the reader feels that he or she is not interested in the particular topic or knows enough about it. However, to those who are just getting acquainted with the topic of the neurophysiological bases of speech and language I recommend starting with chapter 1 and reading on through to the last chapter.

The first chapter is an overview of the development, structure, and functioning of the human central nervous system, particularly the brain. It is perhaps the most complex chapter with respect to terminology and the wealth of facts, but the information contained therein is necessary for a better understanding of the neurophysiological bases of speech and language. When introduced for the first time, each technical term (anatomical, physiological, evolutional, etc.) is given in English and Greek/Latin. Besides the sections on the development, structure, and organization of the central nervous system, the chapter includes sections on sensation and perception and on the neural bases of perception and production of speech. The latter section deals with hearing and the auditory cortex, with movement and speech production, and addresses the various ways in which speech perception and production are related.

Chapter 2 is a brief account of differences between the sexes in neuroanatomy, development, and behavior. Awareness of these differences is important for a better understanding of the linguistic development and functioning of males and females, since these differences frequently become apparent in various aspects of speech/language disorders (e.g., aphasias and developmental dyslexia).

In chapter 3, I present chronologically the major ideas, theories, and historical milestones in research on the mind–brain relationship (particularly with respect to speech and language). In addition to the well-known names (e.g., Broca and Wernicke), the chapter includes persons who have been frequently unjustly neglected in neurolinguistic literature in spite of their important contributions. The chapter sets the stage for the results of research that are discussed throughout the rest of the book, and that span the second half of the 20th century to the present.

Chapter 4 is a review of research methods. It includes the descriptions, with the advantages and the drawbacks, of the techniques that are at present the methods of choice in clinical and behavioral studies (e.g., fMRI), as well as those that are for various reasons used less frequently but their results are available in the literature (e.g., cortical stimulation). The chapter includes a review of the studies of split-brain patients, cortical stimulation studies, radiological methods, electrophysiological methods, ultrasound and radioisotopic techniques, and the most frequent behavioral methods (e.g., dichotic listening, divided visual field, gating, priming, and Stroop).

In chapter 5, I examine different models and theories—from the older, but still influential ones (e.g., Wernicke–Geschwind model) to the most recent that are based on modern technologies (e.g., neural networks). The chapter starts with the short description of the most important principles of the central nervous system functioning (e.g., hierarchical organization, parallel processing, plasticity, and localization of functions), which theories and models explain.

Chapter 6 explains the key terms and dichotomies related to functional cerebral asymmetry (e.g., verbal–spatial, local–global, analytic–holistic), and also some less frequently mentioned ones (e.g., high vs. low frequencies, categorical vs. coordinate). It includes a section on developmental aspects of lateralization, within which the various aspects of asymmetry are considered: neuroanatomical asymmetry, motor asymmetry, asymmetry of the senses, and asymmetry in other species. There is also a section on the factors that affect functional asymmetry of the two hemispheres, and a section on the lateralization of functions, including cerebral representation of various functions.

Chapter 7 deals with the different types of learning and memory, with particular emphasis on speech and language. The existing classifications of learning and memory types are discussed and are related to their neural substrates. There are sections on nervous system plasticity and critical periods, as important factors underlying the acquisition and learning of the first and all subsequent languages.

Finally, chapter 8, albeit the last, is the main chapter of the book, and is as long as the rest of the book. It is subdivided into sections corresponding to different levels of speech and language functions, and includes sections on bilingualism and speech and language disorders. Here are some of the section titles:

- Speech and Language Functions and Their Locations in the Brain
- Anatomic Asymmetries and Lateralization of Speech and Language
- Speech Production and Perception

- Phonetics and Phonology
- Tone and Prosody
- Lexical Level and the Mental Lexicon
- Sentence Level—Semantics and Syntax
- Discourse and Pragmatics
- Reading, Writing, Calculating
- Is Speech Special?
- Language Specificities
- Bilingualism
- Speech and Language Disorders (e.g., Aphasia, Dyslexia)
- Motor Speech Disorders (e.g., Apraxia of Speech, Stuttering)
- Other Causes of Speech and Language Disorders (e.g., Epilepsy, Right-Hemisphere Damage).

The reference list contains more than 600 items and includes the most recent research as well as seminal titles. The glossary has almost 600 terms, which will be particularly helpful to the readers who wish to find more information on topics that are covered in the test. I felt that the book would read more easily if extensive definitions and additional explanations were included in the glossary rather than making frequent digressions in the text. Also, some terms are defined differently in different fields, and in those cases the discrepancies are pointed out. A comprehensive subject index and author index are included at the end.

Relevant figures can be found throughout the text, but there is an added feature that makes the book more reader-friendly. In the appendix there are figures depicting the brain "geography" for easier navigation along the medial–lateral, dorsal–ventral, and other axes (Figure A.1). Brodmann's areas with the cerebral lobes (Figure A.2), the lateral view of the brain with the most important gyri, sulci, and fissures (Figure A.3), the midsagittal view, including the most important brainstem and subcortical structures (Figure A.4), the limbic system (Figure A.5), and the coronal view with the basal ganglia (Figure A.6). Since many brain areas are mentioned in several places and contexts throughout the book, rather than leafing back and forth looking for the fixed page where the area was mentioned for the first time, or repeating the illustrations, the figures may be referred to at any point by turning to the appendix.

Many friends and colleagues have contributed to the making of this book. First of all I'd like to thank Bill Hardcastle for getting me started and Ray Kent for thought-provoking questions. Special thanks go to Damir Horga, Nadja Runjić;, and Meri Tadinac for carefully reading individual chapters and providing helpful suggestions and comments. I am immeasurably grateful to Dana Boatman for being with me every step of the way and paying attention to every little detail—from chapter organization to relevant references and choice of terms—as well as to the substance. She helped solve many dilemmas and suggested numerous improvements. Her words of encouragement have meant a lot. Jordan Bićanić was in charge of all the figures. He even put his vacation on hold until they were all completed, and I am thankful that he could include work on this book in his busy schedule. Many thanks to Ivana Bedeković, Irena Martinović, Tamara Šveljo, and Marica Živko for technical and moral support.

I am grateful to Lawrence Erlbaum Associates and Taylor & Francis Group for giving me the opportunity to write about the topic that has intrigued me for more than a decade. Emily Wilkinson provided guidance and encouragement, and promptly responded to all my queries. Her help is greatly appreciated. I also with to thank Joy Simpson and Nadine Simms for their assistance and patience. Michele Dimont helped bring the manuscript to the final stage with much enthusiasm.

Finally, I wish to thank my husband, Boris, for all his help, patience, support, and love.

Naturally, it would be too pretentious to believe that this book has answers to all questions regarding speech and language. I hope that it will provide the curious with enough information to want to go on searching. Those who stumble upon this text by accident I hope will become interested. Most of all, I encourage readers to share my fascination with the brain, as well as with speech and language, as unique forms of human communication.

—**Vesna Mildner**

1 Central Nervous System

This chapter is an overview of the development, structure, and functioning of the central nervous system, with special emphasis on the brain. All areas that are discussed later, in the chapter on speech and language, are described and explained here, in addition to the structures that are essential for the understanding of the neurobiological basis of speech and language. More information and details, accompanied by excellent illustrations, may be found in a number of other sources (Drubach, 2000; Gazzaniga, Ivry, & Mangun, 2002; Kalat, 1995; Kolb & Whishaw, 1996; Pinel, 2005; Purves et al., 2001; Thompson, 1993; Webster, 1995). For easier reference and navigation through these descriptions, several figures are provided in the appendix. In Figure A.1 there are the major directions (axes): lateral—medial, dorsal—ventral, caudal—rostral, superior—inferior, and anterior—posterior. Brodmann's areas and cortical lobes are shown in Figure A.2. The most frequently mentioned cortical structures are shown in Figures A.3 through A.6. These and other relevant figures are included in the text itself. At the end of this chapter there is a section on the neural bases of speech production and perception and their interrelatedness.

THE DEVELOPMENT OF THE CENTRAL NERVOUS SYSTEM

Immediately after conception a multicellular blastula is formed, with three cell types: ectoderm, mesoderm, and endoderm. Bones and voluntary muscles will subsequently develop from mesodermal cells, and intestinal organs will develop from endodermal cells. The ectoderm will develop into the nervous system, skin, hair, eye lenses, and the inner ears. Two to 3 weeks after conception the neural plate develops on the dorsal side of the embryo, starting as an oval thickening within the ectoderm. The neural plate gradually elongates, with its sides rising and folding inward. Thus the neural groove is formed, developing eventually, when the folds merge, into the neural tube. By the end of the 4th week, three bubbles may be seen at the anterior end of the tube: the forebrain (*prosencephalon*), the midbrain (*mesencephalon*), and the hindbrain (*rhombencephalon*). The rest of the tube is elongated further and, keeping the same diameter, becomes the spinal cord (*medulla spinalis*). The forebrain will eventually become the cerebral cortex (*cortex cerebri*). During the 5th week the forebrain is divided into the *diencephalon* and the *telencephalon*. At the same time the hindbrain is divided into the *metencephalon* and *myelencephalon*. In approximately the 7th gestation week the telencephalon is transformed into cerebral hemispheres, the diencephalon into the thalamus and related structures, while the *metencephalon* develops into the *cerebellum* and the *pons*, and the *myelencephalon* becomes the medulla (*medulla oblongata*).

During the transformation of the neural plate into the neural tube, the number of cells that will eventually develop into the nervous system is relatively constant—approximately 125,000. However, as soon as the neural tube is formed, their number rises quickly (proliferation). In humans that rate is about 250,000 neurons per minute. Proliferation varies in different parts of the neural tube with respect to timing and rate. In each species the cells in different parts of the tube proliferate in unique ways that are responsible for the species-specific folding patterns. The immature neurons that are formed during this process move to other areas (migration) in which they will undergo further differentiation. The process of migration determines the final destination of each neuron. The axons start to grow during migration and their growth progresses at the rate of 7 to 170 μm per hour (Kolb & Whishaw, 1996). Between the eighth and tenth week after conception the cortical plate is formed; it will eventually develop into the cortex. Major cortical areas can be distinguished as early as the end of the first trimester. At the beginning of the third month, the first primary fissures are distinguishable, for example, the one separating the cerebellum from the cerebrum. Between the 12th and the 15th week the so-called subplate zone is developed, which is important for the development of the cortex. At the peak of its development (between the 22nd and the 34th week) the subplate zone is responsible for the temporary organization and functioning. During that time the first regional distinctions appear in the cortex: around the 24th week the lateral (Sylvian) fissure and the central sulcus can be identified; secondary fissures appear around the 28th week; tertiary fissures start to form in the third trimester and their development extends into the postnatal period (Judaš & Kostović, 1997; Kostović, 1979; Pinel, 2005; Spreen, Tupper, Risser, Tuokko, & Edgell, 1984). Further migration is done in the inside-out manner: the first cortical layer to be completed is the deepest one (sixth), followed by the fifth, and so on, to the first layer, or the one nearest to the surface. This means that the neurons that start migrating later have to pass through all the existing layers. During migration the neurons are grouped selectively (aggregation) and form principal cell masses, or layers, in the nervous system. In other words, aggregation is the phase in which the neurons, having completed the migration phase and reached the general area in which they will eventually function in the adult neural system, take their final positions with respect to other neurons, thus forming larger structures of the nervous system. The subsequent phase (differentiation) includes the development of the cell body, its axon and dendrites. In this phase, neurotransmitter specificity is established and synapses are formed (synaptogenesis). Although the first synapses occur as early as the end of the 8th week of pregnancy, the periods of intensive synaptogenesis fall between the 13th and the 16th week and between the 22nd and the 26th week (Judaš & Kostović, 1997). The greatest synaptic density is reached in the first 15 months of life (Gazzaniga et al., 2002). In the normal nervous system development these processes are interconnected and are affected by intrinsic and environmental factors (Kostović, 1979; Pinel, 2005; Spreen et al., 1984). In most cases the axons immediately recognize the path they are supposed to take and select their targets precisely. It is believed that some kind of a molecular sense guides the axons. It is possible that the target releases the necessary molecular signals (Shatz, 1992). Some neurons emit chemical substances that attract particular axons, whereas others emit substances that reject them. Some neurons extend one fiber toward the surface and when the fiber ceases to grow, having reached the existing outer layer, the cell body travels along the fiber to the surface, thus participating in the formation of the cortex. The fiber then becomes the axon, projecting from the cell body (now in the cortex) back to the original place from which the neuron started. This results in the neuron eventually transmitting the information in the direction opposite to that of its growth (Thompson, 1993). The neurons whose axons do not establish synapses degenerate and die. The period of mass cell death (*apoptosis*) and the elimination of unnecessary neurons is a natural developmental process (Kalat, 1995). Owing to great redundancy, pathology may ensue only if the cell death exceeds the normal rate (Strange, 1995). The number of synapses that occur in the early postnatal period (up to the second year of life) gradually decreases (pruning) and the adult values are reached after puberty. Since these processes are the most pronounced in the association areas of the cortex, they are attributed to fine-tuning of associative and commissural connections in the subsequent period of intensive cognitive functions development (Judaš & Kostović, 1997). Postmortem histological analyses of the human brain, as well as glucose metabolism measurements in vivo, have shown that in humans, the development and elimination of synapses peak earlier in the sensory and motor areas of the cortex than in the association cortex (Gazzaniga, Ivry, & Mangun, 2002). For example, the greatest synaptic density in the auditory cortex (in the temporal lobe) is reached around the third month of life as opposed to the frontal lobe association cortex, where it is reached about the 15th month (Huttenlocher & Dabholkar, 1997; after Gazzaniga et al., 2002). In newborns, glucose metabolism is highest in the sensory and motor cortical areas, in the hippocampus and in subcortical areas (thalamus, brainstem, and *vermis* of the cerebellum). Between the second and third month of life it is higher in the occipital and temporal lobes, in the primary visual cortex, and in basal ganglia and the cerebellum. Between the 6th and the 12th month it increases in the frontal lobes. Total glucose level rises continuously until the fourth year, when it evens out and remains practically unchanged until age 10. From then until approximately age 18 it gradually reaches the adult levels (Chugani, Phelps, & Mazziotta, 1987). Myelination starts in the fetal period and in most species goes on until well after birth.

From the eighth to the ninth month of pregnancy brain mass increases rapidly from approximately 1.5 g to about 350 g, which is the average mass at birth (about 10% of total newborn's weight). At the end of the first year, the brain mass is about 1,000 g. During the first 4 years of life it reaches about 80% of the adult brain mass—between 1,250 and 1,500 g. This increase is a result of the increase in size, complexity, and myelination—and not of a greater number of neurons (Kalat, 1995; Kostović, 1979; Spreen, Tupper, Risser, Tuokko, & Edgell, 1984; Strange, 1995). Due to myelination and proliferation of glial cells, the brain volume increases considerably during the first 6 years of life. Although the white matter volume increases linearly with age and evenly in all areas, the gray matter volume increases nonlinearly and its rate varies from area to area (Gazzaniga et al., 2002). Brain growth is accompanied by the functional organization of the nervous system, which reflects its greater sensitivity and ability to react to environmental stimuli. One of the principal indicators of this greater sensitivity is the development of associative fibers and tracts; for example, increasing and more complex interconnectedness is considered a manifestation of information storage and processing. Neurophysiological changes occurring during the 1st year of life are manifested as greater electrical activity of the brain that can be detected by EEG and by measuring event-related potentials (ERPs; Kalat, 1995). Positron emission tomography (PET) has revealed that the thalamus and the brainstem are quite active by the fifth week postnatally, and that most of the cerebral cortex and the lateral part of the cerebellum are much more mature at 3 months than at 5 weeks. Very little activity has been recorded in the frontal lobes until the age of about 7.5 months (Kalat, 1995). Concurrent with many morphological and neurophysiological changes is the development of a number of abilities, such as language (Aitkin, 1990). In most general terms, all people have identical brain structure, but detailed organization is very different from one individual to the next due to genetic factors, developmental factors, and experience. Genetic material in the form of the DNA in the cell nucleus establishes the basis for the structural organization of the brain and the rules of cell functioning, but development and experience will give each individual brain its final form. Even the earliest experiences that we may not consciously remember leave a trace in our brain (Kolb & Whishaw, 1996).

Changes in cortical layers are closely related to changes in connections, especially between the hemispheres. Their growth is slow and dependent on the maturation of the association cortex. Interhemispheric or neocortical connections (commissures) are large bundles of fibers that connect the major cortical parts of the two hemispheres. The largest commissure is the *corpus callosum,* which connects most cortical (homologous) areas of the two hemispheres. It is made up of about 200 million neurons. Its four major parts are the trunk, *splenium* (posterior part), *genu* (anterior part), and the *rostrum* (extending from the *genu* to the anterior commissure). The smaller anterior commissure connects the anterior parts of temporal lobes, and the hippocampal commissure connects the left and the right hippocampus. The hemispheres are also connected via *massa intermedia,* posterior commissure and the optic chiasm (Pinel, 2005). Most interhemispheric connections link the homotopic areas (the corresponding points in the two hemispheres; Spreen et al., 1984), but there are some heterotopic connections as well (Gazzaniga et al., 2002). Cortical areas where the medial part of the body is represented are the most densely connected (Kolb & Whishaw, 1996). It is believed that neocortical commissures transfer very subtle information from one hemisphere to the other and have an integrative function for the two halves of the body and the perceptual space. According to Kalat (1995), information reaching one hemisphere takes about 7 to 13 ms to cross over to the opposite one. Ringo, Doty, Demeter, &

Simard (1994), on the other hand, estimate the time of the transcortical transfer to be about 30 ms. Ivry and Robertson (1999) talk about several milliseconds. In their experiments on cats, Myers and Sperry (as cited in Pinel, 2005) have shown that the task of the corpus callosum is to transfer the learned information from one hemisphere to the other. The first commissures are established around the 50th day of gestation (anterior commissure). Callosal fibers establish the inter-hemispheric connections later and the process continues after birth until as late as age 10 (Kalat, 1995; Lassonde, Sauerwein, Chicoine, & Geoffroy, 1991). Corpus callosum of left-handers was found to be about 11% thicker than that of the right-handers, which was attributed to greater bilateral representation of functions (Kalat, 1995; Kolb & Whishaw, 1996). There is disagreement among authors considering the sex differences in callosal size (for more information, see chap. 2, this volume). Myelination of corpus callosum proceeds during postnatal development and it is one of the parts of the nervous system whose myelination begins and ends last. It is thought that the callosal evolution has an impact on hemispheric specialization (Gazzaniga et al., 2002). In Alzheimer's patients, the area of corpus callosum, especially of its medial part (*splenium*), is significantly smaller than in healthy individuals (Lobaugh, McIntosh, Roy, Caldwell, & Black, 2000).

After the age of 30 the brain mass gradually decreases and by the age of 75 it is approximately 100 g smaller (Kolb & Whishaw, 1996). Although the brains of people in their seventies have fewer neurons than the brains of younger people, in healthy elderly individuals the decrease is compensated for by the dendrites of the remaining neurons becoming longer and branching more (Kalat, 1995). Some recent studies have revealed that in rare cases and in a very limited way in some parts of the brain, particularly in the hippocampus and the olfactory bulb (*bulbus olfactorius*), a small number of neurons may develop after birth and during lifetime (Purves et al., 2001). However, whether these newly formed neurons have any function in the adult nervous system remains to be determined (Drubach, 2000; Gage, 2002; Gazzaniga et al., 2002; Gould, 2002).

STRUCTURE AND ORGANIZATION OF THE CENTRAL NERVOUS SYSTEM

The nervous system consists of nerve cells—neurons—and glial cells (that will be discussed later). The neuron is a functional and structural unit of the brain. It consists of the cell body (soma) with the nucleus built from DNA, and other structures characteristic of cells in general, one or more dendrites, and one axon that ends with the presynaptic axon terminals (Figure 1.1). The neuron transmits information to other cells and receives information from them. The dendrites and the body receive information while the axon transmits information to other neurons. The space between neurons is filled with extracellular fluid so that in general they are not in direct contact.

The size of the smallest neurons is approximately 7 to 8 μm, whereas the largest ones range in size between 120 and 150 μm (Judaš & Kostović, 1997). Axons of some human neurons may be one meter or longer, whereas others do not

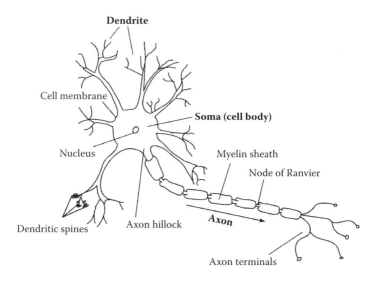

FIGURE 1.1.   A stylized neuron.

exceed several tens or hundreds of micrometers. Most axons are between several millimeters and several centimeters long. The diameter of the thinnest axons is about 0.1 μm. At the end of each axon there are usually several smaller fibers that end with the terminal node. Each node synapses with another cell.

A neuron may have a few short fibers or a huge number. The greater the number of dendrites, the greater the receptive ability of the neuron. In the cerebral cortex, many neurons' dendrites are covered by literally thousands of little processes—dendritic spines. Since each one of them is a postsynaptic part of the synapse, the number of connections is greatly increased. These synapses are most probably excitatory.

All neurons, from the simplest to the most complex organisms, rely on identical electrochemical mechanisms for information transmission. The considerable differences in neuronal organization, for example, in the patterns of their interconnections, are responsible for the functional differences that distinguish, for instance, the humans from other species. Neurons may be grouped into pathways or tracts (a simple series of neurons)—for example, the auditory pathway; into neuronal circles or networks; and into neuronal systems—for example, the auditory system. Each neuron may have connections to thousands of other neurons, which means that it may affect their activity. It can in turn be influenced by thousands of other neurons with excitatory or inhibitory results. There are no unnecessary or reserve neurons—each one has a function. Neuronal populations differ in size, shape, manner of information processing, and transmitters that they use to communicate with other neurons. Those that occupy neighboring positions in the brain and share common functions usually belong to the same population and have identical physical and functional properties. This principle is metaphorically referred to as "Neurons that fire together wire together." This means that some are specialized for visual information, others for auditory stimuli, and still others for emotional expressions. These functions are not interchangeable. However, in spite of such highly specialized properties, there are limited possibilities for the neurons neighboring those that have been injured to take over and assume the new function, different from their original one, which results in the neurofunctional reorganization of the entire affected area. This issue will be addressed in more detail in the context of plasticity in chapter 7, this volume.

Motor (efferent) neurons have richly arborized dendrites, a large body, and a long myelinated axon. They send out their fibers from the nervous system toward the body (parts) and at their ends synapse with muscle fibers and gland cells. They control the activity of skeletal muscles, smooth muscles, and glands. They are controlled by several systems in the brain that are called motor systems.

Sensory (afferent) neurons extend from the body to the brain. Their cell bodies are located along the spinal cord in groups. They are the so-called ganglia. One of their most important properties is selective detection and enhancement of particular stimulus features.

The cerebral cortex is made up of several hundred different types of neurons. They are either pyramidal neurons (principal neurons) or extrapyramidal (interneurons). The principal neurons of a particular area are responsible for the transmission of the final information into other cerebral areas after the processing of incoming information. They are excitatory neurons and make up about 70% of all cortical neurons. They are rich in dendritic spines that contribute to the richness of connections; their axons are long and make projection, association, or commissural fibers. Numerous collateral branches (collaterals) of these axons are the greatest sources of excitatory postsynaptic potentials in the cerebral cortex (Judaš & Kostović, 1997). Interneurons are mainly inhibitory and make up to 30% of all cortical neurons. Their dendrites have no dendritic spines; their axons are short and establish local connections. Neuronal feedback is essential for optimal brain functioning; the brain adjusts its activity on the basis of it.

The number of neurons is greatly (perhaps tenfold) exceeded by the number of glial cells (glia). They make up about 50% of the total brain tissue volume (Judaš & Kostović, 1997). They are not neural cells because they do not transmit information. Their function is not entirely clear, but their roles include absorbing substances in the brain that are not necessary or are excessive (e.g., at the synapses they often absorb excess neurotransmitters); after a brain injury proliferating in the location of neuron damage and removing cell debris, making the so-called glial scars; forming myelin sheaths; establishing the blood–brain barrier; guiding migrating neurons on the path to their final destinations, and so forth (Thompson, 1993; Judaš & Kostović, 1997). Many types of glial cells communicate among themselves and with neurons as well. The neuron–glia–neuron loop is therefore considered to be a more precise description of a communication unit, rather than the simple neuron–neuron connection (Gazzaniga et al., 2002).

The myelin sheath is basically fat. It enables faster propagation of the action potential along axons. There are interruptions in the sheath where the axon is in direct contact with the extracellular fluid, enabling the occurrence of action potentials. These interruptions are the so-called nodes of Ranvier (*nodi Ranvieri*). Myelinated axon segments between the two unmyelinated points are between 200 μm and 1 mm long. Their length depends on the axon type: the greater the axon diameter, the longer the myelinated segments. Consequently, longer myelinated segments, in other words, longer distances between the two nodes, will result in faster impulse conduction. The width of each node is about one μm.

A synapse is a functional connection between two neurons or between a neuron and another target cell (e.g., muscle). It is the point at which the information in the form of a nerve impulse (signal) is transmitted. A tiny space, between 10 to 100 nanometers wide, separates the axon terminal of one cell from the body or a dendrite of another cell with which it communicates. That space is called the synaptic cleft. Synapses can be found only in nerve tissue, because they are formed only between neurons and their target cells. Synapses are functionally asymmetrical (polarized), which means that signal transmission is one-way only. Having said that, it is important to bear in mind the existence of the neuronal feedback—a process that enables communication among nerve cells.

There are two kinds of synapses—chemical and electrical. Most synapses in the brain of mammals are chemical (Figure 1.2; the illustration shows synaptic transmission at a chemical synapse; adapted from Purves et al., 2001). They may be excitatory or inhibitory. Excitatory synapses increase the activity of the target cell, in other words, the probability of occurrence of action potential. Inhibitory synapses decrease target cell activity. The signals are transmitted by means of neurotransmitters that are released (provided that the threshold of activation has been reached) from the presynaptic neuron into the synaptic cleft, from which they are taken up by the corresponding receptors in the postsynaptic membrane. This transfer is very precise and takes less than 1 millisecond. Neurotransmitters are chemical substances that are produced in the presynaptic neuron and stored in the vesicles in the presynaptic axon terminal. About a hundred different kinds of neurotransmitters are known at present. Different neuronal populations produce and react to only one (or a very limited number) type of neurotransmitter. Apart from the excitatory and inhibitory neurotransmitters there are the so-called conditional neurotransmitters, whose activity is affected by the existence of another neurotransmitter or by the neuronal circuit activity (Gazzaniga et al., 2002).

Activation of a single excitatory synapse in the neuron is not sufficient for it to fire: several excitatory synapses have to be activated simultaneously (spatial summation) in order to reach the threshold of action potential. Even simultaneous activation of several synapses may not always result in firing. In such cases these groups of synapses must be activated several times in a row, in short intervals (temporal summation). The same principles of spatial and temporal summation apply to inhibitory synapses. A normal neuron constantly integrates temporal and spatial pieces of information and "makes decisions" on whether to fire or not (neuronal integration). The moment of making a positive decision is the point of reaching the action potential threshold at the axon hillock, which is the result of domination of excitatory over inhibitory effects. It is also possible that a subliminal stimulus (i.e., the one that is not sufficient in itself to reach the action potential thresholds)

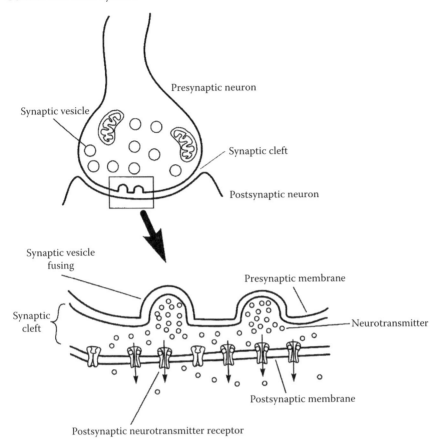

FIGURE 1.2.   Chemical synapse; synaptic transmission. (From Purves et al., 2001. With permission.)

prepares the postsynaptic neuron for the arrival of another subliminal stimulus, which will (owing to that earlier stimulus) reach the action potential threshold. This phenomenon is called *facilitation*. It may be achieved by direct activation of excitatory synapses or by inactivation of inhibitory synapses (Judaš & Kostović, 1997). Experience has a huge effect on the strengthening or weakening of synapses.

As opposed to chemical synapses that exhibit a great deal of plasticity (i.e., may be changed in various ways with increased or decreased activity), electrical synapses are rigid and unchangeable. In electrical synapses there are no synaptic clefts between neurons: their membranes are in direct contact and their cytoplasms are connected through transmembranous channels (gap junction). As a consequence, such neurons have identical potentials, and electrical changes in one of them are immediately reflected on the other. At electrical synapses the transmission is very fast and it may be bidirectional (Purves et al., 2001). Learning and memory would be impossible in a nervous system that had only electrical synapses. However, some electrical synapses have been found in mammalian brains—mainly between cell bodies of neighboring neurons that share the same function.

Nerve impulses are transmitted at the rate of about 1 to 100 meters per second. As it has been mentioned earlier, the rate at which the impulse travels through the axon depends on its diameter (the greater the diameter, the faster the transmission) and on whether it is myelinated or not (the impulse travels faster through myelinated fibers; Sternberg, 2003). The firing rate generally does not exceed 100 times in a second, although some neurons may fire at the very high rate of 1,000 times in a second. A common feature of all neurons is that they function on the all-or-none principle. This means that the action potential will either occur or not. The messages differ in the action potential frequency and the timing of impulses (Ferster & Spruston, 1995; Kalat, 1995). However, neurons may also determine the content of the message that is being transmitted by varying, among other things, the type, quantity, and rate of neurotransmitter release (Drubach, 2000).

Nerves are bundles of nerve fibers. The nerves transmitting the information toward the central nervous system and from it are peripheral nerves. They transmit impulses from the periphery toward the center (sensory fibers, afferent pathways), from the center toward the periphery (motor fibers, efferent pathways), or are positioned between sensory and motor fibers (interneurons). Somatic nerves establish connections with the voluntary skeletal muscles and sense organs. Autonomic nerves are connected with internal organs and glands involved in autonomic aspects of reactions, usually related to emotional behavior (crying, perspiration, some activities of the heart and stomach). All organs are controlled by the sympathetic part of the autonomic nervous system, and some are controlled both by the sympathetic and parasympathetic segment. Peripheral nerves are cranial or spinal.

Cranial nerves (*nervi craniales*) transmit sensory information from the face and head, and commands for motor control over face and head movements. This means that their functions are sensory, motor, or combined. There are 12 pairs of cranial nerves, seven of which are essential for speech production (V through XII). They are numerated from the anterior to the posterior part of the brain:

I   The olfactory nerve (*fila olfactoria*) transmits olfactory information from the nose to the brain (into the *telencephalon*).
II   The optic nerve (*nervus opticus*), actually a part of the visual pathway, transmits visual information from the eyes (it is directly connected to the *diencephalon*).

Nerves III through XII are directly connected to the brainstem:

III   The occulomotor nerve (*nervus occulomotorius*).
IV   The trochlear nerve (*nervus trochlearis*) and VI—the abducens nerve (*nervus abducens*) are responsible for eye muscles.
V   The trigeminal nerve (*nervus trigeminus*) transmits sensory information from the skin of the face and head and innervates the jaw muscles and tensor tympani muscle in the middle ear.

VII　　The facial nerve (*nervus facialis*) has afferent and efferent connections with parts of the face, ear (outer ear, stapedial muscle), tongue, and larynx.

VIII　The vestibulocochlear nerve (*nervus statoacusticus* or *nervus vestibulocochleris*) transmits information about sounds from the ears and about vestibular sense from vestibular part of the inner ear. Some efferent pathways related to that nerve have been found as well (Kent & Tjaden, 1997).

IX　　The glossopharyngeal nerve (*nervus glossopharyngeus*) innervates laryngeal muscles that play an important role in the process of swallowing; it also transmits the sense of taste and sensory information from the outer ear.

X　　The vagus nerve (*nervus vagus*) is important for the autonomic (parasympathetic) control of the heart and other internal organs; it innervates laryngeal and pharyngeal muscles important for phonation; and it transmits the sensations from the outer ear and the sense of taste from the area around epiglottis.

XI　　The accessory nerve (*nervus accessorius*) innervates neck and shoulder muscles as well as the muscles controlling the soft palate.

XII　The hypoglossal nerve (*nervus hypoglossus*) innervates tongue muscles.

There are 31 pairs of spinal nerves (*nervi spinales*). They protrude from the spinal column and innervate the muscles with their motor parts in the anterior portions (they come out from ventral roots). Or they receive afferent information with their sensory parts in the posterior portions (these enter the dorsal roots), to forward it through the spinal cord to the thalamus and the cerebral cortex.

The spinal cord (*medulla spinalis*) is a tube-like structure that extends downward from the brainstem and connects the brain with the parts of the body below the neckline. It is a major thruway for (a) information from the cerebral cortex and other brain structures that control body movements going toward motor neurons (and indirectly through them to the muscles) and toward all the organs in the body (autonomic nervous system), and for (b) information from all receptors, including proprioceptive, and information from some peripheral organs to the brain. The spinal cord is also responsible for reflex muscle and autonomic responses to stimuli. On their way from the brain to the periphery the axons cross over from one side of the tract to the other. Consequently, the motor control of the right side of the body is situated in the left cerebral hemisphere, whereas the right hemisphere controls the left side of the body. Information from the periphery also projects to the hemisphere contralateral to the stimulated side (Drubach, 2000).

The brain (*encephalon*) is a part of the central nervous system (together with the spinal cord). The principal parts of the brain are the following: brainstem, cerebellum, and cerebrum (Figure 1.3).

The brainstem (*truncus cerebri* or *truncus encephalicus*) consists of the medulla (*medulla oblongata*; *myelencephalon*), pons (*pons*; *metencephalon*) and the midbrain (*mesencephalon*). It connects the cerebrum and the cerebellum with the spinal cord, but it also has functions of its own (Drubach, 2000; Judaš & Kostović, 1997; Purves et al., 2001; Webster, 1995). In it there are centers, the

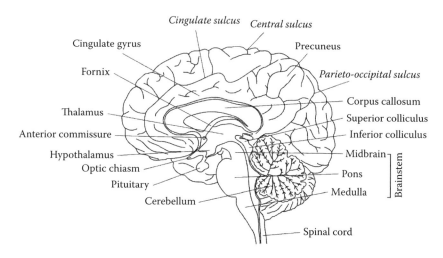

FIGURE 1.3.   Midsagittal view of the brain.

so-called nuclei, made up of groups of neurons, which regulate body temperature; cardiac, respiratory, and gastrointestinal systems; blood vessels; and consciousness. Among other things, they also control the responses to visual and auditory stimuli, movement and, to some extent, wakefulness and sleep. It is believed that motor control of speech stems directly from the basic centers for swallowing and breathing control. Afferent (ascending, sensory) and efferent (descending, motor) pathways go through the brainstem. Reticular formation (*formatio reticularis*) is an important part of the brainstem. It is a heterogeneous set of functionally very different structures (Judaš & Kostović, 1997) through which pass almost all sensory and motor pathways. It is connected with other nuclei in the brainstem, cerebellum, diencephalon and the cerebrum. Injuries to the brainstem may cause paralysis, loss of sensation and/or control of corresponding functions and consciousness, coma, and even death.

The cerebellum is located in the posterior part of the cranial cavity. Its main parts are the cortex, subcortical white matter, and subcortical nuclei. It is one of the philogenetically oldest brain structures. Its surface is convoluted, with fissures, sulci, and gyri much more densely folded than in the cerebrum. It has two hemispheres and a medial part (vermis). The cerebellar cortex is functionally organized in three parts. Various functions are differentiated by specific input–output neuronal connections. On average, its mass is about 145 g. Its cortex is about 1 to 1.5 mm thick and consists of three cellular layers. Despite its relatively small size in proportion to the total brain volume (10%), it contains more than 50% of all neurons of the brain (Judaš & Kostović, 1997). There is a three-pronged connection (cerebellar penduncles) with the rest of the nervous system. Initiation of a voluntary movement (e.g., reaching for an object) will at first reveal a neural activity in the cerebellum (and in the basal ganglia), followed by the activity in the motor cortex of the cerebrum, that has turned out to be responsible for precise performance of fine voluntary movements but not for their initiation

(Thompson, 1993). The cerebellum receives a complex set of sensory information from most modalities: vestibular and auditory, muscles, joints, skin, and the eyes. It is the central place for proprioceptive information. Information related to proprioception, motor planning, and vestibular sense is integrated in the cerebellar cortex. The number of afferent fibers by far exceeds the number of efferent ones; in humans the ratio is about 40 to 1 (Judaš & Kostović, 1997). This means that the cerebellum is an important place for integration and processing of input information before transmitting the output signal to other parts of the brain. On the basis of continuous inflow of sensory information from the periphery, the cerebellum coordinates and smooths out activity of the muscles, and in cooperation with the vestibular system coordinates head movements and body position with all other activities of the body. In other words, it regulates the speed, range, force, and the orientation of movements (Webster, 1995). It seems that the cerebellum plays an important role in learning, particularly in learning and remembering skilled movements, but also in nonmotor learning and numerous cognitive processes (Drubach, 2000). Injuries to the cerebellum may cause clumsiness (particularly purposeful hand movements), balance difficulties, decreased muscle tone, incomprehensible speech, imprecise eye movements, and impaired planning and timing of activities (Drubach, 2000; Kalat, 1995). It might be said that the main role of the cerebellum is to perform temporal calculations that may be used in various perceptive and motor functions, including speech and language. For example, estimating the duration of a sound is impaired in individuals with cerebellar injuries (Gazzaniga et al., 2002; Kent & Tjaden, 1997). As opposed to cerebral injuries, cerebellar injuries cause impairments on the ipsilateral side of the body (due to double crossing of pathways). Body parts are mapped onto the surface of the cerebellar cortex, similarly to the representations found in the cerebral cortex, but due to the lack of association or commissural fibers, each area receives a separate afferent projection and acts as a separate functional unit (Judaš & Kostović, 1997). It is interesting to note that the cytoarchitectonic organization of the cerebellum is identical in all mammals—from mouse to human. The cerebellum and the motor cortex of the cerebrum constitute a constantly active movement control system (Thompson, 1993).

The *diencephalon* is located between the brainstem and the cerebral hemispheres. Its principal parts are the thalamus, hypothalamus, epithalamus, and the subthalamus. Thalamus (originating from the Greek word *thalamos*, meaning bed or bedroom) is a structure almost in the very center of the brain, where numerous fibers synapse and cross. The visual and the auditory signals pass through it and it is also involved in movement control. It has connections with the cerebellum and the basal ganglia. Messages from the limbic system (of which the hypothalamus and epithalamus are important parts) are relayed to the thalamus. The thalamus integrates and interprets signals prior to forwarding them to other parts of the brain. It also plays an important role in memory. With the exception of olfactory information, all stimuli are processed in thalamic nuclei (seven groups in all) before reaching the cerebral cortex. Primary sensory and motor cortical areas receive direct projections from thalamic nuclei. Below the thalamus are the subthalamus and hypothalamus, responsible for emotions, basic body functions, body temperature, pituitary gland activity, hormone release, food and liquid intake, sexual behavior, and circadian rhythms. Below the posterior part of the thalamus (pulvinar) there is the lateral geniculate complex (*corpus geniculatum laterale*) that is a part of the visual system, and the medial geniculate complex (*corpus geniculatum mediale*) that is a part of the auditory system. Recent studies stress the importance of subcortical structures, particularly thalamus and hypothalamus for higher cognitive functions, including language and speech. The hypothalamus is believed to have a role in memory formation (Kent & Tjaden, 1997). Thalamus attracts attention and directs it to verbal information, recall, and so forth. Its role is to enhance and emphasize the information to which the attention is directed at the moment. However, the consequence of thalamic injuries on naming, word finding, arithmetic, verbal short-term memory, and fluency are most frequently transient and short-lived, as opposed to cortical injuries (Bradshaw & Nettleton, 1983). Thalamic injuries typically cause loss of sensation, motor disorders, and consciousness problems.

The cerebrum consists of white (about 39% of volume) and gray (about 61% of volume) matter. There are about 10^{11} to 10^{12} neurons in the cerebrum, of which about 50 billion are directly involved in information processing (Kolb & Whishaw, 1996; Strange, 1995). Each neuron makes about 1,000 to 3,000 connections with other neurons, which means that the number of connections is huge—about 10^{14} (Churchland, 1988). In the cerebral cortex there are about 10 billion neurons.

The mass of the adult brain ranges from 1,100 to 1,700 g. On average, adult male brains weigh approximately 1,450 g, and adult female brains about 1,300 g, which makes about 2.5% of total body mass. The smaller mass of the female brain does not imply poorer abilities. First of all, smaller mass is compensated for by richer connections, and second, it seems that the ratio of brain mass to total body mass is a better indicator of brain development than its absolute mass (Drubach, 2000). For example, whales and elephants have larger brains than humans, but the density of their cortical cells is most likely smaller. The differences in cortical size are also associated with the differences in the cerebral cortex circuits (Hill & Walsh, 2005). In any case, of all the species, humans have the largest brain with respect to their body size. Note also that the newborn's ratio of brain mass to body mass is greater than in the adult (Sternberg, 2003). For as yet unknown reasons, in the past 3 million years there has been an explosion in the size of the human brain, unrecorded in any other species. This sudden growth is mostly attributable to the considerable enlargement of the cortex (Thompson, 1993). The brain is immersed in the cerebrospinal fluid and protected by the firm bony shell of the skull and three tissue layers (meninges). It is connected to the rest of the body (i.e., to the peripheral nervous system) by means of 12 pairs of cranial nerves. The connection with the spinal cord is realized through rich nerve connections (descending efferent and ascending afferent pathways; Judaš & Kostović, 1997). It is generally believed that brains of exceptional people do not differ from those of average individuals with respect to mass, structure, and functioning. However, there is some evidence obtained by magnetic resonance imaging that the correlation between intelligence and brain size is about 0.35 (Kalat, 1995). Moreover, by comparing Einstein's brain with several dozen brains of average people Wittleson found considerable differences in the position of Sylvian fissure as well as in the area and thickness of the inferior temporal lobe (Gazzaniga et al., 2002). Human brains differ from the brains of other primates mainly in the richness of their associative (corticocortical) and projection (subcortical) connections and in quantitatively different organization. For example, the prefrontal area is twice as large as that in other primates, whereas the motor, olfactory, and visual areas are smaller (Kalat, 1995; Kolb & Whishaw, 1996). Philogenetic studies have shown that the proportions of various functional areas change during the development of the species.

White matter consists of bundles of myelinated neuron axons (myelin is responsible for its white color) that connect the two hemispheres (commissural fibers), the cerebral cortex with lower parts of the nervous system (afferent and efferent projection fibers), or that connect various parts of the same hemisphere (short and long association fibers). Deep within the white matter are the ventricles (*ventriculi;* Judaš & Kostović, 1997).

Gray matter is made of the cell bodies and their dendrites. It is found on the surface (cortex cerebri, cortex) and deep within the brain separated from the cortex by white matter (basal ganglia; Webster, 1995). The area of the convoluted surface layer is about 2,200 square cm and its thickness varies between 1.5 and 4.5 mm. The fissures (*fissurae*) and sulci divide the surface into lobes (*lobi*), lobules (*lobuli*), and gyri (Judaš & Kostović, 1997). Most of the cortex is organized into six layers of cells that have ontogenetically developed from the inside out and make up the *neocortex.* This term is synonymous with the term *isocortex,* reflecting the fact that each part of the adult cerebral cortex developed from the same developmental base, and makes up almost 90% of the total cerebral cortex (Judaš & Kostović, 1997). During development, in a smaller part of the isocortex the number of layers either decreases or increases. In evolutionarily older parts of the cortex (allocortex) there are commonly fewer than six layers: two in the paleocortex, three in the archicortex, and five in the mesocortex. These parts make up the limbic system. The five basic functional groups of cortical areas to the largest extent correspond to the basic types of cerebral cortex. They are: (a) primary sensory and motor areas; (b) unimodal association areas; (c) heteromodal association areas; (d) limbic areas; and (e) paralimbic areas. The term *cortex* is commonly used to refer to neocortex. The cells vary in form, size, and distribution across areas, so cytoarchitectonically we talk about nuclei, layers (laminae), areas, and regions that have different cell structure (Judaš & Kostović, 1997). This diversity is partly responsible for the complexity of brain structure. Kolb and Whishaw (1996) have summarized the principles of cortical organization:

1. The cortex is made of many different types of neurons that are organized into six layers (laminae).
2. The cortex is organized into functional columns (columnae), which means that the neurons that share similar functions are grouped into

columns that stretch throughout the cortex, making the cortical column the principal organizational and functional unit.

3. There are multiple representations of sensory and motor functions in the cortex.
4. These functions are plastic.
5. Cortical activity is influenced by feedback from several regions of the forebrain (e.g., from the limbic system or the basal ganglia).
6. The cortex operates on the principles of hierarchical and parallel information processing.

The cerebrum is divided by the longitudinal fissure (*fissura longitudinalis cerebri*) into two hemispheres that are connected by three large systems of commissural fibers: corpus callosum, anterior commissure (*commissura anterior*), and the hippocampal commissure (*commissura hippocampi*). Corpus callosum is the largest and the most important interhemispheric connection. Each hemisphere is divided morphologically into four lobes clearly delimited by anatomical landmarks (fissures and sulci): (a) central sulcus, which is sometimes referred to as Rolandic fissure (*fissura centralis Rolandi*); (b) lateral fissure, also called the Sylvian fissure (*fissura lateralis cerebri Sylvii*); and (c) the parieto–occipital fissure (sulcus) or incision (*fissura s. incisura parietooccipitalis*). The sulci and fissures alternate with gyri. At the bottom of the Sylvian fissure there is the insula that it sometimes referred to as the fifth lobe (Drubach, 2000; Judaš & Kostović, 1997; Figure 1.4).

At the beginning of the 20th century Corbinian Brodmann used different staining techniques on samples of brain tissue to establish a system of cell types with respect to their structure (cytoarchitecture). He drew brain sketches using different symbols to represent cell groups differing in shape, density, and laminar organization, assuming that cells that have the same or similar structure perform

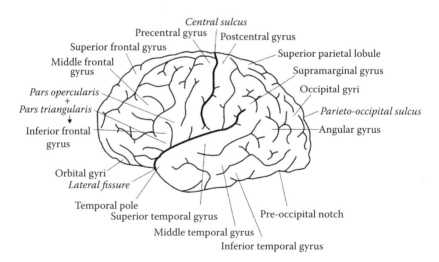

FIGURE 1.4. Lateral view of the brain.

the same or similar functions. This yielded about 50 cytoarchitectonically relatively homogenous areas that are called Brodmann's areas and are marked by
Arabic numerals (Figure 1.5).

The frontal lobe (*lobus frontalis*) is anterior to the central sulcus and above the
lateral fissure. It is the seat of primary and secondary motor areas. The primary
motor area corresponds to Brodmann's area 4. The secondary motor area includes
premotor cortex and the supplementary motor area (dorsolateral and medial parts
of Brodmann's area 6, respectively), Brodmann's areas 8, 44, and 45, and the
posterior cingulate area. Each location in the primary motor areas controls a particular group of muscles on the opposite side of the body. Secondary motor areas
are anterior to the primary ones. Each of them controls several primary centers
and they are responsible for complex movements and voluntary muscle control. In
the language-dominant hemisphere (usually left, but see chap. 8, this volume, for
discussion), in Brodmann's area 44 and probably 45, there are centers that control
speech (Broca's area) and writing. The prefrontal region is responsible for memory storage and retrieval, ethical attitudes, decision making, and psychological
makeup of a person (Judaš & Kostović, 1997). In humans, this region constitutes
about half of the entire frontal lobe. It is connected with almost all other parts of

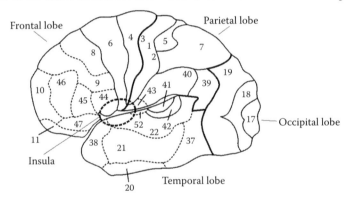

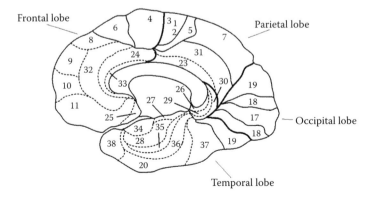

FIGURE 1.5. Brodmann's areas in lateral and midsagittal view, including the four lobes.

the brain and receives information from all sensory areas, memory and emotional stores (Kalat, 1995; Webster, 1995). The prefrontal cortex sends projections into all areas from which it receives them, into premotor and motor regions in both hemispheres. The motor cortex is considered to be a place where a multitude of signals involved in initiating and shaping motor control from other parts of the cortex and deeper levels, such as basal ganglia or the cerebellum, are integrated (McKhann, 1994). It seems that, in addition to the neurons in the primary motor cortex, there are a number of circuits, including the cerebellum, basal ganglia, and the thalamus, that generate motor activity. Consequently, it is logical that the motor aspect of language relies on similar circuits. Almost all types of behavior involve both frontal lobes, so in most tasks, with the exception of higher cognitive functions, unilateral brain injury will have negligible consequences. Frontal lobes are crucial in learning a new task that requires active control. Once the activity has become routine other parts of the brain may assume control (Lieberman, 1991). Raichle (1994) proposed that the parts of the nervous system that are involved in learning certain motor patterns are not the same ones that are used for performing the once learned patterns. Functional magnetic resonance imaging (fMRI) data revealed increased activity in the supplementary motor area and lateral premotor cortex after initial task presentation—when the planning of movement starts. As planning turns into execution the activity shifts toward the more posterior regions, and as the movement becomes more complex, the structures outside the primary motor cortex are activated (Gazzaniga et al., 2002). Some of the manifestations of frontal lobe injuries are impaired motor functions, ignoring of social conventions, inflexible and unorganized behavior, inability to correct errors, perseveration, poor temporal memory, poor egocentric orientation, changed social and sexual behavior, and disorders related to damage of face representations, including language and speech or some of their segments (Kolb & Whishaw, 1996). Positron emission tomography (PET) data have revealed that frontal lobes are activated during internal generation of stimuli (by the subject), as opposed to external stimuli, which has led to the conclusion that they probably play a part in conscious distinction between actual and imagined stimuli (Drubach, 2000). During evolution, frontal lobes of humans have undergone enormous enlargement, particularly in the anterior portions. This enlargement is related to the higher cognitive abilities characteristic of humans (Gazzaniga et al., 2002). In fact, there seems to be a correlation between evolutionary patterns and gene function in humans. Characterization of genes for neurological disorders (such as mental retardation, autism, and dyslexia) that affect intelligence, social organization, and higher order language will hopefully shed more light on human evolutionary history (Hill & Walsh, 2005).

The parietal lobe (*lobus parietalis*) is bordered anteriorly by the central sulcus, posteriorly by the parieto–occipital fissure (sulcus), and laterally by the Sylvian (lateral) fissure. Immediately posterior to the central sulcus there are primary somesthetic centers that receive information from sensory organs (proprioception, touch, pressure, temperature, pain; Brodmann's areas 1, 2, and 3). In the postcentral gyrus there are four parallel representations of the body (Kalat,

1995). A part of that lobe is the angular gyrus (*gyrus angularis*), which plays a very important role in word reading and arithmetic (in the left hemisphere). The inferior parietal lobe is involved in writing, which makes that lobe (together with the temporal lobe) essential for language processing and comprehension. That lobe is also important for orientation on one's own body, particularly with respect to the left–right orientation. The disorders that occur as a consequence of injury to this lobe (apraxia, tactile agnosia, alexia, agraphia, acalculia, autotopagnosia) suggest that it is important for secondary processing of input information (i.e., for coordination of input information from sense organs and output commands to the muscles). It is particularly important for the association and coordination of visual and spatial information (Kalat, 1995). This lobe also seems to be the seat of the short-term/working memory (Kolb & Whishaw, 1996; for more discussion on types of memory see chapter 7, this volume).

The temporal lobe (*lobus temporalis*) is inferior to the lateral (Sylvian) fissure, and extends posteriorly to the parieto–occipital fissure (sulcus). When the lateral fissure is pulled open one to three Heschl's gyri (*gyri temporales transversi Heschl*) are revealed. This area is the seat of cortical representation of the sense of hearing—the auditory cortex (Brodmann's areas 41 and 42). Immediately posterior to Heschl's gyri is a relatively flat area, the so-called *planum temporale*. The posterior part of the superior temporal gyrus (Brodmann's area 22), commonly in the left hemisphere, is the seat of secondary processing of auditory speech stimuli—the center for speech perception (Wernicke's area). Although processing of music stimuli has been associated with right-hemisphere function, there is evidence that hemispheric differences are dependent on proficiency in music (Ivry & Robertson, 1999; Pinel, 2005). Amusia patients reveal that the anterior parts of the superior temporal gyri are responsible for music production and processing (Gazzaniga et al., 2002; Grbavac, 1992). The cortical representation of vestibular function is also in the superior temporal gyrus. The temporal lobe is involved in complex aspects of visual information processing, for example, in face recognition (Kalat, 1995). The temporal lobe in the left hemisphere is the seat of verbal long-term memory (recollection of stories, word lists, etc., regardless of modality of their presentation). The temporal lobe in the right hemisphere is the seat of nonverbal long-term memory (geometrical drawings, faces, tunes etc.; Kolb & Whishaw, 1996). The temporal lobe is also the seat of learning and memory functions that require conscious effort—declarative or explicit learning (Kandel & Hawkins, 1992). Injuries to the temporal lobe cause disorders in stimulus categorization, and Kolb and Whishaw (1996) have grouped the consequences of such disorders into eight groups:

1. Disorders of auditory sense and perception.
2. Disorders of selective attention in the auditory and visual modality.
3. Disorders of visual perception.
4. Disorders in the organization and categorization of verbal material.
5. Disorders in language comprehension, including the inability to use context.

6. Disorders in visual and auditory long-term memory.
7. Personality and affective behavior changes (motivation, fear).
8. Changes in sexual behavior.

Obviously, contribution of the frontal, parietal, and temporal lobes to all of the above processes is additive and probably hierarchically organized. The fact that similar types of behavior may occur after injuries to different areas supports the claims that the same cognitive processes may be disordered in different ways. These cognitive processes are based on joint activities of large areas of neocortical and subcortical tissues, and may therefore be impaired as a consequence of functional disorders or injuries in any of the involved regions (Kolb & Whishaw, 1996).

The occipital lobe (*lobus occipitalis*) is the area posterior to the parieto–occipital fissure (sulcus). It is the seat of the primary visual area (Brodmann's area 17). Next to that area are Brodmann's areas 18 and 19, which are responsible for secondary visual processing. Due to its striped appearance the primary visual area is also known as the striate cortex or the striate area (*area striata*). The neighboring areas are called the extrastriate visual area (*area extrastriata*) (Judaš & Kostović, 1997). The occipital lobe is exclusively responsible for visual information processing (Webster, 1995). Information from the left visual field reaches the right hemisphere, and information from the right visual field travels to the left hemisphere, but almost all regions of the visual cortex are reached by the information from the thalamus and from the opposite hemisphere (Lomber & Payne, 2002). The location of an injury will determine which visual field will be blind. Information about different visual attributes is not stored in one place. The cells responsible for visual perception are highly specialized: some are activated only by vertical lines, others by horizontal lines, whereas others are sensitive to color or specific forms, movements of particular speed, and so forth. Each of the cells contributes to the overall mental image. Apart from being highly specialized, the cells are hierarchically determined, so that the first line processes only the simplest visual data, such as contrast, the second line processes shapes, and the following layer interprets them. In this way, each subsequent layer provides additional data to the mental image until the object is recognized (Drubach, 2000). The processing is not exclusively one way, from periphery to the visual cortex (bottom up); there are also feedback projections from the higher order visual areas that contribute to the analysis of the basic properties of the response and structural properties in the primary visual cortex (top down). In other words, processing of any visual stimulus is actually based on interaction among several cortical areas (networks) at different hierarchical levels (Galuske, Schmidt, Goebel, Lomber, & Payne, 2002). One path goes from the striate area through the extrastriate area into the temporal lobe (ventral pathway) and carries information about the properties and the appearance of the stimulus. This is the so-called *what* pathway, responsible for identification and discrimination of the stimulus. The other path goes into the parietal lobe (dorsal pathway) and carries information about the movement and spatial position of the object. This is the so-called *where* pathway. Knowledge about the object is located in a distributed cortical system, so that the information about particular features is stored in the vicinity of the cortical areas that participate in the perception of these features (Unger-leider, 1995). A person suffering from cortical blindness has normal peripheral vision, but cannot perceive patterns and has no awareness of visual information due to an organic lesion in the visual cortex. Other disorders of visual percep-tion (agnosia) may take the form of impaired ability to recognize colors, faces, objects, depth, movements, and so forth (Drubach, 2000; Kalat, 1995).

The insula got its name from the fact that it is separated from the surrounding areas by a circular sulcus. It is located at the bottom of the Sylvian fissure and cov-ered by parts of the parietal, frontal, and temporal lobes. These parts that hide the insula are called opercula (plural of *operculum*—Latin for lid), and depending on the lobe they belong to, are called the frontal operculum (*operculum frontale*), the fronto–parietal operculum (*operculum frontoparietale*), and the temporal opercu-lum (*operculum temporale*; Judaš & Kostović, 1997). The insula is considered to be an important structure for speech, and there has been some evidence that the insula in the dominant hemisphere, rather than Broca's area, might be the seat of speech motor planning (Dronkers, 1996, 2000; Duffau, Capelle, Lopes, Faillot, & Bitar, 2000). The anterior portion of the insula is active during processing and integration of autonomic and body information. Its posterior part is connected to other neocortical areas; the connections with the cortical and subcortical struc-tures, particularly with the thalamus and basal ganglia, reveal its importance for somatosensory, vestibular, and motor integration. It is an integrative multimodal association area for information arriving from different senses. The insula plays an important part in the cardiovascular, gastrointestinal, vestibular, olfactory, gustatory, visual, auditory, somatosensory, and motor processes. It seems that it plays a part in conditioned learning, affective and emotional components of noci-ception (perception of pain), stress-invoked immunosuppression, mood stability, sleep, and language (Flynn, Benson, & Ardila, 1999).

The association cortex comprises parts of the cerebral cortex that receive data from several modalities, and thus its role is integrative rather than exclusively motor or sensory, which is crucial for higher mental processes. For example, the association cortex at the border between the parietal, temporal, and occipital lobes of the left hemisphere is essential for successful processing of language data. Although for a long time the prevalent opinion had been that most parts of the neocortex are associative, in the past 15 years it has become increasingly clear that the cortex is mainly sensory and motor, and that complex brains do not develop by expansion of the association cortex but rather through the increase of sensory and motor areas and connections among them (Kaas, as cited in Gaz-zaniga et al., 2002).

The limbic system lies along the corpus callosum (Latin word *limbus* means borderline). It is related to biological rhythm, sexual behavior, feelings of fear, anger, and motivation (Figure 1.6). In other words, the limbic system controls and processes emotions, and manages endocrine and autonomic systems. Amygdala are particularly important for the regulation of drives, affective and motivational states, and autonomic and endocrine functions (Judaš & Kostović, 1997; Sternberg,

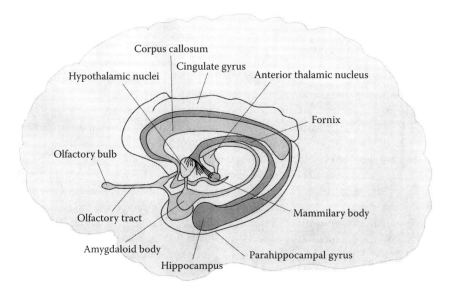

FIGURE 1.6.   The limbic system.

2003). During evolution some parts of the limbic system (e.g., the hippocampus) have assumed other functions as well. It is believed that, in higher animals, the hippocampus is one of the key structures in learning and memory. The hippocampus may host different types of information at the same time and one of its major roles is integrating different details or elements of episodic memory traces and coding current experience, to be subsequently stored in memory (Hampson & Deadwyler, 2002; Payne, Jacobs, Hardt, Lopez, & Nadel, 2002). More on the hippocampus may be found in chapter 7. Within the limbic system the hypothalamus is the key passage for different neuronal circuits (Judaš & Kostović, 1997). The cingulate gyrus (*gyrus cinguli*) is located immediately above the corpus callosum. Physical and mental emotional expressions are integrated in the hypothalamus and in the insula, which explains the fact that each of these two types of emotions may have manifestations characteristic of the other (Drubach, 2000).

Basal ganglia are located deep within the cerebrum (Figure 1.7). This structure is actually a group of nuclei (putamen, globus pallidus, nucleus caudatus, substantia nigra, subthalamus) made of gray matter. They interact with the cerebral cortex, thalamus, reticular formation and parts of the midbrain and spinal cord, and are important for motor functions (primarily voluntary and many involuntary ones), including speech (Webster, 1995). Due to their connections with the association areas of the cerebrum they have a direct influence on the affective, language, and other cognitive processes (Judaš & Kostović, 1997; Lieberman, 1991). Their injury will result in weak and uncoordinated movements (Kalat, 1995), in several types of involuntary movements, such as jerks, tremor, and so forth (Judaš & Kostović, 1997), and in cognitive disorders as well. Parkinson's disease is the most frequent and the most extensively studied neurological disorder related to the basal ganglia.

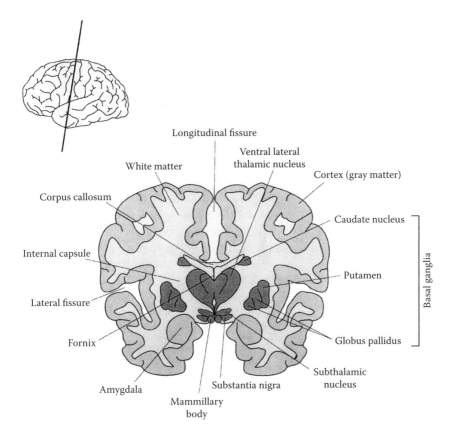

FIGURE 1.7.   Coronal (frontal) view of the brain with the basal ganglia.

Although the cerebellum and basal ganglia are important for planning, initiation, and performance of movements, their roles are different. The cerebellum creates the movement by trial-and-error learning and the final movement is optimal for the particular situation and the set goal. Basal ganglia release the movement from general tonic restraint, allow nonrival positions and movements to develop and prevent rival activity (Thach, Mink, Goodkin, & Keating, 2000). Warren, Smith, Denson, and Waddy (2000) have shown the importance of basal ganglia in speech planning, word recall, and short-term verbal memory. Their 53-year-old bilingual (English–German) patient, who had suffered a stroke in the left posterior *nucleus lentiformis* (a part of the subthalamus, i.e., basal ganglia), presented with apraxia of writing and speech in both languages. Detailed language tests revealed disorders in articulation, fluency, repetition of auditory stimuli, interpretation of complex semantic relations, definition forming, and short-term verbal memory.

The connections between the cortex and subcortical areas are very important for the functioning of the brain, because the injuries in those pathways may cause behavioral disorders that are identical to those caused by injuries in particular functional areas (Kolb & Whishaw, 1996).

The brain's major foodstuffs are glucose and oxygen. Although it is only about 2% of the total body mass, it is responsible for about 20% of total oxygen and about 50% of total glucose consumption (Strange, 1995).

SENSATION AND PERCEPTION

The prerequisites for the occurrence of sensation are (a) the existence of a stimulus; (b) the processes that convert the stimulus into bioelectrical signals suitable for neuronal transmission; and (c) the specific response of the organism to the coded message. All sensory systems are organized hierarchically, in a parallel manner, and topographically (Judaš & Kostović, 1997).

The first intermediary between the outside world and the body is the sensory receptor. It converts the received input energy, which may be mechanical, thermal, chemical or electromagnetic, into electrochemical energy, which fulfills one of the most important requirements of information transfer to the central nervous system (in the form of action potentials). Besides the general functioning principles common to all senses, each sensory modality has its peculiarities. For example, in the visual modality, different receptors are responsible for the black-and-white data/contrast (rod cells of the retina) from those that are responsible for colored input (cone cells). Within a single modality there may exist different receptors for specific stimulus features (different segments of a visual stimulus have been discussed already). In addition to being modality-specific (visual, auditory, gustatory, olfactory, somatosensory), all receptors may transmit the sense of pain in cases of excessive stimulation.

The sensory transduction of the input stimulus into electrochemical energy is followed by neural coding of the stimulus in the primary sensory neurons that are in direct contact with the receptors. Neural coding includes information about stimulus modality, intensity, duration, and location. With the exception of olfaction, information from all sensory organs passes through the thalamus on its way to the cerebrum. The thalamus selects the bits of information to be passed on and directs them to the appropriate location in the cortex. The selected information is transmitted to the primary (modality-specific) areas in both hemispheres. Approximately at the level of the thalamus and the primary cortical areas information is grouped into wholes (*gestalts*). This process ensures the distinction of form from the background, in other words, drawing relevant information from all available stimulus characteristics. Information is then transferred from the primary to the secondary areas, where the wholes (i.e., their meaning) are recognized. Secondary cortical areas are also modality-specific. The term *perception* is used when there is sensory awareness, and that awareness is typically formed at the secondary cortical level. In other words, perception is conscious reception, adoption, and interpretation of external stimuli (exteroception) or those from one's own body (interoception, proprioception). One of the prerequisites of perception is the existence of intracortical phenomena. Conscious sensation may be elicited only if stimulation lasts at least several hundreds of milliseconds (as indicated by electrical stimulation of the sensory cortex in awake patients). Perception is the keenest in the areas of sharpest contrast (Judaš & Kostović, 1997).

Complex information is processed in the tertiary areas, so that the information arriving from the secondary areas is integrated and combined with affective data. In other words, this is where new information is interpreted in the light of previous experience and existing knowledge. That is part of the reason why these areas are also called association areas: a familiar odor may bring to life the image and the sound associated with it, because at some point in our life the stimuli from all three modalities were present at the same time. Pleasant and unpleasant emotions may also be associated with the event. Cerebral (mental) representation of an object, person, or anything else, for that matter, includes the corresponding physical properties, but also the unique affective and experiential components.

Although it is impossible to draw a clear line between sensation and perception, it is generally accepted that sensation is subcortical whereas perception is cortical (Pinel, 2005). To put it more precisely, sensation is the outcome of the activity of receptors and their afferent pathways to appropriate sensory areas in the cortex, and perception is the result of the activity of the cerebral cells after the first synapse in the sensory cortex (Kolb & Whishaw, 1996).

Attention plays a very important role in stimulus perception. In speech, it may be crucial for message comprehension. Some studies have shown that the subjects were able to extract very little information from the message presented to one ear while they were focusing on the other. Many of them had not even noticed that the stimuli presented to the unattended ear were in a foreign language or that it was speech reproduced backwards. Accordingly, very little of the information presented to the unattended ear was stored in memory. Contrary to that, if the other message is physically different or has been changed it will be easier to detect: for example, a male voice presented to one ear and a female voice to the other (Eysenck & Keane, 2000). Escera, Alho, Schröger, and Winkler (2000) found, using event-related potentials (ERP), that very small changes in the properties of an auditory stimulus activate the auditory cortex (temporal lobe) in both hemispheres, even in situations where the stimuli were not attended to.

There is an ongoing controversy about the minimal perceptual unit of speech. There are equally abundant arguments for it to be the sound, the phoneme, the syllable, or the speech measure. The authors, who claim that the smallest unit is the sound or the phoneme, nonetheless believe that the decisions pertaining to sounds and phonemes are made in a wider context—at least to the syllable level. The criterion of processing efficiency does not help resolve the problem either. Namely, smaller units (e.g. phonemes) are less taxing on the memory, but processing is considerably slower than where larger units are involved. On the other hand, larger units, due to their great number of possible combinations, are more demanding on the memory. In any case, it is clear that prelexical processing implies some sort of transformation of acoustic–phonetic information into abstract representations.

Since the main topic of this book is speech, it seems appropriate to shed some additional light on hearing as the primary path of its perception and on movement as the primary means of its production.

NEURAL BASES OF SPEECH PERCEPTION AND PRODUCTION

HEARING, LISTENING AND THE AUDITORY CORTEX

In humans, the first reaction to sound, manifested as startle reflex, occurs approximately 16 weeks before birth. Such a reaction, albeit very primitive, already points to the active relationship between the auditory stimulus and motor reaction to it. More sophisticated reactions, such as orienting reflexes, take longer to develop. The auditory system is ready to receive sound and initiate action potentials at birth. It has been shown that electrical stimulation of the auditory pathway may cause impulses in the auditory cortex even before the final maturation of the synapse between receptor cells and the auditory nerve (Aitkin, 1990). Studies of congenitally deaf cats have revealed that electrical stimulation of the cochlea may result in normal spatial and temporal patterns in their auditory cortex (Klinke, Hartmann, Heid, & Kral, 2002). Keeping in mind the importance of the spectral pattern of auditory stimuli in determining the firing patterns of mature auditory cortical neurons, it is possible that temporal characteristics of surrounding sounds are important factors in synaptogenesis that occurs in the auditory cortex.

The auditory pathway is the path from the peripheral organ (i.e., the ear), to the auditory cortex, structured as a very complex network of connections. Stimuli from each ear are transmitted ipsilaterally and contralaterally along several lines. Approximately one third of the information reaches the same side, and two thirds the opposite. The first neuron of the auditory pathway is located in the inner ear, specifically in the spiral ganglion of the cochlea, and it is in direct contact with the receptors in the organ of Corti. The cochlear nerve (*nervus cochlearis*) is a branch of the vestibulocochlear nerve (*nervus vestibulocochlearis*—the VIII cranial nerve, which is commonly referred to as the auditory nerve), and consists of some 30,000 to 40,000 axons. The vestibular branch (*nervus vestibularis*), which is responsible for balance, consists of some 8,000 to 10,000 axons (Judaš & Kostović, 1997). Axons of the auditory nerve synapse in the ipsilateral cochlear nucleus (*nucleus cochlearis*). In addition to transmitting the tonotopic representation of the cochlea, considerable processing of the auditory signal takes place there. At this level there are at least six different neural responses, resulting from complex interactions and neural processing (Seikel, King, & Drumright, 1997). A number of projections from cochlear nuclei reach the superior olivary nuclei (*nucleus olivaris superior*) at the same level. Some go to the ipsilateral superior olivary nucleus, others to the contralateral side. Neurons in olivary nuclei have two large dendrites each: the right one receives information from the right ear and the right cochlear nucleus, the left one receives information from the left ear and the left cochlear nucleus. These dendrites can detect time differences in the activation from the left and right ear that are as short as several microseconds. This ability is partly responsible for sound localization (Gazzaniga et al., 2002; Thompson, 1993). Superior olivary nuclei are the first location where interaural differences in auditory signal intensity (particularly for high frequencies) and phase (particularly for low frequencies) differences are detected. The differences reflect different stimulation of the left and the right ear by the auditory stimulus due to its position in space relative to the listener. In other words, there are neurons that react to specific stimuli features (the so-called feature detectors) and transmit the recognized and analyzed signal features to the cerebral cortex. In this way the complex sound signals are analyzed into their components. Inferior colliculi (*colliculus inferior*) receive bilateral signals from superior olives and indirectly from cochlear nuclei via the lateral lemniscus (*lemniscus lateralis*). Several responses occur here as well; it seems that at this level the intensity-difference data are combined with the phase-difference data again. Each inferior colliculus is an integration nucleus of the central auditory pathway, where about a dozen projections from the lower auditory nuclei in the brainstem, from the contralateral inferior colliculus, and from the auditory cortex come together (Syka, Popelar, Nwabueze-Ogbo, Kvasnak, & Suta, 2002). The medial geniculate body (*corpus geniculatum mediale*) is the last synapse in the diencephalon (in the thalamus). Here, the tonotopic organization is manifested as the projection of: (a) the ventral part of the medial geniculate ipsilaterally into the primary auditory cortex in the temporal lobe (Brodmann's area 41); (b) the medial part into other regions of the temporal lobe (Brodmann's areas 42 and 43); and (c) the dorsal part into the so-called cortical association areas. The diversity of neural responses has been preserved at this level as well. Some neurons are sensitive to very small intensity differences between signals reaching the two ears (Seikel, King, & Drumright, 1997).

In summary, the cochlea performs the first analysis of complex sound stimuli into their components. Cochlear nuclei, superior olives, and lateral lemniscus nuclei code different aspects of the stimulus (frequency, intensity, timing) and transmit the processed information via six parallel paths into the medial nuclei of inferior colliculi. At the lateral lemniscus level, the left and the right auditory pathways are connected by Probst commissure. This commissure also has crossed projection fibers by means of which the connection with the contralateral inferior colliculus is established. All the information is integrated and synthesized here before being forwarded to the medial geniculate body in the thalamus and subsequently to the primary auditory cortex where the different aspects of the stimulus are to be recognized. The left and the right auditory pathways are connected (in addition to the level of lateral lemniscus) by the inferior colliculi commissure and by corpus callosum at the cortical level. Tonotopic organization is preserved in all auditory nuclei and in auditory cortices of both hemispheres. Cochlear representation is preserved through the auditory pathway, but it multiplies at the central levels. This redundancy is the key to our ability to analyze and understand very complex sounds. Obviously, the auditory pathway is a network of separate but intertwined neural mechanisms that are adapted for the transmission of highly specific, detailed information from periphery to the brain. Cells in the subcortical nuclei react to the wider frequency bands than the cells that are higher in the system. Other sensory systems have parallel ascending pathways, but in the auditory pathway there are more parallel paths than in the other modalities, there are more synapses in the brainstem nuclei, and, finally, after converging, they again go their separate ways into different parts of the auditory cortex (Webster, 1995). Giraud et al. (2000) have found, using the fMRI, that the human auditory system is organized as a hierarchical filter bank with parallel processing, so that each processing level has its preferred stimulus frequency but is able to respond to all others. Such structure makes possible separate transmission of groups of frequencies containing different bits of information, but at the same time preserves the possibility of integration of complementary features in the auditory cortex.

Besides the dorsal surface of the superior temporal gyrus and the small transverse temporal gyri of Heschl, the majority of the human primary auditory cortex (Brodmann's areas 41 and 42) and the neighboring areas of the secondary auditory cortex (Brodmann's area 22) are located deep within the Sylvian (lateral) fissure. There are variations in the location and the size of cortical areas. This is especially true of the primary auditory area, mostly due to the great variability in the Heschl's gyrus (Schönwiesner, Von Cramon, & Rübsamen, 2002). The primary auditory cortex receives input primarily from the opposite ear via the ipsilateral medial geniculate body. At that level the tonotopic representation is realized as columnar organization such that each column is made up of neurons that react to similar frequencies—much like the organization of hair cells in the cochlea. However, Schönwiesner et al. (2002) question the strict tonotopic organization, based on their fMRI studies of humans and other primates in which they found several locations characteristic for each frequency. Takahashi et al. (2002) reported that tonotopic organization is affected by the stimulus intensity: stimuli of higher intensity are less clearly tonotopically organized. Different neurons in the columns react to different elements of the stimulus (e.g., upward or downward frequency or intensity modulation). This is analogous to the already mentioned columnar organization of the primary visual cortex, with the neurons in different columns sensitive to different components of the visual stimulus such as movement, color, slant, and so forth (Scheich, Ohl, & Brechmann, 2002; Seikel et al., 1997). Neuroimaging techniques have revealed that different structures are involved in the processing of sound properties (the ventral "what" path) and location (the dorsal "where" path). In that respect, the auditory and the visual systems are comparable as well (Anourova et al., 2002; Kusmierek, Laszcz, Sadowska, & Kowalska, 2002). Although both pathways are present in both hemispheres, even a unilateral brain injury may cause difficulties in sound recognition and localization (Clarke et al., 2002). With respect to the perception of tactile information, however, Van Boven, Ingeholm, Beauchamp, Bikle, and Ungerleider (2005) found no dorsal/ventral dissociation. In their fMRI study of tactile form and localization processing, they found a hemispheric lateralization effect manifested as selective left intraparietal sulcus activation in the form detection task, and selective activation of the right temporoparietal junction in the location discrimination task, independent of the stimulated hand.

By means of fMRI Binder et al. (2000) have found that parts of the auditory cortex in which spectral information is represented are separated from those where the intensity sensitivity is represented. Both are located on the dorso-lateral surface of the temporal lobe in both hemispheres, and although they involve neighboring regions, there is no overlap. Sound intensity is represented in the caudomedial part of Heschl's gyri and the neighboring parts of the transverse temporal sulcus, whereas spectral information is represented in the rostrolateral part of Heschl's gyri and the neighboring parts of the transverse temporal sulcus.

Due to its location deep within the Sylvian fissure, the auditory cortex is well protected from injury and even the most severe bilateral injuries to the temporal cortex do not result in deafness. Patients with damaged auditory cortex perceive simple auditory stimuli without problems, but they have difficulty in identifying very short stimuli, in discriminating sounds presented in short intervals and in judging the temporal sequence of sounds presented in short intervals. Consequently, patients with extensive auditory cortex damage often complain of difficulties in perceiving fast speech (Pinel, 2005). Damage to the auditory cortex in the left hemisphere, dominant for speech in most people, usually has more serious consequences. Although the auditory cortex is mostly located in the temporal lobe, several areas of the secondary auditory cortex (each of them a tonotopically organized map) extend into the parietal lobe. It has been shown that patients with extensive auditory cortex damage that extends into the parietal lobe have trouble locating the sound source, especially if the injury is in the right hemisphere. The right hemisphere was found to be crucial in the discrimination of the direction of frequency modulation—upward or downward (Scheich et al., 2002).

Despite the fact that speech information has been processed to a great extent before reaching the auditory cortex (a large portion of information necessary to decode speech is processed in subcortical auditory nuclei), many aspects of speech (e.g., speaker variability, coarticulation) are attributed to perception that takes place in the cortex. Durif, Jouffrais, and Rouiller (2002) found that some cortical neurons process both physical properties of sounds and their relevance for behavior. The auditory cortex is not just a final point of bottom-up analysis, but also an important part of the top-down system, that is actively directed toward particular aspects of the sound stimulus, depending on the type of information that needs to be extracted from the input pattern (Scheich et al., 2002). Although there is no clear distinction between auditory projections and auditory processing on the one hand, and areas where speech and language are decoded, on the other, it is believed that conscious processing of speech takes place at the cortical level.

Even very young (1-month-old) infants are able to distinguish sound categories, for example, /p/ versus /b/. Electrophysiological studies have shown that 3-month-old infants have neuronal networks for phonological processing similar to adults (Dehaene-Lambertz & Baillet, 1998). These results used to be taken as evidence of the inborn speech ability to categorize phonemes perceptually. However, it has been found that children are just as successful in distinguishing among nonspeech sounds, and that the ability is present in other mammals as well. Apart from being able to categorize the sounds of their mother tongue, in their first six months of life children learn to normalize across speakers, sound contexts, and prosodic features. Cross-linguistic studies of children have revealed selective sensitivity to their mother's voice and the sounds of the mother tongue, suggesting the influence of prenatal auditory experience. The recognition of the mother tongue and its discrimination from other spoken languages within the first six months relies primarily on prosodic features, only to be followed by the development of sensitivity to segmental features. This is attributed to the fact that, in infant-directed speech, the mothers (or other caregivers) talk more slowly, using higher pitch and more pronounced intonation variations. These suprasegmental features enable babies to distinguish comforting (long, smooth, falling intonation), from warning and disapproval (short, sharp intonation patterns), or calling and drawing attention (rising intonation; MacNeilage, 1997).

MOVEMENT AND SPEECH PRODUCTION

Movement is a readily visible product of cerebral activity directed at acting on the world around us. Movement initiation and coordination are controlled by the brain. The entire course of the movement, from its planning to execution, is hierarchically organized. In this respect it resembles the reception and interpretation of stimuli (in reverse order). The highest wrung on the hierarchical ladder is occupied by groups of neurons whose main purpose is to plan movements. These neurons are located in the tertiary (premotor, association) cortical areas. Actions are planned on the basis of available perceptual data, experience and goals, with the help of the cerebellum and basal ganglia. Tertiary areas are responsible for very complex movements (e.g., speech) and they control primary and secondary motor areas. Secondary areas control and coordinate several muscle groups. The commands are relayed to lower levels until they reach the neurons in the primary motor cortex (Brodmann's area 4) that will activate individual muscles or small muscle groups in order to fulfill the set goal—executing the desired movement. The execution is controlled by motor neurons in the brainstem and the spinal cord by means of commands that reach effector organs, that is, muscles.

Simple movements require minimal processing and are limited mostly to the primary motor and sensory areas. Increasing complexity results in increased activated areas, in such a way that the activation spreads to the regions anterior to the primary motor area in both hemispheres. This bilateral activation can be explained by the activation of some abstract motor plan that is yet to be perfected for a specific activity, or it may reflect activation of several alternative motor plans with the same goal. The one finally selected will result in increased lateralized activity of the motor cortex, related to the activity of the contralateral effector organ, for instance, the hand. This selection process involves the supplementary motor area (Brodmann's area 6) as well. It is particularly important for hand coordination in complex motor tasks. Obviously, the entire process has to be parallel and interactive at the same time.

Feedback is present at all levels. Based on the sensory data the execution programs are modified with the purpose of fulfilling the task optimally and efficiently—yielding maximum results with minimal effort. In the process, the thalamus plays a very important role: it relays information from the sensory areas to the corresponding motor areas. However, the movement does not depend exclusively on feedback involving peripheral data. There are internal representations of movement patterns as well. Even profoundly hearing-impaired patients, who have lost their hearing postlingually, can speak well despite the loss of auditory control. Obviously, kinesthetic feedback is at play here, but it would not be sufficient were it not for fixed movements the patient can rely on. The longer the period without the feedback, the less reliable the patterns will be. As it has already been mentioned above, the cerebellum and basal ganglia also play very important parts in planning, coordination, and execution of movements. It is believed that the cerebellum is particularly important for the functioning of the speech rhythm generator. This means that it is the seat of the neural center for syllable timing that is independent of afferent (sensory and proprioceptive) information or that it actually controls the center (Horga, 1996).

Traditionally, it was believed that the motor cortex was the only starting point of the pyramidal tract (that was thought to be the highest level of motor control). It seems, however, that only about 60% of pyramidal tract motor neurons originate in the motor cortex, whereas the rest of them originate in Brodmann's area 6 and in the parietal lobe. It also seems that the motor cortex is not the place where the movement originates, but rather it is a conduit for information about movement arriving from other cortical and subcortical areas. Studies have shown that the pyramidal tract comprises numerous fibers that originate in the cortex and that influence the sensory transmission at the subcortical level and at the spinal cord level (for a review see Kent & Tjaden, 1997).

In short, the studies of humans and other primates indicate that motor planning involves parallel circuits. One of them—including the parietal lobe, lateral premotor pathways, and the cerebellum—is important for movements in space. The other circuit, that includes the supplementary motor area, basal ganglia and, possibly, the temporal lobe, is activated once the skill has been mastered (Gazzaniga et al., 2002).

The type of functional disorder depends, naturally, on the location and extent of lesion. Lower-level injuries will impair the execution of specific movements of particular muscles or muscle groups. Higher-level injuries will impair planning and coordination, entirely or to a great extent, which will result in impaired execution of all but the simplest movements. In the case of speech production, which requires a very high degree of planning and coordination of numerous muscles, this means that an injury to the tertiary area will impair speech production, despite the preserved ability to move individual muscles involved in speech. Contrary to that, after damage to the area responsible for the movement of one of the articulators, speech may be difficult but not necessarily impossible. For example, damage to Brodmann's areas 6 and 44 will result in speech apraxia that is manifested as nonfluent speech and uncoordinated complex speech movements; damage to Brodmann's area 7 will cause conduction aphasia, manifested as phonological paraphasias, omissions, and transpositions, but without affecting fluency. Stuttering is explained by some authors as a consequence of inappropriate lateralization and/or uncoordinated functioning of both hemispheres. This may be realized as simultaneous and uncoordinated bilateral control or as uncoordinated callosal communication between the two hemispheres. Both explanations are based on the right hemisphere involvement in speech production to the

extent that hinders efficient processing and control by the left hemisphere (generally dominant for speech). In other words, stuttering is a consequence of intra-
and interhemispheric interference between functionally related areas of cerebral
cortex (Webster, as cited in Horga, 1996).

Let's say a few more words about movement in speech. All speech production models assume three phases, of which the second and the third are basically
simultaneous: (a) organization of speech motor programs; (b) realization of these
programs by converting the commands to appropriate muscles into a series of
articulatory movements; and (c) conversion of articulatory movements into actual
speech sound. The articulation program is a part of the speech motor program,
not its synonym (Horga, 1996). The distinction between the articulation and
speech program is clearer if we agree that motor program does not include pre-
defined commands to the articulators, but that it is conditioned by context and the
set goal. In harmony with the goal and the continuous feedback (auditory, tactile,
proprioceptive) it adjusts actual efferent stimuli (i.e., execution of the articulation
program) to the current context (Horga, 1998, 2002a).

It is believed that some common mechanisms are at work in movement in
general, and specifically in speech movement. There is evidence that regions
around Broca's area are not only involved in series of speech movements, but
also in series of movements in general. There are numerous examples of brain
injuries that result in parallel impairment of speech and general motor functioning. Saygin, Wilson, Dronkers, and Bates (2004) have found that not just speech
production but speech comprehension as well may be impaired together with
comprehension of action (pantomime interpretation). They concluded that brain
areas important for the production of language and action are also active in their
comprehension. Moreover, they suggest that brain is organized for action processing. This is not to be confused, however, with the composition of the muscles
themselves—Kent (2004) reviewed a large body of literature and concluded that
speech muscles (mandibular, lingual, palatal and laryngeal) are unique in their
fiber composition, distinguishing them from other muscles in the human body.
Hauk and Pulvermüller (2004) also studied the correlation between action words
and specific cortical areas, and similarly to Saygin et al., suggest a possible role of
mirror neurons in the premotor cortex in language processing. Another argument
in favor of this view is the parallel development of hierarchical organization of
speech (language) and movement.

As opposed to automatic motor behavior patterns controlled by subcortical
structures and reflexes, speech movements are controlled by higher levels. This
may be described as a central neural feedback mechanism that is realized in the
cerebral cortex due to the proximity of motor and sensory association areas; the
effects of motor actions are recorded as patterns of activity in the association cortex, from whence they in turn control the muscles. Although traditionally, swallowing has been considered one of the automatic motor behavior patterns under
subcortical control, there is increasing evidence that the cortex (particularly the
cingulate cortex, the insula, and the inferior frontal gyrus) and the cerebellum
are involved as well (Daniels, Corey, Fraychinaud, Depolo, & Foundas, 2006;

Stickler, Gilmore, Resenbek, & Donovan, 2003; Suzuki et al., 2003; Tasko, Kent, & Westbury, 2002; Watanabe, Abe, Ishikawa, Yamada, & Yamane, 2004).

According to some authors, the center for production of speech patterns is located in the brainstem. This opinion is based on studies that have revealed mechanisms, the so-called pacemakers that keep the rhythm necessary for cyclic life-sustaining functions—for breathing, movement, and chewing—with the assumption that speech, as a higher complex function, has developed from these lower functions. There is, however, evidence to the contrary as well: patterns of muscle activity recorded during speech have been found to be different from those recorded during chewing or some other nonspeech tasks. Gracco (cited in Kent & Tjaden, 1997) suggested a compromise: lower rhythmic functions and speech differ in motor patterns, but share mechanisms for their implementation and principles of organization. For a critical review of related literature see Kent and Tjaden (1997).

Just as in perception, there has been no consensus on the minimal units of the speech motor program and its execution, in other words, the articulation motor program. Distinctive features, individual sounds or phonemes, syllables, words and word groups or short sentences have been discussed as the likely candidates. Studies of both types of programs (speech and articulation alike) converge on the value of approximately seven syllables. This is the average capacity of working memory (the famous 7 ± 2 number) and may be related to the motor speech program, but it is also the average syntagmatic length in speech, which makes it a plausible articulation unit (for review see Horga, 1996). In view of the efficiency and rate of speech, in spite of the enormous number of muscle activations (several hundreds in one second), some preset motor subroutines probably exist. On the basis of the degree of variance among speech segments Horga (1996) opts for phonetic word as this subroutine size.

Besides dealing with the size of the minimal units of speech and articulation motor programs, most speech production models address the question of the relationship between execution—for example, the movement itself—and goal attainment—for example, speech. Here is a very simplified short list of examples:

1. Speech is a series of relatively constant context-independent articulatory gestures (Haskins Laboratories' authors).
2. Movements of the articulators are determined by their relations to all other elements of the system (Chistovich and associates).
3. The physiological model oriented toward the mechanics of speech movements and its acoustic supplements (Peterson; Shoup).
4. Binary functional models that assume phonetic and phonological levels, based on distinctive features founded on the acoustic and articulation characteristics of speech (Jacobson; Fant; Halle; Chomsky).
5. Sound systems of natural languages are harmonized with human perceptual and articulation abilities, so that the sounds that are articulated in natural areas have particular quantal characteristics, in other words,

there are areas where small articulatory changes result in considerable acoustic changes, and areas where large articulatory changes result in negligible acoustic changes (Stevens); distribution of vowels in acoustic space is such that it provides maximum perceptual contrast, regardless of the number of vowels in the system (Liljencrants; Lindblom).

6. Model of speech production based on a closed feedback involving the respiratory, phonatory and articulatory levels on the one hand, and the afferent sensory and proprioceptive feedback, on the other, with the appropriate comparator that continuously coordinates afferent stimuli with the final goal (Fairbanks).

7. The parametrical approach, according to which speech is a unique and complex system with continuous interaction between different levels, oriented toward neural mechanisms of speech production (Liberman).

8. According to several dynamic models that are based on the target theory, and that rely on neurophysiologic foundations of speech, all movements are oriented toward the set goal, without assuming fixed, preset articulatory movements (MacNeilage; Noteboom; Kelso; Saltzman; Tuller). Horga (1996), Kent and Tjaden (1997), Obler and Gjerlow (1999), Eysenck and Keane (2000), and Gazzaniga et al. (2002), among others, have reviewed and discussed such models.

The language network, albeit physically close to the general sensorimotor one, is a separate system. Beatse, Sunaert, Wilm, Van Hecke, and Marchal (2000) have revealed by fMRI that the language network involves the superior temporal gyrus in both hemispheres, the left angular gyrus, the left middle and inferior frontal gyrus, and the cingulate gyrus in both hemispheres. Within the network, the receptive language regions are separate from the expressive ones. The hand, however, is represented in the sensory and motor cortex located in the precentral and postcentral gyrus, respectively.

RELATIONSHIP BETWEEN SPEECH PRODUCTION AND PERCEPTION

The fundamental issue in discussing the neurolinguistic aspects of the relation between speech perception and production is the question of their cerebral representation. In other words, do speech production and perception share a common cerebral representation or are they two neurofunctionally different areas with stronger or weaker connections? Neurolinguistic literature most frequently deals with descriptions of the production (expressive) or the perception side of speech, and their relationship is commonly described by claims that production is more clearly lateralized to the language-dominant hemisphere (usually left) whereas perception is more widely distributed with greater involvement of the nondominant (usually right) hemisphere.

Cortical stimulation studies have revealed that the mouth and face muscles are represented at the points that are responsible for phoneme identification. This supports the motor theory of speech perception—one of the best known and most extensively discussed theories of speech perception (Liberman, Cooper, Shank-weiler, & Studdert-Kennedy, 1967) according to which speech is perceived by means of movements necessary to produce the heard sounds, not by means of the sounds themselves. (The theory is discussed in more detail in chapter 5, this volume.) Penfield and Roberts (as cited in Bradshaw & Nettleton, 1983) have named that region of the brain *the voice control area.* In other words, speech and language comprehension are parts of a single system. In their studies of chimpanzees and speech acquisition in children Premack and Premack (1994) have found that comprehension and production start off as separate systems, but become united on the basis of even very limited experience. Albeit limited, that experience is a necessary prerequisite to initiate the merging of the two systems. Hurford (1994a, 1994b), on the other hand, believes that there is no period in early childhood during which a child might know a new word or structure without being able to use it. Ojemann (1994) also concluded that language processing includes motor mechanisms even without actual production. However, the relationship is not as straightforward as it might seem. Recordings of neural activity have shown that different cells are responsible for speech perception and production, even when the word to be perceived and produced is the same (Creutzfeldt, Ojemann, & Lettich, 1989a, 1989b). The auditory speech perception system shuts down briefly during speech production. Ojemann (1994) believes that the proximity of the neurons responsible for perception and those involved in production may explain the stimulation results. They become parts of the network that has properties not inherent to individual cells. The major brain areas involved in production and comprehension of speech and language are shown in Figure 1.8. Cortical representation of speech and language is discussed in more detail in chapter 8.

Jäncke and Shah (2000) and Specht, Shah, and Jäncke (2000b) also found in their fMRI studies that language production activates parts of the cortex involved in perception and vice versa; language recognition tasks activate classical speech production areas as well.

Kent and Tjaden (1997) discussed possible points of contact and common representations. They may be summarized as three types of connections underlying the integration of speech production and perception: (a) neighboring location of cerebral and cerebellar motor and sensory neurons; (b) existence of *multimodal* neurons, or nerve cells that react to more than one sensory modality; and (c) neural structure that includes parallel and recurrent pathways. Fowler and Galantucci (2005) also provide some evidence of close correlation between mechanisms supporting action and those supporting its perception.

Neighboring Location of Motor and Sensory Neurons

A case in point is the location of motor and somatosensory cortex, in other words, cortical regions responsible for efferent (motor—motor neurons) and afferent (somatosensory—sensory neurons) activities of the body. Although the central sulcus separates the motor (precentral, anterior to the sulcus) from the somatosensory (postcentral, posterior to the sulcus) cortex (see Figure 1.8), some motor

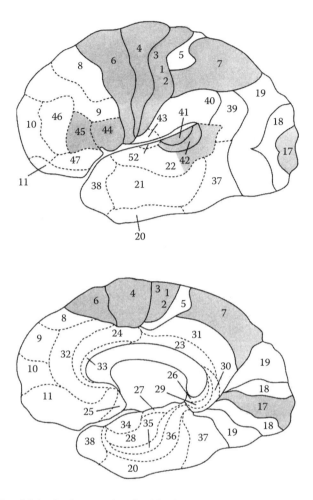

FIGURE 1.8.   Major brain areas involved in the production and perception of speech and language.

neurons can be found immediately next to the sensory ones. In addition to the already mentioned cortical representations of mouth and face muscles involved in speech that share their location with the points responsible for phoneme identification (Ojemann, 1983), motor and sensory neurons are found in the vicinity of each other in the cerebellum as well. Such results, in combination with clinical observations, suggest that among the important roles of the cerebellum are temporal calculations that are used in many perceptual and motor functions, including speech.

Multimodal Neurons

These neurons respond to two or more types of stimuli. They can be found in different animal species: in macaques about 55% are bi- or multimodal (visual and auditory, visual and somesthetic or visual, auditory and somesthetic); in songbirds the pathways that control song also respond to auditory stimuli. Separate sensory pathways allow stimulus distinction with respect to modality, and multisensory pathways make possible integration of stimuli from different modalities (Rosenblum, 2005). This is particularly important for speech because of its multimodal properties, and it has proven to be invaluable in speech and hearing rehabilitation (Guberina, 1992–1993; Pansini, 1995, 2002).

Parallel and Recurrent Pathways

Parallel pathways enable comparisons among various neural representations. In songbirds this explains their ability to learn their species-specific song—by continuously comparing their own song with that of adult birds. These comparisons are possible due to multiple neural mechanisms, modalities, multiple loops and representations of song patterns. They are based on two neural branches that mature at different times. One develops gradually during song acquisition and it is essential for song production in adult birds. The other reaches full maturity very early, quickly reacts to stimuli, and its purpose is quick and recurrent comparison of the bird's own (motor) activity with the model (control, sensory activity). According to Williams (1989), when the species-specific song is acquired, this branch activity decreases (as cited in Kent & Tjaden, 1997). Despite the lack of comparable direct physiological data for humans, Kent and Tjaden (1997) propose the following analogy to speech: (a) different parts of the neural structure mature functionally at different ages, which explains the existence of the sensitive (critical) periods in speech acquisition; (b) different parts of the neural structure have different representations of speech sounds, such as auditory, tactile, motor, or kinesthetic; (c) there are branches that are used for recurrent comparisons of the different elements of sound representations, and as speech acquisition progresses, humans rely on their activity less and less.

2 Sex Differences

There are several aspects of differences between men and women with respect to brain structure, lateralization, and behavior. Before we go on discussing them, it should be stressed that the differences among individuals of the same sex are greater than the differences between sexes.

STRUCTURAL DIFFERENCES

There is no evidence that neural connections or brain architecture are any different in men than in women, although at all ages the average brain mass of men is approximately 10% greater than in women. That difference can probably be attributed to the difference in neuron size rather than number, and it does not imply differences in performance (Spreen, Tupper, Risser, Tuokko, & Edgell, 1984). Differences in mass between the two hemispheres (right hemisphere has greater mass, whereas the left has greater density) are smaller in women than in men. Thicker cortex of the right hemisphere as compared to the left has been found in male, but not in female, fetuses. The shape of the left lateral (Sylvian) fissure corresponds to the right in more women than men. In women, the left *planum temporale* is not as frequently larger than the right as it has been found in men. Relative brain size is different at 2 years of age, and in the hypothalamus, sex differences occur around the fourth year of life (Swaab & Hofman, 1995).

Verchinski et al. (2000) conducted an MRI study on 111 healthy subjects ranging in age between 17 and 54. They reported significantly greater gray matter density in most neocortical regions in women. The greatest sex differences were found in the left middle temporal gyrus (Brodmann's area 22), in the right parietal lobulus, and in the left precuneus. None of the areas in male subjects had greater gray matter density.

Although they reported no statistically significant differences, Amunts, Schleicher, Ditterich, and Zilles (2000) found a trend toward greater asymmetry in cytoarchitecture of Brodmann's areas 44 and 45 (that correspond to Broca's area) in men than in women. Callosal size has been the object of study by several groups of authors. Most have agreed that some parts of corpus callosum are larger in women than in men, but there is no general consensus. Cowell, Allen, Zalatimo, and Denenberg (1992) found that in men, the corpus callosum reaches its maximal width by age 20, and in women much later—between 41 and 50 years of age. These age-dependent differences may be one of the causes of discrepancies in the literature. Besides, the callosal surface size is not a reliable indicator of the actual number of commissural axons (Judaš & Kostović, 1997). In any case, even if the size difference is accepted, it does not necessarily result in different cognitive functioning (Kimura, 1992).

DIFFERENCES IN FUNCTIONAL ORGANIZATION OF THE BRAIN

According to Kimura (1992), sex hormones begin exerting their influence on brain organization so early in ontogenetic development (prenatally) that from the very moment of birth the environment acts on the differently structured brains of girls and boys. She found that 3-year-old boys were better at aiming than girls of the same age and that sex differences in rotating objects in space were evident before puberty. Although the influence is less pronounced in humans than in other animals, early exposure to sex hormones has permanent effects on brain organization. Cohen and Forget (1995) described possible hormonally determined regulation of activities in brain hemispheres during cognitive tasks.

According to Bradshaw and Nettleton (1983), left-hemisphere injuries affect language abilities to a lesser degree in women than in men, due to their less prominent left-lateralization of language functions. Kimura (1983, 1992) does not believe that these different consequences of left-hemisphere damage are due to more bilateral organization of language functions in women. According to her, unilateral focal damage occurs more frequently in posterior areas than in anterior ones, regardless of sex. The difference lies in the fact that in more women, speech and speech-related motor functions are represented in more anterior regions of the left hemisphere as opposed to men, who on average, more frequently have the same functions represented in posterior regions of the left hemisphere. Still, Kimura (1992) reports no evidence of sex differences in functional brain asymmetry with respect to the basic speech, motor, or spatial abilities. Kanasaku, Yamaura, and Kitazawa (2000) also found sex differences in lateralization to vary along the anterior–posterior axis. She did report, however, differences in more abstract verbal tasks. For instance, damage of any hemisphere caused poorer results on verbal tests in women, whereas the results were poorer only in men with left-hemisphere damage. Shaywitz et al.'s (1995) results of fMRI studies of rhyming tasks show that women exhibit more bilateral activation than men. Other authors also report task-specific sex differences (for example, Kitazawa & Kansaku [2005], and Rossell, Bullmore, Williams, & David [2002]).

Developmental dyslexia is more frequent in boys than in girls. Moreover, it has been shown that dyslexic girls still function better than dyslexic boys, which suggests greater plasticity during development (Spreen et al., 1984).

As it has been mentioned at the beginning of this chapter, male and female brains are organized differently from the first days of life. During prenatal development sex hormones control that differentiation. Similar mechanisms probably cause within-sex variation, as suggested by the relationship between levels of some hormones and adult cognitive styles (Kimura, 1992; Sherwin, 2003).

BEHAVIORAL AND COGNITIVE DIFFERENCES

Sex differences in cognitive abilities are most frequently and most consistently manifested in the language and spatial domains (Spreen et al., 1984). In general, it is believed that the two hemispheres are more asymmetrically organized for speech and spatial functions in men than in women. The considerable difference in the size of Brodmann's area 22 (by approximately 11%) is thought to underlie the sex differences in language abilities (Verchinski et al., 2000). On IQ tests, girls score consistently better on verbal tasks and poorer on visuospatial tasks than boys, especially after puberty. It seems that the most pronounced differences in cognitive functions are to be found in the types of abilities and not in the overall intelligence level as measured by IQ (Bradshaw & Nettleton, 1983). On average, men outperform women on some spatial tasks. They are particularly more successful on tests that require mental rotation of an object in space or some other type of manipulation. They are more successful on mathematical reasoning tests and in orienting on a given route. They are also more precise on tests of target-directed motor skills—in other words in aiming and intercepting. Women have greater perceptual speed (they are quicker to find objects that match some target object). Women display greater verbal fluency, including the ability to find words that begin with a given letter or that satisfy some other criterion. Women outperform men in mental arithmetic and remembering landmarks. On precise manual tasks (e.g., O'Connor's dexterimeter) women are faster than men. These differences are manifested in gender distribution in certain occupations (composers, chess players), disorders (developmental dysphasia and dyslexia, stuttering, autism), in normal developmental stages (speech acquisition), and in overall behavior during childhood (Swaab & Hofman, 1995).

Boys tend to investigate more, girls tend to be more social (Bradshaw & Nettleton, 1983). These traits may be encouraged by parents and society. Hereditary factors probably have a stronger impact on spatial skills whereas environmental factors seem to influence verbal abilities more. Sex differences seem to be more pronounced in more authoritarian cultures with rigidly defined gender roles (Bradshaw & Nettleton, 1983). Kimura (1992) believes that human brain organization has been determined by natural selection through generations. During the thousands of years of human brain development people have lived in relatively small groups of hunters and gatherers, with probably clear division of labor between men and women. Men engaged in hunting, which frequently involved covering great distances and developing strategies for finding and overpowering animals. They were responsible for the defense of the group against predators and enemies as well as for design, manufacture, and use of weapons. Women were most probably in charge of tending to home, which involved child care, gathering food nearby, preparing meals, and making clothes. Such specialization assumed different pressures on men and women. Men had to develop skills of aiming and finding their way on the basis of terrain configuration, and women had to develop fine motor skills in a limited space and sensitivity to small differences in the environment as well as in the appearance and behavior of children. These speculations aside, there is no firm evidence that would explain sex differences in cerebral representations of verbal and spatial functions as a consequence of environmental and/or social factors.

Sex differences are not exhausted by the verbal–nonverbal aspects of processing. There are also differences in the degree of lateralization. At first it was believed, probably due to different rates of maturation, that women were more lateralized than men. At present the opposite is more commonly found and believed to be true. Smaller differences between the left and the right hemisphere in women compared with men have been found in studies of morphological asymmetries, clinical studies (women are less affected than men by left-hemisphere trauma), and behavioral studies on healthy subjects. Although, paradoxically, men are more frequently and strongly left-handed than women, they exhibit more pronounced right-visual-field and right-ear advantage for verbal material. Sex differences are as a rule easier to show on verbal material, just as verbal tasks generate stronger and more consistent asymmetries than nonverbal, visuospatial materials (Bradshaw & Nettleton, 1983).

Women frequently exhibit left-visual-field advantage on lexical decision tasks (but not when vocal latencies are measured) early on in the task. On phonological tasks (as revealed by MRI) men exhibit more left-lateralized brain activity compared with women, whose activation is more diffuse (Shaywitz et al., 1995). Women resemble left-handed men by exhibiting the verbal contribution of the right hemisphere, suggesting that in women the areas otherwise reserved for visuospatial processing in the right hemisphere are taken over by the secondary speech mechanisms that facilitate comprehension of difficult and/or unfamiliar material. Moreover, women with right-hemisphere injuries score more poorly on tests of verbal intelligence, but show no signs of dysphasia. It seems that the right hemisphere in women is more active in speech comprehension than in production, which may explain the absence of obvious effects when it is suppressed by the unilateral sodium amytal injection (Bradshaw & Nettleton, 1983). However, it should be said that cerebral blood flow measurements obtained by PET studies have revealed that, both in men and in women, blood flow increases in the left hemisphere during verbal tasks and in the right hemisphere during spatial tasks (Kolb & Whishaw, 1996). McRoberts and Sanders (1992) reported that in the recognition of fundamental frequencies, men were significantly better than women when the stimuli were presented binaurally (i.e., to both hemispheres simultaneously). Dichotic listening tests have revealed no significant sex differences. They speculate that the reason for that may be the differences in relative callosal width. In a study of the relationship between active hand and ear advantage carried out on 72 male and 72 female subjects, Mildner, Stanković, and Petković (2005) reported consistently lower right-ear advantage for male than for female subjects.

Sex differences in verbal and spatial tasks may be a consequence of unequal maturation rates. Early maturing adolescents (typically women) achieve better results on verbal than on spatial tests and are less clearly lateralized. Those who mature more slowly have a chance to stabilize their hemispheric dominance later, which helps spatial abilities if language develops before them. Thus, late maturers (boys) can develop language abilities in the left hemisphere without interference with the right-hemisphere functions. Accordingly, the right hemisphere is free to develop its visuospatial abilities (Bradshaw & Nettleton, 1983). Besides resulting in more pronounced lateralization and separation of functions, an extended period of maturation typical of men might mean a longer critical period during which malfunctions in verbal ability development may occur. Developmental dyslexia in boys may be a consequence of too much reliance on bilaterally represented spatial functions that develop late, which does not happen in girls because they are protected, having had their language skills developed earlier. The greater degree of hemispheric specialization probably puts men at risk with respect to language disorders, because they have no alternative support system in the nondominant hemisphere. So, if the differences are summarized into the different maturation rates it may be concluded that, regardless of gender, early maturers have better developed verbal abilities, whereas late maturers develop better spatial skills. Contrary to this, authors such as Shucard (as cited in Spreen et al., 1984) have reported that sex differences in cognitive functioning are apparent in babies as young as three months.

Sex differences have been attributed to hormonal influences as well. It is possible that sex hormones change male and female brains in such ways that they respond differently to social influences. Some genetic models have also addressed variations in spatial abilities (Kolb & Whishaw, 1996).

Perceptual asymmetries may vary in men and women because of different approaches to the task. For instance, women might prefer verbal strategies during spatial tasks, so that the obtained lateralization effect would not be a measure of sex differences in cerebral lateralization of that particular function, but rather a manifestation of the preferred cognitive style in task solving (Kolb & Whishaw, 1996). Cahill (2003) found sex differences in memory for emotionally arousing events. Right hemispheric processing of global/central aspects of a situation is more pronounced in males, whereas left-hemispheric processing of more local/fine detail aspects is more pronounced in females.

Finally, it is possible that genetic, developmental, and environmental factors predispose men and women for a particular cognitive style, which influences their successfulness in solving verbal and spatial problems. Most probably, gender differences are at least partly under the influence of neurological factors that may be changed by the environment (Kolb & Whishaw, 1996). Sommer, Aleman, Bouma, and Kahn (2004) reviewed 14 studies involving 377 men and 442 women. Their meta-analysis indicated no significant difference in language lateralization between men and women (see also Sommer, Aleman, & Kahn, 2005). They proposed that general sex differences in cognitive performance and the neuronal basis for these cognitive sex differences are not to be found in different language lateralization.

3 Brief History of Neurolinguistics from the Beginnings to the 20th Century

First descriptions of language disorders date back to pharaonic medical texts recorded on papyrus, some 3000 years B.C. The outlines of the first theory of brain and nervous system functions appeared in the first centuries A.D. and were based on ideas originating in the last few centuries B.C. The so-called ventricular theory was based on fluids and their flow, because the scientists of the day believed that something had to move in the brain in order for it to work. That "something" flowed between the sensory and the effector organs and was called animal spirits. The theory held on until the 17th century and Descartes (1596–1650) incorporated it into his hydraulic theory. Some principles of ventricular theory (later also referred to as the medieval cell doctrine) have been kept in the more recent models of brain function developed within cognitive neuroscience (e.g., modular structure according to which the functions are localized in various regions of the brain).

Between the 11th century and Renaissance, written descriptions of medical cases included drawings from which it was obvious that speech production was located, together with memory, in the third ventricle. Moreover, language and memory disorders were commonly described as a single problem. In the 16th century, the first associations between language disorders and certain brain injuries were determined. Different aspects of impaired language function were observed, which may be seen from descriptions of alexia and agraphia, aphasia and even selective aphasia, with preserved internal speech and thought but with seriously impaired speech production. There were also records of aphasia without alexia or agraphia. This was accompanied by descriptions of differences between articulatory control and language production, because clearly, there were patients who had preserved motor functions but could not speak.

In the 17th century, the increasing number of experimental studies of brain brought about abandonment of ventricular theory and acceptance of models that proposed localization of functions in particular brain structures. The Renaissance belief that the nerves relayed information to and from the brain was kept but the idea that nerves were hollow tubes through which energy flowed back and forth was abandoned. Instead, it was posited that information was coded so that different ideas were transmitted by means of different vibrations. The number of descriptions of simultaneous and related occurrences of language disorders and right-sided paralysis increased; descriptions of cognitive function impairments became more thorough, including discussions about acalculia, agrammatism and other disorders, and with discussions about differences between disorders accompanied by agraphia and/or alexia and those without them. Language was still closely associated with memory. The scientists could distinguish language disorders from general cognitive impairments, production from comprehension, lexical errors from sound or letter errors, as well as syntactic and morphological disorders. The brain was believed to function as a whole.

The idea of localization of functions in the brain was adopted and further advanced in the 18th century. It was believed that each ability or trait was connected with a special nerve bundle in the brain. At the time, sensory, moral and intellectual traits and abilities were considered to be equal candidates for localization. Moreover, some authors believed that each word had its own neuronal fiber. Franz Joseph Gall (1758–1828) thought that the shape of the human brain with all the individual traits left a trace on the inside wall of the skull, which could be observed from the outside as bumps. This was called craniology. He also proposed two separate brain areas devoted to two language levels and marked them as *Wortsinn* (for the lexical component) on the left orbit, and immediately above that was the place for expressive speech—*Sprachsinn*.

The relationship between abilities and skull shape established by Gall served as the foundation for phrenology, a very influential pseudoscience that had a significant impact on the 19th century, most closely connected with Johann Gaspar Spurzheim (1776–1832). In line with Gall's descriptions, the phrenologists proposed specific locations in the left and the right hemisphere for different functions that were reflected on the external shape of the skull. There were areas responsible for hope, love, caution, hate, shyness, language and many other functions, abilities and traits; within the brain there were the organs of hope, caution, and so forth. For example, it was believed that people with bulging eyes had exceptionally developed language abilities, because the seat of language functions was thought to lie behind the eyes.

One of the most heated opponents of phrenology was Pierre Jean Marie Flourens (1794–1867). On the basis of his tests on animals he concluded that all senses, perception, and voluntary activities had common brain substrates. In spite of numerous critics, many authors were looking for connections between impaired functions and brain damage as support for phrenology until well into the third decade of the 19th century.

Although not a fervent supporter of phrenology, Jean Baptiste Bouillaud (1796–1881) supported the theory of brain localization, particularly localization of language function in frontal lobes. He offered ample clinical evidence of the connection between frontal lobe injury and loss of speech. Moreover, he described several cases of isolated speech disorders without other motor impairments and with intact nonspeech tongue movements, on the basis of which he concluded that the center for motor control of speech is separate from the center(s) for general motor control. He also distinguished between the organ of spoken language (i.e., speech), located in the white matter, from the organ of memory for words (i.e., lexical representation), located in the gray matter, in both frontal lobes.

Pierre Paul Broca (1824–1880) focused on disorders of speech production because until the sixth decade of the 19th century speech referred only to production, whereas disorders of speech comprehension were not discussed within language proper. At the time comprehension processes of any kind were thought to belong to the mind that was studied by philosophers, theologists, and psychiatrists. By the time his well-known papers were published in the 1860s, a 40-year-long debate about the role of frontal lobes in speech production and about the associations between speech disorders and injuries, and stroke in that region had been raging in medical circles. It was clear from many published case studies that most physicians were aware of the hypothesis about the existence of a language center in frontal lobes. Cases of aphasia without frontal lobe damage were taken as counterarguments, and not as evidence of different types of aphasia. Before Broca's papers, an unknown village doctor, Marc Dax (1770–1837), reported at a medical convention in Montpellier, France, his observations that of his 40 brain-damaged patients who presented with speech problems, none had a right-hemisphere injury. That report went unnoticed, and Dax died a year later, unaware of having anticipated research into lateralization of function. Whitaker (1995) believes that even when Broca's results were published 25 years later, they might have gone unnoticed had not scientists and doctors already begun accepting clinical pathological associations between specific brain regions and particular functions. Broca presented postmortem results of two of his patients, followed by seven more aphasic patients, who had suffered left-hemisphere injuries, specifically in the frontal lobes, anterior to the motor area. Because of these results and his detailed case descriptions, this area—for speech production—is called Broca's area.

Soon after that, authors began characterizing neurologically acquired speech comprehension disorders. Several names were the most prominent: John Hughlings Jackson (1835–1911) and Carl Wernicke (1848–1905), as well as, according to Whitaker (1998a) the unjustly overlooked Theodor Meynert (1833–1892). It became widely accepted that the left hemisphere was responsible for language in general, not just for speech production. Studies showed that left-hemisphere damage caused difficulties in reading, writing, and speech comprehension, which was not the case with right-hemisphere damaged patients. Because of Wernicke's descriptions of sensory aphasia occurring as a consequence of injuries to the posterior superior temporal gyrus (approximately at the point of contact of the temporal and the parietal lobe), the center for speech comprehension was named Wernicke's area. Case studies revealed that apraxia was another consequence of left hemisphere damage. On the basis of these results the left hemisphere became known as the dominant hemisphere, due to its crucial role in the control of all complex behavioral and cognitive processes. Some authors, among whom Whitaker (1998a) particularly points out Henry Charlton Bastian (1837–1915), were aware of the fine differences between various aspects of language functioning and types of memory. Bastian found that function disorders (e.g., aphasia) may be caused by injury to the center itself, to its connections with periphery, or to some other connections. Obviously, his model had some properties of the neural networks models. According to him, words establish connections with percepts and concepts, and during the thought process brain activity is not limited only to strictly localized centers, but there is a widespread activity in various cortical areas in both hemispheres. He proposed that concepts were formed in cortical areas immediately next to sensory centers, which would correspond loosely to the idea of association areas.

Whereas studies by Broca, Wernicke, Bastian, and many others dealt mostly with the taxonomy analysis of the observed phenomena at the word level (or lower), John Hughlings Jackson was the first to give any serious thought to agrammatism. He talked about the propositional nature of language and concluded that propositional meaning did not depend only on constituent words, but also on relationships among words, making the sentence the unit of meaning. Hughlings Jackson also claimed that the right hemisphere was involved in automatic (involuntary) expression and perception. His particular contribution is a description of the motor cortex (precentral gyrus), especially the observation that different parts of the contralateral side of the body are represented in specific locations of the cortex. He also noticed that complete loss of function was rare, and based on that, concluded that a particular type of behavior was managed by many regions of the brain. Another one of his conclusions was that localization of symptoms does not necessarily imply localization of function (Gazzaniga, Ivry, & Mangun, 2002). Arnold Pick (1851–1924) believed that sentence plan (i.e., syntactic structure) preceded the selection of lexical constituents and that content (lexical, open class) words were selected before functional (grammatical, closed class) ones, with surface grammatical form being determined last. He talked about two types of expressive agrammatism: motor (quantitative) and sensory (qualitative), and attributed both to the loss or decrease of control over grammatical devices. He related motor agrammatism to motor aphasia, frontal lobe injuries and telegraphic speech, and sensory agrammatism to temporal lobe injuries, but his emphasis was on expressive aspects of speech.

After the relatively long and very active period of localizationism, a more holistic approach to brain study was adopted at the beginning of the 20th century. One of the most influential proponents of that view was Karl Lashley (1890–1958). In his studies of rat behavior he concluded that there was no single location in the brain whose injury might prevent maze learning. His most important finding was that the extent of the injury, more than its location, will affect a particular function. He defined two important principles: the principle of mass action and the principle of equipotentiality. According to the first, certain types of learning are controlled by the cerebral cortex as a whole (contrary to the view that each cognitive function has a special location in the cortex). Italian physiologist Angelo Mosso (1846–1910) noted a relationship between mental activity and increased number of pulsations in the cortex, in other words, between cerebral blood flow and neuronal activity (Gazzaniga et al., 2002). According to the second principle, which mainly refers to sensory systems, some parts of the system can take over functions from the other parts.

By the second decade of the 20th century it has become clear that the nervous system was built of dynamically polarized nerve cells, whose axons and dendrites were organized into groups, and made specific neural connections by means of synapses. In the 1930s the first motor and sensory maps were produced, and it became obvious that each sensory modality has more than one of those maps. After World War II different methods of imaging and quantifying these connections were designed (more on that in chapter 4, this volume). The obtained results and techniques ensured better understanding of brain physiology and changed the approach to speech and language. However, the key question—does the brain function as a whole or as a set of independent parts—continues to be debated. According to Kosslyn and Andersen (1992), it seems plausible that simple processes are localized, whereas complex functions such as perception, language and others are more widely distributed (as cited in Gazzaniga et al., 2002). This simple distinction does not solve the problem, of course. Rather, it moves it to a different plane: to the question of the level of complexity at which a process is localized, or at what point it becomes complex enough to warrant wider distribution.

4 Research Methods

Methods of research into brain functioning have developed alongside advancements in knowledge and technology. The application of a particular method depends, naturally, on the function we wish to study, subjects, available resources and equipment, and frequently on what is in vogue, or for some other reason the focus of interest, at the particular point in time in the scientific community.

Existing methods may be characterized in several ways: according to the subjects studied (e.g., clinical population vs. healthy subjects); according to the functions studied (e.g., language, motor, etc.); according to type of tasks used (e.g., detection, identification, or discrimination); chronologically (from the oldest to the most recent); or according to the techniques used. Obviously, some overlap is unavoidable and, regardless of the criterion, one method may fit into several categories. This is not an exhaustive list, but it includes brief descriptions of the methods most frequently used in neurolinguistic research on clinical and healthy subjects, as well as those that are, due to their invasiveness, costliness, or relative obsoleteness, used less frequently. Many methods used with healthy subjects are also applicable to clinical patients, such as neuroimaging methods. Since there are advantages and disadvantages to every single one of them, most authors agree that a combination of several different methods on the same subjects will yield the most reliable results. This chapter is limited mainly to the methods acceptable in work with humans, so different lesion methods, genetic and/or pharmacological manipulations, deprivation, and similar methods are not included. Their descriptions may be found in neuroscientific literature (Gazzaniga, Ivry, & Mangun, 2002; Judaš & Kostović, 1997; Purves et al., 2001; Sternberg, 2003).

CLINICAL STUDIES

This large group of subjects includes patients with brain damage, regardless of etiology—trauma (i.e., open or closed head injury), cerebrovascular problems (e.g., stroke), tumor or degenerative diseases and conditions (e.g., Alzheimer's or Parkinson's disease, epilepsy, etc.).

The first documented studies of brain language functions were carried out on clinical patients, particularly in the 19th century. The authors, mainly physicians and surgeons, described observed speech disorders and tried to make connections between their observations and diagnosed brain injuries. Whenever possible they looked for confirmation of their findings in postmortem analyses. They are referred to as diagram makers, because they tried to establish unambiguous relations between injuries and function disorders. In other words, their goal was to draw inferences about the ways different parts of the brain contribute to behavior. The disadvantages of those studies were the strictly localizationist approach, insufficiently defined psychological terms, and unsatisfactory empirical descriptions.

However, brain injuries and their consequences cannot be reduced to the loss of a single component. Damage to one function does not mean that other aspects of cognitive functioning are intact. For instance, formation of scar tissue or disorders in blood supply may affect functioning of neighboring regions. Finally, it is debatable how much we can infer about the functioning of individual components from information about the consequences of their removal. Even the most detailed description of difficulties will not answer the question of how the language system actually works. At best we will find out what aspects of the system have been damaged. Obviously, we cannot reliably make conclusions about functions of the removed area on the basis of facts about how behavior changes when the area has been removed. Furthermore, the key technical issues here are whether the structure in question has been removed entirely and what other structures may have been damaged (Gordon et al., 1994). It is difficult to infer about functioning of the intact brain on the basis of the injured one, because the exact extent of damage or recovery rate is usually not known. It has been shown that more reliable associations between injury and functional disorder may be seen approximately one year after injury. Recovery is most remarkable in the first few weeks and months, but to a certain extent it continues after that initial period (Dronkers & Ludy, 1998). It is also possible that methods to determine functioning are just not sensitive enough to register change. Obviously, one of the more serious drawbacks of forming any conclusions about intact functioning on the basis of clinical cases is that normal functions of the system are not likely to equal those lost by damage. Consequences of injury may be masked by positive symptoms, for instance, events occurring in the injured individual that would not have occurred in a healthy one (Legg, 1989). Moreover, it is usually impossible to control some other characteristics of the patient—the natural aging process, psychological status, other health problems, and so forth.

Another important issue is which results are more reliable: those obtained from large groups of subjects or those based on single case studies? The average behavior of many patients who supposedly suffer from identical disorders or injuries to a particular brain region does not necessarily offer a better insight into cerebral representation of a cognitive function. In averaging, considerable anatomical and functional individual variation may be lost. Moreover, individuals who differ widely not only in the extent of their injuries but also in other characteristics that may significantly affect recovery, such as education, age, socioeconomic status, attitude toward therapy, motivation, and so forth, are frequently studied together as a homogenous group. This approach ignores individual compensatory strategies that also play an important role in recovery and tends to place too much emphasis on some areas of the brain, neglecting others that are seemingly inactive or less active during certain functions. Although group studies are carried out on patients who share some common characteristics of linguistic behavior, or that have been diagnosed with damage to the identical region of the brain, the groups are still quite heterogeneous. Obviously, it is an advantage that individual case studies avoid unjustified overgeneralizations and do not involve large groups of patients with similar cognitive deficits. In this type of study individuals are subjected to large numbers of different tests, which can offer insights into their functional cerebral organization and help to test theories and models of cognitive functioning. One of the most obvious disadvantages of this kind of research, naturally, is the fact that one case cannot serve as a basis for general conclusions, because individual behavior is affected by many different factors (some of which have been mentioned previously) that may not be noticeable or directly measurable. Willmes (1998) and Eysenck and Keane (2000) propose a sensible compromise: start with individual cases and look for what they have in common with other individuals.

Despite all the drawbacks, clinical case studies are a valuable source of data about cognitive and other functioning.

STUDIES OF SPLIT-BRAIN PATIENTS

One type of brain injury is severing of connections between the two hemispheres (commissurotomy). In humans, the most frequent version is cutting the corpus callosum (callosotomy) with the purpose of preventing the spread of epileptic seizures from the affected hemisphere to the healthy one. Another small group of patients without callosal connections are the so-called acallosal patients, in whom the connection was never established. Commissurotomies became the method of choice between the 1940s and 1950s, but were subsequently replaced by increasingly more effective antiepileptic medications. At present the procedure is used only exceptionally, if all other attempts to stop epileptic seizures fail. In cases of nonexistent callosal connections between the two hemispheres, the centers in each of them are intact and each hemisphere can operate on its own. Studies have shown that, under experimental conditions, such patients function as if they had two separate brains, which is not noticeable in everyday life (Milner, Taylor, & Sperry, 1968; Sperry, 1981; Zaidel, Zaidel, & Bogen, 2005).

As it was explained in chapter 1, the corpus callosum is the largest connection between the two hemispheres. It is more than just a vital communication line, because it coordinates hemispheric functioning and behavior. Although we have two hemispheres capable of neural activity and—as hemispherectomy patients show us, we can function with only one—we behave as one mind, not two. Two hemispheres between which the corpus callosum has been severed can learn identical tasks, whereas intact corpus callosum prevents that. In callosotomy patients, one hemisphere has no awareness of the existence or activities of the other. This was supported by observations of perception, learning, cognition, volition, and memory (Levy, Koeppen, & Stanton, 2005). However, the two hemispheres can exchange information, for example, by means of facial expressions that are bilaterally controlled, and via some subcortical connections (Kalat, 1995; Sternberg, 2003).

A typical experiment carried out on split-brain patients looks like this: the patient is seated at a table with test objects hidden from view by a partition. The subject is required to pick up or feel the object within reach with one hand, and to (a) name it, or (b) feel for an identical object with the other hand. The tests are run for each hand separately. Due to crossed connections between the periphery and the brain the right hand has direct access to the left hemisphere, and the left hand to the right hemisphere; because the two hemispheres have been disconnected, the information that reaches the brain cannot be transferred from one hemisphere to the other. Hemispheric differences in language functioning are manifested as the inability of the patient to name the objects felt with the left hand (right hemisphere), with preserved ability to name those felt with the right hand (left hemisphere). The results are highly dependent on the type of commissurotomy—whether it was complete or partial, and if it was partial, how much of the connection was preserved. For example, an intact *splenium* will preserve the connection between occipital lobes, and the anterior commissure will enable transfer of semantic (but not sensory) information (Gazzaniga et al., 2002).

CORTICAL STIMULATION

Cortical stimulations involve administering stimuli to a part of a neural circuit and measuring its consequences at some other point. Stimuli may be electrical or chemical. Although the first results of cortical stimulation in an awake person were reported as early as 1909, the method was used more systematically by Penfield and Roberts (1959) with the purpose of determining cortical locations crucial for language functioning during brain surgery in order to spare them. Since the brain has no pain receptors the procedure is performed while the patient is awake. Electrical stimulation of particular points in the cortex elicits various sensations, images, and experiences that are entered into the so-called stimulation map as the patient describes them. Hence the term *brain mapping*. Stimulation of speech areas causes interference in object naming. Patients may lose the ability to speak entirely or just the ability to name objects presented in pictures. Hesitations, slurred speech, repeated attempts to name the objects, and other effects have also been recorded. Such stimulation maps have been compiled for functions other than speech production and perception as well.

There are several methodological problems to be dealt with here. One is the problem of whether the stimuli are physiologically real in terms of their intensity and/or duration as well as the issue of interpretation of localized stimulation of a system that under natural circumstances most probably receives complex stimulus structures. The main technical problem is how to apply a stimulus of intensity that faithfully reflects the level of activity occurring spontaneously in the brain, and how to determine which structures were affected by stimulation: the brain is structured so that information about the same event may be coded in the activity of a large number of not necessarily neighboring cells. Furthermore, the information on when a cell is inactive is just as important as knowing when it is active, because the brain's electrical activity is temporally organized. If we do not know in advance how the information is represented in the particular brain region, stimulation will not be realistic, and the results will be worthless (Legg,

1989). Besides, it has been shown that human brains do not have identical functional organization of language functions (Whitaker, 1998b).

TRANSCRANIAL MAGNETIC STIMULATION (TMS)

This method is used for experimental purposes on healthy subjects. It simulates injury of a desired brain region. An electrical coil is positioned on the skull over the location of interest. The resultant magnetic field stimulates neural activity on the area of about 1 to 1.5 cm^2 around the coil position. For example, stimulation of the motor cortex activates wrist and finger muscles in about 20 ms; stimulation of the visual cortex causes inability to recognize letters. An obvious disadvantage of this method is that it may be used only to study cortical surface. Furthermore, stimulation effects are very brief, and the timing of the signal beginning and stimulation onset is crucial: in the previously mentioned example of letter recognition, the errors will be elicited only if stimulation is applied 70 to 170 ms after the letter has been presented (Gazzaniga et al., 2002). Another drawback of this method is a well-established risk of inducing seizures, and recently it's been suggested that memory can be affected as well (Boatman, personal communication).

WADA TEST

This method, first introduced by Huhn Wada in 1947, is used clinically to determine the language-dominant hemisphere in patients who are candidates for neurosurgery. The procedure involves injecting the anesthetic sodium amytal into the carotid artery on the side of the neck, which supplies blood to the brain. This temporarily blocks the function of the ipsilateral hemisphere, with practically no effect on the contralateral one. Within seconds of the injection, the hand opposite the injection side starts to drop, because the anesthetized hemisphere cannot control it any longer. During the 5 to 10 minutes the anesthetic is effective the patient is presented with various (mainly linguistic) tasks. For example, reciting the alphabet, days of the week, or months, and naming well-known objects. The procedure is carried out for one side at a time. The patient's inability to perform the tasks successfully is taken as an indication that the anesthetized hemisphere is dominant for that particular activity. With the anesthetized left hemisphere about 95% of right-handers and approximately 70% of left-handers cannot talk at all for about 2 minutes. For several more minutes after that they behave as aphasics—making errors in order and/or naming. With the anesthetized right hemisphere there are typically some minor speech problems, but speech is never inhibited entirely (Kolb & Whishaw, 1996). About one half of the remaining 30% of left-handers behave just the opposite—total failure of speech functions occurs with anesthetized right hemisphere, with some inhibition with the anesthetized left hemisphere. The other half has apparently bilateral speech control because the consequences are the same regardless of the anesthetized hemisphere. The results of Wada tests are usually compared with behavioral tests performed on the same subjects. The main disadvantage of this method is its invasiveness and inappropriateness for healthy subjects. Apart from that, if used on its own, it can only help determine the dominant hemisphere, but not regions of increased activity during a particular function.

NEURORADIOLOGICAL METHODS

A conventional X-ray can reveal, for example, skull fracture, but it is not appropriate for visualizing different brain structures. Somewhat better are contrast techniques. These techniques involve temporary substitution of some of the cerebrospinal fluid with air (nowadays considered obsolete) or injecting the cerebral artery with a dye impermeable to X-rays (angiography); such techniques enable visualization of ventricles and fissures, as well as of the vascular system of the brain. However, they are invasive and their use is only clinically justified. Besides that, they are not appropriate for functional neuroscientific research because they do not provide clear identification or differentiation of gray and white matter structures.

COMPUTERIZED (AXIAL) TOMOGRAPHY—C(A)T

This technique involves computer-supported use of X-rays. It is based on the principle that different biological materials vary in their density, which affects absorption of X-rays. High-density tissues (e.g., bones) absorb a great deal of radiation, neural tissue somewhat less, and low-density materials such as blood or air the least. Due to this it is possible to obtain a three-dimensional image of the living brain by putting together a series of X-ray scans of its horizontal sections. By means of contrast, this procedure offers good view of injury location, with somewhat poorer images of more recent injuries and those closer to the skull. Due to their similar density, it is difficult to distinguish white matter from the gray. Spatial resolution is between 0.5 and 1 cm of tissue (Gazzaniga et al., 2002).

MAGNETIC RESONANCE IMAGING (MRI)

The images are obtained by measuring the energy of waves emitted by hydrogen protons after being activated in the magnetic field. Depending on the model, the magnetic field of an MR machine is more powerful than the earth's magnetic field by about 500 times or more (0.001 vs. 0.5 tesla, or more, even up to 7 tesla). The advantage of this technique is its noninvasiveness—the brain is not exposed to any radiation—but it is relatively slow (it takes about 15 minutes to complete) and noisy. Spatial resolution is less than 1 mm (Gazzaniga et al., 2002). This method provides good images of the brain structure and structural changes (gyri and sulci, white and gray matter, injuries, tumors, or morphological changes such as one finds in Alzheimer's disease patients), but poor functional images (Eysenck & Keane, 2000; Kalat, 1995). A better method for studying brain activity during cognitive functions is functional magnetic resonance imaging, which is based on this technique.

FUNCTIONAL MAGNETIC RESONANCE IMAGING (fMRI)

This method provides a series of functional images of the brain while engaged in a particular activity. It seems that our brains resort to anaerobic metabolism to supply energy necessary for temporary increases in neuronal activity. As a result, the amount of blood oxygen in the activated area increases and the image of brain activity is based on the magnetic properties of hemoglobin, the principal oxygen carrier in the bloodstream. When the oxygen is absorbed, what remains is deoxygenated hemoglobin that is more sensitive and has more powerful magnetic properties. The ratio of oxygenated and deoxygenated hemoglobin can be measured, and this is called the *blood oxygenation level dependent* (BOLD) effect. During increased activity, the amount of oxygen is greater than the possibility of its absorption, so the ratio is usually in favor of oxygenated hemoglobin. This method poses minimal biological risk to the subject, but is counter indicated in patients who wear pacemakers, cochlear implants and/or other metal implants. The signal is obtained by functionally provoking changes in brain tissue (there is no injection or inhalation of radioactive or other substances); it provides anatomic and functional information about each subject, and its spatial resolution is good (1 to 2 mm, i.e., 3 mm^3 of volume). The disadvantages of the technique are that it is an indirect measure of neural activity, and it cannot keep up with the pace of most cognitive processes. Temporal resolution is several seconds: the first changes are visible several seconds after the start of activity, with the greatest increase occurring about 6' to 10 seconds later (Eysenck & Keane, 2000; Gazzaniga et al., 2002; Kalat, 1995; Posner & Raichle, 1997). fMRI is the method of choice for most cognitive neuroscientists. Similarly to PET (see the following for a more detailed description), it is based on subtraction of activity patterns at rest from those recorded during a task. Its great advantage is the practically unlimited number of measurements (Demonet, 1998). Due to this, the BOLD effect may be temporally aligned with a particular event, and combined with multiple repetitions of the same event and averaging (similarly to event-related potentials, see following discussion) it may provide a clearer image of activity in particular brain regions (Gazzaniga et al., 2002). The method is extremely useful in longitudinal studies that monitor recovery from aphasia and the plasticity of language functions (Papke, Hillebrand, Knecht, Deppe, & Heindel, 2000).

RECORDING OF ACTIVITY

These methods are based on the following assumption: if a particular brain region is crucial for a process (e.g., cognitive, motor, or sensory) there will be increased activity in that region when the process is initiated. The technology and techniques of recording brain electrical activity have been developing for approximately 100 years. During this time it has become possible to measure more than just electrical activity, for example, oxygen and glucose consumption, or blood flow in a particular brain region while the subject is performing a task.

Measuring regional cerebral blood flow (rCBF) underlies many techniques, and it is based on the fact that blood flow increases in the activated parts of the nervous system. Several blood flow measurement techniques are in use. One of them involves injecting radioactive, chemically inert gas, xenon (^{133}Xe) into the carotid artery (or inhaling it), and measuring radioactivity accumulated in different parts of ipsilateral cortex. Blood flow may be measured by (functional) infrared spectroscopy (f)NIRS that is based on the brain's permeability to infrared rays. This method actually measures changes in the concentration of deoxygenated and oxygenated hemoglobin. It is noninvasive, fast, and relatively cheap, but its spatial resolution is poor (Cooper & Delpy, 1995).

The problem common to all these techniques is that increased blood flow is present when excitatory and inhibitory neurons are active, which makes the results unreliable with respect to the nature of activity (Colier, Jaquet, van der Hoeven, Hagoort, & Oeseburg, 2000; Posner, 1995). It is also interesting, and should not be neglected when interpreting findings, that people with high blood pressure present a different picture from those whose blood pressure is normal. van der Veen et al. (2000) found their hypertonic patients showed increased bilateral blood flow during cognitive tasks that commonly cause increased activity in only one hemisphere in control subjects. In their patients, even the classical dichotomy between verbal (left-hemisphere controlled) and spatial (right-hemisphere controlled) working memory tasks was substituted by increased blood flow in the left hemisphere regardless of task.

ELECTROPHYSIOLOGICAL METHODS

Some methods of measuring electrical activity register activity of large groups of cells, whereas others record action potentials of single cells.

Single-Unit or Single-Cell Recording

This method was developed some 40 years ago with the aim of studying the activity of single neurons. Because of its invasiveness it is typically used in laboratories on experimental animals, which is its major drawback. A tiny electrode, approximately 1/10000 mm in diameter, is inserted into the animal's brain. This enables measurements of extracellular and intracellular potentials. It is a very sensitive method that can record electrical charges of as little as one millionth of a volt. It has helped provide invaluable information about the functioning of the primary visual cortex (Eysenck & Keane, 2000) as well as data on the auditory cortex in experimental animals. On the basis of obtained results it was possible to make retinotopic and tonotopic maps of primate brain (Gazzaniga et al., 2002; Ivry & Robertson, 1999). Its main advantage is that it can make very precise recordings of neural activity during different time periods—from very short (one second) to as long as several days. Besides its invasiveness, the fact that it offers only information about the single-cell level makes it unsuitable for studying larger brain areas. More recent techniques make possible the recording of activity of several neurons at a time (multiple-cell recording), which takes care of at least one of the disadvantages.

Electroencephalography (EEG)

This method is used to continuously measure brain activity through the skull. It reflects the totality of electrical events in the head, including action potentials and postsynaptic potentials generated by neurons, as well as electrical signals from the skin, muscles, blood, and the eyes. It is suitable for determining the functional state of the brain, but the results can hardly be associated with the activity of individual areas.

Event-Related Potentials (ERP)

In this context we talk of late, so-called cognitive, event-related potentials. The procedure is based on EEG, but the potentials are evoked by a specific stimulus (hence the alternative term *evoked potentials*) and extracted from the EEG record by signal averaging. Electrodes are attached to the scalp before the procedure. The stimuli are presented and ensuing electrical activity is recorded. Underlying the procedure is the fact that EEG contains all the changes in potential that are time-locked with the specific event, such as stimulus presentation, or movement, that become visible by signal averaging over a large number of these events. In the averaging process, the noise (the uninformative part of the signal) is cancelled out and the relevant signal emerges. Ten to 100 repetitions of the same stimulus are usually sufficient to produce a reliable potential that reflects characteristics of the studied brain and stimulus. Each wave is determined by latency and polarity (positivity or negativity). Evoked potentials recorded in the hemisphere contralateral to the auditory stimulus are generally stronger than those recorded in the ipsilateral hemisphere. It has also provided insights into the time course of processing, as well as detailed analysis of the influence of experimental variables. It is possible to compare the effects of two experimental conditions on early or late components of the response: the early component is taken to represent sensory events and the late component is attributed to cognitive ones. For example, P300 is a positive peak that occurs about 300 ms after the stimulus only if the stimulus has some relevance for the subject. Studies with language stimuli have revealed that N400 (a negative peak occurring approximately 400 ms after the stimulus onset) reflects semantic processes (Hagoort & Brown, 1995). It is possible, however, that a large portion of cellular activity relevant for behavior is not manifested as action potentials. A serious disadvantage of this method is its poor spatial resolution (i.e., impossibility of precise spatial localization of the studied activity), and it is also unsuitable for basic cognitive processes. Its principal advantage is good temporal resolution.

Compared with the early evoked potentials (visual, auditory, somatosensory), cognitive potentials are to a certain extent stimulus-independent. This means: (a) they do not necessarily occur every time a stimulus reaches the threshold, even with intact sensory pathways; and (b) they may occur without stimulation if the stimulus is expected. Different modalities can elicit almost identical cognitive evoked potentials. The response is affected by several factors: probability of stimulus occurrence, psychiatric status, selective attention and arousal, habituation, maturity of the central nervous system, aging, and task relevance, to name just a few (Dabić-Jeftić & Mikula, 1994; Praamstra & Stegeman, 1993; Stenberg, Lindgren, Johansson, Olsson, & Rosen, 2000). The response amplitude may be affected by type of stimulus, and even by such fine differences as noun categories. Müller and Kutas (1996) have found that personal names have the same latency (N1 and P2) but greater response amplitude than common nouns, and that the subject's own name, compared with other names elicits an additional response with a peak latency of about 400 ms over parieto-central electrodes and another even later response between 500 and 800 ms over left lateral frontal points.

A word of caution concerning some inconsistencies in presenting the evoked response test results is necessary. Response latency can be expressed in hundreds or single digits, so P1 designates the first positive peak, and P100 a positive peak of 100 ms latency. They may correspond to one another, but not necessarily. Sometimes, both alternatives are present in the same figure. Single digits are used to mark the peaks of same polarity from 1 on, which means that we can have N1 followed by P1, N2, P2, N3, and so on. Additional confusion may be caused by the fact that some authors turn the negative peaks upward and positive downward, whereas the others do not.

Hagoort and Brown (1995) point out, as well as many other authors, that a complete understanding of the neurobiological foundations of language requires the combination of several different methods.

Cortical Cartography

Recently, new combinations of methods have been introduced. One of these techniques is cortical cartography that combines mapping, event-related potentials and fMRI. It provides three-dimensional images of the skull and brain. Temporal aspects may be recorded by 3D movies.

Magnetoencephalography (MEG)

Neurons maintain electrical potentials along the external membrane, and when electrical potentials of many neurons are summed up, it is possible to record them encephalographically. These currents generate magnetic fields that may be recorded on the skull surface providing us with a magnetoencephalogram. This method allows precise (to the order of 1 ms) monitoring of the temporal structure of cognitive processes. It is considered a good direct measure of neural activity, as opposed to fMRI or PET, as the latter two methods reflect blood flow, which is an indirect measure of neural activity (Wang, Sakuma, & Kakigi, 2000). The advantage of MEG over encephalography is the insensitivity of magnetic potentials to the cranial bones and other tissues. Although its spatial resolution is superior to that of encephalography, it still provides relatively rough, hence unsatisfactory, anatomic and structural data. Another disadvantage of MEG is possible interference of other, task-independent sources of magnetism. Although MEG is very sensitive to tangential projections from sulcal structures, it is not as sensitive to radial projections from gyral structures (Boatman, personal communication).

RADIOISOTOPIC METHODS

Positron Emission Tomography (PET)

This technique provides information about metabolic activity of the brain. Metabolism-relevant substances (glucose or oxygen) are marked by a low dose of radiation. The patient is injected with radioactive isotope ^{15}O (tracer), or the isotope is inhaled. Approximately one minute later the radioactive water accumulates in the brain proportional to the local blood flow. During radioactive decay, the tracer emits positrons. As a consequence, an activity performed by the patient (e.g., reading) will reveal parts of the brain that are the most active at that moment. A special apparatus records different levels of radioactivity (i.e., metabolic activity), which results in brain images. The final record is not the absolute level of activity at the moment of task performance, but the result of subtraction of activity patterns at rest from those recorded during a task (similarly to fMRI). Regions with the greatest difference after subtraction are interpreted as areas of highest activity during a function. After 10 minutes no radioactivity can be detected any longer.

One advantage of this method is its applicability to large numbers of different tasks, and also its relatively good spatial resolution (3 to 4 mm, or 5 to 10 mm^3 of volume). Its disadvantages are technical difficulties in application, high price, and invasiveness in exposing the subjects to some (albeit small) doses of radioactivity, in addition to limited temporal resolution, that can be up to 60 s (Eysenck & Keane, 2000; Posner, 1993, 1995). Cognitive processes take one second or less, so it is obvious that this technique will not reveal everything that goes on during testing. Demonet (1998) suggests that it be combined with the results of response-time measurements. Interpretation of results is additionally complicated by the fact that even the subjects' anticipation of what they are about to say changes the final picture of which parts of the nervous system are involved or particularly active. It is also debatable to what extent increased isotope concentration reflects faithfully changes in the neural activity: there are indications that it might be true only for early stages of processing (Eysenck & Keane, 2000). Great intersubject variability precludes attributing specific language processes to limited brain regions (Fromkin, 1995).

Again, it needs to be pointed out that, just as with fMRI, for example, increased activity in a certain area during a task does not necessarily mean that the area plays a crucial role in the task at hand.

Single-Photon Emission Computed Tomography (SPECT)

This scanning technique uses computerized tomography technology, but instead of gamma rays, individual photons emitted by an externally applied substance are recorded. Its resolution is worse than PETs, but due to its lower price it is more suitable for wider use in clinical practice.

ULTRASOUND METHODS

Functional Transcranial Doppler Ultrasonography (fTCD)

This method is used to measure increased blood flow related to an event. It has been proven reliable and valid in lateralization studies. The results are comparable to fMRI and Wada test results, and they are replicable (Anneken et al., 2000; Buchinger et al., 2000; Lohmann et al., 2000; Zavoreo & Demarin, 2004).

SUMMARY

When evaluating methods of brain activity imaging, one must consider whether the information is represented in the brain at the level of the individual cell or at the level of cell groups. If the former is true, changes in the electrical activity of each individual cell may be associated with the function of the system that is based on it. In the latter case, the situation is much more complex. Another issue is the relevance of the recorded change to the brain. In other words, are the other parts of the brain "aware" of the activity? If they are, how do they interpret this increased activity: as relevant for further action or as a sign of some random and/ or functionally irrelevant activity?

Combining several methods may reveal whether the recorded connections are causal or just correlational, possible differences in the timing of activations in different locations in the brain as well as their temporal organization. In tests where the subjects were asked to recognize the objects by feeling them, fMRI revealed that even with their eyes closed their visual areas were activated. Combination with TMS showed that activation of visual representations is necessary for successful recognition by touch (Gazzaniga et al., 2002).

Most neuroimaging studies report average results of group studies, and they have to be interpreted in the light of the discussion at the beginning of this chapter (on the advantages and drawbacks of single case studies and group studies). Although general principles of organization and functioning of the nervous system are common to humans, individual variations are more likely than uniformity.

Methods involving recording of brain activity may lead to results that are different from the ones obtained by cortical stimulation methods, or by observation of clinical cases. Eysenck and Keane (2000) describe amnesiacs whose hippocampi were key structures for declarative or explicit memory. On the other hand, most PET and fMRI studies failed to replicate the findings of high activation in the same structure in healthy subjects during tasks that rely on declarative memory. One of the reasons may be that PET and fMRI show all areas that are active during a task, not just the crucial ones. Furthermore, damage to a part of the brain will result in functional disorder when the affected region is relevant for a particular function, and it may be that functional reorganization of neighboring areas that might take over has not yet taken place. Furthermore, the subjects' ages vary widely across studies: PET and fMRI methods involve mostly young healthy subjects, whereas in brain-injured groups there are older subjects. Increased sophistication and sensitivity of activity recording methods is a mixed blessing: on the one hand, it is their great advantage, and on the other, it makes interpretation much more complicated because registering even the smallest levels of activity frequently makes it difficult to decide which of the recorded active locations is really crucial for the function studied. Another problem is the fact that various techniques may be differently sensitive to the many features of the same function and its representation (Eysenck & Keane, 2000; Gordon et al., 1994). In addition to the recommendation to combine different methods, it seems increasingly necessary to include different tasks that examine the same function (e.g., different language tasks studied by several methods). This is known as *combined tasks analysis (CTA)*. Obviously, if a certain structure proves to be relevant for the same function on several different tasks, it will enable us to make more valid inferences about the relationship between structure and function (Ramsey, Sommer, & Kahn, 2000; Rutten, van Rijen, van Veelen, & Ramsey, 2000; Sternberg, 2003).

BEHAVIORAL METHODS

Since the brain is the organ of behavior, its functions can be studied by studying behavior, as it reflects psychological processes (Legg, 1989). The subjects are presented with different cognitive, sensory, or motor tasks, their solution is associated with physiological manipulations, and on the basis of the obtained results, functions of particular brain areas are defined. Complex psychological processes may be broken down into stages, and researchers can look for associations between individual stages and corresponding brain areas.

Numerous psychological tests include general IQ tests, memory tests, tests of perceptual and motor functions, and various language tests, such as Wechsler's intelligence scale (WAIS), Raven's matrices, and so forth. They can be implemented with a healthy population as well as clinical patients. It is important to have neuropsychological assessments for those who have suffered brain injury—regardless of etiology—for the purpose of choosing a therapy and monitoring recovery. However, clinical assessments are limited by the type of damage, in other words, the patients' ability to understand directions and perform the task. Obviously, someone with a paralyzed right arm as a consequence of stroke will not be able to perform motor tasks that require the use of the right hand.

Response time and the percentage of correct answers (or errors) are the most frequently used indirect measures of task difficulty. However, we must keep in mind the limitations of these measures. For example, the time it takes to give a motor response (e.g., raising one's hand or pressing a button) to a certain cognitive task (e.g., finding the target letter in visual tests, or determining rhyming status in auditory tests), includes time needed to make the decision and the time needed for the actual motor action. Technical limitations of equipment are, of course, additional factors.

The following section includes brief descriptions of the most frequent behavioral experimental methods used in studying language functions.

Paper-and-Pencil Tests

These are all the tests (including language) in which the tasks are presented graphically (as text or images), and the subjects are expected to respond by writing, drawing, or marking.

Word Association Tests

These tests are usually designed in a way that the subjects are presented with one word at a time, and are expected to provide the first word that comes to mind. Variations of the test include providing superordinate terms, synonyms, antonyms, additional members of the same category, and so forth. Another subtype of this test is the so-called *word fluency test* in which the subjects are asked to provide as many words that begin with the target letter or sound as they can in a limited period of time.

Stroop Test

The original Stroop test involved naming the colors in two ways: as blots of different colors and as words designating colors that were printed in letters of (in)congruous colors (e.g., the word *blue* printed in blue or red ink). Response times were longer to incongruous letter–color combinations due to the disagreement between the two bits of information. In a wider sense, the Stroop effect may be elicited by other stimulus combinations (Preston & Lambert, 1969).

The Wisconsin Card Sorting Test (WCST)

Different numbers of symbols varying in color and form are presented on cards. The subject picks up one card at a time and places it on one of the several piles in front of him/her. On the basis of the examiner's reactions, the subject concludes, by trial-and-error, whether the cards should be sorted according to color, shape, or number of symbols. After 10 successful consecutive attempts at correctly sorting cards, the examiner changes the sorting criterion without warning. The subject is supposed to discover the new criterion. Failure on this test—most frequently manifested as perseveration, or insistence on sorting according to the first adopted criterion—reveals disorders of frontal lobe functions.

Priming and Interference

In these tests one stimulus is used to facilitate or interfere with another that is related to the first phonologically, syntactically, lexically, or semantically. The degree of facilitation or interference (measured by response times to the second stimulus) offers information about the organization and relationship between the first stimulus (prime) and the second stimulus (target). For example, in a visual task in which a subject is asked whether the presented letter was *A* or *V*, the response will be faster if before the target *A*, an *a* (prime) rather than *v* is presented briefly. These experiments may reveal temporal sequence and degree of interference between the two competing cognitive processes or representations of different stimuli, but do not tell us much about the functioning of these processes and representations, or about their interference or facilitation (Westbury, 1998).

Shadowing

In auditory tests, the subjects are presented with different stimuli to the left and the right earphone. They are asked to listen carefully and repeat simultaneously with the speaker the message heard in one of the ears. When a sudden change is made in the message presented to the unattended ear (an unexpected sound or switch of the speaker from male to female), the subjects typically start to hesitate or lose continuity. This procedure may reveal language deficits even when they are not noticeable in everyday communication.

The test may also be visual, in which case two stimuli are presented in different locations in space, or in a bimodal manner (e.g., one stimulus is auditory and the other visual). It has been shown that the success of shadowing may be affected by several factors. For example, meaningful stimuli are more easily shadowed than meaningless ones. Shadowing is more successful if the stimuli are further apart in space, if they are presented at different pitch (e.g., male and female voices), and if they are presented at different rates, and so forth (Coren & Ward, 1989).

Gating

This method was introduced by Grosjean (1980). A recorded speech segment (typically one sentence) is spliced into shorter segments (usually about 20 ms) by sound-editing computer software. The subjects are presented with stimuli of progressively longer duration (each time one 20-ms segment is added, yielding stimuli that are, for example, 60, 80, 100, and 120 ms long). The subjects' task is identical at each presentation, or gate: "Say what you heard and/or what you think the entire sentence was." The responses of all subjects constitute a cohort. The subjects are frequently required to grade the certainty of their response (Erdeljac & Mildner, 1999). The procedure is repeated until the subjects guess the entire sentence, or the recorded material comes to an end. Comparison of the subjects' responses and the stimuli, in addition to an analysis of their progression, allows inferences about how much and what kind of information is needed to reach the correct response. The number of activated members of the cohort, and the frequency of their occurrence among subjects, as well as the reduction of their number and the final single response are considered indicators of organization, activation, and functioning of the mental lexicon.

Dichotic Listening

This is one of the most frequently used behavioral lateralization tests with auditory stimuli. In the original version of the test (Kimura, 1961a, 1961b; 1967) the subject hears through the headphones three numbers presented one after another to the left ear, and simultaneously, three different numbers presented to the right ear. During a very brief pause the subject is asked to report as many of the six numbers as possible. Then another triad is presented and responded to, and so on. Some versions of the test include manipulating attention to one ear or the other (Hugdahl & Anderson, 1986; Hugdahl, Anderson, Asbjornsen, & Dalen, 1990; Mildner, 1999; Mildner & Golubić, 2003; Mondor & Bryden, 1992; Obrzut, Boliek, & Obrzut, 1986). Laterality indices, calculated from the subjects' responses, are taken as indicators of ear advantage, i.e., contralateral hemisphere dominance.

Dichotic tests in a wider sense include all auditory tests in which two different stimuli are presented to the two ears at the same time—these can be two signals, or a signal can be presented to one ear and noise to the other. If the untested ear is continuously presented with white noise or murmur, the attention is directed toward the tested ear. The more the distracting stimulus differs from the test stimulus, the greater attention is directed toward the tested ear (Sparks & Geschwind, 1968). For example, if the test stimulus is speech, white noise will direct attention to the tested ear more than if it were speech-based noise (murmur or backward speech). As one channel is loaded more, the response to stimuli in the other one is improved, so the overall response is actually constant (Berlin, 1977). This is equally applicable to healthy subjects and commissurotomized patients.

Such tests have shown that the ear contralateral to the speech-dominant hemisphere is superior to the other ear. In a great majority of people the superior ear is right, and the speech-dominant hemisphere is left—phenomena supported by independent sodium amytal (Wada) tests. Different varieties of the dichotic listening tests have revealed right-ear advantage (REA), with a corresponding left-hemisphere dominance for digits, words, nonsense syllables, formant transitions, backward speech, Morse code, difficult rhythms, phonological tone, and many other speech and language-related stimuli. However, test–retest procedures reveal that only about 50% of the subjects exhibit consistent statistically significant REA for dichotically presented speech sounds. Left-ear advantage (LEA), with a corresponding right-hemisphere dominance, was reported for tunes, music chords, environmental sounds, emotional sounds, tones that are processed independently of the language content, pitch perception, and similar stimuli. No ear advantage, or inconsistent ear advantage, was reported for vowels, isolated fricatives, rhythms, nonmelodic humming (Kolb & Whishaw, 1996), and also for linguistic prosody (Mildner, 2004).

Ivry and Robertson (1999) report results of studies that claim auditory information is indeed lateralized; however, it is not with respect to ear, but with respect to the side of space from whence the sound comes. Accordingly, each ear may have projections in both hemispheres, but sound input from one side of the space will project to the contralateral hemisphere: the sound coming from the right will be projected to the left hemisphere, and the sound coming from the left will be projected to the right hemisphere, along both ipsi- and contralateral pathways.

Divided Visual Field

This is one of the most frequently used behavioral lateralization tests with visual stimuli. It is based on the anatomic and physiological specificity of the visual pathways: all stimuli from the left visual field reach the right cerebral hemisphere, and all stimuli from the right visual field reach the left hemisphere. Since the hemispheres communicate via commissural connections, primarily the corpus callosum, visual information from the two hemispheres is combined in a matter of tens of milliseconds. Nevertheless, it is possible to design the experiment so that very brief stimulation of one or the other visual field by instantaneous presentation of stimuli to the left or to the right of the fixation point results in response-time differences depending on whether the stimuli were verbal or nonverbal and whether they were presented to the left or the right visual field. Some 60 to 70% of right-handers exhibit right-visual-field advantage (RVFA), in other words, left-hemisphere dominance for language material but not for nonlanguage (Pinel, 2005; Tadinac-Babić, 1994, 1999). Since it takes the eye about 150 to 200 ms to shift from the fixation point, in order to get the lateralization effect the stimuli must be kept shorter than that (Gazzaniga et al., 2002).

Dual Tasks

These tasks may tell us something about possible common neural substrates of speech and language functioning and motor activity. The classical experiments of Kinsbourne and others (Chang & Hammong, 1987; Cherry & Kee, 1991; Hicks, 1975; Kinsbourne & Cook, 1971; Singh, 1990; Tsunoda, 1975) have shown that the results of simultaneous tasks that rely on the same neural structures differ from those where processing is controlled from different brain regions. The test typically includes two tasks that have to be carried out at the same time, and it attempts to test the relationship between the two tasks (i.e., between their cerebral representations). It is expected that success on one or both tasks will be poorer if performance requires the activation of identical areas. For example, it has been shown in right-handers that language processing has a significantly greater negative effect on the accuracy and speed of simultaneous motor activity of the right hand than of the left, and that the effect becomes larger as the language processing complexity increases (Mildner, 2000). The same study revealed that even designating one of the two tasks as primary, and purposefully directing attention to it, does not necessarily result in its unhindered performance compared with the secondary one. The two tasks may facilitate or inhibit each other—simultaneity does not necessarily have to cause interference.

It is not quite clear to what extent the results of dual tasks are affected by attention mechanisms and the fact that they share a common neural substrate. Dubost, Beauchet, Najafi, Aminian, and Mourey (2002) studied the relationship between walking and two different cognitive tasks—mental arithmetic and speech production. When performed simultaneously, both cognitive tasks slow down the person's pace and shorten the step, but the walking efficacy is preserved (the subjects' pace is still even). On the other hand, walking affects each of the cognitive tasks differently. Whereas mental arithmetic (working memory) was not affected by walking, word generation (semantic memory) was facilitated by it (expressed as the greater number of words produced while walking than in the speech production task alone).

SUMMARY

Some other lateralization tests look at gesticulations as motor accompaniment and reflection of language functions. Kimura (1973b, 1973c) found that people gesticulate more with the hand contralateral to the language-dominant hemisphere, and that hand gestures accompany linguistic expression. Video recordings of people talking revealed that right-handers make bigger movements with the right side of their mouth than with the left. This was true not only for speech production but also of all complex nonverbal mouth movements. Careful observations have also revealed that right-handers turn their heads and/or eyes to the right while solving verbal problems, but upward and/or to the left when solving numerical or spatial problems (Pinel, 2005). According to some authors, writing posture is indicative of the language-dominant hemisphere, regardless of whether the person is left-handed or right-handed (Levy & Reid, 1976). Namely, if the writing hand wrist is above the finger level, with the hand pointing downward, the language-dominant hemisphere is ipsilateral to the writing hand. If the person writes with the fingers pointing upward (as most people do) the contralateral hemisphere is language-dominant.

The problem of studying lateralization by means of behavioral methods is that in healthy subjects, as opposed to the split-brain patients, we cannot be certain whether the response to the lateralized stimulus is the result of processing in the contralateral hemisphere or whether it reflects joint efforts of both hemispheres after callosal transfer. The most reliable results are obtained if different methods are combined, for example, behavioral methods, with noninvasive activity recording methods, especially if they are compared with disordered functions in clinical patients and the functioning of split-brain patients.

APHASIA TEST BATTERIES

One large subset of neuropsychological methods for studying speech and language functions are tests for aphasics. These are used to test different levels of language functioning—from the most general division into production and perception to tests that tap into specific levels of processing: phonological, syntactic, semantic, and so forth. One of the most widely known and used is the Boston Diagnostic Aphasia Examination (Goodglass & Kaplan, 1983). This battery comprises 34 subtests for 12 language areas, two additional tests of music abilities and seven tests for the assessment of parietal lobes functions. Grammatical-syntactic tests,

tests of nonverbal functions, and profile assessment scales are usually added as well. Many other aphasia tests are in use too, but they all assess four basic language skills, all or some of which may be disordered in aphasia: spontaneous speech, repetition, comprehension, and naming (Juncos-Rabadan, 1994; Turdiu, 1990; Vuletić, 1987).

5 The Central Nervous System

Principles, Theories and Models of Structure, Development and Functioning

On the basis of systematic characteristics, the principles of structure, development, and functioning of the nervous system are established. These principles serve as starting point for the design of theories and models. Empirical and experimental tests and evaluations of theories and models complement existing knowledge. This, in turn, enables us to develop new principles or modify them in such a way that we come to have new models or new versions of the old ones. Due to this obvious interactivity, it seems reasonable to discuss the principles of structure and functioning of the central nervous system in the same chapter with the theories and models that refer to them. The four principles that are discussed in this chapter are hierarchical organization, parallel processing, plasticity, and lateralization of functions.

PRINCIPLES

HIERARCHICAL ORGANIZATION

One of the most important principles of the nervous system structure and functioning is its hierarchical organization (Fischbach, 1992; Kalat, 1995; Kolb & Whishaw, 1996; Webster, 1995). Higher levels provide greater precision. Neurons respond to increasingly abstract aspects of complex stimuli as the distance, measured by the number of synapses from the source, increases. Examples of this principle are reflexes. They are quick precisely because the reflex arc, also measured by the number of synapses, is short. For instance, the cochleo-stapedial reflex (i.e., the response of the stapedius muscle in the middle ear to high sound intensity) is initiated at the level of the superior olive rather than completing the entire auditory pathway that ends in the auditory cortex. On the other hand, phoneme discrimination takes place in the medial geniculate and cortex after the stimulus has passed through a much longer part of the auditory pathway (cochlear nuclei, olivary complex, inferior colliculi).

PARALLEL PROCESSING

Another important principle of the functioning of the nervous system is that bits of information do not travel along a single pathway. Various aspects of the same sensation are processed in parallel ways (Fischbach, 1992; Kalat, 1995; Kolb & Whishaw, 1996; Webster, 1995). Zeki (1992) described examples of visual stimuli. He found that in the brain there is a division of labor manifested in anatomically discrete cortical regions and subregions specialized for different visual functions. There are four parallel systems in charge of different visual properties: one for movement, one for color, and two for shape, of which one is closely related to color and the other is independent. These specialized areas are interrelated directly or through other areas. Signal integration in the parietal or temporal lobe proceeds through local circuits. Some of these areas are fully developed at birth (the so-called V1 region—where the entire retinal map is located—is synonymous with the primary visual area in traditional terminology). The development of other areas is completed after birth, which indicates that their maturation depends on experience.

Auditory stimuli behave in a similar manner. Sound localization depends on interaural differences in phase and amplitude, and these differences are processed along several paths in three synaptic relays in the brain. Phase differences provide information about the location on the horizontal plane, whereas amplitude differences provide information about the location on the vertical plane. In humans, as little as 3° shift on the horizontal plane (i.e., a temporal difference of only several μs in the activation of the dendrites of the left and right cochlear nuclei) is sufficient to identify the difference in sound source location (Kalat, 1995; Webster, 1995). This type of parallel processing is probably characteristic of other sensory systems, association areas, and motor pathways as well. Primates have about a dozen different cortical maps for visual stimuli, about six for auditory (Lieberman, 1991), and four for the somatosensory ones (Kalat, 1995).

PLASTICITY

The third principle of the structure, development, and functioning of the central nervous system—primarily the brain—is its plasticity. This is the ability of the central nervous system to adapt or change under the influence of exogenous or endogenous factors. There are three main types of plasticity: (a) changes in connections that occur after birth, as a consequence of interactions with the environment; (b) changes in connections that occur after lesions; and (c) changes induced by learning and experience. The term *developmental plasticity* that is often found in literature refers to the first, and partly the third type. Plasticity is closely related to the notion of functional reorganization—a phenomenon referring to the change in (cerebral) representation of a function or sensory modality. The change may be caused by lesions or natural aging processes, but also by practice and learning. Functional reorganization may be manifested as a change in the size of the cortical area where the particular function or sensory organ is represented, or as a different location of representations. For example, if one finger is amputated, the neighboring fingers will be represented on a greater area than before, at the expense of the amputated finger. Shifting of speech representation to the opposite hemisphere is sometimes found in patients with brain injuries in the speech-dominant hemisphere. Without plasticity, functional reorganization would be impossible. This topic is discussed in more detail in chapter 7, this volume.

LATERALIZATION OF FUNCTIONS

The fourth important principle of brain functioning is lateralization of functions. Since the brain appears to be anatomically symmetrical, early works on the biological foundations of behavior assumed that functions were symmetrically organized as well. However, more detailed studies have revealed that the brain is not exactly symmetrical and that the two hemispheres function differently; in other words, they are both anatomically and functionally asymmetrical. This was supported by findings that lesions to homotopic regions in the left and the right hemisphere have different consequences for behavior and functioning in general. Hence the term lateralization of functions.

After many repeated unsuccessful attempts to associate the site of lesion with a function disorder, the localizationist approach of the late 18th century was replaced by a holistic one—understanding and describing cerebral functions as a process in which each behavior requires interaction of many different structures as a whole. Therefore, the first attempts to relate language deficits to left-hemisphere damage went largely unnoticed. Broca emphasized the difference between anterior and posterior injuries, but only as Wernicke's findings on the importance of the left hemisphere for language functioning emerged. As a consequence, the left hemisphere was called the dominant or principal hemisphere, whereas the right hemisphere was treated as less important or minor. In this volume, as indeed in most contemporary literature, the term *dominant* may refer equally to both hemispheres. It is used in the sense of being primarily involved in the processing of a function, not in the sense of being more important in general. The few authors who studied right-hemisphere functions at the turn of the 19th century (e.g., Hughlings-Jackson and Balint) found that damage to that hemisphere most frequently resulted in deficits in spatial functioning (perception of objects in space and orientation in space). This was the foundation of the propositions that language and spatial functioning are two basic human cognitive abilities, each represented in a hemisphere of its own.

Primary sensory processing and motor functioning are bilaterally represented. Lateralization occurs in higher, more complex functions, such as language, spatial processing, music, and so forth, so that at the highest levels of processing the two hemispheres have different roles. Lateralization of function is discussed in more detail in a separate chapter.

THEORIES AND MODELS

The brain consists of numerous cortical areas and subcortical nuclei that differ in afferent and efferent connections, appearance under the microscope, and characteristics of their physiological reactions. It is, therefore, logical that their contributions to psychological processes are different as well. Although phrenology turned out to be unacceptable, anatomical studies have shown that some areas have direct connections with the motor system, others with the sensory, and still others are to be found between motor and sensory areas. Accordingly, some areas are closely connected with a particular sensory modality, others with movements, whereas others exhibit complex response properties that are neither exclusively motor, nor solely sensory. The parts that are most closely connected with specific functions are those having the closest connections with the sensory organs. Experimental and clinical data have shown that damage to different parts of the brain may have considerable consequences for behavior and cognitive functions.

Theories and models of central nervous system functioning, especially of the brain, attempt to address several key issues: (a) where does a particular function take place? (b) What is its course? and (c) how autonomous is it? The processing may proceed in parallel (more aspects or levels are processed at the same time) or serially (one at a time); processing may be one-way (bottom-up or top-down) or there may be more or less interaction (between levels or within one level), with total or partial autonomy of processing at each level. Processing may go on in separate and specific brain structures or it may be more diffuse. Active theories posit the existence of very complex transformations of neural information and programs that may be compared, and on the basis of that comparison perceptive decisions may be made. Each level is connected to other levels and processing proceeds in a parallel manner in all of them—there is no necessary order of levels of processing (e.g., acoustic material serves as a basis for certain hypotheses, but at the same time as a test of the existing ones). Passive theories are as a rule one-way—processing is only bottom-up or top-down, with no interaction among levels. Obviously, each model may belong to several categories (e.g., localistic and serial). Furthermore, not all models deal with all or the same components of language functioning—some are limited to language production, others to perception or word recognition.

In this chapter, I discuss some of the most influential and most widely quoted general theories and models of structure and functioning of the central nervous system. This includes the application to language functioning, as well as some specifically linguistic theories.

PARALLEL OR SERIAL PROCESSING?

The first models of sensory system functioning were serial. According to them, the information flowed between components, but only through a single channel. Later, it became acceptable to talk about parallel models that were believed to represent sensory functions better than the serial ones. In parallel models, the information may be relayed among components through different channels. Although there is ample evidence for parallel processing in sensory systems, the nature of language processing is not so easily agreed upon (Gazzaniga, Ivry, & Mangun, 2002). Examples of serial processing are Levelt's (1989) model of speech production and the Wernicke–Geschwind model of language functioning. These models are discussed in more detail later.

Serial or cascade models were supported and discussed, among others, by Bentin, Mouchetant-Rostaing, Giard, Echallier, and Pernier (1999) and Schmitt, Muente, and Kutas (2000). On the other hand, Starreveld (2000) does not agree with the serial model of speech production.

LOCALISTIC MODELS

A principal characteristic of localistic models is establishing direct connections between structure, condition, and functioning of a particular brain region with behavior. According to these models, focal injury to some brain region will result in specific patterns of cognitive deficits, because brain functions are assumed to be localized. An obvious drawback of these models is the inability to deal with cases of disordered functions without damage to "responsible" brain regions, and with cases of preserved function in spite of damage to corresponding regions. The models are acceptable to the extent that it has been shown that particular functions are in fact localized within specific brain regions, with the higher functions (e.g., attention and thought) spread over greater areas of the cortex and including subcortical parts. Some advocates of these models were Broca, who localized the speech production center in the left frontal lobe; Wernicke, who localized the speech perception center in the left temporal lobe; and Hughlings–Jackson, who associated motor activity with the posterior parts of the frontal lobe, on the basis of postmortem examinations of his epileptic patients. One of the first models was Lichtheim's in 1885. It consisted of three main parts and connections among them. They were: (a) Wernicke's area with the phonological store, (b) Broca's area with programs for planning and execution of speech, and (c) an area where concepts were stored. Lichtheim's was a classic localizationist approach, elaborated later by Geschwind and Galaburda (Galaburda, 1994; Gazzaniga et al., 2002).

On the basis of the properties of the Hebbian synapse, Pulvermüller (1992) calls functional neuronal groups *cell assemblies.* Turner and Frackowiak (1995) call these restricted areas *cortical fields* (each field comprises about 10^6 to 10^7 neurons) and consider them to be the substrates of specific processes. However, these cannot be counted as true representatives of localistic theories because, in essence, their approach relies on neural networks.

For some 30 years now, all discussions about localization of language functions have included the Wernicke–Geschwind model. In spite of its inconsistencies and imperfections, over the years the model has instigated research and discussions about cortical representation of language. Before the model was proposed, there had been attempts to describe localization and lateralization of language functions on the basis of deficits in language functions (chap. 3 on the history of neurolinguistics). These localistic theories lost ground at the beginning of the 20th century to holistic theories that see the brain functions as a whole. Geschwind incorporated these ideas into the so-called Wernicke–Geschwind model based on a theory stemming from the belief that damage to language areas in the left hemisphere and/or connections between them caused aphasia and other language disorders.

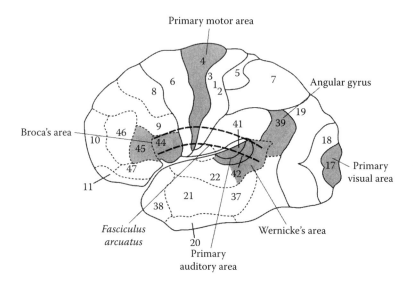

FIGURE 5.1. Wernicke–Geschwind model of speech and language.

Wernicke–Geschwind Model

The Wernicke–Geschwind model consists of seven components: primary visual cortex, primary auditory cortex, primary motor cortex, angular gyrus, arcuate fasciculus, Wernicke's area, and Broca's area. All the components are located in the left hemisphere (primarily in the precentral and the postcentral areas, immediately anterior and posterior to the central sulcus, where face representations are located). The model is shown in Figure 5.1.

When we read aloud, the signal arriving in the primary visual cortex is relayed to the angular gyrus, which transforms the visual form of the word into its auditory code and transfers it to Wernicke's area where comprehension takes place. Wernicke's area initiates appropriate responses in the arcuate fasciculus. In Broca's area the signal activates the appropriate articulation program that activates neurons of face and mouth in the primary motor cortex, and finally, muscles that participate in word articulation.

This model belongs to the group of localistic and serial models, because it involves a series of responses that occur in linear succession, and this is one of its most serious drawbacks. Any model that involves any number of highly localized cortical centers connected linearly, is not a true description of actual brain functioning and cannot be applied to complex cognitive processes. Broca's and Wernicke's aphasias are, in fact, primarily but not exclusively expressive and sensory, respectively. Moreover, it has been found that these types of aphasia do not necessarily ensue from damage to Broca's and Wernicke's areas.

The model was not supported by the examples of patients who had, for medical reasons, undergone surgical removal of parts of the cortex that are supposedly components of the model. For example, if the entire Broca's area was removed, but with little or no surrounding tissue, the patients had no speech difficulties. Similar examples from clinical practice may be found for other components of the model as well. The advocates of the model explain this phenomenon by the fact that the patients had longstanding neurological disorders before the surgical procedure, which might have resulted in some functional reorganization prior to surgery. However, the model is not supported by cases of sudden brain injury caused by trauma or illness. Only extensive damage involving three lobes caused difficulties proposed by the model (Pinel, 2005). It has also been consistently found that extensive damage to the anterior regions is associated with articulation problems as opposed to equally extensive damage to posterior regions. CAT scans have shown that damage limited to Broca's and Wernicke's areas does not cause language problems, and that in all patients presenting with language difficulties there had been some subcortical damage. All studies confirmed a greater probability that extensive damage to left anterior parts would cause difficulties in language expression, as opposed to damage to posterior parts, and that comprehension difficulties would be caused by extensive posterior damage, rather than by anterior damage. Additional explanations were supplied by Kimura (1983; see also chapter 2, this volume) and Hier, Yoon, Mohr, Price, and Wolf (1994).

Cortical stimulation of large (widely distributed) numbers of sites in the left hemisphere cause speech arrest or selective speech deficits (inability to name objects, incorrect naming, counting, etc.). Aphasic symptoms occurred very rarely in response to right-hemisphere stimulation. Contrary to the model's predictions, cortical areas that were affected by stimulation in terms of language functions were found well outside the language areas defined by the model. Another important result emerged from these studies: individual differences were substantial among subjects in the organization of language abilities. Ojemann (as cited in Pinel, 2005) proposed that the language cortex is organized like a mosaic, in which columns of tissue responsible for a certain function are widely distributed throughout the entire cortical language area. He also concluded, on the basis of results from a series of recording and stimulation studies (Ojemann, 1994), that there were separate systems of neurons and basic areas for additional language dimensions. Different components of each system obviously work in parallel. The neurobiological substrate of language probably involves (mainly) separate processing of each language dimension, but with the systems related to each dimension active at the same time. Human language, like so many other functions in the primate cortex, is probably processed in multiple parallel distributed systems. Scanning techniques have revealed increased activity during speech in the left frontal, temporal and parietal lobes, as well as in the left thalamus and basal ganglia (Kalat, 1995).

Gordon et al. (1994) present evidence that confirm the existence of fine subdivisions in representation of language and related functions and conclude that a considerable number of these subdivisions may be controlled by higher mechanisms. Evidence may be found in the speech perception system, as well as in verbal and visual semantic systems and their connections to other language subsystems, including phonology and its connections. Global regulation and coordination is supported by the same data about semantic processing difficulties.

With respect to neuroanatomic connections, cortical stimulation maps differ from the classical language function maps. First, Broca's and Wernicke's areas are probably spatially more circumscribed for any individual than is usually shown. Second, other areas crucial for language may be identified more reliably, for example, those related to the posterior connections between the temporal and occipital lobe.

As expected, resection of the speech cortex can cause acute deficits, but recovery is quick—within several days or weeks. Such speedy recovery of even those skills that had taken longer to acquire (e.g., reading) suggests that, in normal situations, there are multiple but latent copies of language functions and representations (Gordon et al., 1994).

The serial Wernicke–Geschwind model is challenged by the cases of deficits in reading aloud. According to the so-called *dual-route models* proposing that the reading process is in fact mediated by two different pathways of neural activity, there are two different systems of reading aloud. One is the *lexical procedure*, which is based on the information about pronunciation of written words stored in our vocabulary. The other one is the *nonlexical procedure*, which is based on general rules of pronunciation that enable us to read unfamiliar and nonsense words. Patients who have trouble with one procedure but not with the other are taken as strong support for these models. For example, in surface dyslexia, the nonlexical procedure is intact, but the patients have considerable difficulty reading words that require unusual pronunciation (impaired lexical procedure) and most frequently pronounce words in accordance with the rules (e.g., reading /ei/ instead of /æ/ in *have* as if the word rhymed with *cave*). With impaired nonlexical procedure but intact lexical procedure, the patients are typically unable to pronounce nonwords, but their ability to read real words is spared. PET scans have shown that looking at words activates only the occipital lobe with no additional activation in Wernicke's area or in the angular gyrus; the frontal lobe processes spoken and written language in the same way (Pinel, 2005). Furthermore, the activity recorded in the right hemisphere during these studies is not predicted by the model. Obviously, these results cast serious doubt over any serial model of language processing.

The problems with the Wernicke–Gerschwind model, as indeed with any localistic model, may be summarized in the following points: (a) localization of language system parts is identical in all healthy subjects; (b) specific functions of subregions of the language cortex are derived from the connections of these subregions with the motor and sensory cortical regions. These features are problematic, because they do not take into consideration the nature of many components of language processing, and are in disagreement with the evidence of variability in language function localization (Caplan, 1988).

Despite the problems we have discussed with the Wernicke–Geschwind model, in combination with the observed language difficulties in brain-damaged people, it can provide sufficient information about the general location of damage.

Hierarchical Models

These models are based on the principle of hierarchical organization primarily of sensory systems, such as visual, tactile, auditory, olfactory, and gustatory. The main path goes from each sensory organ to the thalamus, a group of nuclei located at the top of the brainstem. Nuclei responsible for individual sensory modalities relay the majority of the arriving information from the sensory organ to the limited part of the neocortex that is the primary sensory cortex for that particular sensory system. The complexity of coding increases with proximity to the neocortex. A large portion of outputs from each area of the primary sensory cortex are relayed to the neighboring cortical area—the secondary sensory cortex for that sensory modality. According to the traditional model, the association cortex is an area of cortical tissue not yet entirely understood that is the final destination of the sensations, loosely defined. It is believed that association cortex connects activities of different sensory systems, that it transforms the sensory input into the programs necessary for motor output, and that it mediates complex cognitive activities, such as reasoning and memory. There are multiple representations of sensory information in visual, auditory and somatosensory systems. At the highest levels, the functions are lateralized. Injuries to primary visual, auditory, and somatosensory systems cause serious deficits in sensory discrimination, which are manifested as significantly reduced sensory acuity. When secondary regions are damaged, acuity is frequently preserved, but not the ability to recognize objects, shapes, or patterns.

It is assumed that the hierarchical stages are closely connected. A generally accepted view is that structures at increasingly higher levels of the sensory system have a less and less sensory and more and more perceptive role. This is based on the notion that each level of the system analyzes the input from the previous level, adding to the complexity of analysis.

The Triune Brain

According to MacLean (as cited in Spreen et al., 1984), the mammalian brain may be anatomically and conceptually divided into three hierarchical systems that make up a whole. The first system comprises upper parts of the spinal cord, the midbrain, the diencephalon, and the basal ganglia. On the evolutionary scale this system corresponds to the lowest developmental level. This part plays a crucial role in instinctive activities necessary for survival of the individual and the species. The second part corresponds to the limbic system and is on a higher evolutionary level. It is involved in the integration of emotional expressions and self-awareness, and it may inhibit and suppress the first part. The third part corresponds to the cortex, and according to MacLean, it is responsible for nonemotional, integrative, detailed analysis of the external world. In humans, these properties are represented by language in the left hemisphere, enabling us to reason and think about future actions. The third part may override the first two and, in terms of evolution, it is on the highest level. Such a division corresponds to the ontogenetic development of the central nervous system. Van der Vlugt (1979;

cited in Spreen, 1984) divides this ontogenetic development into three stages as well, with each developmental stage depending on previous ones, and each subsequent structure having increasingly more refined and more complex adaptive and integrative functions.

Luria's Model of Functional Systems

Luria (1973, 1982) worked out three functional units of the brain that are responsible for reception, interpretation, and use of sensory information. These units act serially, producing behavior. Any weakness in any of the structures may affect processing in another.

The First Functional Unit

The arousal unit (upper and lower parts of the brainstem, reticular formation and hippocampus) is primarily responsible for arousal level, attention, motivation, and reasoning or impulsiveness. Inappropriate arousal or attention may have a negative impact on information processing that takes place in the second unit, which in turn may influence planning performed by the third unit.

The Second Functional Unit

The sensory (input) unit (posterior cortical areas, including the occipital, temporal, and parietal lobes with the accompanying projection zones) is responsible for reception, processing, and storing of information. In this unit the information is processed (in parallel or serially) and coded; it is also responsible for integration of information from different sensory modalities. This unit is, to some extent, involved in every task.

The Third Functional Unit

The motor unit (for output and planning, located in the frontal lobe and associated areas) is responsible for planning and programming of behavior, as well as for actual performance. This unit depends on the efficient functioning of other units and is probably in highest correlation with intelligence. It is the highest functional level of the brain.

Sensory and motor units may be further divided into primary, secondary, and tertiary areas, which represent levels of increasing complexity and integration in information processing.

The first functional unit may be identified with selective attention; the second with sensory data, information processing, motor responses, and cerebral dominance; and the third unit may be identified with planning, organization, and higher-order language functioning. It should be kept in mind that several functional units in the brain participate in production of behavior; there is no direct one-to-one correspondence between a cerebral area and particular behavior.

Luria related his theory to ontogenetic development of brain and behavior. Secondary zones cannot develop before the primary zones have fully developed. Only after the secondary (gnostic) zones have been developed can higher cortical zones become operative. The tertiary zones become dominant in adults.

This hierarchical development of the three zones is mirrored in the development from the maximally modal specificity of the primary zones to the supramodal organizational and interpretative functions of the tertiary zones. This means that the primary areas are maximally modality-specific, whereas the tertiary areas are associative and integrative across sensory modalities. The development entails progressive lateralization of functions as well: left and the right primary areas have identical roles in an individual's functioning, but hand dominance and language development require functional organization and specificities that develop concurrently with the secondary and tertiary areas and are radically different in the two hemispheres.

Performance at any level does not predict the quality of performance at subsequent levels. Since psychological functions dependent on tertiary zones develop in late childhood or adolescence, clear differences between children and adults in this respect can be expected.

Luria reserved a special place for the role of language in a child's development. Newborns have only the basic ability to express themselves by movement, crying or facial expressions (*the first signal system*), but older children begin to complement their actions with verbal expressions and eventually develop *the second signal system*. With the maturation of the tertiary cerebral zones (according to Luria, occurring around age 6), language becomes more sophisticated, and accompanying motor actions are no longer necessary (this does not pertain to normal hand gesturing accompanying speech). Language does not have to be overt any longer—it becomes internalized, and it mediates and directs behavior.

Kolb and Whishaw (1996) address several drawbacks of Luria's model. First, it is practically impossible to set a clear distinction between sensory and motor functions at any level of the nervous system, particularly when it comes to the cerebral cortex. Besides, the model does not predict the possibility of different perceptions of the same object under changed circumstances. Another difficulty is that the model does not allow the possibility of information bypassing the frontal lobe or primary motor cortex. Finally, it does not predict parallel sensory-motor systems, for the existence of which there is anatomical evidence.

One of the hierarchical models of perceptual speech analysis was proposed by Chistovich (1984). Her model posits the existence of hierarchically organized stages of perceptual analysis—auditory, phonetic, morphological, syntactic, and semantic. The result of analysis at one level is not final—at the higher level the ambiguous decision may be resolved. Each level operates on its units: at the morphological level decisions cannot be made about phonemes, for example, but only about morphemes, yet the higher levels may influence the outcome of the lower levels. Processing is parallel (at several levels simultaneously: morphological, phonological) and interactive (mutual influence of different levels). Some sort of normalization mechanism is assumed that takes care of stimuli arriving from different speakers. The model also posits that perceptual decisions are formed on the basis of (auditory) feature detectors. Perception starts at the subphonemic level because a decision is reached before the entire phonemic segment has been produced.

Jurgens' Model of Neural Vocalization Control

Jurgens (as cited in Kent & Tjaden, 1997) proposed a three-subsystem model of neural vocalization control, based on the studies of human and animal vocalizations.

Subsystem I
This is primarily responsible for coordination of breathing, movements of the larynx and upper respiratory pathways. It includes reticular formation, and motor and sensory nuclei of the brainstem and spinal cord responsible for phonation. Apart from coordinating muscle activity, this subsystem may have subroutines necessary for genetically programmed vocalization patterns.

Subsystem II
This initiates the vocal expression and selects among the existing vocalization patterns. It is hierarchically organized into three levels:

• Lowest level—periaqueductal gray and the surrounding tegmentum in the midbrain. This structure plays an important role in vocal expression of emotions.
• Middle level—subcortical limbic structures including the hypothalamus, medial part of the thalamus, amygdala, etc. These same structures are involved in regulating emotions. Their role is integration of external stimuli with the internal motivational ones.
• Highest level—anterior cingulate—the role of this structure is to maintain control of emotional states.

Subsystem III
This comprises the motor cortex and its primary input–output structures, primary somatosensory cortex, cerebellum, ventrolateral part of the thalamus, putamen, nucleus ruber, and the pyramidal tract. This subsystem executes fine voluntary control of vocalization patterns.

Obviously, this is also a hierarchical model. Kent and Tjaden (1997) proposed a somewhat more elaborate variant of the model. Their model also has three main subsystems, but they have modified Jurgens' subsystem III so that it reflects a greater number of connections and specific functions of some structures. It includes more inputs to the motor cortex, particularly from premotor areas. Basically, their model predicts parallel connections and processing.

MODULAR MODELS

Legg (1989) claims that the brain owes its resistance to damage to its modular structure. As opposed to the interactive principle of functioning, in which damage to any part causes collapse of the entire system (because the subregions are connected to each other), modular structure is such that groups of components are functionally isolated from each other. Accordingly, if one group is damaged, the remaining ones will continue to function normally. Modularity can be achieved in two ways: (a) functionally independent modules are created so that each of them performs a different function (complementary system); or (b) several identical modules exist, each of which is capable of performing equal functions (redundant system). Processing is exclusively bottom-up. A higher level cannot be reached before completing the lower one. Modularity has found support in the fact that brain damage results in very specific consequences limited to the damaged area. Specificity does not only imply that a function is lost or weakened by damage, but also that the part survives lesions to other parts that result in different consequences. Legg (1989) concludes that the brain functions on the principle of the redundant modular system (because if it were interactive, it would be much more susceptible to damage), and that the only operative difference between the interactive and the redundant modular system is the degree of dysfunction resulting from damage to individual components.

According to Fodor's (1983) modular model of the mind language does not belong to the central system. It is an input system, and input systems have modular structure. This modular structure is determined by several features. First, the input system receives information from several sensory systems, but it processes them in particular ways. For example, during reading the language input system translates information from the visual modality to the phonological or speech representation modality. Second, processing is one-way, bottom-up, which means that higher cognitive modules do not affect the lower ones (e.g., sentence context does not affect phonemic processing). In cases of ambiguities, both (or all) word meanings are activated and forwarded to higher levels, and ambiguity is resolved by context only after both (or all) meanings have reached the level of context. Third, each module has its place in a particular region of the brain. Hence, modular models are at the same time predominantly localistic.

During speech production, actual speech output is preceded by several preparatory stages that are superordinate in terms of cognitive level. One of the most frequently quoted models in the past 15 years is Levelt's (1989; Levelt, Roelofs, & Meyer, 1999). According to his theory, word preparation is accomplished through the stages of conceptual preparation, lexical selection, morphological and phonological encoding, as well as phonetic encoding, which is followed by articulation. In the process, the result (i.e., the language product—speech) is monitored by means of the speaker's speech comprehension mechanism. The model includes macroplanning (a decision about what we want to convey to the listener) and microplanning (choosing words and defining their roles). The output of the planning stage is the conceptual message that is forwarded to the formulator, which supplies the message with appropriate grammatical and phonological form (grammatical encoding). During the process, the surface structure of the message is computed. In this surface structure, lemmas are the lowest-level elements. Lemmas are stored in the mental lexicon, and they contain all syntactic and semantic characteristics of the word. Since the concepts are organized with respect to meaning, in a task where the subjects are required to name an object in the picture, activation of one concept will activate semantically related concepts, and the lemma eventually selected will belong to the term that corresponds to the picture (lexical selection). The lemma then activates the lexeme (word form) with its phonological and phonotactic data, followed by appropriate phonetic encoding based on the data, resulting in the activation of the sound form of the word. Articulation is the final process that results in the spoken word by mapping phonetic gestures to articulators. In summary, the model essentially consists of the following six stages: conceptual preparation (→ lexical concepts), lexical selection (→ lemma), morphological encoding (→ basic word form), phonological encoding (→ syllabification), phonetic encoding (→ preparation of speech sounds), articulation (→ spoken word) (Eysenck & Keane, 2000).

Since this model is modular and serial, phonological processing cannot take place before the lemma has been chosen. Therefore, phonological information has no effect on lemma selection. Auditory-perceptive self-monitoring is the only form, albeit very limited, of feedback (Levelt et al., 1999). The model is illustrated in Figure 5.2. Some ERP studies have confirmed that lemma selection precedes phonological activation at the level of the lexeme (Gazzaniga et al., 2002).

Different approaches to studying language functions and models of language function organization more or less confirm that language is modular in the sense that it is autonomous with respect to other higher cortical functions, and that it involves submodules (e.g., syntax, lexicon) that are functionally autonomous. This autonomy, however, cannot be interpreted as exclusively one-way processing or the existence of separate neurological structures for individual submodules, but only as relatively independent functioning (Blumstein, 1988).

Cascade Models

These models are similar to modular ones. They include different, but mutually connected neural modules, each of which is responsible for a different level of processing of word information or some other data. In terms of word recognition, they propose that lexical access is autonomous, independent of higher levels, but that lexical selection may be equally affected by the sensory (bottom-up) and by contextual (top-down) levels. Examples of serial or cascade models are supplied by Bentin et al. (1999) and Schmitt et al. (2000). They report data from studies in which subjects were required to name pictures in two concurrent tasks. The semantic task was to decide whether the picture depicted an object or an animal; the phonological task was to decide whether the name of the object starts with a vowel or a consonant. They claim that semantic processing starts before phonological.

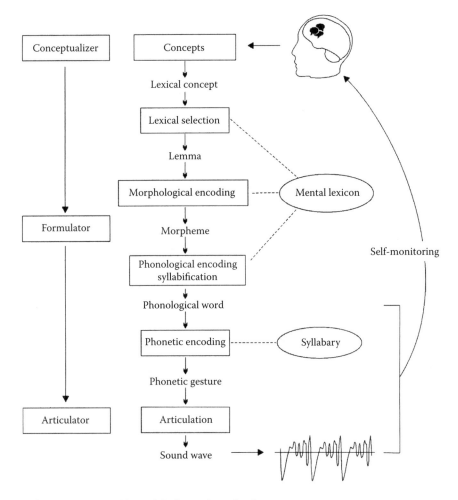

FIGURE 5.2. Levelt's model of speech production.

INTERACTIVE MODELS

Contrary to modular models, interactive models propose some degree of influence of one processing level on another (both toward the higher and toward the lower levels), and a combination of top-down and bottom-up processing. According to interactive models, phonological activation starts immediately after the beginning of semantic and syntactic activation and proceeds simultaneously. Not only can all types of information participate in word recognition, but context may affect sensory data even before they become available, by changing the activation status of the word form. According to these models ambiguity is not possible, because only those words will be activated that are in harmony with the familiar context. Most of these models do not predict the existence of words as ready-made forms, but a particular word is recognized if within the neural network circuit certain nodes are activated simultaneously (Eysenck & Keane, 2000; Gazzaniga et al., 2002; Pinel, 2005).

The models posit some feedback among levels, but also among elements within each level. Two types of processing are at work here: (a) data-driven processing (bottom-up) that starts with input data; (b) concept-driven processing (top-down) that starts with thought processes. These are active models, because they predict active cooperation between different levels taking into consideration context, expectations and attention, as opposed to the passive models in which processing is one way—only bottom-up. The interactivity assumes, naturally, simultaneous processing at several levels, but also some degree of hierarchy. A large number of models involve some measure of distinctive feature analysis at lower levels, which may be reflected in the name of the theory or model or just in its description. In auditory perception, the process starts from the bottom and proceeds upward. At the auditory level, speech segments are not separated, but acoustic analysis takes place (for more details see chap. 1). Processing continues through the phonetic level (where decisions are made about the pronounced sound), and on to the phonological level (where the results of phonetic analysis are compared and coordinated with the specificities of the language at hand). Models and their diagrams vary in the amount of detail within the basic levels, but common to them all, even when it is not explicitly specified, is comparison of the input signal with some already existing patterns (template matching).

CONNECTIONIST MODELS

Classical connectionist models are those in which one processing continues after another. In that sense the components are related, but they are still predominantly localistic and serial models. An example is the Wernicke–Geschwind model discussed previously, but also the much older model by Lichtheim (discussed in this chapter). More recently, the connectionist approach assumes interactivity and parallel processing, as well as wide spatial distribution, due to which these models are said to be based on parallel distributed processing. Contrary to the localistic models, the connectionist models assume widely represented functions and connections among all segments of processing. The first computer-aided connectionist models were designed by McClelland and Rumelhart (1986). Since they include basic units or nodes mutually connected into networks, they are most frequently referred to as network models or neural network models. The first discussions in which neural networks were mentioned date back to the 1940s (Lončarić, 2002).

NEURAL NETWORKS

Many studies have shown that hardly any function can be reliably localized in a particular spot, that performance of a cognitive task (e.g., speech) activates

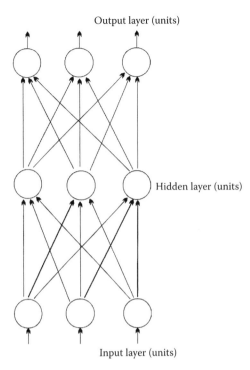

Output layer (units)

Hidden layer (units)

Input layer (units)

FIGURE 5.3.   Example of a simple neural network.

simultaneously several separate cerebral areas, and that stimulation of a limited area may elicit any number of different responses. Language and speech functioning can therefore be interpreted as coordinated activity of more different assemblies within a single unitary network (cortical or neural). As it has already been mentioned previously, it is believed that basic functions are localized in specific locations in the cerebral cortex, whereas complex functions involve parallel processing of information in widely distributed networks that spread over cortical and subcortical structures.

Neural network models consist of three layers: the input layer (units), the hidden layer (units), and the output layer (units). The units (that actually represent neurons) are connected and these connections facilitate or inhibit (increase or decrease) activation levels of the specific reception unit. Each unit receives input from the preceding layer and relays its signals to the next layer (Figure 5.3). Each input has a value—weight. The activation level of each unit depends on the weighted sum of all inputs. Hidden units provide information necessary for correct mapping of the input layer to the output layer by changing the strength of connections between units. This is accomplished by developing a set of rules for learning, in other words, a quantitative description of necessary changes in processing, depending on the final outcome. During the practice phase, neural networks "learn" to respond to given inputs with a particular output, by modifying the connections between units, so that each actual output is compared with the target output, and in case of discrepancies the weights are changed. The rule for weight adjustment is called *back propagation algorithm* (back prop), because the error message is relayed through the network in the opposite direction—from output units (back) to input units. Rumelhart (1986) called this procedure *supervised learning* (as cited in Ainsworth, 1997; Gazzaniga et al., 2002). A trained network, in fact, resembles natural systems: it generalizes responses to the patterns that had not been explicitly used during practice, and its efficacy gradually decreases as individual units are eliminated.

When we say that many areas function as a network, it means that they consist of mutually highly interconnected sets of neurons that function as units during a higher cortical activity. Neural networks are adaptable; they can learn to differentiate among patterns of input stimuli and to respond to each one of them in an appropriate manner. Information in the neural network is distributed, and each cell contributes to the recognition of every pattern. Particular cells do, however, respond selectively to specific patterns, but there are many of them for each type, and they are distributed throughout the network. This means that complex functions are represented within mutually interconnected areas that together make an assembly. Several conclusions may be drawn: (a) each individual cerebral area has the neural basis for several different types of behavior, and it can be part of several assemblies; (b) damage to one area will probably result in multiple deficits of some function; and (c) different aspects of the same complex function may be impaired depending on which of the many cortical areas and their connections have been injured. It can also be said that the brain consists of a number of smaller areas that function as overlapping neural networks.

Network models that include programmed cell death (*apoptosis*) are even closer to the actual functioning of the brain. Such models have shown that artificial neural networks may successfully solve difficult problems if there are more neurons at the beginning than will be eventually needed. The least useful neurons die away gradually after learning has taken place, and the learned solution can be preserved even with a smaller number of units than was necessary for initial learning—this is obviously similar to the living brain (Brown, Hulme, Hyland, & Mitchell, 1994). Although there are recurrent networks as well as feed-forward networks, speech and language functioning requires a model that predicts a combination of bottom-up and top-down processing.

Damage to the network causes overall inefficacy without specific deficits. The actual behavior of the network depends on the extent of damage: after mild damage the remaining cells may take over some of the function affected by damage; more serious damage makes the connections within the network sparse. The cells within the network recognize and respond to input patterns by mutual excitation and inhibition. As a consequence, damaged networks react more slowly, and it is possible that the normal excitation threshold is never reached, which results in malfunction (Deane, 1992).

It seems that impulses relayed by neural pathways to the higher cortical areas code information digitally: During each functional state some neuronal fibers are active while others are at rest. Neural networks are more resistant to localized damage than single neuronal tracts. According to the model of neural networks connected by nerve tracts, the brain functions as a series of parallel processors that interact by means of information channels that integrate them into a whole (Deane, 1992).

In short, networks have great data processing capabilities. They are resistant to damage, quick and adaptable, which makes them a good model of brain functioning (Lieberman, 1991).

Neural network models can engage in some highly sophisticated cognitive processes. Many consequences of brain damage resemble closely what one would get by damaging a network system (be it individual neurons, or connections among them). Seidenberg and McClelland (1989) constructed a language acquisition network. By switching off individual units of the network they simulated brain damage, which resulted in their network behaving as a dyslexic.

In studies of speech production, neural network models have been used to simulate articulatory movements on the basis of the data obtained by electromyographic recordings (e.g., the relationships among different articulator positions, speed, acceleration, etc.), or on the basis of experimental results about the influence of changes in the rate of speech and phonetic environment on the kinematics of speech movements (Löfqvist, 1997).

On the basis of their PET results, Friston et al. (as cited in Kent & Tjaden, 1997) proposed a model of word production based on the neural network models. Their model comprises three neural systems: (a) a distributed word representation store; (b) an afferent system that relays information to the store; and (c) a modulating system that changes the sensitivity of the neurons in the store. The store is located in the left hemisphere, in Wernicke's area, and the modulation system is located in the left dorsolateral prefrontal cortex.

Simpler versions of the neural network models cannot include temporal variations in speech and are therefore not suitable for speech recognition, but more complex models, with more than one hidden layer, achieve better results because they can learn to recognize different acoustic properties, such as second-formant transitions, vowel onsets, and so forth—independent of temporal organization (Ainsworth, 1997). It seems that we have yet to design a model that would solve all the problems of speech recognition or that would integrate all aspects of speech and language functioning into a whole.

The theory of neuronal group selection functions similarly to neural or cortical networks. According to this theory, different populations of neurons are structured by the interaction between genetic and experiential factors. The theory predicts exchange of signals by means of parallel and reciprocal connections among groups of neurons (*reentrant signaling*) and it attempts to explain such a wide selection of phenomena as perception, motor responses, language, and consciousness (Kent & Tjaden, 1997).

Spatialization of form hypothesis (parietal hypothesis) predicts that language processing (grammatical competence) is represented in the part(s) of the brain whose primary function is the representation of body image (schema), in other words, processing of spatial structures, especially with respect to one's own body. This is a direct isomorphism between spatial and grammatical knowledge. The cerebral area responsible for this function is located in the region where auditory, visual, kinesthetic and inputs from other sensory modalities converge and are integrated (Deane, 1992). The requirements are best met by the inferior parietal lobe. In other words, according to this hypothesis, the seat of grammatical (syntactic) competence should be in the inferior parietal lobe, and not, as traditionally assumed, in the frontal lobe, particularly Broca's area. According to this hypothesis, aphasia can be explained by the loss of awareness about one's own body.

Pansini's (1988) notion of spatioception (spatial perception) as a necessary prerequisite for speech acquisition includes five sensory systems: tactile, proprioceptive, vestibular, auditory, and visual. Stimuli from these five modalities converge in the part of the brain predicted by parietal hypothesis—on the border between the parietal, temporal and occipital lobes. Regardless of whether they are taken as five sensory modalities that take part in perception of space or as a new modality—spatioceptive—the underlying idea is that without them speech acquisition would be impossible just as spatial and language relations (grammar, primarily syntax, is based on these rules and relations) would be unthinkable. This idea is in agreement with the parietal hypothesis about the representation of language functions in the brain. A study of the relationship between space and native versus foreign language revealed a very strong effect of language on the preference of the left or the right hemispace (Mildner, 2002): When the processing was in the native language the subjects preferred reaching into the left hemisphere, and when the stimuli were in a foreign language they preferred the right hemispace.

Here is some evidence in support of the parietal hypothesis (Deane, 1992):

1. The inferior parietal lobe is the seat of bodily awareness and orientation toward extrapersonal space. It integrates somatosensory information. Moreover, this is the only cortical area in which information from many modalities is available at the same time. There is ample clinical evidence and evidence from primate experiments to support this claim.
2. The abilities to represent and manipulate complex spatial relations are located in the inferior parietal lobe. This includes the ability to recognize complex objects on the basis of the nature and arrangement of their components (right hemisphere in humans).
3. The inferior parietal lobe seems to be necessary for constructing sequential plans of action—for manipulation of a series of actions as mental entities (left hemisphere in right-handers). The left hemisphere is responsible for mental manipulation of abstract structures. Damage to the parietal lobe causes various symptoms: global aphasia, agrammatism, reading difficulties, and disorders of grammar and logic, and so forth.
4. The right inferior parietal lobe has only visuospatial and somatic functions and is considerably more efficient in spatial processing than the corresponding area in the left hemisphere. Homotopic areas in the left

hemisphere have a key role in hand–eye coordination and in general in hand movements. The hand is basically a parietal lobe organ (as extremities in general, it is the part of the body whose main function is interaction with the environment).

The parietal hypothesis predicts that the greatest damage to structural thought (→ grammar) will occur as a consequence of injury to the margins of the inferior parietal lobe, and that the nature of the deficit will depend on connections that have been severed. This, in turn, is defined by functional brain geometry (Deane, 1992). According to the hypothesis, aphasia will occur after injury to any segment of the network, not only as a consequence of direct damage in the injured area, but also because the injured area can no longer be activated, or the result of its activity is not a desirable input to other parts of the network. This may explain why there are so few cases of aphasia that can be clearly categorized, as well as cases of, for example, Broca's aphasia without actual damage to Broca's area.

Damasio and Damasio (1992) represent language processing in the brain through three sets of interacting structures. Their description is similar to Luria's model of three functional units (see previous discussion), but it is interactive and to some extent it relies on neural networks as well.

The first set consists of a large group of neural structures in both hemispheres that represent nonlanguage interactions between body and environment, realized by means of various sensory and motor systems; in other words, everything that a person does, perceives, or feels. The brain categorizes these nonlanguage representations (based on shape, color, order, emotional state, etc.) and creates a new level of representation for the results of this categorization. This is how humans organize objects, events, and relations. Subsequent layers of categories and symbolic representations are the basis of abstraction and metaphor.

The second set comprises a smaller number of neural structures, mainly located in the left hemisphere, that represent phonemes, their combinations and syntactic rules for combining words. When stimulated from within the brain, they produce words and sentences that will be said or written. When stimulated by the environment, by means of speech or writing, they engage in initial processing of auditory or visual language signals.

The third set (also mainly in the left hemisphere), acts as a mediator between the first two sets. This set may start with the concept and initiate word production, or it may receive words and stimulate the brain to retrieve appropriate concepts. Besides selecting appropriate words to denote a particular concept, these intermediary systems control the production of sentence structures that express relations among concepts.

Neural structures that serve as mediators between concepts and words are located along the occipitotemporal axis. It seems that mediation for the many general terms occurs in the posterior part of the axis, whereas the most specific ones are mediated by the most anterior part, near the left temporal pole. Damasio and Damasio (1992) conclude this on the basis of clinical cases of focal injuries in different parts of the left temporal pole (see also Gazzaniga, 1994). Depending on the location of the injury, there may be selective damage to common or proper nouns. Injury to some parts of the temporal lobe may impair access to verbs and function words, but also the grammatical structure of the sentences produced by the patients.

In general, Damasio and Damasio (1992) redefine the notion of "images" in the brain—physical representations of different concepts and experiences. They claim that the brain preserves a trace of neural activity that was elicited in the sensory and motor cortex during interaction with an object or a person, rather than a permanent record of actual "pictorial" representations of objects or persons, as was traditionally believed. These traces are patterns of synaptic connections that may repeatedly combine separate sets of activities defining an object or an event. Each trace may initiate related traces as well. In other words, besides preserving the representations of the external world, the brain records how the body reacts to the outside world. This interaction is represented in simultaneous microperceptions and microactivities in separate functional regions. These separate activities are united in neural assemblies in many areas of "convergence" in the brain, which would correspond to the traditional notion of association areas, as well as Turner and Frackowiak's (1995) notion of cortical fields, or the Hebbian cell assemblies, as suggested by Pulvermüller (1992). The brain also categorizes information so that related events and concepts may be reactivated together. This possibility is based on the physiological principle that the neurons that are active together tend to group together (see the "fire together–wire together" principle in chap. 1, this volume). Activity within such a network may serve both expression and comprehension. It is precisely due to categorizing percepts and actions simultaneously along many different dimensions that symbolic representations (e.g., metaphors) are possible (Damasio & Damasio, 1992).

Localistic and connectionist approaches actually agree on the three areas in which focal lesions may impair language processing: (a) in Broca's area, that affects speech production; (b) in Wernicke's area, that affects speech comprehension; and (c) in the angular gyrus, that disrupts written language and mathematical operations and may result in severe aphasia (Deane, 1992).

OTHER THEORIES AND MODELS

Many other theories and models of language functioning may be found in the literature. General language models that do not deal specifically with neurofunctional organization of speech and language activity have three layers in common:

1. The conceptual layer—the highest, language-independent level, where thought processes take place.
2. The language layer—in which concepts are given names and are being manipulated (where the signified and the signifier get paired up); the language-specific layer contains all language rules, including syntax, morphology, etc.

3. The speech layer—where the message is materialized in the process of speech production, or where the first processing of input signals starts in the process of speech perception.

Among the best described models and theories of speech perception and/or recognition that do not go into specific neurofunctional substrates are the motor theory of speech (Liberman, Cooper, Shankweiler, & Studdert-Kennedy, 1967), theory of acoustic invariance (Blumstein & Stevens, 1979), analysis-by-synthesis model (Halle & Stevens, 1959), Logogen theory of word recognition (Morton, 1979), cohort theory (Marslen-Wilson, 1980; Marslen-Wilson & Tyler, 1980; Marslen-Wilson & Warren, 1994), TRACE model (McClelland, 1991; McClelland & Elman, 1986), native language magnet theory (Kuhl, Williams, Lacerda, Stevens, & Lindblom, 1992), Markoff's hidden models (short review in Ainsworth, 1997), RACE, Shortlist (review in McQueen & Cutler, 1997), and the neighborhood activation model (Luce & Pisoni, 1998). Some of them are briefly presented in the following section, but this is by no means an exhaustive list. Descriptions of more models and theories can be found in Eysenck and Keane (2000), Gazzaniga et al. (2002), Horga (1996), Ladefoged (2004), Lieberman and Blumstein (1988), Luce & McLennan (2005), McQueen and Cutler (1997), Moore (1997), Pinel (2005), and Sternberg (2003).

Motor Theory of Speech Perception

According to this theory (Liberman et al., 1967), perception is based on speech production, with the following hypotheses:

1. Since humans are both recipients and producers of speech, it is rational to assume the existence of a single mechanism.
2. Since invariant (i.e., constant) commands to articulators must exist in order to produce the same consonant in different vowel environments, it is logical to assume that the perceptual system makes use of these commands. Imitation may be cortical (not necessarily realized at the level of peripheral speech organs).
3. The hypothesis is valid at the suprasegmental level as well.

Several facts and observations support this theory:

1. During speech acquisition, the relationship between acoustic speech signals and sets of articulatory gestures is established by imitation.
2. People move their lips silently to facilitate understanding.
3. Speech perception in aphasics is impaired if they are asked to clench their teeth/keep their tongue between the teeth, which immobilizes their speech muscles.
4. Lip and face reading.
5. Electromyographic measurements have shown that the relationship between muscle activity patterns for a particular sound and its perceptual

result is stronger than the relationship between acoustic properties of the sound and its perception.

6. Neuroanatomically, there are points that are shared by speech production and perception—their stimulation may impair phoneme identification as well as face and lip movements characteristic of speech.

However, there are also some inconsistencies and problems with the theory:

1. Electromyographic data have shown that gestures are as variable as the acoustic signal. The same target (acoustic outcome) may be achieved by different movements (e.g., in cases of perturbed speech, such as when bite-block is introduced).
2. In the speech acquisition process comprehension precedes production.
3. The theory has not answered the question of how the listener extracts relevant data from the acoustic signal. At what level of the perceptual process does articulation come in? Besides, if auditory analysis is at the level at which its results can be compared with articulatory patterns, then it must be possible to bring auditory processing to the final decision without the help of articulatory patterns. Avoiding the mediators is more efficient.
4. Processes that would relate listening and articulation, regardless of level, would probably be very complex and therefore very slow, which again goes against the efficacy requirement.
5. In different types of aphasia speech production and perception are not equally impaired.
6. Simultaneous interpreting.
7. Neuroanatomically, there are sufficient examples of different and separate representations of speech production and perception processes.

Liberman and Mattingly (1985) proposed a revised motor theory of speech, with partly independently functioning modules. The phenomenon of the so-called duplex perception, which suggests the existence of speech and nonspeech modules for the same stimuli, is also taken to support the motor theory (more on duplex perception can be found in chap. 8, this volume).

Analysis by Synthesis

Halle and Stevens' theory (1959) is related to the motor theory—perception is to some extent based on production, but analysis-by-synthesis does not posit actual motor commands. In the process of comparing the input signal with an internally generated referent (listeners decode the acoustic signal by internally generating corresponding signals) the listeners perceive the one that best matches one of the existing internal models. This is called template matching. The process of identifying the phonetic aspect of an utterance goes through several stages: (a) peripheral analysis (preliminary analysis), during which the speech signal is broken down into distinctive features, yielding a rough, hypothetical matrix of phonetic segments and features; (b) dynamic analysis of the matrix by means of a series of generative rules, resulting in a phonemic decision; and (c) comparison of the original pattern and possible solutions (iteratively by means of generative rules) gives a final solution that is transmitted to higher perceptual levels.

The main components of the theory are the following: (a) some sort of articulatory description is interpolated between auditory analysis and final perceptual decision; (b) the process is dynamic—analysis is carried out by active synthesis of patterns at a particular stage of the entire process. The calculations resemble those that, in speech production, result in motor activity (on the basis of afferent feedback actual movements are modified to reach the desired target).

Chomsky and Halle (1968) proposed a variant of the theory. According to them, comparisons between the input signal and the patterns stored in memory are carried out at phonological and syntactic levels, rather than at the level of neuroacoustic signal processing, as in Stevens. The input signal is the initial impulse that enables the listeners to set hypotheses about the content of the speech message, relying on their linguistic and general knowledge, and to test the hypotheses as the signal goes on. Top-down processing plays a very important role. Decisions made at the lower level are hypothetical, and the final decision is made when data from both directions are merged or when the information received by lower-level processing is confirmed by information coming from higher levels.

Auditory Theory

According to Fant's theory (1967), acoustic analysis of the signal is sufficient for speech perception. It proceeds as primary auditory analysis, followed by analysis that determines distinctive features (feature analysis) and finally auditory features are combined into phonemes, syllables, morphemes, and words. The relaying of the message to the speech center in the brain includes motor and sensory components. The theory allows interactions between these mechanisms.

Neural (Phonetic, Linguistic) Feature Detectors

This theory of Jakobson, Fant, and Halle (1976) proposes neural assemblies that react to different segments of the speech signal (features) and that are in harmony with production capabilities and programs. The following experimental and empirical evidence is taken in support of the theory: (a) selective adaptation—after multiple repetition of a voiced sound (more than 100 times) subjects identify more stimuli as voiceless; (b) speech errors are usually off by one feature and the substitutions are systematic; (c) aphasias; (d) perception of sounds under difficult circumstances.

Theory of Acoustic Invariance

Blumstein and Stevens' theory (1979) assumes invariance in the acoustic signal. The mechanisms of vowel perception are applied, with two additional assumptions in case of place of articulation in stops: (a) moment of release and the first

20 ms are crucial—they carry information about place of articulation (before formant transitions); (b) combination of spectral features (compact/diffuse and gravis/acute). The authors claim that the theory enables 85% accurate identification of initial stops followed by vowels, somewhat lower in the final position. The theory does not deny the importance of other cues (e.g., transitions). This theory also assumes template matching.

The Cohort Theory

According to this theory (Marslen-Wilson & Tyler, 1980; Marslen-Wilson & Warren, 1994), word recognition proceeds in several steps: (a) at the beginning of auditory presentation all words familiar to the listener that start with the same sound(s) as the one presented are activated (→ initial cohort); (b) by increasing the duration of the presented stimulus, words that no longer correspond to further information, semantic or some other context, are eliminated; (c) processing continues until contextual information, and information available from the word itself become sufficient to single out one word (→ point of recognition). In the original theory the key role is played by the word onset: the word will not be recognized if the first phoneme is unclear or ambiguous. Context is important from the very beginning. The modified theory assumes different activation levels of candidate words (words that have identical endings are activated but with some delay). Context effects occur later.

Trace Model

McClelland's model (McClelland & Elman, 1986; McClelland, 1991) posits individual processing units (nodes) at three levels: features, phonemes, and words. Feature nodes are connected with phoneme nodes, and phoneme nodes with word nodes. Connections between levels are two-way and facilitatory. Connections among nodes at the same level are inhibitory. Nodes affect each other proportionately to their activation levels and strength of interconnections. Spreading of excitation and inhibition among nodes develops an activation pattern, or trace. The recognized word is determined on the basis of the activation level of candidate words.

One of the main disadvantages of this model is attributing too much importance to top-down processing: according to the model, nonwords would be inhibited, which is true only in difficult listening conditions. Another problem is that the model cannot be generalized to different speaking rates, because it assumes fixed timing patterns between levels. The model does not account for learning.

The Neighborhood Activation Model (NAM)

The neighborhood activation model (Luce & Pisoni, 1998) is a spoken word recognition model aimed at dealing with the representation and structural organization of the mental lexicon. According to this model, a spoken word activates a set (neighborhood) of words in memory that sound like the input word (which is phonologically similar), and that subsequently compete for recognition. The model takes into account the number of words in a neighborhood, the degree of their phonetic similarity, and the frequencies of their occurrence in the language. It predicts that a high-density neighborhood (in which many words share segments or sequences of segments) will affect word recognition in such a way that these words will be recognized more slowly and less accurately than words from a low-density neighborhood. The main problem of the model is its inapplicability to nonsense words, i.e., to the sublexical level.

PARSYN

PARSYN (Luce, Goldinger, Auer, & Vitevich, 2000) is a localist connectionist version of the NAM model. It is an improvement of NAM in light of its ability to account for the sublexical level as well. It consists of three levels (layers) of interconnected units: an input allophone level, a pattern allophone level, and a word level. The fact that it proposes an allophonic rather than a phonemic intermediate level of representation makes it unique among similar models, such as Trace or Shortlist. Between-level connections are facilitative and within-level connections are inhibitory, with some exceptions. The word level inhibits the lower (pattern) level when a single word gains advantage over its competitors and each unit at this level is capable of inhibiting other word units.

The Mirror–Neuron System

It has been suggested that mirror neurons may be a basis for higher level cognitive skills such as language and theory of mind (Rizzolatti & Arbib, 1998; Rizzolatti & Craighero, 2004). Mirror neurons are neurons that fire not only when the individual performs an action, but also when observing someone else performing the same action, and are therefore believed to underlie imitation learning and mind reading. This enables us to anticipate other people's actions and to empathize. They were found in primate (specifically monkey) and bird brains by means of electrophysiological studies, and their existence in human brains is confirmed by correlations between actions and observations and by scanning and neuroimaging techniques (Hauk & Pulvermüller, 2004; Saygin, Wilson, Dronkers, & Bates, 2004). Some mental disorders (e.g., autism) are thought to be a consequence of deficits in the mirror–neuron system. With respect to evolution of language, according to this theory, verbal language has evolved from gestural language (as had been suggested by Kimura, 1975).

6 Lateralization and Localization of Functions

In chapter 3 on neurolinguistics, I introduced some of the key terms related to descriptions of neural, primarily cerebral, substrates of speech and language. These are *lateralization, localization,* and *specialization,* and the related terms *representation* and *mapping.* Before we proceed with a systematic analysis of the relationship between speech and language functioning and brain activity, which is the central topic of the book, each of these terms are briefly defined.

The term *lateralization* refers to relatively greater control of a certain function by the left or the right hemisphere. If during some function, the left hemisphere is more active than the right it is said that the function is left lateralized; if the right hemisphere is more active than the left, the function is right lateralized. A synonymous term is *functional asymmetry.*

The term *localization* implies that some function has a specific neural substrate, a locality in the brain where it is realized. The term *specialization* means that some cerebral structure is particularly "skilled" in performing some function: this may refer to one of the hemispheres (e.g., it is commonly said that the left hemisphere is specialized for language) or to some area (e.g., Broca's area is specialized for language production). The terms *representation* and *mapping* refer to the representation of organs, functions, and so forth in the cerebral cortex.

LATERALIZATION OF FUNCTIONS

Studies of communication disorders have traditionally been oriented toward left hemisphere damage, because it was believed to be the seat of speech and language, and for that matter, communication. Hence the term *dominant hemisphere,* which implied that the right hemisphere was less important and, in terms of communication, silent. Although by the end of the 19th century it was known that the right hemisphere had an important role in perception, it was not until the 1940s and the first callosotomies that the language capabilities of the right hemisphere became interesting to researchers. The first studies confirmed that the right hemisphere was involved in visual perception, but they also showed that it can decode simple language patterns. Cognitive disorders and communication deficits started to be associated with right-hemisphere damage in the past 40 years or so. In the late 1960s, dichotic listening and tachistoscopic studies made it possible to study functional differences between the two hemispheres in healthy subjects. More research followed analyzing differences between the hemispheres in cognitive styles, or strategies implemented in information processing. Besides its dominant role in language functioning, the left hemisphere turned out to be crucial for analytic, linear, rule-based processing (e.g., language rules).

On the other hand, the right hemisphere was found to be important not only for visual and spatial information processing, but also for holistic, nonlinear, or parallel processing. This means that it is crucial for information synthesis, grasping the whole picture (*gestalt*), and processing of new data before any processing rules have been formed. It was noticed that right-hemisphere damage may affect one's body image, visual memory, visual perception, spatial orientation, or awareness about one's illness. The right hemisphere began to be considered the seat of artistic talent and creativity, uninhibited by rules, adaptable and capable of processing new, unfamiliar data. Simultaneously, *communication* ceased being synonymous with language and speech, and the term was extended to include body language and other nonverbal forms.

At present, the general opinion is that the left hemisphere is specialized for language, arithmetic, detail analysis, logical thought, temporal and sequential analysis, and serial processing of sensory data. The right hemisphere is believed to be specialized for emotions, intuition, recognition of faces and emotional facial expressions, artistic achievements, attention, recognition of tunes and other musical abilities, visuospatial analysis, and parallel processing of sensory data. These supposed specializations are frequently summarized into several dichotomies. It is said that the left hemisphere is specialized for verbal functions, as opposed to the right, nonverbal, hemisphere. In the same context, the left hemisphere is specialized for language functions and the right hemisphere for visuospatial ones. With respect to the type of data processing, the left hemisphere is referred to as more analytic, specialized for detailed functions, as opposed to the right hemisphere that provides a comprehensive image of the world, because it is apparently specialized for holistic information processing. It is also said that the left hemisphere is specialized for propositional functions and the right hemisphere for appositional ones. With the advancement of computer techniques and the development of models of cognitive functioning some new dichotomies surfaced. Kosslyn (1987) believes that the left hemisphere is specialized for categorical data (e.g., where something is, in a relational sense— whether an object is below or above some other object, what its relation is to the observation point, etc.). On the other hand, the right hemisphere is specialized for coordinate information (the exact location of the objects, distances among them and between each of them and the observer). Robertson, Sergent, and some others (Gazzaniga, Ivry, & Mangun, 2002; Volberg & Hubner, 2004) suggested the local–global dichotomy, in which the left hemisphere is better at local stimuli processing, whereas the right hemisphere is superior in global information processing. Ivry and Robertson (1999) differentiate the two hemispheres in the way frequency data are represented, rather than along the lines of comprehensive cognitive functions (e.g., music or language). Their hypothesis refers to auditory and visual (spatial) data (to be discussed later).

Another dichotomy emerged recently. Behavioral tests have revealed indirectly that the right hemisphere registers events as they happen, but the left hemisphere analyzes, interprets and draws inferences about them. The left hemisphere uses an interpreter to construct theories by means of which it assimilates newly perceived data into a meaningful whole—this is basically learning and experience forming. The process makes it slower and less precise when the task is mere recognition. On the contrary, the right hemisphere is very precise in registering the stimuli because it engages in no other operation on them (Gazzaniga et al., 2002). Naturally, in an intact brain these two procedures and strategies are simultaneous and complementary, resulting in satisfactory precision and analysis.

In their critical review of functional hemispheric asymmetry studies that had been carried out during a 100-year period, Friedman and Polson (1981) summarized several key issues:

1. Relatively small changes in stimuli, instructions to the subjects or other task properties, may result in the opposite direction of increased activity or change the dominant peripheral organ (e.g., ear or visual field).
2. Most studies cannot be replicated in other laboratories or by different methods.
3. There is great variability in subjects' responses on tasks that are expected to reveal laterality effects, even in homogenous groups.
4. There are intrasubject inconsistencies in the exhibited degree of laterality on different tasks that are used to study the same function.
5. There is no acceptable global theory that would explain even the established regularities. Malamed and Zaidel (1993) also pointed to the influence of language and task effects on lateralized word recognition.

Despite the fact that even the most fervent advocates of division of labor between the two hemispheres have not without a doubt proven that the two hemispheres are in opposition to each other, it has become popular to categorize people into left-hemisphere or right-hemisphere groups. In other words, it is common to separate those who, with respect to their cognitive style, rely more on the type of functioning characteristic of one or the other hemisphere. Many self-help and popular psychology books are full of advice on how to use the neuroscientific facts and the "facts" in everyday behavior and communication (Howard, 2000).

One of the pitfalls overlooked by the authors who tend to overemphasize the differences between the hemispheres with respect to their information processing characteristics, is attaching cause-and-effect properties to relations. In fact what may be revealed is correlations, and not necessarily the influence of one property, activity, or behavior on another.

The right hemisphere seems to be organized more diffusely than the left, so the functions are not as clearly localized. Due to this, some sensory or motor disorders resulting from focal lesions to the right hemisphere are not as severe as when they affect homotopic areas in the left hemisphere. Some authors have attributed this to the fact that the ratio of the white to gray matter is higher in the right hemisphere than in the left, which supposedly accounts for better inter-area connections in the right hemisphere, as opposed to the better intra-area connections in the left. Accordingly, damage to one area in the right hemisphere causes many different disorders, and injuries to different areas may cause identical disorders.

In a healthy population the two hemispheres do not act independently. Differences occurring in response times or some other differences between visual fields, ears or hands may be interpreted as delayed transfer from one hemisphere to the other, as disintegration of stimuli during transfer, as relative functional superiority of one hemisphere for a particular mode of action or as a result of attention.

Ringo and colleagues (cited in Gazzaniga et al., 2002) have shown, by using a neural network model, that slow interhemispheric transfer of information results in relatively independent activity of the two hemispheres. Each hemisphere in the model processes the task relatively successfully and quickly, but the communication between them is slow, resulting in greater probability that different processing abilities will develop. Since it takes about 30 ms for information to cross from one hemisphere into the other, and that is relatively slow, Ringo and coworkers believe this to be the basis for functional asymmetries.

What are the advantages of having a functionally asymmetrical brain? Hemispheric specialization for different types of processing, or specific activities, may be interpreted as a way to increase functional capacity of the brain: redundancy is reduced, but capabilities to act are considerably increased (Gazzaniga et al., 2002). According to Kertesz (as cited in Kent & Tjaden, 1997) asymmetric representation ensures adaptability, due to complementarity of functions. In speech, this complementarity may be found, for example, between segmental and suprasegmental (prosodic) features, between short-term and long-term operations, between local and global procedures, or between high-frequency and low-frequency characteristics. Each hemisphere processes the type of data that are optimal for its structure. This increases processing precision and efficacy, but still allows final integration of processed data. Functional asymmetry is desirable in motor control as well, particularly in fast and precise movements characteristic of speech. Peters (1992) believes that symmetrical control would require precise coordination between the two hemispheres, and account for different lengths of the left and the right *n. recurrens* that innervate larynx muscles. In fact, some authors claim that bilateral control of speech is one of the causes of stuttering and other speech production disorders (see chapter 8, this volume).

According to some theories of lateralization of cerebral functions, there is some sort of cooperation and interaction between the two hemispheres, and according to others, each hemisphere has unique functions of its own. The problem with both conflicting views is that they rely on speculation rather than on hard evidence.

Advocates of the former group (interactive) share the idea that both hemispheres are able to perform all functions, but do not. As to why that might be so, different versions of interactive theories have different answers. Some claim that the hemispheres function simultaneously, but are engaged in different aspects of processing. Others say that one hemisphere inhibits the activity of the other. For example, the left hemisphere inhibits language processing in the right hemisphere. Although from the developmental point of view, these models are acceptable, the problem is that physiological mechanisms of inhibition are not clearly defined. The third group of answers is based on the models of information processing and they predict that the hemispheres receive different kinds of information and, consequently, perform different analyses, or that some mechanism enables each hemisphere to pay attention to a specific type of information. However, these models fail to define mechanisms that would be responsible for selective attention (Kolb & Whishaw, 1996).

The second line of thought gave rise to the notion of hemispheres as representatives of different types of cognitive processing (analytic vs. holistic) and in charge of processing different types of material (verbal vs. nonverbal).

VERBAL VERSUS NONVERBAL AND LANGUAGE VERSUS SPATIAL INFORMATION

In spite of similarities in general perceptual functions between the left and the right hemisphere, there are subtle differences in the type of processing the stimuli features. Both hemispheres are active in all tasks, including language and spatial ones, but they use the information available in sensory data in different ways.

The most frequent dichotomy used to describe functional cerebral asymmetry is the verbal versus nonverbal or language versus spatial data processing. Studies of brain-damaged patients, as well as healthy subjects, have emphasized the role of the left hemisphere in language (more at the motor than at the receptive level). Auditory experience is not essential for left-hemisphere specialization for language. Evidence can be found in profoundly hearing-impaired subjects who had never heard speech. A right-ear advantage (i.e., left-hemisphere dominance) was found for all verbal material, meaningful as well as meaningless, even for linguistic tone. Left-ear advantage (i.e., right-hemisphere dominance) was found for simple, nonverbal acoustic stimuli, such as pitch, harmony, intensity, musical chords, tunes (in some cases) including humming, environmental sounds, nonverbal vocalizations, such as laughing, crying and sighing, sonar signals, emotional tones and intonation curves (Bradshaw & Nettleton, 1983; Kolb & Whishaw, 1996; Springer & Deutsch, 1997; Webster, 1995).

Such interpretations of cerebral asymmetry were supported by studies of memory and intelligence carried out independently of asymmetry research itself. Within theories of memory, the concept of a dual coding system was developed: verbal and iconic. Advocates of the theory claim that these two types of material are represented and processed through two separate and functionally independent, albeit interconnected, symbolic systems. According to them, the iconic system operates directly, analogously, and its output has a synchronous and spatial character that allows dynamic transformations with respect to visual and spatial features such as size, location, orientation, rotation, reflexion, distortion, and substitution of imagined objects. The verbal system is specialized for processing language and sequential information involved in speech production. The authors found support for their theory in studies that have shown that verbal and iconic information may be acquired, coded, stored and retrieved independently, with minimal interference, and involving independent and different types of forgetting (Bradshaw & Nettleton, 1983; Kalat, 1995; Kolb & Whishaw, 1996). Intelligence testing has for quite some time now recognized the two main sets of abilities: verbal and performance. Performance sets in general include abilities related to pattern and space perception (Bradshaw & Nettleton, 1983).

Studies with nonhuman primates as well as PET and fMRI results of human studies on processing spatial information have revealed that spatial tasks activated the right hemisphere considerably more than the left, whereas nonspatial tasks (linguistic and nonlinguistic alike) activated both hemispheres, with somewhat greater activation of the left than the right. Verbal tasks did not elicit such clear results. Contrary to humans, monkeys exhibited smaller differences between the two hemispheres with respect to the nature of the task (Goldman-Rakic, 2000).

Disconnection of the two hemispheres usually results in the inability to access language (generally left-lateralized) to described percepts and events in right hemispace. This, however, does not change nonverbal listening aspects. Such patients are able to localize the sounds as long as they are not speech stimuli. If the stimuli are words or just parts of words, comprehension or memory is impaired (Aitkin, 1990).

Processing of speech sounds, even of meaningless syllables such as *pa, ta, ka, ba, da, ga,* reveals great differences between hemispheres in split-brain patients. Efron (1990) does not attribute these differences (nor the ones found in dichotic listening studies in healthy subjects) to physiological suppression at the cerebral level as proposed by Kimura (1961a, 1961b), or to the difference between direct and indirect access, but to the tendency to pay attention to one side or the other. This tendency is stronger in split-brain patients than in people with intact corpus callosum. It might be concluded that left–right asymmetry in dichotic tests does not reveal hemisphere specialization for particular kinds of stimuli (e.g., music or language). Efron (1990) found, in his studies with visual stimuli, that people start scanning the stimulus from right to left more frequently than in the other direction, and concluded that this might underlie the right-ear advantage in dichotic tests. However, he failed to account for left-ear advantage for musical stimuli in dichotic listening tests. Finally, he concluded that his hypothesis allowed left-visual-field advantage as well, because it is not based on the assumption of asymmetry between the left and the right hemisphere functioning.

The left temporal lobe is responsible for the perception of short auditory stimuli (shorter than 90 ms), sound distinction (patients with damage to this region need longer pauses between stimuli in order to be able to distinguish them), and for recognition of sound sequences. Speech sounds are also distinguished better in the left hemisphere than in the right (see chap. 8, this volume). The left hemisphere is dominant for selective auditory attention as well. On the other hand, the right hemisphere seems to be dominant for music (Kolb & Whishaw, 1996).

It appears that musical elements—pitch, duration, height, loudness, and rhythm—are separate entities, because injuries affect them in different ways

(Bradshaw & Nettleton, 1983). Since corresponding elements exist in speech as well, analogous division of functions may be expected.

For auditory stimuli in general, it has been found that the right ear (left hemisphere) has an advantage over the left ear (right hemisphere) in dealing with verbal information, and that the opposite is true for nonverbal information. Ipsilateral pathways are partly or completely suppressed by contralateral activation. Verbal information presented to the left ear is degraded in the right hemisphere (which is reached first) or during transfer across the corpus callosum into the left hemisphere where verbal information is eventually processed. As it has been said before (see chap. 1, this volume), there are more nerve fibers in contralateral auditory pathways according to neurophysiologic evidence, and contralateral stimulation elicits greater cortical activity. In dichotic listening tests Kimura (1961b) found right-ear advantage for repetition of digits, and concluded that the left hemisphere is dominant for numbers. After that, many dichotic listening studies have been carried out for verbal and nonverbal stimuli.

Behavioral tests with very small children have shown that most of them, just like adults, exhibit right-ear advantage (left-hemisphere dominance) for verbal stimuli, and left-ear advantage (right-hemisphere dominance) for music (Spreen, Tupper, Risser, Tuokko, & Edgell, 1984).

Activity was recorded in both hemispheres, contrary to some other studies in which greater blood flow was found in the right hemisphere while distinguishing tones with respect to their temporal patterns, as opposed to the increased blood flow in the left hemisphere when the stimuli were words. This is in agreement with the neuromagnetic reactions to vowel onsets that have been recorded in both hemispheres. It seems that the difference is quantitative rather than qualitative: the amount of tissue activated by speech sounds is greater in the left hemisphere than in the right (Aitkin, 1990).

Sidtis (as cited in Bradshaw & Nettleton, 1983) concludes that the right hemisphere is specialized for analysis of harmony information during steady states of complex tones, and not for musical perception as such. Left-ear advantage is greater for more complex (with more overtones) musical signals.

Studies with visual stimuli have shown that the left hemisphere is dominant for letters and digits. For letters, right-visual-field advantage is greatest for stops, followed by fricatives, and it is the smallest for vowels. The left hemisphere is dominant when the letters are nominally identical (e.g., Aa or Bb), whereas the right hemisphere is dominant when the pairs contain physically identical letters (e.g., AA or bb).

Lohmann et al. (2000) found, by using fTCD, marked double dissociation in lateralization of language and spatial attention in 10 out of 12 of their subjects: in subjects with left-hemisphere dominance for language spatial attention increased activity in the right hemisphere, whereas in subjects with right-hemisphere dominance for language, spatial attention elicited activity in the left hemisphere. In two subjects both functions were lateralized to the right. In a study with Croatian–English unbalanced bilinguals Mildner (2002) found a clear dissociation between languages and preferred hemispace: when the auditory stimuli were in the native language (Croatian) the subjects preferred the left hemispace, when the stimuli were in the foreign language (English) they preferred the right hemispace.

Right-handers with right-hemisphere damage have difficulty performing spatial tasks. They lose their way, forget the paths they had taken many times, and they have problems understanding complex diagrams and pictures (Thompson, 1993).

Besides its role in spatial abilities, the right hemisphere is involved in non-speech communication—facial expressions, body language, and intonation. In a way, the corpus callosum eliminates the need for bilateral multiplication of structures; in evolutionary terms, this might have enabled the development of higher functions such as spoken communication (Levy, Koeppen, & Stanton, 2005).

At the simple visuospatial level, the right hemisphere is almost exclusively the active domain. This is also true of recognition of objects by separating the figure from the background, or on the basis of incomplete pictures. At the level of visual construction, when parts are integrated into a whole, both hemispheres may be involved. In general, the more complex the task, the greater the involvement of both hemispheres. The simpler the task, the abilities necessary for its performance rely more on the right hemisphere.

Left temporal lobe damage causes disorders in verbal memory and verbal intelligence. Damage to the corresponding area in the right temporal lobe results in difficulties in reading, recall, and recognition of nonverbal visual and auditory patterns, as well as a decrease in nonverbal IQ. Injuries to the left frontal and fronto-medial area decrease verbal fluency. Identical injuries in the right hemisphere affect rapid production of abstract, meaningless patterns.

One of the functions of the corpus callosum, besides information transfer, is allocation of attention in order to ensure focal unity. Disconnection results in problems with unilateral directing of attention, and the consequences are poorer information processing capabilities (Posner & Dehaene, 1994). It is, therefore, possible that the corpus callosum also plays an inhibitory role, which is manifested as prevention of synkinesia. It may also inhibit the development of language functions in the right hemisphere. It has been found that people with bilateral speech control often stutter, probably due to rival access to the single speech apparatus from two hemispheres. It has also been suggested that bilateral representation of language may diminish spatial abilities, probably because right-hemisphere language ability inhibits spatial functioning (Bradshaw & Nettleton, 1983).

Split-brain patients' behavior suggests that the right hemisphere may comprehend simple speech, read simple names, and that the left hand may comply with verbal commands (if they are not too complex), reach for named objects and select the appropriate object. The right hand is still dominant for writing, as in healthy subjects, but the left hand is used for drawing and model construction. The right hemisphere is superior in many spatial tasks, including copying of drawings, facial expression recognition, and so forth. The right hemisphere is better than the left in recognition of faces, but the left is superior when purposeful facial expressions have to be made (Gazzaniga et al., 2002). That hemisphere can recognize and identify social relations, pictures of people, family members, acquaintances, pets, and personal belongings, as well as pictures of historical or public persons. Both hemispheres have general awareness of body states, such as hunger or fatigue (Kolb & Whishaw, 1996).

In general, consequences of damage to the right hemisphere suggest that the following may be some of its functions (Bradshaw & Nettleton, 1983; Galić, 2002; Kalat, 1995; Myers, 1999): understanding spatial relations among objects and within objects in extrapersonal space; recognition and processing of complex visual patterns; precise perception, memory and recognition of abstract or meaningless forms that are too complex to be described verbally; ability to copy given forms and block design; face recognition; ability to understand and produce different musical aspects (although rhythm is usually unaffected by injury); appreciation of humor; control of emotions (particularly in the frontal and medial temporal lobe); recognition of emotional aspects of the stimulus; facial expression and recognition of emotions.

Experiments with tachistoscopically presented visual and visuospatial and language stimuli also support the claim that the right visual field (hence, left cerebral hemisphere) has advantage over the left for language stimuli, and that the left-visual-field advantage in visuospatial stimuli is the sign of right-hemisphere dominance for that type of material. However, it has been shown that retest results were in poor correlation with the original ones. Namely, only 42% of subjects exhibited right-visual-field advantage on both tests.

When distinguishing the so-called spatial, nonspatial and verbal tasks, one should keep in mind that it is impossible to exclude the verbal element entirely, even in the "clearly" spatial tasks, because it is impossible to control the amount of verbalization that goes on during the task. It is equally difficult to conceive of a nonspatial task with absolutely no spatial processing involved.

ANALYTIC VERSUS HOLISTIC APPROACH TO PROCESSING

Analytic versus holistic dichotomy is based on the premise that there are some advantages to locating the areas of the brain that perform similar functions into the same hemisphere, and that there are two basic types of reasoning: analytic and synthetic, each requiring different neural circuits. During evolution, functions that require analytic reasoning separated from those requiring synthetic thought, so that analytic and synthetic mechanisms positioned themselves in the left and right hemisphere, respectively. The left hemisphere operates in a more logical, analytic and computer-like mode, analyzing the stimulus sequentially, extracting relevant details, and giving them verbal labels. The right hemisphere is primarily a synthesizer that deals predominantly with the overall stimulus configuration, and organizes and processes information as gestalts or wholes (Levy, 1969; Pinel, 2005).

It seems that the right hemisphere is aware of the cognitive potential of the left, but not the other way around. With respect to visuospatial abilities, it has been shown that the right hemisphere is capable of storing and producing drawings and patterns that are acceptable as a whole, but lacking in detail. Results of the left-hemisphere activity are rich in detail, but without these details making any sense as a whole. The left hemisphere is better at analyzing a whole into constituent parts, whereas the right is more successful at recognizing the overall stimulus configuration and matching parts with appropriate wholes. In general, it has been shown that the right hemisphere is better at tasks that involve holistic, gestalt approach, whereas the left is better at analytic tasks, regardless of sensory modality. It has also been found that laterality differences are more marked at the motor than at the sensory level, in verbal and nonverbal tasks alike (Bradshaw & Nettleton, 1983).

Consequences of left-hemisphere damage indicate that it controls voluntary movements (injuries to specific areas frequently cause apraxia) as well as the ability to find one's way in a building or city (i.e., the position of a body in space). Contrary to that, the right hemisphere controls spatial perception in the sense of understanding space regardless of the subject's position in it. Patients suffering from left-hemisphere damage omit details in their drawings, but keep the spatial relations among elements, and in general preserve the overall coherence of the form. On the other hand, right-hemisphere patients have no difficulties with details, but have too many elements that are poorly connected into a coherent whole, with relations among elements and their spatial arrangement typically full of errors (Bradshaw & Nettleton, 1983; Galić, 2002; Kalat, 1995; Kolb & Whishaw, 1996; Webster, 1995).

The right hemisphere is dominant in face recognition (measured as response times and accuracy) if the responses are supplied manually. If verbal response is required, response time superiority is lost. In some individuals, recognition of familiar faces activates the left hemisphere more than the right. If the faces are to be distinguished by only one feature (obviously an analytic procedure), the left hemisphere is better. Yovel, Levy, Grabowecky, and Paller (2003) concluded on the basis of their ERP results that the two hemispheres exchange information at early stages of face processing. Facial representation is better if facial information is presented directly to the right hemisphere than to the left. It is best when both hemispheres receive facial information. In general, for visual stimuli, in terms of pattern recognition, the superiority of the right visual field is more probable (i.e., left-hemisphere dominance) for familiar and simple forms that are easily named. Left-visual-field advantage (right-hemisphere dominance) was found for letters or words that are difficult, unfamiliar and presented very briefly to the subjects. This again suggests that the differences between the two hemispheres are relative and quantitative rather than absolute or qualitative, which in turn is in agreement with the fact that there is no structure, at any level of analysis, that might exist in only one half of the intact brain (Gazzaniga, 1994).

SERIAL OR SEQUENTIAL VERSUS PARALLEL PROCESSING

From the evolutionary point of view, it is probably more correct to look at the serial, segmental motor specialization of the left hemisphere as the origin, and the right hemisphere as basically acting in a less specialized manner. The right hemisphere may mediate in different relatively unspecialized, more primitive, and possibly unconnected functions that have been "expelled" from the left hemisphere. Even activities that the right hemisphere is believed to be specialized in are less clearly defined, less well supported by evidence, and less unique. However, the contribution of the right hemisphere to social, affective, esthetic, and even cognitive competence should not be neglected (Bradshaw & Nettleton, 1983; Myers, 1999).

In line with this reasoning is Sussman's paradigm (Bradshaw & Nettleton, 1983; Sussman, 1994), according to which the left hemisphere is specialized for sensorimotor integration of movements related to speech as well as for movements of arms and legs, hands, fingers, and orofacial muscles, even when they are not associated with phoneme production. Most likely it is not a coincidence that the cortical representations of hands, mouth, and ears are so close to each other in humans and that all of them are relatively much larger than the corresponding areas in apes. Only humans are capable of using complex tools and verbal and gestural communication, and all of these activities require sequential, timed syntactic mechanisms in order to flexibly generate new rule-based sequences.

Problems arise when brain functions are studied using simple verbal-nonverbal oppositions because: (a) the right hemisphere has considerable language abilities, albeit more receptive than expressive; (b) the left hemisphere is superior in some visuospatial tasks that rely on strategies involving analytical extraction of significant or distinctive features or elements; (c) the right hemisphere is not dominant for music in all aspects, particularly in cases where the sequential or time-dependent nature of sound stimuli is relevant (e.g., in judging temporal sequence, duration, simultaneity, rhythm, or in categorical perception). Moreover, clinical and healthy-subject studies indicate that the left hemisphere is perhaps uniquely specialized with respect to temporal order, sequencing, and segmentation at sensory and motor levels alike. Motor level involves control of rapid changes in the position of hands, legs, fingers and articulators. It seems that the left hemisphere acts as a dynamic, kinesthetic and proprioceptive, time-dependent control system for attaining goals within the body, whereas the right hemisphere acts through static, exteroceptive, visuospatial functions, mainly outside the body. This notion is supported by work with dysphasic and dyslexic children who seem to suffer from deficits in perception of temporal order of nonverbal auditory stimuli (Bradshaw & Nettleton, 1983). In other words, left-hemisphere mediation in language is possibly based on the need for analytic, time-dependent, and sequential coding (primarily at the expressive level, but to some extent at the receptive level as well), rather than on its symbolic or phonological attributes.

LOCAL VERSUS GLOBAL DATA REPRESENTATION

Robertson and her coworkers (as cited in Gazzaniga et al., 2002) studied patients with unilateral brain damage and concluded that the left hemisphere is superior to the right in representation of local data, whereas the right hemisphere is better in processing global data. One of the common methods of research into differences between the local and global approach involves presentation of shapes of capital letters consisting of capital letter of smaller size (as in the examples that follow). The local elements may be identical to the global ones or they may be different (i.e., the same or a different letter).

Example 1: Local and global elements are identical (T).

TTTTTTTTTT
T
T
T
T
T
T

Example 2: Local (T) and global (L) elements are different.

T
T
T
T
T
T
T T T T

Robertson (1982, as cited in Gazzaniga et al., 2002), got similar results working with split-brain patients using language (letters) and nonlanguage forms (geometric shapes), as did Sergent in tests with healthy subjects (as cited in Gazzaniga et al., 2002).

HIGH FREQUENCIES VERSUS LOW FREQUENCIES

Ivry and Robertson (1999) claim that there are small but important differences between the hemispheres in the early stages of data processing. Interaction of these initial asymmetries with higher order systems enhances these differences, and the final result of data processing seems qualitatively asymmetrical.

Dichotic tests had indicated (based on the left-ear advantage) that the right hemisphere is mainly dominant for pure tones. However, Efron (1990) cautions that in some subjects, ear advantage changes with the pitch of tones used in experiments. Differences among presented tones expressed as a simple pitch difference between the higher and the lower tone or as pitch ratio between the two presented tones calculated as their average (central frequency) affect ear advantage in different ways. In approximately 43% of subjects the ear advantage shifts from the left to the right ear with the increase of the simple frequency difference between the presented tones. In about 24% the situation is exactly the opposite and in about 33% of subjects there is no difference. Similar results were obtained for the relation between central frequency and ear advantage: Some subjects exhibited right-ear advantage for all central frequencies (the tones used in the tests were between 200 Hz and 4,800 Hz); some exhibited left-ear advantage for all central frequencies; and in others higher central frequency caused the right ear to take over. In subjects with very strong ear advantage (regardless of side) a very large intensity difference between the two presented tones was needed to eliminate the ear advantage effect. Efron and coworkers interpreted this ear advantage in pitch processing as being the property of the peripheral part of the auditory system—up to the level of the brainstem (see Efron, 1990, for review). Their conclusions were based on tests with healthy subjects and on the behavior of split-brain patients. Ear advantage for pitch may occur in the inner ear, as the difference between the two cochleae in frequency tuning, or in the brainstem, where the frequency data arriving from the two ears are combined.

Ivry and Robertson (1999) also studied the influence of relative pitch on lateralization. According to their theory of hemispheric asymmetries in perception (double filtering by frequency, DFF, theory), the differences between the two hemispheres are based on frequency characteristics of the stimulus. The right hemisphere prefers the low frequencies, and the left hemisphere the high ones. These differences may be found in auditory stimuli (where different-frequency tones are psychoacoustically perceived as different pitch), but in spatial and temporal data as well. Processing of spatial data is mediated by vision. High frequencies in the temporal domain refer to rapid changes, preferred by the left hemisphere or slow changes to which the right hemisphere is more inclined. Regardless of modality, asymmetries are caused by attention. Both hemispheres are equally capable of processing and representation of the entire data spectrum, which means that there are no considerable differences between them at the level of early sensory processes. At a higher level the nature of the task will direct attention to particular features of information at hand and at that point the effect of lateralization based on relative frequency will occur.

On the basis of their observations Ivry and Robertson (1999) concluded that the left hemisphere enhances information on a relatively finer scale (i.e., high frequencies) whereas the right hemisphere does it on a larger scale (i.e., low frequencies). The theory deals with the perception of visual and auditory stimuli (visual perception actually refers to spatial data processing). It is founded on three principal ideas: (a) frequency-based representations include information about different multiple scales; (b) frequency information is asymmetrically represented in the left and the right cerebral hemisphere; and (c) selective attention causes laterality that is elicited by relative rather than absolute frequency. According to their theory, perception proceeds through three stages.

Stage 1: Sensory Representation of Frequency Information
At this stage there are no consistent differences between the two hemispheres. They can both represent any frequency information from the environment. Sensory representation is mainly symmetrical. This stage corresponds to detection, which means that both hemispheres are capable of determining whether the signal was present, regardless of its features and side of presentation (e.g., to which

visual field it was presented). In auditory stimuli some differences were found in sensitivity between the left and the right ear, but only in men—the right ear was more sensitive than the left, particularly for frequencies between 2,000 and 6,000 Hz. Ivry and Robertson ignored the difference, because it did not refer to relative frequency.

Stage 2: The First Frequency Filtering Stage—
Selection of Task-Relevant Information
At this stage the attention is selectively allocated to stimulus aspects that are the most relevant for the goal at hand. This process of selection of relevant stimulus features causes laterality effects that occur in the form of relative frequency. This enhances the segment of the auditory or spatial spectrum that is relevant for the current situation or task.

Stage 3: The Second Frequency Filtering Stage—Asymmetric
Processing of Selected Information in Cerebral Hemispheres
After being selected at Stage 2, relevant information undergoes additional filtering at Stage 3. Identification and discrimination, which are in fact higher order analyses, take place at this stage. During these procedures the differences between the hemispheres become obvious. Right-hemisphere processing is characterized by low-pass filtering (i.e., passing the low frequencies with simultaneous attenuation of the high ones), and left-hemisphere processing is characterized by high-pass filtering (i.e., passing the high frequencies, with simultaneous attenuation of the high ones). The outcomes of such different filtering procedures actually underlie many observed laterality effects in perception.

Although filtering is involved in both the second and the third stage, these two procedures are independent. They may be impaired independently of each other and their neural substrates are separate.

Ivry and Robertson (1999) believe that both hemispheres are capable of representing all elements of an image, but the quality of these representations is different. It seems that the visual system of humans and other animals has developed different strategies for each hemisphere: The right hemisphere favors global features of an image, and the left prefers the details. Global features correspond to low frequencies, and local features correspond to detailed, or high frequencies. Hence, the differences in representation occur above the sensory level, due to the different types of processing spectral information in the left and the right hemisphere. It may be concluded that simple detection is not lateralized—both hemispheres are equally capable of it, regardless of the nature of the stimulus. However, when further processing (be it discrimination or identification, as more complex and demanding segments of perception) requires selection of a frequency, functional asymmetry occurs.

With respect to speech, the dichotomy between high-frequency and low-frequency stimuli is best illustrated by the fact that comprehension of individual sounds requires analysis and presence of high frequencies (left hemisphere), whereas recognition of prosody requires low frequencies (right hemisphere).

Many independent studies have revealed just such a division of dominance. The local–global dichotomy fits here as well. Obviously, recognition of individual sounds, particularly of consonants, involves processing of local features, as opposed to prosody, that involves processing of global features.

CATEGORICAL VERSUS COORDINATE

Kosslyn (1987) compared hemispheric specialization with a snowball: The initial asymmetry is manifested as specialization for a particular type of problem (categorical or coordinate); then this specialization is further enhanced depending on specific task requirements. He believes that left-hemisphere specialization for speech production was crucial for evolutionary development of the left hemisphere as the one specialized for categorical tasks. Namely, speech production must be fast and therefore coordinated by a single center (one hemisphere). Since speech is by its very nature categorical, its lateralization into the left hemisphere has made that hemisphere specialized for categorical types of processing. The need for a single control center that can rapidly and successfully manage sequential movements is not limited solely to speech movements. Such control is necessary for nonspeech movements of articulators, and for any type of motor activity in general. Moreover, Corballis (as cited in Gazzaniga et al., 2002) proposes that the development and use of tools have contributed to the specialization of the left hemisphere for control of skilled movements (e.g., speech).

DEVELOPMENTAL ASPECTS OF LATERALIZATION

Two different theories have tried to explain the notion of lateralization of functions. According to Lenneberg (1967) cerebral hemispheres of children from birth to about the second year of life have equal potentials to become a neural substrate for language or other kinds of lateralized functions. Damage to either hemisphere may be equally incapacitating for speech acquisition in children. From the second year until puberty the left hemisphere becomes increasingly more important for language. As the right hemisphere loses its initial language capabilities, cortical plasticity that enables recovery after damage, decreases. After puberty, all throughout adulthood, left-lateralized control of language functions remains relatively unchanged. This theory is based on clinical cases of recovery after aphasia in childhood that have shown that children who had suffered left-hemisphere damage before age 2, have right-lateralized speech. Children who had suffered brain damage between the ages of 2 and 6 had bilaterally represented speech, and those who were injured after the age of 6 had permanent speech disorders similar to those found in adult aphasics.

The other theory is based on empirical data about early behavioral and anatomic asymmetries (Hynd, Obrzut, Weed, & Hynd, 1979; Kinsbourne, 1976). According to it, lateralized functioning does not develop gradually: cerebral hemispheres are programmed to function asymmetrically from the moment of birth in such a way that the left hemisphere controls language and motor functions of most people. Krashen (1973) reviewed clinical and dichotic literature and concluded that hemispheres are not equipotent for language functioning at birth and that behavioral asymmetries do not increase with age, reaching their maximum in puberty. He believed that the ratio of speech disorders in children age 5 or older was the same as in adults, and only right-hemisphere lesions occurring earlier than the age of 5 had some impact on speech abilities. This could have been the consequence of a general cognitive deficit impacting speech. However, Satz, Bakker, Teunissen, Goebel, and Van der Vlugt (1975) did find in their dichotic tests of children that the degree of laterality increased until approximately age 11, with some asymmetry for language functions noticeable around age 5. A dichotic listening study of elementary schoolchildren—unbalanced Croatian-English bilinguals—revealed that around ages 10 to 11 most children do not exhibit clear laterality effects (Mildner & Podnar, unpublished data). It is safe to assume that faster and more satisfactory (albeit almost never complete) recovery of language processes occurs after an early left-hemisphere lesion more so than has been found when damage occurs at an older age; this can be explained by the gradual decrease in neural plasticity. According to Kertesz and McCabe (1977), the inverse relation between the age of aphasia onset and the degree of recovery persists in adults as well. Such a progressive decrease of plasticity is not related to development of lateralization and some areas of the same hemisphere that had not been allocated to any particular function before damage may be activated in the course of recovery (Rasmussen & Milner, 1977).

Morphologic brain asymmetries can be seen at birth or even before, although they may simply indicate preprogrammed structural bias underlying functional asymmetries that develop later. Newborns exhibit marked asymmetry of responses to sensory stimulation, with a lower threshold on their right side and a greater tendency to turn toward the right. These effects do not seem to be dependent on previous asymmetrical head position. It is not quite clear whether this asymmetry can be attributed to sensory sensitivity or to motor turning bias (Bradshaw & Nettleton, 1983).

It is possible that hemispheric specialization for language functioning is not related to motor asymmetries. This is supported by the considerable percentage of left-lateralized language in left-handers, and some cases of bilateral or right-hemisphere language representation in right-handers. Previc (as cited in Gazzaniga et al., 2002) proposed a theory that left-hemisphere dominance for language is primarily related to structural asymmetries in the skull. Most people have somewhat larger orofacial bones on the left side of the face, which indirectly influences ear structure and has a negative impact on the projection of auditory information in the right hemisphere, particularly in the frequency range important for speech. Handedness is determined by the position of the fetus in the womb, and since most fetuses are turned with their right side toward the mother's front, the left vestibular organ (specifically the left utricle) receives more stimulation. This results in the better developed vestibular system in the right hemisphere. As a consequence, children rely more on their left side for balance and body posture, leaving the right side (i.e., right hand) free for investigation. This theory is not quite supported by exact measurements, and the correlations have not been established for individuals, but rather averaged across the entire sample.

According to some authors, functional asymmetry of the brain is the prerequisite for full realization of human language potentials, and the absence of such asymmetry is believed to be the cause of numerous difficulties in various intellectual areas. However, Anneken et al. (2000) found no direct or firm connection between the degree of language lateralization (measured by fTCD during word generation task) and success on standard language tests. Lohmann et al. (2000) found by the same method that normal development does not require lateralization of language and spatial functions to different hemispheres.

Amunts, Schleicher, Ditterich, and Zilles (2000) applied a postmortem staining technique on the brains of 34 individuals who died at ages 4 months to 85 years, to carry out cytoarchitectonic analysis of Brodmann's areas 44 and 45 in both hemispheres. They found that during postnatal development there are considerable changes in those areas that are manifested as different laminar patterns. Differences in laminar structure imply different organization of input–output structures in Broca's area in the two hemispheres. Asymmetry in Broca's area was found in newborns. Although the differences failed to reach statistical significance, there was a tendency toward greater asymmetry in male brains than in female ones. Considerable changes in asymmetry were observed between newborns and children ages 1 to 5, and between children ages 5 to 12 and adults. However, no changes were found between younger and older children. Developmental changes were more noticeable in right than in left Brodmann's areas 44 and 45, even in adult brains. This provides one explanation for the smaller asymmetry in children than in adults for language tasks.

The overall architecture of neural circuits is probably present at birth and subsequent events are related to establishing particular local connections and eventual branching, as well as to the use of specific receptor architecture in neural networks (Gazzaniga, 1994). ERP studies of 20-month-old babies revealed that lateralization is correlated with the number of words in their repertoire, not their age. Children with rich vocabulary had left-lateralized brain activity while listening to words, whereas those with a relatively smaller vocabulary exhibited bilateral activation in identical conditions (Gazzaniga et al., 2002). Showing that some linguistic knowledge exists at birth would suggest that the key issue is establishing the appropriate number of neurons and connections. With the exception of some smaller cortical sulci, the newborns' brains are impossible to distinguish from adult ones with respect to convolutions. Besides, it seems that architectonic differentiation is already present at birth, in the sense that it is possible to distinguish all adult cytoarchitectonic areas. Neuronal density is considerably greater than in the adult brain, but myelination of cortico-cortical pathways has not reached full maturity. Asymmetry of the future language areas is noticeable between the 20th and 30th week of gestation, which means that it precedes exposure to language. In any case, the near-adult differentiation is present at birth, only to be perfected later.

Corballis (as cited in Gazzaniga et al., 2002) proposes the existence of a laterality gene that is uniquely human, and that determines left-hemisphere dominance for language and hand use. He also believes that postnatal development, during which lateralization is fixed, is programmed to be asymmetrical. He also points out that equipotentiality of the right hemisphere for language acquisition has to be interpreted as an unrealized possibility that has been inhibited by some processes.

Studies of hand preference have yielded many contradictory results, frequently due to poor methodology and criteria. As already mentioned, one suggestion is that the hemispheres differ in maturation rates, so that there are periods when one hemisphere is faster than the other, and then the roles are reversed. All this is combined with a great deal of individual differences. Right-handedness is fixed by age 5, possibly even by the end of the first year of life, and may be related to speech acquisition. The results may depend on whether bimanual or unimanual activities have been assessed. There is evidence of very early asymmetries in holding, reaching and dropping, although their significance is not very clear. There is also evidence of correlations between head posture asymmetries and later handedness (Bradshaw & Nettleton, 1983; Kolb & Whishaw, 1996). However, developmental patterns in hand preference may reflect the way in which the child learns how to lift and manipulate objects. Hand performance measurements offer no clear evidence of developmental changes, and such changes cannot be assessed before the third year of life (Bradshaw & Nettleton, 1983).

Registering evoked potentials during visual and auditory stimulation has shown that even in very small children there are stimulus-dependent asymmetries in brain electrical activity. Auditory stimuli elicited greater activity in the left temporal lobe, and visual stimuli resulted in greater activity in the right occipital lobe (Spreen et al., 1984). Molfese and Molfese (1979) showed that newborns are capable of differentiating acoustic cues and that children have an adult-like ability to use phonemically relevant cues in a categorical manner, which suggests some sort of hemispheric specialization for language in early childhood. There is evidence that perceptual mechanisms needed for speech sound discrimination relying on formant transitions and voice onset time (VOT) are lateralized at birth (Bradshaw & Nettleton, 1983).

Contrary to Lenneberg's claims, cases of childhood aphasia after right-hemisphere damage are much less frequent than after left-hemisphere damage. Many potential artifacts may enhance what seems to be right-hemisphere aphasia in very young people: the nature and degree of brain damage in early childhood; the limitations of testing methods suitable for children and their interaction with the environment; and speech may be one of very rare available organized responses in children's repertoire. As opposed to Lenneberg, Wada's tests suggest that it is not probable that early left-hemisphere damage will result in speech being taken over by the right hemisphere. The left hemisphere, unless completely removed, will probably become and/or remain dominant for language, in spite of substantial damage. In other words, whenever possible there is intrahemispheric rather than interhemispheric functional reorganization. Left-hemisphere damage in childhood actually does generally result in some degree of aphasia, although it is more transient than in adults. In some cases, left-hemisphere damage occurring before 5 to 7 years of age may initiate a shift of language function to the otherwise nondominant right hemisphere, but after that age intrahemispheric reorganization will be more frequent. When the damaged left hemisphere is incapable of plastic reorganization (which is the real key to recovery), the right hemisphere takes control over speech, but subsequent testing in adulthood reveals that such speech is never as perfect as when speech processes are managed by the left hemisphere. The residual permanent deficits reveal limitations of early plasticity of interhemispheric reorganization (Bradshaw & Nettleton, 1983).

Cases of childhood hemispherectomy imply that at birth both hemispheres are capable of acquiring language, and that injury to either hemisphere does not impede development of seemingly normal speech. However, the right hemisphere is never quite as successful as the left. During the periods of fastest development, the left hemisphere actively participates in production and perception of speech, and the linguistic potential of the right hemisphere gradually decreases. The left hemisphere becomes firmly dedicated to speech, and these functions can no longer be "squeezed out" by rival functions that may try to shift into it from the injured right hemisphere. On the other hand, the remaining language potential of the right hemisphere indicates that it is not irreversibly dedicated to nonlanguage functions, although transfer of language functions to the right may be at the expense of its nonlanguage, primarily spatial capabilities (Kimura, 1975).

Khan, Frisk, and Taylor (1999) found that children with very low birth weight, when they reach ages 8 to 10, use their cortical resources differently from control children: They exhibit smaller functional asymmetry. However, response speed and accuracy do not differ significantly between the two groups.

By puberty, the right-hemisphere potential for language acquisition decreases to the point where it is able to mediate little or no propositional speech after left hemispherectomy. This ontogenetic decrease of neural plasticity may be achieved by active suppression by the left hemisphere via the maturing corpus callosum. It is therefore possible that acallosal patients have bilateral language representation, due to the absence of inhibitory pathways. We could even suppose that in healthy children laterality would decrease with maturity, were it not for mutual inhibition of secondary abilities exerted by one hemisphere on the other by means of the developing connections. Some skills may undergo a decrease in asymmetric organization as they become fixed and integrated into the child's repertoire. Witelson (as cited in Bradshaw & Nettleton, 1983) claims that it is even possible that environmental factors, for example, language experience, influence the degree of left-hemisphere control. She presented evidence of less frequent cases of aphasia in the illiterate and severely hearing impaired population, and in support of the idea that total language deprivation until puberty may result in subsequent right-hemisphere mediation of language processes. A case in point is Genie, who had practically no exposure to language until age 13. When she was tested for lateralization of language functions after years of socialization and deliberate language coaching, she exhibited right-hemisphere language.

Healthy subjects, even as young as 3, gesticulate more freely with their right hand while talking, and exhibit greater interference with right-hand than with left-hand tapping while performing a concurrent verbal task. Right-ear advantage occurs around age 4. Although some authors speak of developmental aspects of the advantage, many more do not.

Among the artifacts in such developmental studies is the type of testing that varies greatly across studies, but also the kind of required distinctions. Memory measures, rather than perceptual functions, are used with older children. On the other hand, with younger subjects perceptual measures have to be used, despite the probability of weaker laterality effects that have been found at the perceptual level. Ceiling and floor effects may blur laterality differences. Ability to direct attention develops with age, and this particular factor has been shown to increase ear advantage. When attention aspects are controlled, there is no developmental increase in right-ear advantage. In the visual modality, young subjects may not want or be able to keep their gaze at the fixation point. Some functions may not have developed in young children, and cannot be in their processing or response repertoires. When novel, unknown, or difficult letters or words are being read for the first time, left-visual-field (right hemisphere) advantage may initially occur even in adults. This is the consequence of involvement of the right hemisphere in preprocessing novel tasks, and reading is in itself a novel task for very young children—unfamiliar and difficult as well.

It is difficult to design suitable tests for nonverbal right-hemisphere processing in young subjects. Even in adults it is usually more difficult to demonstrate nonverbal right-hemisphere superiorities. But even in that area there is no hard evidence of developmental effects in lateralization. Some authors claim, on the basis of behavioral tests, that the right hemisphere matures more slowly than the left, although other evidence (e.g., anatomic) suggests just the opposite. However, there is plenty of anatomic evidence for continuous developmental myelination of the corpus callosum and possibly also of the inferior part of the parietal lobe until puberty (Bradshaw & Nettleton, 1983).

It may be concluded that the hemispheres are not equipotential at birth and there is no solid evidence in favor of the developmental nature of asymmetries, which would suggest that asymmetries might reach their peak in puberty or even at age 5. A developmental decrease of plasticity can explain better recovery from early aphasia, but that phenomenon is not correlated with the development of lateralization. Later on, until puberty, the left hemisphere becomes firmly involved in language, mostly as a consequence of the considerably decreased neural plasticity. Hemispheric specialization increases with age only with respect to the child's repertoire of asymmetrically organized functions. These functions probably emerge at some crucial developmental periods, such as puberty (hormone-dependent) and possibly around the fifth year of life (when language is stabilized). It is possible that there is different hemispheric development related to these (and possibly some others) critical periods, which may also interact with a general decrease in neural plasticity (Gazzaniga et al., 2002).

Lateralization of functions has its neural substrate as well.

NEUROANATOMIC ASYMMETRIES

Even in 29-week-old fetuses the left *planum temporale* is larger than the right in about 90% of cases (Wada, as cited in Spreen at al., 1984), and the Sylvian fissure is longer on the left side than on the right. Magnetic resonance imaging revealed a high correlation between the absence of this asymmetry and the occurrence of developmental dyslexia in children (Gazzaniga et al., 2002). In the left hemisphere the Sylvian fissure has a less prominent upward curl than in the right, and this is noticeable in 16-week-old fetuses. As a consequence, the parieto-temporal region located ventrally to the Sylvian fissure is larger on the right, and such an enlarged area has a particular role in sensory integration of spatial characteristics. The inferior part of the postcentral gyrus (parietal operculum) that belongs to Wernicke's area and receives kinesthetic input from the articulators is also larger in the left hemisphere. Habib, Robichon, Levrier, Khalil, and Salamon (1995) found that, ontogenetically, parietal operculum asymmetry precedes planum asymmetry and that the highest found positive correlation with right-handedness is parallel enlargement of the parietal operculum and *planum temporale* in the left hemisphere. It has to be pointed out, however, that modern three-dimensional imaging techniques (MR) have revealed that the surface of that cortical region is larger in the left hemisphere in 5 out of 10 subjects, and in 5 out of 10 it is larger in the right hemisphere (Gazzaniga et al., 2002).

In the right hemisphere there is frequently an additional Heschl's gyrus, whereas in the left hemisphere there is only one. Kolb and Whishaw (1996) consider this complementary asymmetry between the two hemispheres to be a possible anatomic foundation for the functional division of labor between the temporal lobes into language (left hemisphere) and music (right hemisphere) functions. The location, direction, extent, and consistency of these morphologic asymmetries indicate that they may be the neurological substrate of language (Bradshaw & Nettleton, 1983).

Prefrontal areas, which include Broca's area for speech production, seem smaller on the left side, because the visible brain surface is larger on the right by about one third. However, given the greater degree of folding in the left hemisphere it is highly probable that the total cortical surface is greater in the left than in the right hemisphere (Bradshaw & Nettleton, 1983; Kolb & Whishaw, 1996). This different organization probably reflects functional differences between homologous areas of the left and the right hemisphere, the left being involved in speech production, and the right in tone of voice (Kolb & Whishaw, 1996).

There is more tissue in the right hemisphere and its mass is greater. The left occipital pole protrudes toward the back more than the right. Anterior parietal and posterior occipital areas are commonly larger on the left. The right frontal pole and the central (prefrontal) part of the right hemisphere are commonly wider than on the left, and the right frontal pole is usually longer than the left. Wider and longer anterior parts of the right hemisphere and posterior parts of the left give the human brain a torqued look in counterclockwise direction (Bradshaw & Nettleton, 1983).

Density of the left hemisphere is greater than that of the right and the ratio of gray and white matter is greater in favor of gray in the left hemisphere, particularly in frontal and precentral areas. This means that one of the right-hemisphere characteristics may be better connections among different areas, as opposed to better within-area organization in the left hemisphere. It is believed that a consequence of these differences is the left hemisphere's greater capability for unimodal processing and specific representations of sensory and motor functions, contrary to the right hemisphere that has more association cortex. This ensures multimodal processing; hence, one of the most prominent differences between the hemispheres is their mode of action: The right is adapted for holistic processing, and the left for analytical (Bradshaw & Nettleton, 1983).

Asymmetries are visible at lower levels as well. For example, in about 80% of the cases, more neuronal fibers connect motor cortical areas in the left hemisphere via contralateral pathways with right extremities, as well as motor areas of the right hemisphere via ipsilateral pathways also with the right extremities, than is the case with the left. In other words, the right hand is better innervated by motor fibers than the left, which may explain such a high proportion of right-handers in the population (Bradshaw & Nettleton, 1983).

The main artery in the left hemisphere is located near speech and language areas, whereas in the right hemisphere it is in the superior part of the parietal lobe that is involved in spatial information processing. Distribution of various neurotransmitters is asymmetric at cortical and subcortical levels (Kolb & Whishaw, 1996) as is the cell appearance, as for example, their columnar pattern (Gazzaniga et al., 2002).

At present there is not much evidence about systematic asymmetries at subcortical levels, with the exception of the thalamus. There is electrophysiological evidence of the asymmetric participation of the thalamus in language functions (Bradshaw & Nettleton, 1983; Kolb & Whishaw, 1996; Sternberg, 2003).

Having listed the most obvious neuroanatomic (and cytoarchitectonic) asymmetries, we should emphasize several points of caution: (a) a doubtless correlation between the size of an area and its functional significance cannot always be established; (b) successful performance of a function does not necessarily require more tissue, larger area, and so forth; (c) it seems that cortical mass is not as important as the specialized circuits that are localized in one hemisphere or the other; (d) boundaries and limitations of cortical asymmetries are not straightforward or easy to define. Finally, if the three-dimensional reconstruction algorithm that takes into consideration the natural curvature of the cortical surface is applied to the posterior temporal lobe, the area is not in fact asymmetrical (Gazzaniga, 1994).

SENSORY ASYMMETRIES

Olfaction is the only predominantly ipsilateral sensory modality. All other senses are bilaterally represented in the brain.

In audition there is the greatest degree of doubling of hemispheric functions—the stimulus from each ear projects to both sides of the brain, so that approximately two thirds of the information is relayed to the contralateral hemisphere and one third to the ipsilateral one. Chen, Halpern, Bly, Edelman, and Schlaug (2000) found a significant correlation between asymmetry in *planum temporale* and absolute pitch. If exposure to music and music training start early (preferably before age 7) the probability of developing absolute pitch is greater in individuals with greater asymmetry in favor of the left hemisphere (i.e., in those whose right *planum temporale* is considerably smaller than the left).

Vision is more clearly lateralized to the side opposite to the peripheral sensory organ. Somatosensory modality is mostly contralateral, with pain and temperature having both ipsi- and contralateral components. In the tactile modality, it has been found that the left side of the body (hand, sole, etc.) has a lower absolute threshold for pressure sensitivity than the right. Studies have revealed superiority of the right hand for sequential tasks and of the left for simultaneous tasks. If two tasks controlled by the same hemisphere are performed concurrently (e.g., verbalization and right-hand movements) there is interference (Bradshaw & Nettleton, 1983; Mildner, 2000). Some exceptions have been reported for female subjects and left-handers (Hicks, 1975). Left-hand movements may even improve concurrent verbalizations (Kinsbourne & Cook, 1971). Motor control is mainly contralateral, especially for precise finger movements.

MOTOR ASYMMETRIES

Archeological findings indicate, judging by the earliest traces of tools and paintings dating to the Paleolithic time, that most humans were right-handed (Bradshaw & Nettleton, 1983). The ontogenetically earliest examples of motor asymmetry can be seen in the walking reflex of newborns. They may also be manifested as more frequent head turning to the right while lying on their back. It has also been found that more newborns turn their head to the right when touched on their right cheek, than to the left as response to touching of their left cheek. Children prefer one hand for reaching and holding objects. This hand preference is fixed after the third year of life; earlier fixed asymmetry may be a sign of some pathology (Bradshaw & Nettleton, 1983; Spreen, Tupper, Risser, Tuokko, & Edgell, 1984).

Different theories of hand preference may be grouped into those that stress impact of the environment, structure, hormones, or heritage (Kolb & Whishaw, 1996).

A very high correlation was found between the preferred (dominant) hand and the preferred (dominant) foot. Such dominance may be recorded by asking subjects to fill out questionnaires about which hand or foot they prefer in some everyday activities (brushing teeth, lighting a match, kicking the ball, etc.) or by observing them perform these activities. Searleman (1980) found that the correlation between language function lateralization and the dominant (preferred) foot is higher than is the case with the dominant (preferred) hand. He attributed this to the fact that left-handedness is still stigmatized in some societies, and foot dominance does not attract as much attention. It is, therefore, foot dominance that is a true measure of motor asymmetry, because it is not influenced by social conventions and expectations. He corroborated his claim with the fact that subjects who had reported left-foot preference had the greatest percentage of left-ear advantage.

Various methods have shown that motor asymmetries in favor of left extremities do not necessarily change language function lateralization. Left-hemisphere dominance for language is more widespread than right-handedness, and reversed dominance is rarer than left-handedness. However, right-handers exhibit more consistent lateralization of language functions to the left hemisphere, and left-handers exhibit less stability of left-hemisphere dominance in test–retest situations involving visually or auditorily presented language material. In general, the contribution of the right hemisphere is more probable in left-handers than in right-handers. Their language functions recover faster after left-hemisphere injury but they are more prone to dysphasia after right-hemisphere damage. Some authors have found that the degree of right-handedness is more important for prediction of language lateralization than its direction. Data on the influence of familial sinistrality on language lateralization are inconclusive. If such influence exists, it is more noticeable in left-handers than in right-handers. Similarly, a reliable correlation between parents' dominance of extremities and that of their children has not been established. Levy and Reid's (1976) hypothesis about hand posture during writing as an indication of language representation has not been definitively confirmed either.

ASYMMETRIES IN OTHER SPECIES

Many animals exhibit foot or paw preferences. These asymmetries are mostly unsystematic with respect to members of a species (the ratio is approximately 50:50), and frequently within one and the same member across tasks: In some activities the animal will prefer the right foot or paw, in others the left. With respect to the structural cerebral asymmetries, it was found that rats have a thicker cortex in the right hemisphere than in the left. Various experiments have shown that their right hemisphere is important for complex tasks, new situations and aggression, and that it is more under the influence of environmental factors. Studies of birds have revealed that left-hemisphere damage impairs their song, but that their brains are plastic as well, because their right hemispheres can take over control of song if damage occurred before it has developed completely. Plasticity is also manifested in their ability to acquire a new song repertoire each year (Bradshaw & Nettleton, 1983; Nottebohm, 1994). Chickens and pigeons solve different types of tasks if they are presented only to the left or to the right eye (Gazzaniga et al., 2002). In apes, neuroanatomic asymmetries similar to humans' have been found: a longer and less steeply sloping left Sylvian fissure, and in other mammals the right hemisphere is also heavier than the left. Anatomic asymmetries found in other species seem to support the claim that human brain asymmetry is not directly related to language or the preferred hand (Kolb & Whishaw, 1996).

FACTORS INFLUENCING FUNCTIONAL CEREBRAL ASYMMETRY

Many factors cause and modify laterality. They may increase or decrease effects of laterality, change their direction or eliminate them entirely. Efron (1990) listed about 30 such factors and grouped them along criteria of subjects (e.g., age, sex, dominant hand, education, culture, language, processing strategies, motivation, attention, skill, etc.), stimuli (size, complexity, amount, difficulty, duration, contrast, degree to which they can be verbalized, etc.), or research method (detection, response time, recognition, event-related potentials, etc.). It has been shown that laterality effects (i.e., greater activity of one or the other hemisphere in a particular task) depend on many other details: familiarity with the task, instructions, type of material, kind of response required, sensory modality, and many others. Their very number and diversity, and the fact that so many of them are difficult or impossible to control in any given task, even when we are aware of them, makes one wonder how much experiments aimed at revealing hemispheric specialization for that particular task in fact tell us about the activity and not about some of the listed factors. Besides, each specific task or area of research brings in additional variables (more on that in the section on bilingualism).

Carpentier, Pugh, Studholme, Spencer, and Constable (2000a) conducted fMRI studies of brain areas that might be affected by the sensory modality. They defined common, modality-independent areas that probably perform more abstract calculations (e.g., syntactic or pragmatic processing), and those that are modality-specific. These specialized areas (e.g., Wernicke's area in the right hemisphere, left fusiform gyrus, Broca's area in Brodmann's area 44, supramarginal gyrus) seem to carry out procedures that are important for establishing connections between abstract language dimensions, which increases knowledge and skill of the entire language network. Their results indicate that the area in the temporal lobe of the right hemisphere that is homotopic to Wernicke's area in the left hemisphere plays a special part in speech recognition. Furthermore, they have shown that, depending on whether the stimulus was auditory or visual, processing is different in Brodmann's areas 44 and 45 (although they both constitute Broca's area) and in some other regions. In short, they have shown that in the visual modality, functional asymmetry, manifested as language lateralization, is more marked than in the auditory modality. A general conclusion that may be drawn from their research might be that language processing does not proceed within a unique network, but in several networks whose action is combined in order to improve sentence processing. In other words, language is built of simpler components whose combinations determine specific types of complexity and diversity.

Gender differences in cognitive tasks have been studied and described extensively, particularly with respect to verbal and spatial processing. Men seem to be better at spatial tasks and women outperform men on phonological tests. Earlier studies using fMRI have revealed differences in brain activation during phonological processing: bilateral activation was found in women and primarily left-lateralized activity was recorded in men. Gur et al. (2000) compared men and women on two tasks—verbal (producing analogies to presented stimuli) and spatial (estimation of line orientation). During verbal processing, expected changes in left-hemisphere activity, particularly in the inferior temporal lobe and in the *planum temporale*, were found in all subjects, but only men exhibited increased activation of these areas in the right hemisphere during spatial tasks. The network of cortical regions that were activated by these tasks included lateral and medial frontal, medial temporal, parieto-occipital and occipital regions. Activation was greater in the left hemisphere during verbal tasks and in the right during spatial ones. Men differed from women in their activity of the left hemisphere during spatial tasks. Making the tasks more difficult resulted in wider activation during verbal tasks, but in more limited activation during spatial tasks. The authors concluded that insufficient activation in a particular hemisphere in regions directly involved in task performance accounts for sex differences in various tasks, and sex differences in spatial tasks are based on bilateral activation in a distributed cognitive system. Sex differences are discussed in more detail in a separate chapter.

Differences in ear or visual field advantage may occur (even in the same subjects and for the same stimuli) as a consequence of a forced or self-imposed processing strategy, which implies that the manner of stimulus processing is more important than the stimulus itself. However, characteristics of the stimulus may also be crucial. Differences in visual-field advantage may depend on image sharpness, duration of exposure, retinal eccentricity, frequency range of its constituents, and so forth. In the auditory modality, Hagberg et al. (2000) have recorded by PET that listening to a regular series of pulses (e.g., drum beating) elicited activation in the left superior temporal gyrus (Brodmann's area 40), as opposed to the irregular series that elicited bilateral activation in Brodmann's areas 40 and 43, as well as in the right cerebellar hemisphere.

The importance of attention in dichotic listening became clear as the first studies were done in 1950s. It is discussed more comprehensively by Mondor and Bryden (1992) and Hugdahl et al. (2000). They checked the effects of attention by PET recordings of changes in brain activity of healthy subjects during listening to music (instrumental) and speech (CV syllables) stimuli in different attention conditions: when it was directed to the right ear, to the left ear, or to both ears simultaneously (divided attention). Directing attention to one ear or the other significantly reduced the activity in both temporal lobes, compared with the condition of divided attention. Syllables activated the classical language areas (Broca's and Wernicke's) and music stimuli activated areas in the visual association cortex, cerebellum, and hippocampus. They interpreted these results as a facilitatory effect of attention on auditory processing because the activity of the primary auditory cortex is decreased when attention is consciously manipulated. Increased activity in the parietal lobe, which was also recorded during the tasks, was attributed to activation of the attentional network that is common to all modalities. The significant effect of attention was also found by Mildner (1999) in a dichotic listening task.

ERP studies have shown that auditory stimuli that are attended to elicit signals of higher amplitude than those that have been ignored. This difference is manifested as the first large negative polarity (auditory N1 potential). Its latency is somewhat less than 90 ms, but even shorter latencies have been recorded. Hillyard and coworkers (as cited in Gazzaniga et al. 2002) found, using MRI, greater sensory activity elicited by auditory stimuli in the primary auditory cortex that receives stimuli from the attended side as early as 20 to 50 ms after stimulus onset. These results support early selection attention theories. According to these theories, the stimuli to which attention has been directed are facilitated, and the others are inhibited in early processing stages, before more complex stimulus features are to be processed in higher cortical areas. The time it takes the auditory stimulus to reach the cerebral cortex is approximately 20 ms, and the greatest activity was recorded 20 to 50 ms after stimulus onset in Heschl's gyrus. It has to be emphasized that intentional, conscious manipulation of attention does not affect the subcortical level of the auditory pathway.

Alho et al. (1999) also reported the influence of attention on brain activation. Their PET scans showed that attending to the right ear activates the auditory cortex mainly in the left hemisphere, and vice versa. This selective activation of one or the other hemisphere, depending on the side of stimulus presentation, is mediated by executive control mechanisms in the frontal lobes, where increased activity related to auditory attention was in fact recorded. Manipulation of attention was found to be important in some concurrent verbal-motor tasks with auditorily presented language material, more so for native than for foreign language (Mildner, Stanković, & Petković, 2005).

Similar results were obtained for visual stimuli. Although they were present, differences in early activity recorded in the primary visual cortex (Brodmann's area 17) with 50 to 80 ms latencies, were less affected by spatial attention than differences in later (80 to 200 ms) activity found in extrastriate visual areas. Attending to other, nonspatial, object features (e.g., to color or orientation) produced no reliable results, but it has shown that directing attention to a particular isolated object feature (e.g., color) may affect the areas in the extrastriate cortex that are specialized for processing these features. This is more evidence in support of the claim that selective attention influences perception before the analysis of all features has been completed. Despite the effects of selectivity, attention facilitates processing of all features of the attended object. This is explained by the fact that attention facilitates synchronization of neuronal firing, which makes processing more efficient. Clinical electrical cortical stimulation of human patients has confirmed that selective attention affects the activity of the corresponding sensory modality. Even reflex attention has similar effects to intentional manipulation of attention, but the neural mechanisms are not quite the same (Gazzaniga et al., 2002).

PET and fMRI techniques have also revealed attention-dependent activity in areas other than those where particular sensory modalities are represented: in the thalamus, basal ganglia, insula, frontal cortex, anterior cingulate, posterior parietal lobe, and temporal lobe. The parietal lobe was found to play a very important role in attention manipulation. It is the seat of representations of spatial relations, it controls intentional orientation toward a relevant location in space, and it connects subcortical structures (particularly pulvinar) with the temporal lobes.

The most frequent attentional deficits are neglect and extinction. They are typically a consequence of brain damage (particularly of the parietal lobe) and affect the side contralateral to the side of the injury. It has been shown that even stimuli presented to the otherwise neglected field are processed without awareness about it. For example, a meaningful word presented to the neglected visual field will be processed at the semantic level without the patient's awareness of even seeing the word. Details of a familiar scene or space (a room or a city square) that the patient may not have remembered, from his/her perspective at the moment of description, on the neglected side, will be included in the description if the patient's imagined position is changed. These examples corroborate the claim that neglect is an attention deficit rather than a memory or processing disorder. Extinction is a milder form of attention deficit. It refers to the state when a person is able to register stimuli in either side of the space, regardless of injury side, but if two stimuli occur at the same time, one on each side, the patient does not attend to the one contralateral to the injured side (Judaš & Kostović, 1997). It should be pointed out, however, that the term *extinction* may be defined differently in some psychology textbooks, where it refers to the gradual decrease in conditioned response intensity under certain circumstances (Zarevski, 1994).

Garavan et al. (2002) found that similar brain areas are activated when switching attention within one modality (verbal or visuospatial) and from one modality to another. These areas include the dorsolateral prefrontal cortex, anterior cingulate, the area immediately anterior to the supplementary motor area, bilateral premotor cortex, bilateral inferior temporal lobulus and the precuneus. In addition to these areas, intermodality switching of attention activates the right middle frontal gyrus (Brodmann's areas 9 and 10). Dubost, Beachet, Najafi, Aminian, and Mourey (2002) concluded that allocation of attention is different for working memory than for semantic memory.

Signal processing is an active process at almost all levels, and it depends considerably on the nature and requirements of the task at hand. Perceptual mechanisms, regardless of modality, are not mere processors of sensory data—processing is modified according to the situation. The final result, be it behavior or a percept, is a whole. It is not quite clear whether this whole is a product of constant interaction between the two hemispheres or whether each hemisphere processes the stimuli on its own, according to its own strategies, style and preferences, with the final outcome being the result of the activity of the hemisphere that was more successful in the competition. In any case, hemispheric specialization is one of the essential characteristics of cognitive processes.

All evidence suggests that the differences between the hemispheres are relative, quantitative, and a matter of degree, rather than absolute or qualitative. The degree of specialization may vary from one person to the next and may depend on gender, preferred hand, or literacy, among other factors. Visible consequences of injuries seem to support the model of exclusive hemispheric specialization, whereas laterality differences in healthy subjects probably reflect the time needed for interhemispheric transfer and/or signal degradation during such transfer. Severe clinical consequences may be a result of the existence of intact interhemispheric connections that are inhibitory rather than facilitatory. For example, after removing the damaged hemisphere or a portion of it, or after severing the connections with the left hemisphere, the right hemisphere may realize its language potential (that is in fact considerable) more efficiently. In healthy subjects, the inhibitory influences probably take care of rivalry between the hemispheres in processing identical types of stimuli. Split-brain studies reveal the quantitative and relative nature of functional differences: each hemisphere is capable of functioning in any processing mode, but at different competence levels and in different directions. For example, even left-hemisphere superiority in processing stops decreases if the timing is slowed down. In healthy subjects, the intensity or temporal advantage given to the inferior ear or visual field does not eliminate or change laterality effects, as would be expected if laterality differences depended on interhemispheric transfer from the incompetent to the exclusively functional hemisphere. Quantitative asymmetry may seem qualitative if it is large enough, if analytic processing requires greater processing capability than holistic, and if the left hemisphere is more powerful in arithmetic operations than the right in its early development, regardless of the reasons for such ontogenetic differences.

Finally, it should be stressed that many brain functions are symmetrical, particularly in the primary sensory and motor areas. In many functions, intrahemispheric differences are greater than the interhemispheric ones. For example, although frontal lobes are asymmetrical, the functions of the left and the right frontal lobe are more similar than the functions of different lobes in the same hemisphere. Furthermore, the differences between the two hemispheres are relative rather than absolute. It should be pointed out again, that asymmetry does not mean exclusivity. Both hemispheres are generally capable of and involved in performing any cognitive task, but their contributions may differ. Although experience and the environment may influence the manner of stimulus processing, there is no evidence that the environment changes the organization of cerebral hemispheres. Having discussed the pitfalls of oversimplification and the nuances of functional asymmetries, we can nevertheless summarize that in the gross cerebral organization, with respect to lateralization, the left hemisphere is primarily dominant for language and the right is dominant for spatial processing.

LOCALIZATION OF FUNCTIONS

Localization of functions refers to the possible neurophysiologic substrate of sensations or behavior. The notion closely related to it is that of cerebral representation of sensations and/or functions, in other words, defining regions of greatest cerebral activity while performing an action or experiencing a sensation as a result of an external stimulus. For example, it is commonly said that the phonological store is represented at the junction of the parietal, occipital, and temporal lobes.

Different brain study techniques, among the first the cortical stimulation method, have revealed organized, topographic maps in the cortex. For example, body surface is represented in the postcentral gyrus; the tonotopic organization present in the cochlea is preserved in the temporal lobe so that high frequencies

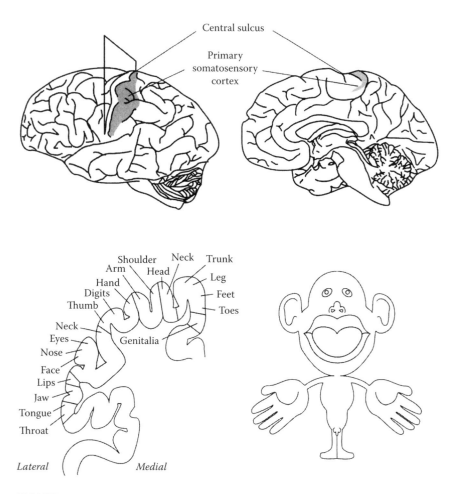

FIGURE 6.1. Human primary somatosensory cortex—mapping of periphery onto the postcentral gyrus. (From Purves et al., 2001. With permision.)

are represented more posteriorly in relation to the more anteriorly represented low frequencies, and so forth (Fischbach, 1992; Levy et al., 2005; Pinel, 2005). The area of the corresponding primary sensory cerebral cortex is directly proportional to the density of innervation of peripheral areas (Figure 6.1; the homunculus represents the relative size of the particular cortical areas devoted to corresponding body parts; Purves et al., 2001). In other words, the most densely innervated peripheral areas (e.g., lips, palms, and soles) take up the relatively greatest portion of the primary sensory cerebral cortex (Penfield & Rasmussen, 1950).

The effectors are represented in the primary motor areas located in the precentral gyrus. The size of the area in which an effector is represented does not reflect its size, but rather its importance and the amount of control necessary to manage it. That is why, for example, fingers are represented in a relatively greater

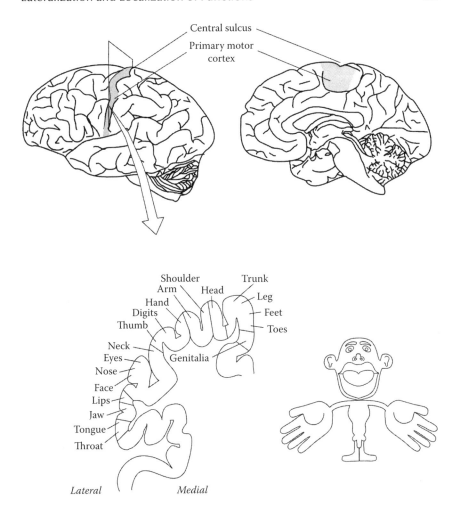

FIGURE 6.2. Human primary motor cortex—mapping of periphery onto the precentral gyrus. (From Purves et al., 2001. With permission.)

cortical area than toes (Figure 6.2; Purves et al., 2001). Each cerebral hemisphere controls the opposite side of the body, and each cerebellar hemisphere controls the ipsilateral side, due to the double crossing of pathways.

Different authors disagree about the number of identifiable brain areas. The number varies between several to about 200. All agree, however, on the basic sensory (auditory, visual, and areas onto which body surface is mapped) and motor areas. Whereas the anatomy of the principal motor and sensory systems is quite well known, the patterns of connections among association cortices and large subcortical nuclei have not been determined. It has become clear that primary sensory areas are not clearly separated, with association areas between them, as previously thought. The majority of these so-called association areas include, in fact, many specific sensory representations (Bradshaw & Nettleton, 1983; Kalat,

1995; Levy, Koeppen, & Stanton, 2005). Sensory and motor processes involve surprisingly many areas, richly connected with each other and with the thalamus. It is interesting that the basic organization of primary sensory and motor areas in the cerebral cortex is very similar in all mammals. However, with the higher place on the mammalian evolutionary scale, the absolute brain size and the relative amount of association cortex increase (Thompson, 1993).

Cortical maps are not fixed. Their appearance and organization may be affected by onset and course of illness, as well as recovery of function after injury, normal learning, involving changes in peripheral receptors or nerves (more on that in the section on plasticity). Cortical areas that no longer receive stimuli from the original peripheral organ or modality are taken over (flooded) by representations from neighboring organs or other modalities. For example, disconnection between a finger and its cortical representation results in the reaction of that area to stimuli arriving from the neighboring finger; tonotopic organization may be modified by increased exposure to selected tones, so that the representation of the practiced tones will cover a larger area; partial injuries to the retina may result in reorganization of the visual cortex. The most obvious cross-modal changes can be found in the multimodal areas of the superior temporal lobe that receives visual and auditory stimuli anyway (Gazzaniga et al., 2002), but functional reorganization is possible in other sensory combinations (vibrotactile aids in hearing impaired persons are based on this).

Neuroimaging methods (e.g., PET, SPECT) enable us to visualize how many different areas in both hemispheres are metabolically active during cognitive processes. The maps obtained for particular activities reveal that neural circuits underlying the cognitive processes are located in anatomically separate areas, but also that these areas may be activated by very different cognitive functions. Even before such methods became available for research in healthy subjects, there had been clinical reports of identical functional disorder after damage to different parts of the brain in different patients, as well as cases where focal lesions to a specific area had not necessarily caused identical functional deficits in different patients. Obviously, complex cognitive activities, such as language or spatial data processing, cannot be simply and straightforwardly related to strictly localized areas in the brain. These and similar results have given rise to attempts to discover and interpret different contributions of the two hemispheres to the common task, rather than to rigidly categorize activities into left-hemisphere and right-hemisphere.

The highest correlation between lesion location and cognitive dysfunction was found for language. More than 95% of patients who have suffered a stroke in the left fronto-parietal region are bound to present with some kind of aphasia. This high correlation definitely points to the importance of the region for language, but it does not necessarily imply that it is the exact or the only seat of language functions. This argument is supported by cases of aphasics without injury to language areas and cases of patients with extensive damage to the regions without aphasic symptoms. Obviously, despite the importance of this region that has been confirmed by numerous cases, other brain areas that are active in the process should not be neglected. Similarly, it has been shown that spatial representation is a result of joint functioning of both hemispheres. Due to these and similar examples, Efron (1990) proposes the term *support* rather than *specialization,* it is more accurate to say that certain parts of the brain or neural circuits, for which the correlation between location and function has been established, support that particular function—it is not a matter of specialization.

The human auditory cortex is very sensitive to small changes in the auditory stimulus. Rupp, Hack, Schneider, Stippich, and Scherg (2000) found, using the MEG technique, that interruptions of the auditory signal as brief as 3 ms have their neural representations in the brain. In their fMRI studies of healthy subjects Hall et al. (2000) found that complex acoustic stimuli activate secondary auditory areas more than the simple ones, just as it had been found in electrophysiological animal studies. They compared differences in activation between modulated and static tones and between complex and simple tones and found that in all cases the primary auditory cortex and neighboring areas, including the planum temporale, were activated bilaterally, although differences associated with signal complexity were not statistically significant. Ducommun et al. (2000) found in their ERP study that sound movement and location are processed in different cerebral areas. Of the 22 maps obtained by measuring the brain's electrical activity, 15 represented auditory stimulation in general, three represented sound location and were located mainly in the temporal lobe, and four represented movement and were located mainly in the frontal lobes with some activity in the temporal lobe.

Stimulation of the anterior part of Heschl's gyrus elicits simple auditory sensations and damage to that area may cause deafness. When stimuli are presented posteriorly, anteriorly, or laterally to the auditory area, different sensations occur. Sounds are received more frequently by the language nondominant temporal lobe (usually right). Stimulation of the speech cortex immediately next to the auditory cortex actually inhibited speech (aphasia) but did not cause any vocalizations.

Listening to word lists, simple sounds, including the 1,000 Hz pure tone and music, and silent reading of visually presented words elicited activity in the temporal gyrus. It was found that: (a) responses of all neural units were speech-specific, namely, they were not evoked by simple stimuli; (b) semantic content was irrelevant, in other words, the unit could respond to various words, differing in temporal and spectral content; (c) attention was an important variable as opposed to comprehension, and soft speech evoked no response. Finally, music was found to suppress the activity of the examined population of units.

Motor cortex functioning was studied in primates by electrical cortical stimulation. The studies revealed that their cerebral cortex was organized into efferent microzones, each of which represented an individual muscle or a basic move, but also that the response of individual muscles or muscle groups that work together (in synergy) may be elicited by stimulation of several different nonneighboring areas of the motor cortex. Similar results were obtained when brain activity during voluntary hand movements was recorded by fMRI. Contrary to traditional views that motor functions of different parts of the body were systematically mapped onto the motor cortex (Figure 6.2), overlapping cortical representations of finger and wrist movements were found, as well as multiple representations of all fingers and the wrist in the precentral gyrus. Multiple efferent microzones were found in regions of the primates' motor cortex where mouth and face muscles were represented. Electric cortical stimulation revealed two very important facts: (a) face representation in the motor cortex partly overlaps with and surrounds the area where jaw and tongue movements are represented; and (b) besides the expected contralateral facial movements, microstimulations elicited ipsilateral movements as well, which suggests a certain degree of bilateral control (for a brief review see Kent & Tjaden, 1997). By analogy to human behavior, particularly with respect to the consequences of brain injury, these findings may explain observations that a spatially circumscribed injury does not necessarily result in a severe and irreversible functional disorder.

Fabri, Polonara, Salvolini, and Manzoni (2002) showed that in humans, similarly to nonhuman primates, parts of the skin along the body midline are represented bilaterally in the primary somatosensory cortex. A very noticeable mapping of peripheral organs onto the cerebral cortex was found in rodents. Each vibrissa in the snout is represented by a column of its own in the somatosensory cortex (Cybulska-Klosowicz & Kossut, 2002).

Butler et al. (2000) found by PET that reaching for objects that had previously been presented kinesthetically (by touch) or visually, activates cerebral structures that are associated with these modalities in both hemispheres: the sensorimotor cortex, supplementary motor area, and the cerebellum for the kinesthetically presented stimuli, and in the primary and the secondary visual cortex for the visually presented stimuli. Interhemispheric differences were recorded with respect to the hemispace in which the stimulus was located. Regardless of modality, when the stimulus was in the left visual field (i.e., on the left side of the body) sensory-motor, parietal, and occipital areas in the right hemisphere (and the left cerebellar hemisphere) were activated. When the stimulus was on the right side of the body (i.e., in the right visual field) activation was more bilateral. This confirmed the importance of the right hemisphere in processing kinesthetic spatial information and right-hemisphere dominance in visuospatial processing.

As stated previously, spatial data are processed mainly in the right hemisphere (in the inferior temporal and superior frontal lobe, specifically in the angular and superior precentral gyrus). Bilateral activation was recorded in the lingual/para-hippocampal region only when the task was to determine the position of a given object with respect to a reference point in the surroundings (allocentric processing), but not in other spatial tasks (Committeri et al., 2002). Studies of metabolism showed that the spatial representation mechanism includes neural networks with inputs from cortical and subcortical structures (Myers, 1999).

Grube, Ruebsamen, and Von Cramon (2002) found that, regardless of a sound spectral composition, left-hemisphere injured persons had only partially impaired ability to determine its location in space, whereas right-hemisphere patients had serious difficulties in such tasks. This confirmed the functional importance of the right primary auditory cortex in sound localization.

Clarke et al. (2002), like many other authors, have shown that in healthy subjects identification and discrimination of auditory stimuli are supported by neural networks different from those supporting sound localization. During recognition (identification and discrimination alike), the middle temporal gyrus and the precuneus in both hemispheres, as well as the posterior part of the left inferior frontal gyrus, were more active than during sound localization. Apparently, these structures constitute the "what" path. Contrary to that, sound localization activated the inferior part of the temporal lobe and posterior parts of the middle and inferior frontal gyri in both hemispheres more than its recognition, which implies involvement of these structures in the "where" path. In patients with right-hemisphere focal injuries, auditory stimuli activated the spared areas of the right hemisphere. Both types of tasks activated Heschl's gyrus and varying amounts of the surrounding cortex in the intact left hemisphere (albeit less than in healthy subjects), but not the pathways specialized for one or the other type of task. All patients had difficulties in sound localization. It seems that right-hemisphere damage significantly impairs auditory processing of the opposite, healthy, left hemisphere, particularly its specialized networks.

Nirkko, Baader, Loevblad, Milani, and Wiesendanger (2000) found that violin playing, and possibly music production in general, involves the area of frontal operculum in both hemispheres. Parsons et al. (2002) found, by using PET, that music production (e.g., finishing a tune, harmonizing) in nonmusicians activates the midbrain, left insula, cerebellum, basal ganglia, left middle temporal lobe (Brodmann's areas 21 and 39), parts of the medial frontal lobe (Brodmann's areas 6 and 25), and the right inferior frontal gyrus (Brodmann's area 47). Harmonizing activated some specific areas in the right hemisphere (Brodmann's areas 20, 40, and 45). Neither the control speech task (finishing incomplete sentences) nor mere repetition of melodies has activated these areas.

Most patients who suffer from *prosopagnosia* (inability to recognize faces) have lesions in the occipital and/or temporal lobes, as revealed by fMRI and other neuroimaging techniques. There are two areas in the temporal lobe that are activated more during recognition of faces than of any other objects: superior temporal sulcus and inferior temporal gyrus. Furthermore, the ventral surface of the temporal lobe (fusiform gyrus, particularly in the right hemisphere) is activated more by faces than by inanimate objects or meaningless forms (patterns). In the left hemisphere there was no difference between reactions to faces and reactions to inanimate objects. Although some other stimuli (e.g., pictures of birds or cars) elicited activity in the area that is considered responsible for face recognition, a series of letters never evoked any considerable activation in the area. These stimuli activated primarily the left hemisphere, its inferior part of the occipital lobe, along the border between the occipital and the temporal lobe (Gazzaniga et al., 2002).

Patients with frontal lobe and white matter damage subsequent to traumatic brain injury have severe problems with attention and concentration. This is particularly obvious when concentrated attention is required during a longer period of time. A 0.58 correlation was found between the severity of the injury and problems related to inability of sustained attention at the level necessary to continually perform a task successfully. Different kinds of memory are represented differently. This issue is discussed in more detail in chapter 7, this volume.

On the basis of the observations of autistic children, Baron-Cohen concluded that theory of mind probably has a cerebral representation of its own. His model proposes that it may be distributed, involving processing of emotions (probably in the amygdala) and some aspects of face processing (probably the superior temporal sulcus). Two studies (one SPECT and one PET) using different tasks suggest the activity in the right orbito-frontal cortex and the left medial frontal cortex (Gazzaniga et al., 2002).

LATERALIZATION AND LOCALIZATION OF EMOTIONS

Expressing one's own emotions and reacting to the emotions of others are important components of speech communication. Early 20th-century authors who studied emotional functioning emphasized the separation of emotions from other functions—primarily cognitive ones—and believed that emotional activity may be limited to the limbic system. These views were modified in the 1980s, due to an increasing body of evidence suggesting that some parts of the limbic system are functionally closer to cognitive than to emotional activities (e.g., the relationship between the hippocampus and learning and memory), and that processing of emotions is not restricted to the limbic system.

The analysis of neural substrates of emotions revealed that neural systems supporting emotional functioning are both dependent and independent of those supporting cognitive actions. Certain structures are specific to emotional functioning, particularly the amygdala and the orbito-frontal cortex. The amygdala are a small almond-shaped group of neurons, immediately anterior to the hippocampus in both hemispheres. They are involved primarily in processing negative emotions (e.g., fear), but they also participate, to a somewhat lesser degree, in responses to positive and neutral stimuli. They play a very important role in learning and memory. The orbito-frontal cortex is a part of the prefrontal cortex that constitutes the base of the frontal cortex and is adjacent to the upper orbital wall just above the eyes (Brodmann's area 47). Its main task is to manage and control our actions in social and emotional situations.

Berthoz et al. (2000) listed medial and middle prefrontal and cingulate regions in both hemispheres as key structures in the processing of emotions. They claim that inability to recognize and express emotions, that is believed to be a personality trait, may be related to the differences in cerebral activity during processing of emotional stimuli that depends on their (un)pleasantness.

Iidaka et al. (2000) studied (by fMRI) brain activity during recognition of faces with neutral, negative (angry or disgusted) and positive (happy) expressions. In addition to the common cortical and subcortical regions that constitute a unique neural network, they found areas specific for negative and positive expressions. The common network comprises the bilateral prefrontal region (Brodmann's area 46), the fusiform gyrus (Brodmann's area 37), and the amygdala. Areas specific to negative, as opposed to neutral, expressions were the left amygdala, the parahippocampal gyrus, and the right middle temporal gyrus (Brodmann's area 21). Areas specific to positive, as opposed to neutral, expressions were the prefrontal area (Brodmann's area 46), and the right inferior and middle temporal gyrus (Brodmann's areas 37 and 21). Direct comparison of activity elicited by negative and positive facial expressions revealed functional hemispheric asymmetry: negative expressions activated mainly the left hemisphere (Brodmann's areas 45/46, 6, and 21), whereas positive expressions activated predominantly the right hemisphere (Brodmann's areas 10 and 46, the fusiform gyrus in Brodmann's area 37, and Brodmann's area 7). Finally, the authors concluded that positive facial expressions are processed holistically, in the right hemisphere, whereas the processing of negative expressions requires a more analytical processing in the left hemisphere. However, Simon-Thomas, Role, and Knight (2005) found that emotional responses to aversive pictures selectively facilitated right-hemisphere processing during higher cognitive task performance.

In line with some earlier studies that reported modality-specific cerebral activation in response to emotional stimuli, Heining et al. (2000) found (using fMRI) that identical emotions (anger, disgust, fear, sadness) elicit greater cerebral activation when presented auditorily than when presented visually. The common region activated in most emotions, regardless of presentation modality, was the cerebellum. It may, therefore, be inferred that it is essential in processing emotional content in general. In the auditory modality all emotions activated the auditory cortex in both hemispheres and the anterior cingulate. The cingulate activity is related to its role in attention, because it is obvious that the auditory modality requires a greater amount of attention. Almost all visually presented emotions activated the visual cortex. The activity of some emotion-specific structures was recorded as well: visually presented emotions expressing fear and auditorily presented anger activated the amygdala; auditorily presented expressions of disgust activated the left insula (in accordance with earlier studies). However, contrary to earlier studies, no activity was recorded in the amygdala during presentation of emotions expressing sadness, regardless of modality.

With respect to lateralization in brain-damaged patients, a double dissociation was found between understanding meaning based on language and emotional prosody: the left hemisphere was crucial for the linguistic aspect, and the right hemisphere for prosody (more on that in the last chapter). Similarly to recognition of emotions, their expression depends mainly on the right hemisphere. However, it seems that two different neural pathways control emotional facial expressions, depending on whether they are intentional or spontaneous. The former are controlled by the left hemisphere, and they involve the cortex, whereas the latter are under bilateral control, with no cortical activity. Healthy subjects' data do not suggest such pronounced right-hemisphere dominance as found in clinical patients, but they do confirm the relatively greater involvement of the right hemisphere, compared with the left, during emotional functions (Gazzaniga et al., 2002). An interesting correlation between affective style and differences in the left and right hemisphere electrical activity during rest was found by EEG. Individuals that rate themselves more positively (e.g., as happier) on the scale of positive and negative personality traits exhibit relatively greater activity in the medial part of the left frontal lobe, and those who rate themselves more negatively (e.g., anxious) exhibit relatively greater activity in the corresponding area of the right frontal lobe. Asymmetries have been found in newborns as well. Babies with relatively higher activity in the right hemisphere cry more when separated from their mothers, as opposed to those who had greater activity in the left hemisphere (Gazzaniga et al., 2002).

Clinical and experimental data have indicated that the right hemisphere is more closely related to processing of emotional content than the left. Judaš and Kostović (1997) offered the following summary:

1. Emotional facial expressions presented to the left visual field (right hemisphere) are recognized faster and more accurately.
2. Emotional facial movements are usually more prominent on the left side (i.e., contralaterally to the hemisphere controlling the appropriate muscles).
3. Right-hemisphere injury causes more difficulties in recognizing emotional facial expressions than left-hemisphere injury.
4. Split-brain patients recognize emotionally relevant events only if presented to their left visual field.

Many clinical cases confirmed that emotions and mood in general are not exclusively associated with the limbic system, their primary neurophysiological substrate, but with cortical structures as well. The theory of right-hemisphere dominance for affective behavior was proposed on the basis of studies of right-hemisphere patients and healthy subjects that included behavioral tests and EEG measurements, among other methods. According to the theory, the right hemisphere is dominant for perception, recognition, and expression of emotions. Some authors have found that affective problems are encountered in patients with either left or right hemisphere damage, but that left-hemisphere damage results in cognitive deficits, whereas right-hemisphere damage causes emotional problems. Another hypothesis related to the possible laterality of affective functions proposes that the importance of the two hemispheres in emotional behavior is different, depending on the valence (emotional value) of the stimulus (Ortigue et al., 2004). According to that hypothesis, the right hemisphere is better at processing negative emotions, whereas the left hemisphere is superior at processing positive emotions. Although this dichotomy might account for cases of right-hemisphere patients who respond to negative emotions less strongly and see everything in a more positive light than left-hemisphere patients, clinical cases are not conclusive in that respect (for review, see Myers, 1999).

According to Myers (1999), affective and emotional disorders caused by right-hemisphere damage are manifested as:

1. Impaired recognition and production of nonverbal emotional information (decreased use of facial expressions in expressing emotions, decreased sensitivity to facial expressions of others, decreased use of gestures, inappropriate body posture).

2. Impaired understanding of verbally expressed emotions (difficulties in understanding emotions conveyed verbally in stories, pictures and films, as well as decreased recognition of emotional prosody).
3. Impaired verbal expression of emotions (impoverished use of emotions in conversation and storytelling, decreased use of prosody in expressing emotions, and decreased recall of emotionally colored events and memories).

Emotional and affective problems may take different forms and intensity, or they may be absent entirely. The most frequent manifestations of right-hemisphere damage at that level are depression, states of confusion—which may include restlessness—disorientation, delirium, psychoses, indifference, and lack of awareness of one's own condition. In this volume, when we talk about consequences of right-hemisphere damage in affective and emotional aspects of communication, we refer to individuals who do not present with actual psychological problems, but only to those who have cognitive difficulties.

SUMMARY

In a great majority of people, the left hemisphere is without a doubt dominant for language processes. Asymmetric brain morphology and consequences of lesions confirm that. Are earlier analytic and segmental specializations of the left hemisphere accountable for that? In other words, have language mechanisms been drawn to the left hemisphere during evolution or even ontogenetic development and then subjected to further neural development in the left hemisphere due to its already existing analytic segmental specialization? If we were to adopt such a viewpoint, we would consider the left hemisphere as specialized, not for symbolic functions as such, but for carrying out some kinds of motor activity that may be used in communication. On the other hand, are all observed language superiorities of the left hemisphere really just manifestations of analytic and sequential processing of the left hemisphere? There is plenty of evidence of the left-hemisphere analytic or segmental superiority, regardless of the phonological or verbal component. Some authors point out the advantage of speech and verbal processes with respect to left-hemisphere dominance, particularly unilateral motor control of the speech apparatus. According to them, speech is a species-specific ability. It is, therefore, controlled by the specialized left-hemisphere mechanism that enables humans to overcome limited resolution capabilities of the ears and the lack of acoustic invariance in the speech signal. It is believed that this mechanism is responsible for the phonological and the sound system that determines basic speech sounds and implements rules for their combinations into meaningful words, as well as for syntactic rules for combining these words into phrases or sentences. This leaves the right hemisphere free to engage in another important aspect of survival—visuospatial orientation and functioning.

7 Learning and Memory

One of the most impressive characteristics of the brain is its ability to learn how to create internal representations that make possible various skills: speech, recognition of faces and objects, sports, arts, and so forth. At the neurophysiologic level, learning is based on changes in synaptic activity induced by the influence of one neuron on another (Hinton, 1992; Rose, 1995). It seems that in these learning processes, the brain uses so-called population codes, in which the information is represented by an entire population of active neurons. For example, as the brain coordinates eye movements, the process is coded by the activity of a population of nerve cells, each of which represents a somewhat different movement. The final outcome, the actual movement, is the result of all constituent movements coded by active cells. If for some reason some of the cells are not active, the movement will be different than anticipated, but not impossible.

All learning is based on one of the key principles of the structure, development, and functioning of the nervous system: plasticity.

PLASTICITY

As previously discussed in chapter 5 on the principles, models, and theories, (neural) plasticity may be manifested in several ways. Developmental plasticity involves changes in connections that occur after birth as a consequence of interactions with the environment. These changes make possible the process of learning and acquiring new experiences but are also a result of these processes and are present until old age. Another type of plasticity refers to the ability to recover functions after brain damage (or more generally, after damage to the central nervous system).

Several decades ago the development of the nervous system was thought to be unchangeable: it was believed that neural connections were genetically determined with little influence from the environment on synaptogenesis. In other words, the connections among the neurons making up the nervous system were thought to be fixed once established. However, it eventually became clear that the genetic code determines just a set of rules for brain structure. Two principal rules are genetically determined: (a) the time when different cell groups appear (e.g., the ones that are predetermined to form the cortex or the hypothalamus), and (b) relative positions of cells and their terminals at the end of the process. The brain develops in an orderly and organized fashion: cells in certain areas occur and establish connections before cells in other areas (Changeaux, 1983). Neuronal activity cannot be chaotic either. It is defined temporally and spatially and is associated with particular synapse types. Temporal determination of action potentials is crucial in determining which synaptic connections are to be maintained and strengthened, and which are to be eliminated (Shatz, 1992). Obviously, distribution and connection patterns of earlier cells determine distribution and connection patterns of those that appear later on. Such a developmental mechanism is efficient, but probably not very precise. It provides similar overall brain structure within the species but not a well-formed mature nervous system. Under certain circumstances some synaptic connections may change, and this capacity to adapt is the basis of neural plasticity. Plasticity underlies the continuity of mental life (Aitkin, 1990; Fischbach, 1992). From the neurophysiologic point of view, action potentials do not just encode information—their metabolic consequences change pathways along which they travel. Plasticity increases the complexity of molecular characteristics or functions of cells (Fischbach, 1992). Grachev and Apkarian (2000) studied chemical changes related to establishment of new synaptic connections and found that the thalamus, sensorimotor cortex, and the cingulate might play a key role in plastic changes associated with normal aging. The fact that cortical connections in the somatosensory system are modified constantly, based on relevant activities is also related to plasticity. There is ample evidence that considerable reorganizations may occur in some cortical areas as consequences of the changes in peripheral receptors. For example, early sensory hearing loss will result in the reorganization of the representation of the auditory periphery in the primary auditory cortex in such a way that the intact (peripheral) hearing cells are represented in a much larger area than is the case in people with normal hearing (Harrison, Smith, Nagasawa, Stanton, & Mound, 1992). This is the basis of auditory hypersensitivity (i.e., recruitment), which typically accompanies sensory hearing loss. Somatosensory cortical maps seem very plastic, at least in primates, although there are limits to the expansion of a particular cortical area after peripheral changes. In the primary sensory areas, the brain refines the connections to the level of high precision during critical periods in early life, by means of unsupervised learning. During these critical periods (but not before or after) synaptic connections among neurons are very plastic and they react vigorously to changes in the patterns of neural activity (Stryker, 1995). In other words, cortical maps (for more on cortical maps see chapter 6, this volume) change constantly under the influence of the use of sensory pathways. It is believed that fine-tuning of connections in later developmental stages may require an activity-dependent associative synaptic mechanism (Kandel & Hawkins, 1992; see also Levy, Koeppen, & Stanton, 2005).

Singer (1995) proposed two complementary strategies that the brain uses to analyze and form representations of an infinite number of possible relations among the components of sensory and motor patterns. The first strategy is the analysis and representation of relationships that occur frequently, by means of broadly tuned cells that selectively respond to certain features. The other is a dynamic combination of these cells into functional units. Both strategies depend on experience, but the former is predominant in the prenatal and early postnatal period, whereas the latter reflects adaptability and probably underlies the ability to form representations of new perceptual and motor patterns throughout life. Attention and relevance of the activity for the individual are important prerequisites, especially for the latter strategy (Maunsell, 1995; Singer, 1995): attention paid to certain aspects of the stimulus may increase neuronal responses by as much as 50% to 100%.

The brain starts to function even before all circuits and connections have been completely developed. Neuronal connections are elaborated and perfected from the initial immature structure that only in general terms resembles the patterns of the adult brain. Although people are born with almost all neurons that they are ever going to have, brain mass at birth is only about one fourth of the adult brain. The brain enlarges because the neurons grow, the number of axons and dendrites increases, as well as the number of their connections (Shatz, 1992; Strange, 1995).

Developmental plasticity is, obviously, fine-tuning of connections within the nervous system and it depends on experience during postnatal period. At first, there is an excess of connections among cells, and then their number gradually decreases. This overabundance is probably manifested as overreacting of cells to stimuli in early life periods. This responsiveness gradually decreases as a function of later experience.

Neuronal activity is a prerequisite for developing the precision characteristic of the adult brain—the brain has to be stimulated. Functional properties of neurons, as well as their structure acquire their specificities during postnatal development. The sequence of developmental changes in arborization indicates that the mature pattern of connections is established by means of reshaping the axons through selective growth or withdrawal of different branches (Shatz, 1992).

The greatest changes in the primate brain occur in its cortex during the postnatal period, especially until puberty. This is attributed to the fact that the cortex is the most susceptible to postnatal experience. The relatively large size of the primate cortex (especially in humans) compared with other species, is associated with its higher cognitive functions (Johnson, 2000). This is particularly true of the frontal regions that are the last to fully develop in the postnatal period. Developmental changes that may be found in children during the early postnatal period (before 12 months of age) are a consequence of the maturation of the frontal lobes.

Neural development results in cognitive changes, but the opposite is true as well. Some of its aspects may be a function of the interaction between neurocognitive systems of the organism and the environment. In addition to context, knowledge, and other factors, past experience can also have a powerful effect on the reception and perception of new stimuli, as well as on the reorganization of the cortical regions that used to be considered exclusively primary sensory areas (Gilbert, Das, Ito, Kapadia, & Westheimer, 2000; Kosslyn, Thompson, Kim, & Alpert, 2000).

Interestingly, the effect of experience is first manifested as decreased activation of sensory and motor cortical areas. This is explained by the selectivity of neuronal populations that participate in the representation of familiar stimuli, because experience has "taught" them which features are relevant. After the initial decrease, additional cells become gradually active (Turner & Frackowiak, 1995; Ungerleider, 1995). At the same time, changes in activation of other regions (cerebellum, prefrontal cortex) occur, which may be compared with the previously mentioned results of Raichle (1994).

According to Changeux (1983), the connections among cell groups are genetically determined but not stable. Unstable synapses may be reinforced or weakened—depending on the overall activity of the postsynaptic cell, which is input-dependent. The input may be a result of spontaneous activity in the network that may be enhanced by environmental effects. This is selective stabilization, which means at the neuronal level learning is actually the process of elimination. A manifestation of learning is cortical reorganization in the absence of sensory stimuli. For example, congenitally deaf individuals were found to be more sensitive to events occurring at the periphery of their visual fields than hearing subjects; furthermore, visual stimuli activated parts of their cerebral cortex that are activated by auditory stimuli in hearing persons (in the temporal lobe). These results of ERP studies are interpreted as stabilization or reinforcement of visual afferent connections in the areas that would otherwise remain unused due to the absence of auditory stimulation ordinarily represented in these regions. In this context, Neville (1991) concludes that development of language competence (she is specifically talking about grammar) is necessary for the left hemisphere to become specialized for language. As it is discussed elsewhere in this volume, this is not necessarily applicable exclusively to oral language: the left hemisphere is specialized for language in congenitally deaf individuals who use sign language.

One of the important facts resulting from studies of connections between neural development and behavior is that the relationship is two-way: behavior is not just a consequence of neural development, it is an active contributor to it. Orientation of sensory organs toward particular types of stimuli within the developing nervous system makes possible specialization for processing of information about biologically relevant stimuli.

Le Carret, Petrescu, Amieva, Fabrigoule, and Allard (2002) used fMRI to compare the brain activity of young and old adults while they were solving tasks that required selective attention. In young subjects, they found bilateral activity in the occipital and superior parietal areas, which are responsible for visuospatial processing. In older subjects, they found decreased activity in the posterior parietal regions and bilateral activation of the dorsolateral prefrontal cortex. This indicates that, in order for cognitive abilities to be maintained, functional changes occur in cortical network activity: the areas that become less efficient with age (e.g., visuospatial) are functionally replaced or aided by other resources in the more frontal regions. Hagoort, Wassenaar, and Brown (2003) provide evidence from an ERP study of agrammatic patients, nonagrammatic aphasics and controls for the compensation of a syntactic deficit by a greater reliance on another route in mapping sound onto meaning. This form of plasticity is referred to as multiple-route plasticity.

As discussed at the beginning of the chapter, plasticity is also manifested as the ability to recover after injury or some other nervous system dysfunction.

Several variables may affect recovery after brain damage (Kalat, 1995; Legg, 1989). An example of relatively rapid reorganization is vestibular compensation. Because of this mechanism, asymmetry in the sense of balance that occurs as a consequence of unequal responsiveness of the vestibular system in the left or the right inner ear (manifested as ataxia) is very quickly compensated, primarily in the cerebellum, but also at the level of the vestibular nucleus in the brainstem (Dutia, 2002). On the other hand, there are cases of very slow reorganization: Gazzaniga et al. (2002) reported on patients who started "speaking" from their right hemispheres as long as 10 years after callosotomy.

After a stroke in one hemisphere, sensorimotor representations of arms or legs are frequently reorganized in both hemispheres. In the intact hemisphere, this is attributed to the fact that the extremities that had not been affected are used more, which changes their cerebral representation accordingly (Rossini, 2002). Such activation of the cortical regions in the intact hemisphere has been recorded by PET and MRI after various types of cortical and subcortical lesions. Weiler (as cited in Runjić, 1996) calls this activation the auxiliary mechanism.

The age at which the brain injury occurs plays an important role in recovery, but that influence is not straightforward. On the one hand, the developing brain has greater capabilities for compensating for the deficits occurring after localized damage. On the other hand, precisely because development has not been completed by the time of injury in young people, the risk of other disorders in subsequent development is increased. After a left hemispherectomy in early childhood, language functions are likely to transfer to the right hemisphere with minimal functional deficits (Boatman et al., 1999; Lassonde, Sauerwein, Chicoine, & Geoffroy, 1991).

Obviously, the site of injury is closely related to the prognosis for recovery, but apart from location itself, the rate at which damage occurred is also important. For example, a gradually developing tumor will cause less severe functional disorders than a sudden focal injury or stroke. The extent of damage is frequently more important than its location. Weiler (as cited in Runjić, 1996) concluded that the potential for functional reorganization is smaller and the outcome poorer if the affected motor area is larger. It has also been found that appropriate care and attention immediately after surgery resulted in alleviation or complete disappearance of symptoms, which suggests that the time and quality of the postoperative experience also play important roles in recovery.

It is presumed that the mechanism of recovery is based primarily on the fact that intact systems go back to normal activity levels, rather than a damaged system being replaced by another one, but this hypothesis lacks sufficient evidence. LeVere (as cited by Legg, 1989) concluded that even partial damage of the system may change its function to the degree that a patient may even stop using it entirely in spite of the fact that some residual function is still possible. The consequence of this is overrating the extent of damage.

Other mechanisms of recovery that have been proposed in the past (with varying degrees of empirical support) include: taking over the function of the damaged region by the intact ones that had not had that particular function before; adopting new problem-solving strategies; and limited regeneration that is primarily manifested as sprouting of new axon terminals at undamaged axons. In a great many cases the reorganization occurs in the same hemisphere (Milner, 1994). The brain has the ability to reorganize after peripheral injury or deprivation so that it allows neighboring (intact) areas to expand to the area normally occupied by the input from the (now) deprived sensory organs. In blind individuals, it has been found that additional cortical areas participate in active recognition of auditory and somatosensory stimuli. There is also some indication of enhanced automatic processing of changes in auditory stimuli. Data suggest compensatory changes in the auditory and somatosensory modality after early visual deprivation. This plasticity is possibly not limited to particular developmental periods but may to some extent be feasible throughout life (Kujala et al., 1995; Rauschecker, 1995). Bellman Thiran et al. (2002) recorded by fMRI the functional reorganization in the brain of their 60-year-old patient suffering from progressive aphasia due to atrophy of the left temporal lobe.

Plasticity that is related to learning and experience, but which also enables functional reorganization after injury, is associated with notion of the so-called critical periods.

CRITICAL PERIODS

Critical period is the time span between the onset of an anatomically or functionally determined biobehavioral system and its maturation. During this immature phase the system may be under the influence of positive or negative exogenous stimuli with more or less permanent consequences (Colombo, 1982; Spreen, Tupper, Risser, Tuokko, & Edgell, 1984).

Critical periods occur even prenatally. The most sensitive at a particular point are the organs and systems that undergo the most intensive cell growth. The systems that have not yet reached their level of rapid growth and development as well as those that have already completed that stage are less affected by external influences (e.g., teratogenous drugs).

It is believed that the initial phases of axon growth and selection of the paths of migration are independent of their activity. The genetically determined part of the program can be seen in the high degree of structural completeness that is reached during the embryonic stage. However, when axon terminals reach their designated areas, the selection of specific targets is under the influence of nerve impulses originating in the brain or stimulated by exogenous events. Synaptogenesis during a critical period may be determined by the type of competition among axons; the axons that have been activated in the optimal manner have priority (Fischbach, 1992; Shatz, 1992).

According to Spreen et al. (1984), the following criteria have to be met in order for a period to be called critical: (a) the beginning and the end that can be identified; (b) an intrinsic component (i.e., sensitivity of the organism to some maturational event); and (c) an extrinsic component (i.e., an external stimulus to which the organism is sensitive).

It is possible to compare the developmental periods of the brain with the critical, sensitive (Spreen et al., 1984), or optimal (Andrilović & Čudina, 1990) periods in the development of the organism. These periods are defined as windows of time during which the organism is particularly susceptible and/or vulnerable (i.e., more sensitive) to the environmental influences, and that involve prenatal and postnatal period. Coren and Ward (1989) define the critical period as "… an interval during which sensory experience is essential if perceptual development is to proceed normally" (p. 509). In postnatal development the importance of these periods is manifested in acquiring early experiences (Shatz, 1992), establishing basic social relationships, and learning. Moreover, developmental stages of the brain, which are closely associated with the notion of plasticity, are the foundation of behavior that is explained by the onset or offset of a critical period. Studies in anatomy, biology, physiology, and developmental neurobiology have shown that the brain does not develop continuously or evenly, but rather in spurts. These brain growth spurts are chronologically predictable and alternate with plateaus. About 85% to 90% of children of average and above-average abilities go through several phases of brain growth spurts: between the 3rd and 10th months of life, between the 2nd and 4th years, between the 6th and 8th years, between the 10th and 12th years, and between the 14th and 16th years of age (or later; Epstein, 1980). Some authors question the methodology of Epstein's studies and challenge the replicability of his results, but there is agreement as to the existence of brain growth spurts, with a word of caution that these phases are not necessarily simultaneous in all brain areas: some areas are at a plateau, whereas others are undergoing rapid growth (Greenough, Black, & Wallace, 1987). However, Chugani, Phelps, and Mazziotta (1987) measured glucose consumption (as an indicator of activity) in eight cortical and three subcortical areas, as well as in the cerebellar cortex, and in the brainstem and found that by the age of 2, children reach adult (19 to 30 years of age) levels in all measured areas; these values increase until ages 3 to 8, when they are about twice the adult levels, after which time there is a decrease. At ages 9 to 15 the levels are still somewhat higher than in adults.

One of the key issues is the relationship between brain growth and development on the one hand, and mental functions and learning on the other. The visual cortex is a good example of the close connection between anatomic changes and functional development. Synaptogenesis is closely related to the development of visual functions: at birth, there are only about 10% of connections, whereas rich synaptic connections are established rapidly at the age of approximately 4 months corresponding to the time of development of visual acuity and the ability to track objects (Huttenlocher, 1990). Huttenlocher's studies confirmed Epstein's (1980) claims that brain size increases are due to the increase in the amount of protein. In neurons, this increase in the amount of protein is manifested as elongation and arborization of axons and dendrites, despite the decrease in the number of synapses per neuron between late childhood and age 16 (Huttenlocher, 1990). The process results in a remarkable increase in the complexity of neural networks during later developmental stages, which is manifested as greater complexity of cognitive processes in the brain. Lassonde et al. (1991) associate the maturation of the corpus callosum with periods of greater plasticity. On the other hand, during plateau phases in brain growth and development there is practically no increase in brain mass or complexity of neural networks (Epstein, 1980). The importance of the age factor in learning has been confirmed for various skills—from sports to arts. Chen, Halpern, Bly, Edelman, and Schlaug (2000) found in their fMRI studies that early exposure to music and commencement of music education is important for the development of absolute pitch. However, they also stressed the importance of the necessary anatomic prerequisite—smaller right than left *planum temporale.*

Locke (1994) believes that the sensitive period for language acquisition is a developmental framework that includes several phases. These phases are sensitive to external and internal events and vary in the degree of sensitivity. The constituent systems of the overall language system are turned on and supported by different processes, and each of them has its own subsystem and course. The consequence of these variations is a series of dynamically variable interactions that cannot be recognized or explained by the existing theories of language development. The notion of sensitive periods in language acquisition is supported by evidence from acquisition of sign language by the deaf. Lieberman (1991) found that individuals who acquired sign language earlier performed better at the morphological level than those who acquired it at a later age. Foreign language learning literature provides ample evidence that the ability to learn a foreign language to the level of near-native competence decreases sharply after ages 6 to 8. Around age 14 the ability reaches and remains at the adult level. Most of these data do not, unfortunately, tell us much about the acquisition of the first (native) language, because they do not address the initial activation and the development of the learning systems and processes involved in mastering a language. Another flaw in most approaches to language acquisition and learning is that they treat language as a unitary ability, not as different systems—e.g., phonology, morphology, syntax, lexicon—which would be more appropriate, because the abilities that support these systems are different and do not develop simultaneously (Hyltenstam, 1992; Locke, 1994).

Language development begins with the orientation of the child toward language manifestations—the physical activity of people who talk—which provides children with information about language. Vocal learning and the first words are preceded by (socially) cognitive operations: studying and interpreting eye movements with respect to utterances, learning and application of the rules of turn-taking in vocalizations, orientation toward and imitation of prosody, communicative pointing, assimilation of phonetic patterns, and interpretation of the mental activities of others. Combined with perceptual experience and motor development, these procedures enable children to manage (native) language situations in spite of their limited language capacity (Locke, 1994). What Lenneberg neglected in his claims that language acquisition starts around the second year of life is that the crucial part of the critical period for language is the preverbal phase. The amount of attention the children get from their mothers or other care providers and the extent of the imitations they produce by their own vocalizations were found to be in positive correlation with the size of their expressive vocabulary at 21 months of age. According to Locke (1994), there is a vocal learning phase and three linguistic phases in language acquisition. They occur in specific order and partly overlap. Each phase affects the next but is also under the influence of the preceding one, and they are all affected by neuromaturational events and social stimulation. The vocal learning phase and the first linguistic phase (acquisition of utterances) are primarily affective and social. Their goal is to master the prosody of the language and form a collection of utterances. The function of the second linguistic phase (structure analysis and computation) is analytical. In this phase, previously stored forms are analyzed into syllables and segments. This process enables discovery of regularities and acquisition of grammar, including phonology, morphology, and syntax. The third linguistic phase (integration and elaboration) extends throughout the lifetime and is in fact the basis for lexical learning (i.e., enrichment of vocabulary). Preliminary results of Plumet, Gil, and Gaonac (2002) suggest that practice may improve and maintain cognitive functions (e.g., verbal fluency and memory) well into old age.

Contrary to the critical periods discussed previously, referring primarily to different phases before and including puberty, Lenneberg's (1967) notion of the critical period in language acquisition includes the entire preadolescent period, as the optimal time for language acquisition as opposed to the (post)adolescent period. On the basis of evidence from stroke patients, children with Down syndrome, and the experiences of foreign-language learners, Hurford (1991) also places the critical period for language acquisition in the time before puberty. Deane (1992) associates language acquisition with the rate of development of the parietal lobe, which is, according to him, the seat of language function as an integral process at three levels (phonological, syntactic, and cognitive, or semantic–pragmatic). According to his hypothesis, grammatical competence is represented in brain regions whose primary function is to represent body image, which means that they are to be found in the areas where bits of information from different sensory modalities converge and are integrated: in the inferior parietal lobe, at the border between the temporal, occipital, and parietal lobes. Since neurological measurements reveal rapid development of the parietal lobe between birth and the 2nd year of life (with further, somewhat slower maturation until age 10), Deane believes that it is possible that "… the stages of development in first language acquisition reflect stages in the maturation of the inferior parietal lobe …" (p. 297). Johnson and Newport (1989) tested the critical period hypothesis (in addition to numerous other tests of motivation, identification, etc.) on Korean and Chinese subjects who had arrived in the United States at different ages. Their knowledge of American English was measured by comprehensive syntactic and morphological tests. With respect to critical periods they concluded that: (a) there is a significant correlation between the age of arrival in the United States and the results on all types of syntactic and morphological tests; (b) subjects who had arrived in the United States before the age of 7 had results comparable to native speakers of American English, whereas those who arrived after the age of 7 exhibited a noticeable drop in competence until puberty; (c) subjects who had arrived as adults scored on average significantly more poorly than those who had arrived before puberty, but competence did not decrease as a function of increasing postadolescent age of arrival. Their general conclusions (which they found support for in many studies by other authors) are that the notion of the critical period may be extended from the → native language acquisition proper to foreign language learning, but that the capacities diminish differently than defined by Lenneberg (1967). A drop in competence does not occur in puberty, but as early as around 7 years of age. Interestingly, after age 7, the number of synapses in the frontal lobe starts to decrease (although the functions of that cortical region are not yet understood completely, it is clear that it plays an important role in complex intellectual processes). As it has been mentioned above, cerebral metabolism measurements have shown that metabolic activity of the human cortex increases rapidly in the early postnatal period, remains above adult levels during childhood, and decreases to adult levels during puberty (Chugani, Phelps, & Mazziotta, 1987; Huttenlocher, 1990).

The importance of critical periods in language acquisition has been confirmed by (luckily rare) examples of speech and language deprivation without organic etiology. These are the cases of the so-called *feral children,* who for various reasons had no exposure to speech and language communication at the optimal age. The best documented example is Genie, who had lived in isolation (imposed by her parents) until she was 13. Her speech and language development (but also her social development and interactions) started when she was found, but in spite of enormous efforts and time spent in teaching and coaching, her competence never reached the level of children who had been growing up surrounded by speech. Even 4 years after she began stringing words into first sentences her speech was still confused and telegraphic. She could not distinguish passive from active verb forms and confused her pronouns. Her language and, it is interesting to note, her nonlanguage functions were lateralized to the right hemisphere.

Learning is usually classified as associative and nonassociative. During associative learning the individuals learn about relationships between two events or about consequences of their own behavior. It may be simple (classical and instrumental conditioning) or complex (explicit or implicit). Nonassociative learning occurs when individuals learn and remember the features of the stimulus to which they are exposed. It may be manifested as habituation or sensitization.

The process of acquiring information and skills (learning) and the result of that process (memory) regardless of whether it is conscious or unconscious, proceed through several stages (Figure 7.1). The first stage is encoding, during which the material to be learned is presented and processed. Encoding consists of two

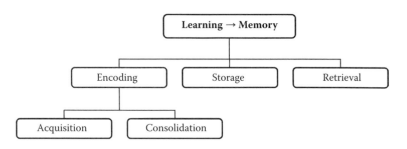

FIGURE 7.1.   Stages of learning and memory.

steps: First, the input data are registered by the senses and subjected to sensory analysis (acquisition), and then they are consolidated. The second stage is storage, during which some of the available information is stored in the memory system. During the third stage (retrieval) the stored material is retrieved from memory in the form of a conscious representation, recognition or as some form of learned behavior.

Animal studies have shown that acquisition, storage, and retrieval are separate neural processes: one or more of them may proceed independently of the others (Webster, 1995). It has also been found that specific neural pathways participate in each learning task, depending on the nature of the task. In a particular situation the changes occur in the majority of the pathways, but not necessarily in all of their parts. It is, therefore, more plausible that data are stored in a wider area, rather than in a small number of structures (Levy et al., 2005).

TYPES OF MEMORY

Memory is most frequently characterized according to the duration of information retention (sensory, short-term/working, and long-term; see Figure 7.2) and with respect to the type of information storage (declarative or explicit vs. nondeclarative or implicit). The latter classification is used in long-term memory. Each of these groups has characteristics and subgroups of its own. They are briefly reviewed here. For more detailed explanations and discussions of different types of memory see Zarevski (1994) and Gazzaniga et al. (2002).

SENSORY MEMORY

The duration of this type of memory ranges from less than one second to several seconds. It is sometimes referred to as sensory trace(s). The traces disappear very quickly; most often we are not even aware of them, and the capacity for this type of memory is relatively large. Information representations are sensory rather than semantic and are manifested as brief traces of neural activity in cortical areas that correspond to the projections of various senses. If the information was auditory this type of memory is called echoic. The visual modality will produce iconic

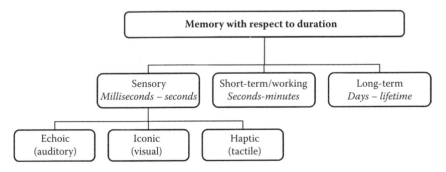

FIGURE 7.2. Types of memory with respect to duration.

memory. Tactile information will result in haptic memory. Echoic memory may last from two to three seconds, but the traces start to dwindle after 300 to 500 ms (according to some authors even after 100 to 200 ms; Levy et al., 2005). Iconic memory lasts not longer than half a second (according to some authors not longer than 300 ms). Kölsch, Schroger, and Tervaniemi (1999) found that sensory memory, specifically echoic memory, may be modified by practice. If the stimulus is "worth" remembering, it is passed on to short-term/working memory.

SHORT-TERM/WORKING MEMORY

This type of memory is measured in seconds and minutes. It enables us to remember someone's phone number or address long enough to dial it or write it down. It is accessible to consciousness, but its capacity is very limited: five to nine individual pieces of information (the well-known Miller's 7±2 number). One of the common ways of overcoming this limitation is grouping data before subjecting them to memory. A series of 12 digits (e.g., 257986105337) will be much easier to remember than six two-digit numbers (25, 79, 86, 10, 53, 37) or than four three-digit ones (257, 986, 105, 337). Many different mnemonic techniques are recommended in the popular literature (e.g., Howard, 2000). The serial position effect is closely related to the notion of short-term memory. It has been found that the elements at the end of the list and those at the beginning are the easiest to remember. These two effects are known as the recency effect and the primacy effect, respectively. They are based on different mechanisms. Primacy effect is based on the transfer from the short-term to long-term memory by repetition. Recency effect is based on retention in short-term memory (Gazzaniga et al., 2002). The time elapsed from the stimulus and the time allowed for response are the most important factors that determine which of the two effects will prevail (Petz, 1992).

The term *working memory* evolved from the term *short-term memory* (as opposed to long-term memory). Short-term memory used to be described as a single short-term storage of limited capacity, responsible for various memory phenomena. It was also thought to be responsible for learning and recall. Several memory models proposed that storage of sensory data into long-term memory proceeds via short-term memory. However, clinical studies have shown that patients with severely impaired short-term memory may have intact long-term memory, which was in contradiction to the notion of short-term memory as a single system. It was, therefore, replaced by the term working memory, to designate short-term limited-capacity information storage where mental operations on the content of the storage may be performed as well. As opposed to the earlier models that described short-term memory only as one-way input to long-term memory, working memory may receive data from sensory memory, but from long-term memory as well, and may be a place for processing of such data. Because of this, working memory cannot be viewed as a single system. It comprises at least two components: storage and processing units. Baddeley and coworkers (as cited in Baddeley, 2000) propose a three-part model in which a *central executive* regulates and controls attention and is hierarchically superordinate to two active systems:

(a) *the articulatory/phonological loop*, and (b) *the visuospatial sketchpad*. The central executive coordinates their connections with the long-term memory. It is comparable to the *supervisory attentional system* of Norman and Shallice (as cited in Gazzaniga et al., 2002) that coordinates and plans activities, stops routine performance of learned behaviors when new circumstances that require different behavior occur, and so on.

The phonological loop contains and maintains speech information. It comprises two components: short-term (transient) speech storage, where the trace remains for only about two seconds, and the process of articulatory control. This process may best be described as subvocal (silent) articulation or a practice that keeps the speech material in the storage and supplies new speech by the process of subvocalization, regardless of the fact that the original data input may not have been auditory or spoken. It has been shown that working memory uses acoustic rather than semantic code during practice. It is assumed that auditory speech information has automatic and obligatory access to the storage. The phonological loop is very important for the acquisition of new vocabulary, which involves long-term phonological learning.

The visuospatial sketchpad involves short-term storage and control processes responsible for registering visual and spatial information and its restoration by repetition, or practice. The visuospatial sketchpad is also included in long-term memory, but these two subsystems are independent of each other.

Their relative independence has support in neuropsychological research. It has been found that difficulties in phonological working memory, manifested as a decreased ability to hold a series of words in working memory, occurs because of injury to the left supramarginal gyrus (Brodmann's area 40; see Figure 7.3). The phonological loop includes the left premotor area (Brodmann's area 44). On the other hand, the visuospatial sketchpad is damaged after injury to the parieto-occipital areas of either hemisphere. Right-hemisphere damage results in poorer nonverbal visuospatial short-term memory, whereas damage to homologous areas in the left hemisphere results in difficulties in short-term memory of visually presented language material (Gazzaniga et al., 2002).

Neuroimaging studies of healthy subjects have revealed that the anatomic network of verbal working memory comprises mostly frontal regions (Brodmann's areas 44, 10, 9, 6) during repetitions within the articulatory loop, and posterior regions (Brodmann's areas 40 and 7) constitute the temporary phonological store. On the other hand, the anterior cingulate (Brodmann's area 32) and the dorsolateral prefrontal cortex (Brodmann's area 46) are active during selection, manipulation, error control, and affective regulation. During complex tasks or in some pathological conditions (e.g., in chronic fatigue syndrome), some right-hemisphere areas exhibit increased activity (Lange et al., 2000). Fiez et al. (as cited in Gazzaniga et al., 2002) analyzed the results of several PET studies and concluded that tasks that include verbal practice (i.e., those that belong in the phonological loop) elicit increased blood flow in inferior regions of the left lateral prefrontal cortex (Brodmann's areas 44 and 45) and in the right cerebellar hemisphere. They attributed this cerebellar activity to the subvocal repetition, and

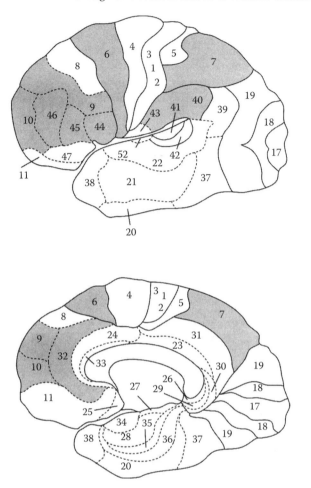

FIGURE 7.3. Activation of brain areas—various stages and types of memory and learning.

activity in Broca's area to phonological (re)coding. Crosson et al. (1999) found by fMRI that various posterior regions of the left hemisphere participate in decoding and storage of information, depending on whether the data in working memory are semantic, phonological or orthographic, which was in agreement with earlier literature on the mechanisms for processing of these types of data. During tasks that required involvement of working memory they found additional activation in the left frontal lobe, including the premotor cortex, but in subcortical structures as well. They concluded that there were different forms of verbal working memory, and that it was necessary to reconsider the premotor cortex functions. Walter et al. (2000) studied working memory during verbal (recognition of visually presented letters) and visuospatial (determining the position of visually presented letters) tasks by fMRI and found that verbal tasks activated left-hemisphere structures (inferior frontal gyrus, superior temporal gyrus, and fusiform gyrus) more than the visuospatial tasks. These tasks activated medial *precuneus*, the right superior frontal lobe and the left superior temporal lobe. D'Arcy, Ryner, Richter, Service, and Connolly (2004) also confirmed left-hemisphere dominance for verbal memory.

Suchan, Gayk, and Daum (2002) used the ERP method to study the visuospatial working memory, and recorded mainly the left lateralized positive peak with the 600 ms latency, over frontal lobes and a pronounced negativity over the right parietal lobe. They also concluded that different neural circuits are activated during processing of visuospatial information, depending on memory and attention requirements. Schmidt et al. (2002) reported similar results. In their fMRI study they recorded activity in the frontal, parietal, and temporal lobes of both hemispheres during manipulation of three-dimensional objects in virtual space. Chambers, Stokes, and Mattingly (2004) reported modality-specific attentional processing in the parietal cortex.

Saur, Erb, Grodd, and Kammer (2002) studied the differences between visual processing of colors and spatial configuration with the aim of discovering possible differences that would correspond to the ventral ("what") and the dorsal ("where") pathways. Their data have suggested domain-specific processing of stimuli within working memory in the frontal lobes: during memorizing colors (the "what" pathway) there was increased activity in the middle frontal gyrus, whereas during memorizing the spatial arrangement of dots (the "where" pathway) there was increased activity in the premotor regions. Moreover, in addition to the frontal "what" pathway they recorded simultaneous activation of the posterior "what" pathway (ventral), and in addition to the frontal "where" pathway there was simultaneous activity in the posterior "where" pathway (dorsal). These differences were noticed at cellular level as well (Gazzaniga et al., 2002).

Schizophrenic patients and healthy controls have similar activation patterns during visuospatial and verbal tasks related to working memory (Brodmann's areas 44/45, 9/46, 6, 7, and 40, and the cerebellum). However, contrary to control subjects, in whom greater activation was found mainly in the left hemisphere during verbal but not for visuospatial tasks, they do not exhibit domain-specific lateralization, only overall greater activity (Walter et al., 2000).

The central executive function is perhaps the most important, but also the least investigated segment of the working memory. Clinical studies suggest that its neurophysiologic substrate is in the frontal lobes of both hemispheres, particularly in the lateral prefrontal areas. Prefrontal areas are considered to be a temporary repository of representations and information that are held here while they are essential for performing the task at hand. When a new stimulus arrives, a temporary representation is retrieved and established in prefrontal cortex by means of connections with posterior regions where the representations are stored permanently. Patients with damage to these regions cannot control the direction of attention, which is manifested as perseveration on one and the same response, or as a reaction to the first stimulus that comes along, regardless of its relevance to the organism in general or to the actual situation. Alzheimer's patients exhibit a pronounced disorder of the attention direction mechanism. In these patients it is manifested as the inability to coordinate two concurrent tasks from different subsystems, and the disorder becomes more serious as the condition progresses. These data support the description of working memory as the ability to simultaneously store and process information (Baddeley, 2000).

On the other hand, Goldman-Rakic (2000) concluded on the basis of registering brain activity in monkeys that the central executive is distributed in the same areas where information is stored. According to her, it comprises specific modules for information processing, each with its own sensory and mnemonic properties and elements for motor and motivational control, rather than being a single control system with hierarchically lower slave subsystems. In other words, in the prefrontal cortex, there are several working memory domains, and not a single working memory with different ongoing processes. On the basis of clinical, experimental, and neurobiological data she concludes that the prefrontal cortex has a specialized function that is replicated in all or almost all cortical subparts, particularly in the cerebellum and basal ganglia. At the same time, interactions between these working-memory centers and other areas in specific cortical networks make up the brain structure for higher cognitive functions. Prefrontal cortical damage does not impede acquiring knowledge of the world, but it does prevent its use in control of behavior.

Although the term *working memory* has its roots in the classical term *short-term memory,* it seems that the more general model of the relationship between memory and cognition has been adopted. Working memory is involved in processing language data, in formation and understanding of utterances, but also in cognitive processes in general.

LONG-TERM MEMORY

This type of memory is measured by days, months, and years. With respect to the characteristics of the stored information it is usually grouped into declarative and nondeclarative, and it has been found that these two types of memory are differently represented in the brain (Kandel & Hawkins, 1992).

Declarative memory is also called explicit or direct, and it refers to knowledge (and experiences) that can be consciously accessed. It may be further divided into episodic and semantic memory. Episodic memory is knowledge of events that concern us personally (memory of the first day of school, wedding, the most embarrassing situation, etc.); it is therefore frequently referred to as autobiographic memory, and it is temporally marked. Semantic memory contains knowledge of facts that we have read, learned in school, seen on television, and so forth, without particular details about the process of acquiring such knowledge, which makes it temporally unmarked. Semantic memory underlies the mental lexicon (see chap. 8, this volume).

Nondeclarative memory is also called *implicit* or *indirect.* It is sometimes used synonymously with the term *procedural memory,* but most authors agree that nondeclarative memory comprises subtypes other than procedural memory (Kalat, 1995; Thompson, 1993). Besides procedural memory, nondeclarative memory includes the perceptual representation system, classical conditioning, and nonassociative learning (Gazzaniga et al., 2002). What is common to all these subtypes is that they all involve knowledge that has been acquired and stored without explicit memory of that process. It is an unintentional, unconscious form of knowledge retention. Procedural memory involves the ability to perform a motor or cognitive skill (e.g., skiing or reading) without conscious knowledge or deliberation about how the skill is performed. Knowledge retained in the perceptual representation system may be discovered by priming and memory tests. Classical conditioning is also referred to as Pavlovian conditioning. As mentioned previously, nonassociative learning involves habituation and sensitization.

Explicit memory is typically studied by means of recall and recognition tests that require intentional recall of information from some specific earlier learning situation. On the other hand, implicit memory is tested by tasks that do not require conscious recall of specific episodes or events. PET studies have shown that implicit memory may be further categorized into perceptual and conceptual implicit memory, because perceptual and conceptual priming tasks affected different parts of the brain (Baddeley, 2000; Schacter, 2000).

The above classification of long-term memory is based mainly on neuropsychological tests and observations of brain-damaged patients. It has been noticed that different types of memory are affected differently by injury: some types may be completely disordered without deficits in the others. Amnesic patients are believed to have deficits in the episodic learning mechanism, which is manifested as difficulties in adding on to the existing semantic memory, namely, its updating. In such patients implicit procedural learning capabilities are usually preserved, which is explained by the fact that such learning is possible without reliance on episodic learning (memory; Baddeley, 2000). Posthypnotic amnesia affects episodic but not semantic memory and it dissociates explicit from implicit memory (Sternberg, 2003). Drubach (2000) pointed out another difference between declarative and nondeclarative memory: Plasticity of the brain for declarative learning remains relatively constant throughout the lifetime (with the exception of very old people), whereas plasticity for nondeclarative learning is the greatest in early childhood. According to some authors, native (first) language and foreign (second) language are acquired or learned by means of different types of memory. The former rely on nondeclarative memory, and the latter on declarative (Paradis, 1994, 2004). In Figure 7.4 different types of long-term memory are shown.

NEURAL SUBSTRATES OF MEMORY

The most important structures involved in declarative memory (episodic and semantic) are: (a) the medial part of the thalamus with the associated connections within the internal medullar lamina, and (b) the hippocampal formation with the neighboring anatomically related parts of the cortex (medial temporal lobe). Since most patients suffering amnesia caused by injury have poor episodic and semantic memory, it would seem logical that both types of memory depend on the same brain area. However, it has been found that episodic and semantic memories

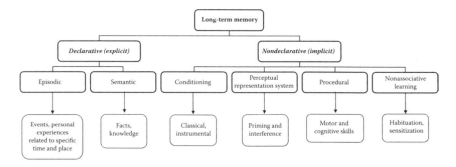

FIGURE 7.4.   Long-term memory.

are represented in neighboring brain regions that are commonly affected in amnesiacs (Baddeley, 2000). Although no differences were found between the consequences on episodic and semantic memory after injury to these parts, it seems that severe frontal lobe damage has a negative effect on episodic, but not on semantic memory (Squire & Zola, 2000). Rajah and Mcintosh (2005) suggested, on the basis of their combined ERP and PET studies, that activation differences between episodic and semantic retrieval may reflect variation along a continuum of processing during task performance within a single memory system.

The hippocampus turned out to be the most active when explicit recall involved experience with the test material, rather than an attempt to remember information. Several different studies have confirmed that the hippocampus is the most important structure in coding new data and retrieval of recent information that requires explicit recall (Gazzaniga et al., 2002).

Guillem, Rougier, and Claverie (1999) have found in their ERP studies that previous exposure to a stimulus facilitates each subsequent processing of an identical stimulus. They recorded electrical activity in different parts of the brain during a continuous memorization task in order to determine which parts contribute to short-term and long-term effects of stimulus repetition. Their results indicate that there are multiple anatomic and functional memory systems in the human brain (a short-term semantic activation system and a long-term episodic memory system) and structures that connect and coordinate the functioning of memory. Saykin et al. (2000) studied Alzheimer's patients and found double dissociation between structural and functional changes in the systems that support semantic as opposed to episodic memory. Namely, atrophy in the left inferior frontal gyrus was associated with deficits in semantic processing, whereas atrophy of the hippocampus was associated with episodic memory disorders. Episodic memory is the cognitive function that is affected first and foremost in Alzheimer's patients, similarly to memory changes that occur as a function of normal aging (Bernard, Desgranges, Eustache, & Baron, 2002).

The theoretical hypotheses about the importance of the inferior temporal lobe for semantic memory were supported by Papps, Best, and O'Carroll (2000). They studied a patient who had suffered considerable damage to the left temporal and parietal lobes. Many comprehensive tests have revealed good functioning of her semantic memory and even relatively intact neurological and neuropsychological functioning, probably owing to the spared left inferior and medial temporal lobe. Rossion et al. (2000) found by measuring cerebral blood flow during PET scans that recall of semantic information about visual characteristics of objects and their categorization are located in the left occipito-temporal regions. Their study has not confirmed prefrontal activity, which they attributed to the fact that their study involved direct processing of visual stimuli. Simultaneous activation of the left prefrontal areas may be elicited by a similar task, but through media-tion of language operations. Semantic coding and information recall involve the left prefrontal cortex, primarily Broca's area (Brodmann's area 44) and neighbor-ing parts (Brodmann's areas 45 and 46). This lateralization is not affected by the type of the task (verbal vs. nonverbal) (Gazzaniga et al., 2002).

In their PET study, Krause et al. (1999) found that an important role in epi-sodic memory, regardless of modality (visual or auditory) or word characteristics (abstract or imageable), is played by *precuneus,* a part of the multimodal associa-tion area in the medial temporal lobe above its border with the occipital lobe.

Activity in the right prefrontal cortex is greater when the subjects are trying to retrieve knowledge related to episodic memory than when they try to access other types of memory (Eysenck & Keane, 2000). The results of clinical and animal studies were compared with the PET and fMRI studies on healthy subjects. Tasks that tapped into episodic memory have shown that at the encoding stage (i.e., dur-ing acquisition of new knowledge) the right hippocampus and the left prefrontal cortex are activated, whereas recall of stored information activates the right pre-frontal cortex. Several authors have found, using different tasks, that (neo)cortical areas are the most active, with task-dependent functional asymmetries: encoding activated the left hemisphere more than the right, and recall activated the right hemisphere more than the left. These asymmetries were affected by the nature of the task as well—language and pictorial tasks elicited opposite results (Bernard et al., 2002; Gazzaniga et al., 2002).

Episodic memory is better for emotionally charged stimuli than for neutral. Furthermore, the results of the study by Beauregard, Breault, and Bourgouin (2000) suggest that the emotional valence of information may affect neural net-works involved in the recall of memorized material (i.e., negative and positive events do not activate identical areas) as opposed to working memory that is not influenced by emotional content (Perlstein, Bradley, & Lang, 2000). Moreover, they found that men and women differed in the neural substrates responsible for memorizing pleasant and unpleasant stimuli, and that greater areas were acti-vated in men than in women, regardless of whether the stimuli were pleasant or unpleasant. In women, memory of unpleasant stimuli was located predominantly in the right hemisphere (Brodmann's areas 37 and 47), whereas in men it included Brodmann's area 37 in both hemispheres, Brodmann's area 18 in the left hemi-sphere, Brodmann's area 36 in the right hemisphere and the right insula. Recall of pleasant stimuli activated Brodmann's areas 21 and 37 in the right hemisphere and Brodmann's area 19 in the left hemisphere in women, whereas in men, under

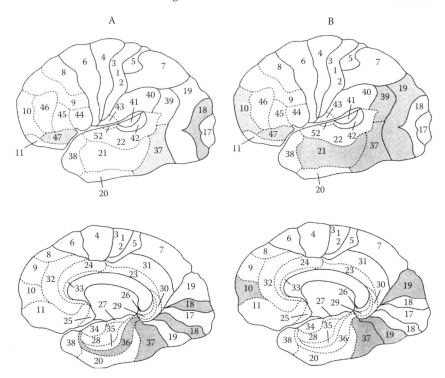

FIGURE 7.5. Brain areas responsible for processing emotional stimuli (A = unpleasant stimuli; B = pleasant stimuli).

identical conditions, Brodmann's areas 10 and 47 of the right hemisphere and bilateral Brodmann's areas 37 and 39 were activated (see Figure 7.5).

The motor cortex was found to be important for implicit procedural learning of movement patterns. Activation was found in the *putamen* (basal ganglia) and in the supplementary motor cortex. All these areas make a common network—the cortico-subcortical motor loop—that regulates voluntary movements. On the other hand, when the subjects were aware of learning movements (explicit learning, or memory), the increased activity was found in: the right premotor cortex, the dorsolateral premotor cortex typically associated with working memory, the anterior cingulate, the parts of the parietal lobe that control attention, and the lateral parts of the temporal lobe believed to contain records of explicit memory (Gazzaniga et al., 2002). Declarative memory is associated with temporal lobe activity, including the hippocampus, whereas procedural memory includes specific sensory and motor systems that are active during a particular task (Kandel, 2002). Amygdala are important for learning social behavior, which is related to their role in processing emotional information (see chap. 6, this volume). The perceptual representation system, which is also a subtype of implicit learning, does not activate the hippocampus.

In general, it is believed that normal memory functions rely heavily on the hippocampus. This is especially true for memorizing new data and associative memory. One of the best known and most frequently quoted cases in neuroscientific literature is H. M., who had undergone a bilateral resection of the medial temporal lobe, and subsequently could not acquire any new knowledge. He could not even learn how to get to his new home although it was on the same street, just a couple of houses away from the address at which he used to live before the operation. He also suffered from retrograde amnesia reaching back 3 years prior to surgery. Apart from such severe cases, there are many milder or transient forms of amnesia. There is a positive correlation between the amount of damaged hippocampal tissue and the severity of amnesia (Scoville & Milner, 2000). Namely, only bilateral removal of these parts caused such serious deficits, whereas removal of the medial part of the right temporal lobe (including the hippocampus and the hippocampal gyrus) had no negative effects on the patients' memory. Further studies have established that the medial part of the temporal lobe is not crucial for short-term memory. Due to the temporal characteristics of retrograde amnesia (which affects the period closest to the onset of amnesia and extends back into the past up to several years at the most), it is believed that damage to the hippocampus affects consolidation of new knowledge, but not access to the already consolidated information. It follows that the neocortex is the seat of long-term memory, whereas the hippocampus, albeit crucial for the process of consolidation, is not necessary for storage or recall of consolidated knowledge (Gazzaniga et al., 2002). On the other hand, Kali and Dayan (2002) proposed a model of neocortical functioning according to which both the hippocampus and the medial temporal lobe are essential for acquisition and recall of declarative data.

The most prominent difference between types of memory, with respect to their neural substrates, was found between short-term and long-term memory. These differences are not limited to different brain areas that are selectively activated during processes belonging to one or the other type—they are present at the cellular level as well. Short-term/working memory is associated with rapid and temporary changes at the cellular level, namely, the internal structure of nerve cells; with the strengthening of synaptic connections, and only if the number of synapses actually increases, knowledge will be consolidated (Drubach, 2000; Webster, 1995). Long-term memory requires gene activation, establishing new connections and, according to Kandel (2002), synthesis of new proteins. The difference between short-term and long-term memory is manifested by strong double dissociation: Individuals suffering from short-term memory disorders have intact long-term memory and vice versa.

Consequences of brain damage that are manifested as amnesia or some types of language disorders (e.g., aphasia) suggest that learning and memory have both the temporal and the categorial structure. It seems that all chunks of knowledge acquired within the same time period are stored together, and that information is organized and stored in categories (e.g., tools, fruits, animals). However, it seems less plausible that information is stored in separate compartments, as suggested by Drubach (2000). We are probably dealing with multiple representations of the same concept or information formed during acquisition, storage, and manipulation of knowledge.

In summary, it can be said that:

1. The hippocampus participates in formation and consolidation of new episodic and possibly semantic memories.
2. The prefrontal cortex is responsible for encoding and recall of information.
3. Episodic and semantic information is stored in the temporal lobe.
4. The association cortex is the seat of perceptual priming.

Other cortical and subcortical areas participate in acquisition of skills and habits as well. Although practically the entire brain is active during encoding, storing, and recall of information (i.e., in learning and memory) each type of memory relies on a specific structure. Kopp, Schroger, and Lipka (2006) found different networks to be engaged in different recall modes too. These differences are best manifested as selective deficits in different types of memory as consequences of damage or degenerative changes occurring in the brain, but they can also be revealed by neuroimaging methods in healthy subjects.

8 Speech and Language

Language seems to have appeared on the evolution scale when people became skillful in movement and categorizing actions, and in forming and categorizing mental representations of objects, events, and relationships. Ontogenetic development mimics these phylogenies, which can be seen in speech acquisition in children: Children's brains form and recall concepts and initiate actions before they utter their first word, form sentences, and start using the language in its entirety (Damasio & Damasio, 1992). In the course of speech and language development a veritable explosion of object naming and vocabulary expansion occurs concurrently with the development of categorizing abilities, namely, between the 14th and 18th months of life (Lieberman, 1991). However, maturation of language processes is not necessarily dependent on the maturation of conceptual processes, because children with deficits in their conceptual systems are capable of acquiring grammar. This would imply that the neuronal structure necessary for mastering syntactic procedures may develop independently (Damasio & Damasio, 1992). Still, the brain uses the same mechanisms for language representation that are used for representation of other entities. This means that information about the neural basis of representations of external events and objects and their relationships provide insight into the representation of language processes and their relations with other processes.

Although mechanisms of action are the same and the elements of the neuronal structure (neurons, synapses, neurotransmitters, etc.) are shared with other species, it is believed that language is a uniquely human ability with its biological substrate. This is particularly true of speech: whereas some form of language-like symbolic communication is possible in some primates (e.g., chimpanzees), speech communication is used only by humans (Lieberman, 1991). There is evidence that nonhuman primates use vocalizations for more than just signaling simple emotional and behavioral situations; some form of "conversation" exists among members of some primate species, which suggests a relatively elaborate cortical organization of their vocalizations, similar to humans' (Aitkin, 1990). However, cortical and subcortical pathways in humans and other primates differ, and human cortical areas devoted to speech do not correspond anatomically to those involved in primate vocalizations. Moreover, the consequences of injuries to relevant areas involved in human speech and primate vocalizations are not identical.

Humans have the innate biological ability to perceive and produce all possible phonetic features of the sounds of any language. The process of language acquisition includes activation of specific features characteristic of the native language, and loss of those that are not used. Literature dealing with innateness of brain mechanisms adapted to speech perception is abundant (for reviews see Chomsky, 2000; Flores d'Arcais, 1988; Hulit & Howard, 2002; Jenkins, 2000; Kess, 1992; Lieberman, 1991; Oberecker, Friedrich, & Friederici, 2005; Oller, 2000). Researchers agree that humans have inbuilt genetically transferable neural mechanisms that facilitate perception of sounds related to human speech. Although many animals have brain mechanisms tuned to species-specific vocalizations, a human set of detectors is much more sophisticated and efficient. As little as several hundred milliseconds are sufficient to perceive an entire syllable (Lieberman, 1991). There is analogy at the syntactic level as well: besides the innateness of the ability to produce linguistically organized elements, speakers of different languages have learned to attach specific importance to different syntactic features as a function of comprehension.

With respect to brain mechanisms, Lieberman (1991) divided evolution of language into two stages. At the first stage, gross motor control is lateralized. This is consistent with Kimura's (1975) association of movement and speech production. Evolution of brain mechanisms that enable fast encoding of human speech, syntax, and some cognitive aspects is characteristic of the second stage. Since the first stage is to some extent present in other animals, there had to be a reason for the second stage to develop only in humans. Lieberman believes that the need for quick and reliable communication resulted in the brain being equipped with a highly efficient information processor that enhances the human ability to use syntax and ensures application of previously acquired knowledge and rules or principles to new problems. This quick and reliable information was provided by quick and precise sound communication—in other words, the capacity for speech has made the human brain special. Lieberman places the first stage at the time of *Homo erectus* (more than 1 million years ago) who began making tools, which facilitated lateralization, just as the use of those tools did also. The need for vocal communication probably occurred in order to free the hands and to communicate across distances and in poor visibility conditions. Changes in brain organization that enabled this form of communication occurred at the cortical and subcortical level and *Homo sapiens* (who lived some 100,000 to 120,000 years ago) fossils reveal that the vocal tract similar to ours, which enabled speech, was already in place. It is somewhat more difficult to date the adaptation to syntax and abstract cognitive processes, but it may be assumed that the process paralleled that of speech development.

Chomsky (2000) believes that language developed by a combination of conceptual and computational abilities. We share conceptual ability with other primates and it enables us to perceive and form categories and symbols and to draw inferences. The computational ability enables us to build words, phrases, and utterances from (sub)lexical units, which are then poured (mapped) into sound and meaning.

Right-handedness and left-hemisphere lateralization are considered to be among the greatest evolutionary achievements. These two processes are related and are particularly important for studying neural control of speech. It is believed that this control shifts to higher levels with evolutionary development. Lower animal species are believed to have neural control of vocalizations exclusively in subcortical structures. In primates, this control is located in the cingulate gyrus, but only humans have voluntary control of vocalization in the cerebral cortex. This has been used as explanation of the fact that chimpanzees can master sign language (i.e., they are capable of adopting a system of understanding and manipulating symbols) but they cannot talk. It should be stressed, however, that chimpanzees on the one hand are capable of voluntary vocalizations (e.g., different vocalizations for different kinds of food, which are understood by other members) and their vocal tract anatomy, on the other hand, precludes human-like speech (Lieberman, 1991).

Asymmetry in vocal control in animals has been found in several species, particularly in songbirds. Although at first it had seemed that this asymmetry was not accompanied by asymmetries in use of extremities, it was found that preferences did exist, but that they were task dependent: Reaching for an object is more frequently done with the left hand whereas object manipulation and postural support is carried out by the right. These noticeable asymmetries are accompanied by appropriate specialization of the contralateral hemisphere: The right hemisphere became specialized for visuospatial relations, and the left for processing of data that are relevant for body posture. This left-hemisphere specialization transferred to other activities, including language (Hellige, 1990, 1993).

SPEECH AND LANGUAGE FUNCTIONS AND THEIR LOCATION IN THE BRAIN

New, more sophisticated and objective methods and tools for studying language functioning increasingly support those authors who have suggested that division of labor between the two hemispheres is not strictly determined, and that the asymmetries are more a matter of degree than of exclusive (in)activity. One of the examples that support this view is recovery of language functions after injury to brain regions traditionally referred to as language centers. In the 1980s it was believed that during functional reorganization (e.g., after injury) the hemisphere dominant for a particular function keeps its priority and that the areas neighboring the incapacitated (until then optimal) areas are recruited, with the transfer to the nondominant hemisphere occurring only if the damage covers a very large area. However, PET studies have revealed that after damage to the left posterior temporal lobe, that roughly corresponds to Wernicke's area for speech perception, homotopic areas of the right hemisphere gradually take over speech perception functions, resulting in eventual recovery from aphasia (Ivry & Robertson, 1999). Crosson et al. (2005) suggest that the dominant basal ganglia could play a role in spontaneous reorganization of language production functions to the right hemisphere. This does not imply going back to the notion of equipotentiality according to which both hemispheres are equally capable of performing any function. It is still obvious that the representations in the two hemispheres are different, but they are organized in such a way that information essential for the situation and task at hand are used optimally.

Although brain functions began to be more systematically described in the 19th century, descriptions of aphasic symptoms dating back to the 17th century made possible inferences about the left hemisphere being specialized for language (Whitaker, 1995). Around the end of the 1950s the relationship between the dominant hand and aphasia caused by unilateral damage was confirmed. It was found that the left hemisphere is dominant for speech in practically all right-handers and in a great majority of left-handers. Subsequent sodium amytal tests revealed that these ratios were indeed high (more than 90% for right-handers and about 70% for left-handers), and Kimura's dichotic listening tests (Kimura, 1961b) confirmed these results in healthy subjects.

Geschwind (as cited in Caplan, 1988) found that there are special anatomic characteristics of the brain regions involved in language functioning, based on the relationship between association areas of different sensory modalities in the inferior parietal lobe, around Sylvian fissure, that are considered to be crucial for object naming. The development of that particular cortical region with respect to myelination and cytoarchitecture that differ from surrounding tissue, also implies specialization of that area. As far as we know, that region subserves language functions, independent of the actual language, acquisition method, number of languages a person knows, literacy, or any environmental factor. This structure is genetically determined, but with individual variations (Varga-Khadem, Gadian, Copp, & Mishkin, 2005). In general, it seems that actual performance and early sensory registration are more narrowly localized than abstract aspects, which are represented in wider areas, with greater interindividual variation (Caplan, 1988; Weinberger, 2004). However, similar peculiarities in structure and transfer of learned material from one modality to another have been found in great apes as well (Dingwall, 1988).

Linguistic knowledge is widely represented in the adult brain (Bates, 1994). Although some areas may play a more important part in a particular language activity than others, knowledge itself is not strictly localized. Gazzaniga (1994) proposes that there should exist brain areas that are responsible for grammar, but that the evidence of lexicon localization would be much more difficult to find, because it reflects learned information, which makes it a part of the general memory and knowledge systems in the brain. The grammatical system is supposedly discrete, and therefore readily localizable, as opposed to the lexicon, that is distributed, and therefore resistant to complete damage.

Several brain areas are considered essential for speech production and perception. Apart from the primary areas that are in perception the first point of input (e.g., the primary auditory or visual cortex), and in production the final point of output from the cerebrum (the primary motor cortex), these are Broca's area, Wernicke's area, and the supplementary motor area (the premotor area).

Broca's area (Brodmann's areas 44 and 45) is located in the frontal lobe of the language-dominant (typically left) hemisphere. For a long time it was believed to be the center for speech production, containing programs for turning concepts and rules into words and utterances. Damage to it was expected to cause Broca's aphasia (more on different types of aphasia can be found later in this chapter).

Numerous studies, supported by different methods of registering cerebral activity (Gazzaniga, Ivry, & Mangun, 2002; Hellige, 1990, 1993; Kent & Tjaden, 1997; Pinel, 2005; Springer & Deutsch, 1997), have shown, however, that there is not necessarily a direct correlation between speech production and activation of this area. On the one hand, there were cases of Broca's area activation in tasks that did not require speech production, and on the other, some tasks that required actual speech (e.g., automatic listing) did not activate Broca's area. Disagreements among authors, even clearly contradictory results, may be explained by considerable methodological differences across studies, but also by the process of averaging results within large groups of subjects, which necessarily hides individual differences (on the advantages and drawbacks of group and case studies see chap. 4, this volume). Müller (2000) argues that Broca's area should be discussed within the working memory functions of the inferior frontal lobes, rather than exclusively as a seat of a particular language function. D'Esposito et al. (as cited in Kent & Tjaden, 1997) also claimed that the prefrontal cortex was involved in working memory. Similarly, Stowe (2000) believes that the left inferior frontal gyrus supports temporary storage of language material during linguistic tasks, rather than being directly involved in computations of syntactic representations. His neuroimaging study has revealed that this area is not activated by simple sentences, but rather by complex sentences and word-list maintenance. In any case, it may be concluded that Broca's area does not play such a unique role in speech production as was believed on the basis of clinical studies. MRI studies have shown that the neighboring cortical area, the left inferior frontal lobe, anterior to Broca's area (Brodmann's areas 47 to 10) is activated during word production. This activity occurs during semantic processing, but also during production of speech. It is absent during silent (subvocal) word production or when listening to words, as well as during nonspeech movements of the lips, tongue, or the lower jaw (McCarthy, Blamire, Rothman, Gruetter, & Shulman, 1993). Petrides et al. (as cited in Kent & Tjaden, 1997) conducted a PET study of subjects during verbal recall and found increased blood flow in the part of the frontal lobe corresponding to Brodmann's area 45. They concluded that this cortical area was important for recall of verbal information from long-term memory. In approximately the same area (Brodmann's areas 45–47) Demb et al. (as cited in Kent & Tjaden, 1997) found (by fMRI) increased activation during semantic encoding and associated this cortical area with recall of semantic information. Research into motor disorders such as dysarthria or apraxia of speech have revealed that the successful organization of the motor aspect of speech requires intact Broca's area, surrounding regions that extend along the inferior frontal lobe into the temporal lobe, including its first gyrus and the insula, and deep into the white matter. There are numerous cortical and subcortical connections important for human communication in the insula, and an intact insula seems to be essential for all aspects of speech and language behavior (Bennett & Netsell, 1999; Dronkers, 2004).

Wernicke's area (Brodmann's area 22) is located in the temporal lobe of the language-dominant hemisphere (typically left) and is referred to as the center for comprehension and perception of speech and language. According to traditional

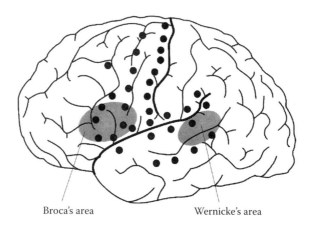

Broca's area   Wernicke's area

FIGURE 8.1.   The relationship between traditional speech production and perception areas; activation points during speech and language processing. The darker dots correspond to greater activity.

descriptions of speech and language processes, this (together with Brodmann's areas 42 and 37) is the store of sounds and phonological representations of words that are activated in order to recognize appropriate visual and auditory information such as speech and language. The most striking manifestations of injury to this area are failure to comprehend speech with preserved fluent but incomprehensible and/or nonsensical speech. A common name for these disorders is Wernicke's aphasia. There are interindividual variations in the size and location of Wernicke's center. Neuroimaging methods have revealed increased blood flow in the left parieto-temporal cortical region during passive listening to words. Interestingly, although it has been claimed that speech played backwards activates the same areas as meaningful speech, some authors found considerable differences in the activation of the left temporal lobe between conditions in which words were represented in their original form and those in which they were played backwards (Kent & Tjaden, 1997). No single cortical area for reading and listening to words has been found, so it is assumed that the representations of word meanings are not strictly localized, but rather dependent on the activation of semantic features and their relationships, which is more widely distributed over large cortical areas (Gazzaniga, Ivry, & Mangun, 2002; Howard et al., 1992).

Figure 8.1 illustrates the discrepancies between the location of the traditional speech production and perception areas (Broca's and Wernicke's, respectively) and the points that were found to be involved in speech and language production by intraoperative electrical cortical stimulation (Purves et al., 2001)—the darker the dots the greater activity was recorded.

The supplementary motor area or premotor area (Brodmann's area 6) is located immediately anterior to the motor cortex that separates it from the central sulcus. PET scans have revealed that this area is activated during various motor tasks, especially when the movements were internally motivated. Since speech production is in fact a set of such movements, activation of this area during speech is to be expected. Increased blood flow in the area was recorded during motor activities that, when performed in sequence and repeated, constitute a complex movement. This is true of actual movements as well as of the imagined ones, with little spatial differences in representation, and with some overlap of activated areas. Brain scans of patients with difficulties in speech have revealed areas of excessive activity in their left supplementary motor areas. Cerebral blood flow measurements of healthy subjects revealed increased blood flow in this area during verbal and nonverbal naming tasks. In the 1950s it was found that vocalizations can be elicited in humans by electrical cortical stimulation of the supplementary motor area (Kent & Tjaden, 1997). It is interesting to note that stimulation of speech motor centers results in simple vocalization if the person is silent, but if vocalization is already in progress, stimulation of the same point will result in slowing speech or in speech arrest.

Electrical stimulation of the areas in which face representations are located in the precentral gyrus and in the supplementary motor area (the superior and middle aspects of the precentral gyrus) may elicit vocalizations but not comprehensible words in the patient who was not speaking at the time. Other stimuli within and outside of the precentral motor area, as well as those in the vicinity of Broca's and Wernicke's area, inhibited ongoing speech. There were no remarkable differences in inhibitory effects, regardless of whether the current was applied to Wernicke's, Broca's, or the supplementary motor area. Intent to vocalize is associated with the activity in the supplementary motor area (the source of the motor commands directed toward Broca's area), whereas feedback, which involves the auditory cortex and the temporal lobe (Wernicke's area), controls and modifies signals that travel from motor centers to the muscles used in speech. These mechanisms are normally lateralized to one (typically left) hemisphere, but the motor center may shift to the opposite side after damage to the original area.

Language cannot be observed as a unitary function localized in one place. Damasio and Damasio (1992) claim that what is traditionally called visual image of objects or persons is actually a trace of neuronal activity that the contact with that object or person has elicited. Language function alike should be observed as a combination of activations of different levels and areas in the brain.

ANATOMIC ASYMMETRIES AND LATERALIZATION OF SPEECH AND LANGUAGE

The differences in the structure and appearance of the left and the right hemisphere have been described earlier (see chap. 1, this volume). The fact that these asymmetries have been found in fetal brains implies functional asymmetries, and it has been generally accepted that the left hemisphere is structurally specialized for language activities even before speech development. The total area of the left hemisphere region where Broca's area is located, the so-called frontal operculum, is greater than in the right hemisphere. This is generally true of the *planum temporale* as well. However, it must be kept in mind that people with more asymmetric brains are not necessarily more likely to have highly lateral-ized language functions: although the left hemisphere is dominant for speech in almost 95% of individuals, only 65% have a larger *planum temporale*. Anatomic asymmetries and developmental aspects of lateralization are discussed in more detail in chapter 6.

Although most authors stress that functional lateralization in the brain is an important prerequisite for optimal development of language abilities, Anneken et al. (2000) did not find a direct correlation between the degree of hemispheric lat-erality of language and language abilities in their functional transcranial Doppler ultrasonography study of healthy subjects during a word generation task. Earlier, Benson and Zaidel (ac cited in Kolb & Whishaw, 1996) concluded that the only language function that could be considered strictly left-hemisphere lateralized is syntax, which involves several elements: production, timing and correct sequence of movements necessary for speech, and understanding of grammatical rules. Other functions are to a greater extent right-hemisphere functions as well.

Evidence of lateralization and/or localization of language functions are typi-cally found in several areas: clinical cases, split-brain patients, and studies involv-ing healthy subjects.

SPLIT-BRAIN PATIENTS

This is a group of individuals with no interhemispheric connections, regardless of whether these connections had been severed or whether they had never developed.

There is great variability in the right-hemisphere language functions in this group of patients. In some of them speech comprehension is nearly normal, whereas in others it is very poor. Speech production has not improved even sev-eral years after surgery in some, whereas in others the expressive aspect of speech developed within a year. It would be logical to assume that this variability is a function of the extent of callosotomy, and dependent on whether other connec-tions between the hemispheres had been cut (e.g., anterior commissure), but the correlation has not been proven. Preoperative pathology seems to be the most important factor in the development of speech and language functions in the right hemisphere. Naturally, the question arises as to how the preoperatively language-dominant hemisphere responds to the new circumstances of speech and language development in the right, now rival, hemisphere. Research has shown that in most cases, behaviors generated by the right hemisphere, now itself capable of speech and language functions, are built into the awareness of the left hemisphere that is still in charge.

Around the end of the 19th century it was believed that the right hemisphere could produce automatic speech, exclamations and familiar phrases, but that its principal activity was restricted to lexical decoding and speech comprehension. It used to be taken for granted that, since the right hemisphere could not talk it was incapable of speech comprehension as well. Kohn (1980), among others, con-cluded that language abilities of the right hemisphere are restricted to the seman-tic level and connotative meaning, less noticeable at the syntactic or phonological level, with very limited expressive competence. It was shown later that the right hemisphere has a surprising ability to comprehend speech. Zaidel (1985) has found that the right hemisphere can understand common spoken or written words, as well as simple grammatical and syntactic principles. Latent language abilities of the right hemisphere will probably become most obvious in cases of early left-hemisphere injury, especially in women and right-handers, in nonphonological and nonarticulatory materials and situations (Bradshaw & Nettleton, 1983). Kolb and Whishaw (1996) concluded that the right hemisphere has good recognition capabilities, but that it could not initiate speech, because it does not have access to the left-hemisphere speech mechanisms. The idea that the left hemisphere is superior to the right in all important activities was modified by evidence that the right hemisphere is generally superior in tasks that involve spatial abilities.

The right hemisphere can understand verbs, produce verbal commands, or associate an appropriate noun with a given verb, as long as verbal response is not required. Its comprehension of written material is considerably poorer than when information is presented auditorily. However, it has great difficulty in processing words in noise. It seems to possess a considerable lexicon, but it is probably connotative, associative, and abstract as opposed to the precise, denotative, and phonological lexicon of the left hemisphere. Right-hemisphere function in language situations is primarily supportive with respect to the left hemisphere in the sense that it probably identifies input information by means of visual and auditory gestalts and manages extralinguistic context (Bradshaw & Nettleton, 1983).

The left-hemisphere approach to language functions is based on feature analysis, whereas the right-hemisphere strategy in pattern recognition is holistic. In general, each hemisphere has a wide range of cognitive competence that is sufficient to support different behaviors, including those that would under certain circumstances be better performed by the opposite hemisphere. Even in commissurotomized patients, connotative, affective, and semantically diffuse information may "spill over" into the other hemisphere (as opposed to specifically denotative information) by subcortical pathways. Otherwise, each hemisphere has independent perceptual, memory, and cognitive abilities (Zaidel, Zaidel, & Bogen, 2005). With respect to language functions, studies of commissurotomized patients have shown that the left hemisphere is not only necessary for language, but that it is sufficient. On the other hand, the right hemisphere loses its preoperative language functions.

Another interesting finding resulted from split-brain studies. It was found that phonetic coding was necessary for communication between the hemispheres. It is not clear, however, whether this transfer is based on the activity of the midbrain and the brainstem in general, or on the afferent information supplied by the speech muscles. It was also found that interhemispheric interactions occur at the level of semantics and attention. In other words, cognitive data activated in one hemisphere may affect some processes in the other. Subcortical structures seem to play a very important role in this information transfer. Semantic priming studies have shown that the effects of priming occur at the level of semantic representation, rather than at the perceptual or phonological level.

Zaidel found (as cited in Bradshaw & Nettleton, 1983) that the separated right hemisphere can write and it is aware of meaning, but in normal circumstances it is prevented by the left hemisphere from responding vocally. Auditory comprehension of the right hemisphere is poorer for low-frequency, abstract words, or for more complex or lengthy instructions, possibly due to its small short-term verbal capacity. It seems to lack rules for grapheme-to-phoneme mapping and reads words ideographically, as visual structures (gestalts). The isolated right hemisphere may concatenate letters and words and perform simple writing tasks (mostly printed letters) and can recognize many written words, not just concrete nouns, as it used to be believed. It can recognize and select objects on the basis of abstract descriptions or definitions of their use provided auditorily. It is anomic: it knows the characteristics and use of an object, but not its name. The most markedly left-lateralized is the expressive aspect of language, followed by writing, and comprehension the least.

According to the same author, the left hemisphere plays a leading role in semantic associations, although the right hemisphere has a surprisingly rich auditory lexicon. Interestingly though, the isolated left hemisphere also has difficulties in fast reading and spoken vocabulary. The linguistic "mental" age of the right hemisphere is not comparable with any stage of normal native language acquisition, contrary to previous claims that it corresponds to the initial stages of speech and language acquisition (Zaidel, Zaidel, & Bogen, 2005).

Individuals with disconnected hemispheres can read material presented to their left visual field, that is projected to their right hemisphere, and can make simple semantic decisions, but they are incapable of understanding grammatically complex sentences. Their right hemisphere can determine whether something is a word or a nonword and recognize some nouns (Gazzaniga, 2000). It has hardly any syntactic capabilities (this is, of course, true of people with left-hemisphere language, not of the minority in whom language is lateralized to the right hemisphere). On the other hand, Zaidel (1985) found that the right hemisphere is superior to the left in processing auditory linguistic tasks in these patients.

In summary, theoretically, it is possible that there are two lexicons—one in each hemisphere. However, such organization is very rare. Most frequently, the lexicon is represented in the left hemisphere, with a wide distribution in healthy subjects. The right hemisphere stores word information in an unorganized way. Syntax is generally represented in the left hemisphere. The right hemisphere's syntactic abilities are very limited—it can recognize whether a sentence is grammatical or not. Speech production is probably the segment of speech and language functioning that is most firmly rooted in the left hemisphere, although in some cases it may be controlled by the right hemisphere.

HEALTHY SUBJECTS

Obviously, for ethical reasons, the only acceptable studies are those using non-invasive techniques and behavioral methods, and the most reliable results are obtained by combining several of them.

Shankweiler and Studdert-Kennedy (1975) found a significant positive correlation between the degree of right-handedness and right-ear advantage. Similar to Kimura (1973b, 1975) they concluded that cerebral lateralization for speech perception and manual praxia should be interpreted as a matter of degree and as two components originating from the same source. Kolb and Whishaw (1996) reviewed studies in which bilateral organization of speech was not found in any right-handers, as opposed to nonright-handers in whom considerable speech disorders were found upon anesthetizing either side with sodium amytal. However, even this bilateral organization was not quite symmetrical: anesthetizing one hemisphere resulted in anomia, whereas anesthetizing the other caused sequencing problems (e.g., days of the week).

Mondor and Bryden (1992) found that right-hemisphere dominance may be elicited by directing attention to the left ear, but also that this is possible only in easier tasks. As soon as the auditory identification task becomes more difficult, the right ear (left hemisphere) becomes dominant, despite the instructions.

In the visual modality, the advantage of the left visual field (i.e., right hemisphere) was found for pairs of physically similar letters (e.g., E F) and for processing letters of an unusual or ornate alphabet. The right hemisphere can also take over the processing of simple verbal material if the dominant hemisphere is busy with some other primary task.

Holloway et al. (2000) studied language lateralization in two patients suffering from temporal lobe epilepsy, aged 15 and 16. In their left-handed patient, during silent generation of verbs to auditorily presented nouns, they found (by fMRI) increased activity in the right hemisphere, particularly in the areas that correspond to Broca's and Wernicke's, and in the premotor cortex. Somewhat lower activity was found in the left hemisphere, in Broca's area (inferior frontal gyrus) and in the cerebellum. An additional Wada test confirmed right-hemisphere dominance for language. The right-handed patient exhibited a mirror image: the greatest activation was recorded in the left hemisphere, in Broca's and Wernicke's areas and in the premotor cortex, whereas somewhat lower activity was recorded in the right hemisphere in the area homotopic to Broca's, and in the cerebellum. A Wada test confirmed left-hemisphere dominance for language functions. Malagoli et al. (2000) found bilateral activity (recorded by PET) during language production in a left-handed patient suffering from a glioma tumor in the left posterior frontal lobe. It is not quite clear whether bilateral activity is a consequence of the left hemisphere tumor or the fact that the patient was left-handed.

Nowicka and Szatkowska (2002) tested the differences between men and women in the degree of laterality of language functions, using the ERP technique. The task was based on memory for verbal stimuli. They presented their right-handed male and female subjects with nouns located at the center of the screen, to the left of the fixation point (i.e., to the left visual field—right hemisphere) and to the right of the fixation point (i.e., to the right visual field—left hemisphere). After presentation of the target word, a list of nouns was presented in a column centered on the screen, and the subjects were asked to identify the target noun. The gender differences were manifested in the following way: in men, direct stimulation of the right, or language-nondominant hemisphere (target nouns presented to the left visual field) did not facilitate memorization. Direct stimulation of the left, or language-dominant hemisphere (target nouns presented to the right visual field) elicited a pronounced response (recorded as evoked potential) associated with memorization, in both hemispheres. On the contrary, in women, direct stimulation of any hemisphere facilitated memorization in both hemispheres. The authors took this as support of the claims that language functions were more markedly lateralized in men than in women.

In the rest of this chapter, unless otherwise specified, cerebral representation of speech and language functions will be discussed on the basis of studies in right-handers, regardless of gender. Namely, despite numerous claims about significant differences in cerebral organization between men and women, within-sex variations are most frequently greater than those between sexes, and there are studies that explicitly refute sex differences in this context (see discussion in chap. 2, this volume). Right-hemisphere activity in language functions will be reviewed in parallel to that of the left hemisphere, in light of its (right hemisphere's) important contribution to optimal linguistic functioning. In view of the fact that different aspects of language are represented differently and that their cerebral organization is affected by many factors, the chapter is organized so as to address various aspects of neurolinguistic organization.

SPEECH PRODUCTION AND PERCEPTION

Speech Production

Cerebral blood flow measurements during various language activities provided precise data on the parts of the cerebral cortex that are active during listening, reading, and repetition of visually or auditorily presented words, or during verb association to given nouns. While subjects look at written words, the secondary visual cortex in the occipital lobe is activated. While listening to nouns, bilateral activity in the primary and secondary auditory cortex in both temporal lobes is noticeable. It has been found that there is no overlap between areas activated during listening to and viewing words, which means that word processing in these two modalities is independent. Repetition of nouns out loud activated regions along the right lateral sulcus, as well as areas along the central sulci of both hemispheres, specifically motor and sensory areas involving face representation, and the supplementary motor area. Associating verbs with nouns elicited activity in the left prefrontal cortex, immediately anterior to Broca's area and in the medial part of the cortex, just above the anterior part of corpus callosum. While subjects were repeating words, the stimulus seemed to travel directly from the secondary sensory areas to output areas of the central sulcus. When the task involved semantic processing (verb association) the signals appeared to take an alternate route from sensory areas, through the frontal lobe to motor areas of the central sulcus, without going through the primary visual cortex (Pinel, 2005). Gazzaniga (1994) talks about three types of conceptual deficits in patients suffering from temporal lobe damage: (a) anterior injury affects the most detailed type of identification of conceptual patterns (e.g., my dog); (b) injury to the more posterior part of the inferior temporal lobe results in the loss of subcategories (e.g., Maltese, Dalmatian); (c) injury to the even more posterior regions restricts the identification to a superordinate category (e.g., animal), with no ability to distinguish among various mammals. Interestingly, automatic repetition (e.g., listing days of the week) several times in a row does not increase activity in Broca's area, contrary to expectations based on sodium amytal tests (Kolb & Whishaw, 1996). Penfield and Roberts (as cited in Kolb & Whishaw, 1996) claimed that the thalamus coordinated the activity of cortical speech areas.

According to Raichle (1994), the human brain generates responses in two ways: one is nonautomatic, which requires attention, and the other is automatic and operates without particular effort on the part of the speaker. The nonautomatic mechanism is located primarily in the language-dominant (typically left) cerebral hemisphere and partly in the right cerebellar hemisphere, whereas the automatic mechanism is bilaterally represented. Although Raichle got these results by means of PET on healthy subjects, he claims that they can be related to specific aphasic difficulties. Flores d'Arcais (1988) concluded that the use of the results of the language perception process is selective, or controlled, rather than automatic. In light of Raichle's observations, only automatic processing would be more or less bilateral, and use of the results would be controlled by the dominant hemisphere.

Regional cerebral blood flow measurements yielded controversial results. Ryding et al. (as cited in Kent & Tjaden, 1997) found right-hemisphere dominance for automatic speech (listing days of the week) and symmetrical activation when the subjects were humming nursery rhymes. According to other authors, the same method revealed no interhemispheric differences (Kent & Tjaden, 1997).

Earlier studies involving automatic speech, such as listing days of the week, months of the year, or phoneme repetition, have revealed that this particular type of language function does not activate cortical language regions as anticipated, and that different automatic speech-motor tasks do not yield identical results with respect to the degree of cortical activation. Bookheimer, Zeffiro, Blaxton, Gaillard, and Theodore (2000) studied several types of automatic speech varying in complexity using PET. In eight healthy subjects they measured differences in cerebral blood flow, with special emphasis on Broca's and Wernicke's areas, during several automatic speech-motor tasks: tongue movements, repetition of phoneme series, listing months of the year, and reciting prose. All tasks resulted in increased activation in the areas responsible for articulatory and auditory processing, but only tasks involving words (as opposed to phoneme repetition) revealed a left-lateralized increase in blood flow in the section of the temporal lobe that corresponds to Wernicke's area (posterior superior part); only reciting prose increased activity in the part of the left hemisphere that corresponds to Broca's center. This study has shown that the type of automatic tasks used to study brain activity is an important factor, because, obviously, more complex tasks will elicit a more noticeable left lateralization, similarly to nonautomatic speech and language tasks.

Abrahams et al. (2000) used fMRI to measure activation of different brain regions while their healthy subjects were generating words starting with a given letter and naming visually presented objects. A word-generation task elicited increased activation mostly in the left hemisphere, with some bilateral activity. The most activated were the supplementary motor area (Brodmann's area 6), anterior cingulate (Brodmann's areas 32 and 24), inferior frontal gyrus (Brodmann's areas 44 and 45), dorsolateral prefrontal cortex (Brodmann's areas 9 and 46), inferior parietal lobe (Brodmann's area 40), insula and anterior part of the thalamus. At the same time, the naming task elicited the highest degree of activity in Brodmann's areas 44, 45 and 24, that correspond to the inferior frontal gyrus, and the anterior cingulate in the left hemisphere. Activation of the greater area during a word-generation task, especially in the anterior frontal regions, corresponds to greater executive requirements of this type of task.

Speech and language disorders may disrupt different stages of the process. Patients suffering from anomia are usually capable of describing the pictured object quite well, but they cannot produce the appropriate word. The difficulties are not articulatory, but at the lexeme level. Semantic paraphasias, common in Wernicke's aphasia patients, reflect the inappropriate selection of terms, lemmas, or lexemes. Phonemic paraphasias, that are also present in Wernicke's aphasia patients, reflect errors at the phonological level, as a consequence of phoneme/sound substitutions. Broca's aphasia is frequently accompanied with dysarthria that affects articulators, and these patients speak with a lot of effort because they cannot control their articulator muscles.

Neuroimaging techniques applied during picture naming and word generation tasks revealed activity in the left basal temporal regions and in the left frontal operculum (Broca's area). Cortical stimulation of the basal temporal regions caused a transient inability to generate words. It is believed that the frontal operculum activation is associated with phonological encoding during speech production. The process of articulation activates posterior parts of Broca's area (Brodmann's area 44), but also the bilateral motor cortex, supplementary motor area (Brodmann's area 6), and the insula. Damage to the insula results in apraxia of speech in patients suffering from Broca's aphasia.

Lurito et al. (2000) used fMRI to measure brain activity in their healthy subjects while they were naming subvocally visually presented objects. They recorded activity in the traditional language areas (Wernicke's—left posterior superior temporal gyrus; and Broca's—left inferior frontal gyrus), left posterior fusiform gyrus (one of the gyri at the border between the occipital and temporal lobes, corresponding to Brodmann's area 37), and several areas in the left middle temporal gyrus. In addition, they also registered activity in the premotor cortex and in the superior cerebellum in both hemispheres, as well as in the supplementary motor area near the border between the hemispheres. Their results are in agreement with data reported earlier about predominant left-hemisphere activation in language tasks, obtained by PET (review in Murtha, as cited in Lurito et al., 2000). Interestingly, they reported no activity in the primary or secondary visual cortex, despite the fact that the stimuli were presented visually.

Kent and Tjaden (1997) summarized the neural substrates of speech production by listing the primary neural structures responsible for particular functions. Intent is located in the fronto-limbic formations of the brain; linguistic-symbolic processing in the cortico-cortical connections; motor speech programming or planning in Wernicke's area, Broca's area, premotor cortex, supplementary motor area, inferior parietal lobule, inferior dorsolateral cortex, cerebellum, and basal nuclei; coordination in the basal nuclei, the cerebellum and in the motor cortex; whereas execution is primarily supported by the pyramidal and extrapyramidal motor pathways. Note that the same structure may be involved in more than one process. For example, the cerebellum may be active during motor programming and motor coordination.

Disorders of intention will result in mutism and problems with linguistic–symbolic processing; motor speech programming or planning will be manifested as aphasia and/or apraxia of speech. The consequence of deficits in coordination and execution will be dysarthria (speech and language disorders are discussed in more detail at the end of this chapter).

Smaller variability in activation was found in the frontal regions that are traditionally regarded as speech production areas (i.e., involved in motor aspects of language) more so than in temporal and parieto-temporal regions that have traditionally been associated with more abstract aspects of language functioning (word access, lexico-semantic activation, etc.). In their seven patients (seven epileptics and two with brain tumor) Corina et al. (2000), using the cortical stimulation method, clearly defined Brodmann's areas 44 and 45 (frontal operculum) and Brodmann's area 6 (supplementary motor area) as language areas, whereas stimulation of temporal (Brodmann's area 22) and temporo-parietal regions (Brodmann's areas 39 and 40) caused naming problems less reliably. Parallel recording of activity by fMRI confirmed these results, but also revealed somewhat wider activity than was found by cortical stimulation. Carpentier et al. (2000b) emphasize that cortical stimulation is a more reliable method for defining language production than language perception areas. They claim that fMRI is the method of choice for determining the latter.

Various research methods have shown that language perception tasks (e.g., listening to stories or tasks that elicit language production—different types of word generation or automatic production, such as counting, listing days of the week or months) typically elicit marked left lateralization (Pujol, 1999; Tzorio, 1998; Wildgruber, 1996—all cited in Staudt et al., 2000).

Ramsey, Sommer, and Kahn (2000) applied several different language tasks to their subjects (verb generation, antonym generation, deciding on the category of the presented word) and found, by fMRI, marked left lateralization of language functions. They stress the importance of combining different tasks, because they believe it is more probable that the areas involved in a number of different but related tasks are in fact more crucial for language functioning than those that are active only in some of the tasks.

SPEECH PERCEPTION

Bentin, Mouchetant-Rastaing, Giard, Echallier, and Pernier (1999) measured evoked potentials during different visually presented stimuli, and their tests revealed the following:

1. Words, nonwords, series of consonants, series of alphanumeric symbols, and series of patterns elicited a sharp negativity 170 ms after stimulus onset, in temporo-occipital points, with double dissociation with respect to the type of stimuli. Orthographic stimuli elicited higher activity in the left hemisphere than in the right, whereas nonorthographic stimuli elicited higher activity in the right hemisphere than in the left.
2. In the phonetic–phonological task (rhyming status), the greatest activity was found 320 ms after stimulus onset, and this negativity was elicited by pronounceable stimuli, and not by the unpronounceable ones, regardless of their rhyming status; bilateral activity was recorded in the middle temporal lobe, but it was significantly higher in the left than in the right hemisphere.
3. The phonological–lexical task (detection of words among a series of consonants and nonwords, and detection of nonwords among meaningful words) elicited a 350 ms negativity when the stimuli were allowed by the phonological system, but not when the stimuli were phonologically "illegal." The distribution resembled that found at the earlier peak, corresponding to the phonetic–phonological task, but it was a little wider and involved parieto-temporal areas that had not been activated by the rhyming task.
4. The semantic task (differentiating abstract words from concrete words, nonwords and a series of consonants) elicited a 450 ms negativity, which was associated with the distinction of phonologically legal from the phonologically illegal words, but also with the distinction of meaningful from the meaningless (but phonologically acceptable) words (i.e., nonwords). In addition to the regions activated in the lexical task, this task also activated fronto-central points.

The authors concluded that their results supported the hypotheses about the cascade model of processing, which involves different, but mutually related neural modules, each of which is responsible for a different level of processing word information.

It has already been shown that processing auditorily presented sentences activates perisylvian cortex in both hemispheres. Meyer, Alter, Friederici, and von Cramon (2000) used fMRI to study the differences in activation of various brain areas while the subjects listened to normal German sentences, syntactically correct nonsensical sentences, and incomprehensible sentences obtained by filtering normal speech so that only intonation and intensity had been kept. They found bilateral supratemporal cortex activation during listening to normal sentences. Contrary to that, both conditions of listening to incomprehensible sentences activated the entire perisylvian cortex in both hemispheres, with the sentences with preserved prosody eliciting marked lateralization to the right hemisphere and decreased activity in the supratemporal cortex. The authors attributed the increased activation in the fronto-opercular region (restricted to this particular condition) to the attempts at scanning the incomprehensible speech-like stimulus for language information.

Staudt et al. (2000) used fMRI to study language functions in four persons with congenital right hemiparesis without cognitive deficits. Three patients had injury on the left, deep within the white matter (periventricularly), and one had damage to the left insula and putamen. Even in individuals with small damage deep within the white matter, functional reorganization of language areas in the brain was noticed, especially with respect to speech production. Although speech perception (which they tested by recording activity during listening to a story) remained lateralized to the left hemisphere, speech production (subvocal generation of a series of words so that each subsequent word began with the last sound of the preceding word, and automatic speech—listing months of the year) shifted to the right hemisphere. Three patients with periventricular damage had completely right-lateralized activation of the primary motor cortex, with almost no activity in Broca's area in the left hemisphere. The patient with damage to the insula and the putamen exhibited bilateral activation of the inferior frontal lobes during word generation, but right-lateralized activation of the motor cortex during automatic speech. Two patients exhibited activation of the left cerebellar hemisphere, contrary to typical activation during language functions. The cerebellum has doubly crossed pathways to the periphery, so its ipsilateral connections are stronger than the contralateral ones (which is the case with the cerebrum—for more details, see chap. 1, this volume).

During recovery from left-hemisphere injury, speech perception (e.g., comprehension of words and sentences) returns to the original condition more rapidly than speech production (e.g., naming or word generation; Boatman et al., 1999). This also supports the claims that perceptual language functions are more widely represented in the brain than expressive, that is, speech production. With the help of fTCD, Buchinger et al. (2000) found in their healthy subjects that receptive functions are indeed more bilaterally represented than those for production, regardless of the hemispheric dominance for language. On preliminary tests, 11 of their subjects exhibited left-lateralized language and 6 of them had language lateralized to the right hemisphere.

Jäncke and Shah (2000) used fMRI to record brain activity during a task that involved detection of stop + vowel /a/ combinations. They found a high correlation between activation of the left superior temporal gyrus and the inferior frontal gyrus (regions that correspond to the traditional speech centers), and that the degree of activation was directly correlated with the accuracy of target syllables detection. On the basis of those results, they concluded that these areas constitute a neural network that is at its most efficient when a number of neurons are activated simultaneously. Similarly, in different language tasks involving same-type syllables presented visually and auditorily (repetition, detection of the target syllable in a series, subvocal repetition, paying attention to the stimulus without overt response) Specht et al. (2000b) found (by fMRI) activation of the inferior frontal gyrus in both hemispheres, regardless of modality (visual or auditory) or type of response (vocal or subvocal). This bilateral activation of premotor areas is probably associated with activation of motor programs, on the one hand (which supports motor theory of speech perception), and with the phonological loop of the working memory, on the other.

Crozier et al. (2000) found (using fMRI) activation of language areas during processing of sequence at the sentence and letter levels, with additional activation of Brodmann's areas 6 and 8 in both hemispheres, and of the left supplementary motor area (Brodmann's area 6) and left angular gyrus during processing letters. They concluded that these areas probably played a special role in the analysis of relationships among elements in a sequence.

Bottini et al. (as cited in Kent & Tjaden, 1997) studied (by PET) comprehension of metaphoric and literal meaning and found bilateral activation during the process of metaphor comprehension, but not during attempts to comprehend literal sentences or in the lexical decision process. The same technique revealed bilateral activation during comprehending sign language and oral language in the hearing impaired. Bilateral activation did not necessarily entail equal activity in homotopic parts of the two hemispheres. For example, Demonet et al. (as cited in Kent & Tjaden, 1997) found different activation in their right-handed subjects during semantic and phonological processing. The task in which the stimuli were words (semantic) activated both hemispheres, with the activity in the right hemisphere restricted to the angular gyrus, whereas phoneme processing activated the left hemisphere. Karbe et al. (as cited in Kent & Tjaden, 1997) also found bilateral, but uneven, activation during repetition of isolated words. The entire *planum temporale* of both hemispheres was active during the task, but Brodmann's area 22 (which roughly corresponds to Wernicke's center for speech perception) was activated more in the left hemisphere than in the right.

Nakai et al. (2000) showed by fMRI that discrimination of stories, when presented simultaneously by two speakers (phonological task), requires only phonological processing in Wernicke's area (Brodmann's area 22). Contrary to that, discrimination between the stories presented by the same speaker (semantic task), involves, in addition to Brodmann's area 22, additional processing in the frontal association cortex: bilaterally in Brodmann's areas 6 (premotor area), 44 and 45 (posterior part of the inferior frontal lobe), and in Brodmann's area 8 (prefrontal cortex) of the right hemisphere, as well as in the cingulate gyrus and anterior to the supplementary motor area (Brodmann's areas 32 and 24). They concluded that working memory, selective attention, syntactic and semantic processing, and prosody are organized as a universal system for auditory discrimination.

Brockway (2000) conducted several tests involving processing of different language material on 36 healthy subjects and 12 patients diagnosed with tumor or epileptic focus in the left temporal lobe during which he recorded (by fMRI) brain activity in eight regions chosen as relevant on the basis of preliminary measurements (the so-called regions of interest). In the majority of healthy subjects (89%) and patients (92%), significantly greater activation was found in the left than in the right hemisphere at the junction of the temporal, parietal, and occipital lobes during the activity of making conclusions about a story on the basis of questions. When generating nouns starting with a given sound, 64% of the healthy subjects exhibited greater activation in the left than in the right superior temporal gyrus. Subsequent application of the Wada test to the patients and intraoperative cortical stimulation confirmed the fMRI results.

Parts of the lateral temporal lobe, particularly the superior temporal gyrus and the transverse temporal gyrus are activated during subvocal lipreading in hearing subjects. These regions are considered to be responsible for primary (Brodmann's area 41), secondary (Brodmann's area 42), and higher levels (Brodmann's area 22) of speech processing (MacSweeney et al., 2000).

Klopp, Halgren, Marinkovic, and Nenov (1999) found (by ERP technique) clear anatomic, temporal, and cognitive specificities in the fusiform gyrus during face recognition, as opposed to word recognition.

Vocal perception in primates has many features in common with speech perception in humans. One of them is the left-hemisphere superiority in perception of species-specific vocalizations, use of temporal features in identification of different calls, and their use for surrounding objects and events. The neural basis of these similarities seems to be in the primate auditory and prefrontal cortex (Ghanzanfar & Hauser, 1999).

PHONETICS AND PHONOLOGY

Although it is difficult to separate phonemic level from other levels of speech and language processing, it seems that the area activated the most during phonological processing is the middle temporal gyrus—typically, but not always in the left hemisphere (Gazzaniga, Ivry, & Magnun, 2002).

Paulesu et al. (as cited in Kent & Tjaden, 1997) studied the verbal component of the working/short-term memory (the articulatory loop) by recording brain activity during memorizing letters and during assessment of their rhyming status. By comparing activation patterns associated with these two tasks they determined the primary location of the phonological store. During phonological processing they found bilateral activation in Brodmann's areas 44, 33, 42 and 40, as well as in both insulas. They therefore concluded that these were the neurofunctional centers of the articulatory loop. They designated Brodmann's area 40 as the primary location of the phonological store, because there they recorded activity during short-term memory tasks (which, according to them, involves the phonological store and subvocal repetition), but not during assessment of the rhyming status (which involves only subvocal repetition). Activation was recorded in the supplementary motor cortex as well, in the cerebellum and in the sensorimotor cortex (Brodmann's areas 1, 2, 3 and 4) despite the fact that there was no loud speech involved during the test. The authors interpreted their results as automatic switching on of these areas, because they are a part of the general neural network of planning and execution of language functions.

Frackowiak (1994) recorded (by fMRI) activation of the left inferior frontal and superior temporal lobes during phonological processing. The left inferior temporal lobe, at the junction with the parietal and occipital lobes, was identified by Turner and Frackowiak (1995) as the phonological store by means of PET. It remains to be seen whether the size of this area changes as a function of experience, for example, by learning new languages, just as the area of the active motor cortex changes as a result of practicing a motor task.

For years it was thought that the anatomic seat of the phonological store is in the supramarginal and the angular gyri of the speech-dominant hemisphere. This hypothesis was supported by many neuroimaging studies. However, upon detailed analysis of the published experimental results, Becker, MacAndrew, and Fiez (1999) discovered two possible locations of the phonological store in the parietal lobe. Neither of these stores had the kind of functional organization that would be consistent with the working-memory model of Baddeley and Hitch (as cited in Baddeley, 2000), which among other things assumes a subsystem whose function is maintaining verbal information during processing, the so-called verbal slave system.

In the study in which they measured evoked potentials during phonological processing (assessing rhyming status) and lexical tasks (word recognition and semantic categorization) in healthy subjects, Anglilli, Dobel, Rockstroh, Stegagno, and Ebert (2000) found greater activation in the left than in the right frontal lobe, with the smaller degree of laterality during word recognition and an even smaller one in the semantic categorization task.

Gutbrod et al. (2000) found (by fMRI) that phonological processing (deciding whether a pair of visually presented words rhymes or not) elicits the greatest amount of activation in the left inferior frontal gyrus.

Celsis et al. (1999) found higher activity (measured by ERP) when the same speech stimulus (fricative /f/) had to be detected in the nonspeech environment than was the case in speech. The negative peak had approximately equal latency (between 250 and 280 ms) but its amplitude was higher and particularly prominent in the left temporo-parietal region. Based on that, the authors conclude that this area is involved in the autonomous, modular process of speech perception, as opposed to other sounds. In other words, Celsis and colleagues believe these findings support the existence of a special speech mode of processing.

Using MEG, Gootjes, Raiji, Salmelin, and Hari (1999) found that in the left hemisphere vowels elicited a significantly higher activity (37 to 79%) than tones, whereas in the right hemisphere there were no differences with respect to the type of stimuli.

Lowe et al. (as cited in Scheef, Kuhl, Neugebauer, Schoeb, & Schild, 2000) reported that Wernicke's center processes speech signals selectively, namely, that the "real" speech signal is not processed in the same location as backward speech. Contrary to that, Scheef et al. (2000) found that normal speech, as well as backward speech, activates auditory association areas of the central part of the superior and middle temporal gyrus, where the system of phonological recognition is probably located. They claim that speech reproduced backward is recognized as speech of an unfamiliar language.

ERP studies have shown that negative peaks N170, N200, and N320 reflect orthographic and phonological processing (Bentin, as cited in Simon, Bernard,

Lalonde, & Rebai, 2002), with their amplitude and latencies reflecting differ-ences between words and nonwords. This is in agreement with response-time measurements. In summary: (a) response times to words are shorter than to nonwords, regardless of their frequency of occurrence; and (b) practice short-ens response time. Longer response times to longer nonwords and longer less frequent words had their equivalent in the amplitude and latency of the N320 peak, which corroborates the hypothesis that word frequency is the property processed at the lexical and phonological level, and that word length is the result of the phonological circuit that correlates with the N320 peak (Simon et al., 2002). Martin, Kaine, and Kirby (2006) found in their ERP study that nonwords elicited greater N200 and P300 amplitudes regardless of reading proficiency, but that larger amplitude P200s were elicited by poor readers when process-ing nonwords. Their data provide evidence for separable lexical and sublexical phonological decoding procedures and support the notion of a core phonological deficit in poor readers.

Jaramillo, Alku, and Paavilainen (1999) used the ERP method to compare processing of changes in the duration of speech and nonspeech sounds in healthy subjects. They found that these changes were processed differently in vowels than in tones, and that there were no interhemispheric differences. In tones, occur-rence of a tone longer than the referent tone elicited greater mismatch negativity (MMN) than occurrence of a tone shorter than the referent. In vowels the reaction was exactly the opposite: vowels shorter than the referent vowel elicited greater negativity than the ones that lasted longer than the referent vowel.

Boulanouar et al. (2000) found (by fMRI) that listening to tones increases activity in the left superior temporal gyrus and that detection of phonological changes activates the left supramarginal gyrus. During listening to syllables there was bilateral activation of the superior temporal gyrus (as opposed to dyslexics, in whom the activation was found in the middle temporal gyrus).

Native speakers of Thai (a tone language that utilizes pitch as phonologi-cal feature) exhibited right-ear advantage in tests involving word discrimination based on tone. When the same stimuli were presented outside of speech context, the right-ear advantage was lost (Bradshaw & Nettleton, 1983). Hsieh, Gandour, Wong, and Hutchins (2000) found using the PET technique in the tasks involving discrimination of vowels, consonants, and tones in Chinese, increased activation in the left premotor cortex for all stimuli in native speakers of Chinese. In native speakers of English, left-lateralized activity was recorded for vowels and conso-nants, and right-lateralized activity for tones. Mildner (2004) compared response times, consistency, and categorization in labeling short- and long-falling accents in Croatian and found no reliable ear advantage, as opposed to Moen (1993) who found right-ear advantage for Norwegian phonological tone, but in agreement with von Koss Torkildsen (2002). It is possible that Croatian subjects' responses reflect the nonlateralized activity of subcortical regions (Baum & Pell, 1999) or a simultaneous activity of both hemispheres relying on different cues: left hemi-sphere on segmental information, right hemisphere on pitch variation, as sug-gested earlier by Toepel and Alter (2002).

Shtyrov, Kujala, Palva, Ilmoniemi, and Naatanen (2000a, 2000b) compared cortical magnetic fields activated by stop + vowel syllables and corresponding nonspeech sounds, and found no asymmetry for any type of stimuli.

Mathiak, Hertrich, Lutzenberger, and Ackermann (2000) found right-ear advantage (left-hemisphere dominance) during recognition of CV syllables, which they interpreted as left-hemisphere superiority in coding formant transitions. The asymmetry was confirmed by MEG recordings of brain activity during identical tasks. However, asymmetry was found only when the subjects' attention was directed to the task. If they were distracted by visual stimuli during the task, activation was bilateral.

By the fMRI method Burton, Small, and Blumstein (2000) examined the relation between the segmentation of speech stimuli within a speech discrimination task (same–different) and activation of anterior (lateral-frontal) brain areas. The activity was found in the frontal regions only when the task required segmentation (e.g., distinguishing the first consonant in CVC words that differ in other sounds as well), but not when the test words differed with respect to voicing of the first sound. Contrary to the control condition of distinguishing tones, speech stimuli activated the superior part of the temporal lobe, which suggests a speech processing mode. The authors concluded that the phonological processing per se does not necessarily activate frontal regions; that part of the brain was activated by the segmentation processes in speech perception. Namely, during segmentation, the results of phonological processing are temporarily stored in working memory until such time as the final decision about the arriving verbal data can be made.

In addition to determining that the right ear (i.e., left hemisphere) is significantly dominant for consonant perception and also dominant (but statistically insignificant) for vowel perception, Blumstein, Goodglass, and Tartter (1975) showed by retesting subjects that ear advantage for vowels is very weak and unstable at repeated testing. Ear advantage in vowel perception may be obtained if their perception is made more difficult by shortening them, presenting them in noise or by masking the speaker's pitch (Bradshaw & Nettleton, 1983). In difficult listening conditions (filtered words as stimuli to one ear with concurrent white noise presented to the untested ear) Dudaš (1989) found right-ear advantage for all words, with more expressed asymmetry for words that consisted mainly of consonants. Absence of laterality (i.e., ear advantage, which is frequently reported for vowels in dichotic listening experiments) may be explained by the actual absence of lateralization of the perception process, or by the nature of the stimulus, or its presentation, which are not sensitive enough to reveal laterality. The size of the laterality effect may depend on the degree to which the information conveyed by the signal presented to the left ear is degraded on its way to the left hemisphere (across cerebral commissures; Porter & Berlin, 1975). In terms of different types of sounds, research has revealed right-ear advantage for consonants, mostly stops, and smaller or no ear advantage for vowels. As mentioned previously, even if ear advantage for vowel perception is found at some point, it is usually unreliable and unstable, and may even be reversed (manifested as left-ear advantage). Bradshaw and Nettleton (1983) explain this difference between the two extremes in sound categories by the fact that stops are typically short and their identification requires a great deal of restructuring and phonetic processing. This probably involves a special phonetic processor located in the left hemisphere. Right-ear advantage was obtained more reliably when the vowels were presented in noise or shortened. Synthesized vowels exhibit right-ear advantage when the subject is uncertain as to the size of the vocal tract, and the left hemisphere is probably expected to carry out the process of normalization necessary for correct speech perception, regardless of the speaker's age or gender. Right-ear advantage was found for vowels in the absence of contextual information. It seems that ear advantage in vowel perception is affected by the complexity of the required discrimination. Vowels typically convey little information to the listeners, as opposed to the highly coded stops that are acoustically very complex. Besides, vowel duration is usually longer and therefore easier to discriminate than consonants. In other words, consonants are more apt to be distorted and lost than vowels if they are presented to the "wrong" (i.e., nondominant) hemisphere. As mentioned above, if presented in unfavorable listening conditions, but also if the subject anticipates speech stimuli, the vowels will elicit right-ear advantage. If the same material is presented outside the language context, when the subjects expect nonspeech signals, left-ear advantage will emerge.

Molfese (1980) claims that his study was the first to report the results of recording cerebral neuroelectric responses during phoneme processing. His results suggest that the phoneme (sound) is processed as an isolated and independent unit in the cortex. He found that several cerebral regions take part in vowel discrimination, regardless of the surrounding context: although transition frequencies changed depending on CV combinations, two components of the electric response were associated with phoneme classes, not acoustic parameters. Molfese concludes that at some level, phoneme is the basic perceptual language unit. Pulvermüller (1992) also proposes cell assemblies in the primary auditory cortex that might correspond to phoneme distinctive features, which are supposedly functionally associated in the early stages of speech acquisition, in accordance with syllabification rules of the particular language (compare also Kean, 1995). Such views are consistent with the motor theory of speech perception (Liberman et al., 1967).

In synthesized fricatives, right-ear advantage emerges only when formant transitions (which require complex analysis and decoding) are included in the signal, not when other cues that are ordinarily sufficient for their perception (e.g., noise at the point of articulator constriction) are present (Bradshaw & Nettleton, 1983; Kolb & Whishaw, 1996).

Liquids and semivowels elicit smaller right-ear advantage than "real" consonants, but still greater than vowels (Ahonniska, Cantell, Tolvanen, & Lyytinen, 1993). It seems that in speech, the left hemisphere is responsible for processing rapid acoustic changes.

Ackermann, Lutzenberger, and Hertrich (1999) used MEG to examine hemispheric lateralization of neural coding of temporal characteristics of speech, particularly voice onset time (VOT). They found that the ordinary, expected stimuli elicited bilateral, symmetric distribution and that activation time was significantly affected by VOT. Unusual VOT elicited significantly earlier activation in the left hemisphere than in the right. They also concluded that processing speed was an important factor of hemispheric specialization for language. On the basis of the brain's electrical activity recorded during speech perception Molfese (1978) found that phoneme identification involves a series of complex cortical events. He came to several important conclusions: (a) the two hemispheres respond to different VOT values in different ways; (b) both hemispheres are active in information processing during a task; (c) several different processes go on in the same hemisphere; and (d) distinction between voiced and voiceless consonants is a right-hemisphere process.

Some authors have shown that voiced stops elicit larger right-ear dominance than their voiceless counterparts, and that the right ear is better for gravis than acute stops (Mildner, 1993; Studdert-Kennedy & Shankweiler, 1970). Molfese (1978, 1980) and Cohen and Segalowitz (1990) reported that the right hemisphere was dominant for distinguishing consonants along the voicing feature, whereas the left was dominant for distinguishing them on the basis of place of articulation. Cohen, Gelinas, Lassonde, and Geoggroy (1991) demonstrated that it is more difficult to distinguish the stops on the basis of their place of articulation than on the basis of their voicing feature, especially if the signal was presented to the left ear (right hemisphere) first. Based on her observations that right-hemisphere patients had intact phonemic processing, Myers (1999) concluded that the seat of phonological processes is in the left hemisphere. However, right-hemisphere damage does present problems in sound recognition (Gazzaniga et al., 2002). Studies of clinical cases have shown that the left hemisphere is superior in morpho-phonemic processing, but that the right one is better at the logographic level (extraphonological reading and comprehension). Furthermore, left-hemisphere patients cannot distinguish sounds based on their place of articulation (e.g., b–d, d–g) within the same voicing category, but are capable of distinguishing voiced from voiceless (e.g., p–b, t–d). This, along with the similar results obtained by objective methods, such as ERP, but also dichotic listening tests in noise (Mildner, 1993), implies that the right hemisphere mediates one of the basic distinctive features in speech sounds—voicing. As fMRI studies have shown, the inferior frontal gyrus is activated during solving a phonological task. In subjects whose phonological processing speed was significantly affected by regularity, a greater right-hemisphere involvement was found relative to other subjects (Eysenck & Keane, 2000). On the other hand, the left hemisphere, sensitive to rapid changes in formant transitions, which makes it superior in recognition of the consonant place of articulation, is similarly sensitive to such cues outside the speech context.

Rivera-Gaxiola, Csibra, Johnson, and Karmiloff-Smith (2000) used the ERP method to study electrical brain activity during listening to several types of phonetic oppositions. Some of them were phonemic, or present in the subjects' native language (English) (e.g., /b/ vs. /d/), whereas others were not (e.g., allophones of the phoneme /b/; oppositions that are phonemic in Hindi, but not in English, such as dental vs. retroflex /d/). All oppositions elicited increased neuronal activity, although the subjects reported being aware only of the first distinction (i.e., phonemic). They concluded that the universal perceptual capabilities of newborns and very young children are not irreversibly lost during acquisition of their native speech phonological system, but that considerable neuronal reorganization makes the process more efficient by neglecting contrasts that are not distinctive in a particular language.

A study measuring response times and accuracy in a task that involved determining the rhyming status of pairs of words showed that the response times to rhyming pairs were shorter than to nonrhyming pairs, but also that there were no statistically significant differences between the ears. The results indicate symmetrical phonological processing (it should be stressed, however, that the subjects were women and that the task was in fact perceptual, and both factors may have contributed to the absence of functional asymmetry; Mildner & Rukavina, 1994, 1996b).

TONE AND PROSODY

Production and perception of prosody are accomplished in two ways. Language prosody helps with understanding and solving possible ambiguities at the word or sentence level (higher levels are discussed in the section on pragmatics), and emotional (affective) prosody reveals condition, attitudes, and mood of the speaker as well as the emotional content of the conversation. The first role is manifested as a distinction of sentences depending on intonation and accent position (emphatic stress). For example, the sentence *John was early* may be interpreted in several different ways, depending on the combination of accent and intonation:

John was early.　(= John, not someone else, was early.)

John was **early**.　(= John was early, he wasn't late and he wasn't on time.)

John was early?　(= Was it John that was early?)

John was **early**?　(= Is it really true that John was in fact early—not late, not on time?)

These combinations may be supplemented by emotional content that will add a tone of pleasant surprise that John for once was early, or annoyance that he was earlier than we had expected and we are therefore not ready for his arrival, and so on.

Even a single word may have frequently contradictory meanings, depending on the tone. For example, the word *Coming!* in response to the command *Come here!* besides the fact of arriving may express annoyance, respect, joy, or impatience; it may even reveal the physical state of the person coming, for example, if the person is tired or walking is for some reason painful.

Prosody is generally realized by combining three features: tone, duration, and intensity. Languages use these features to varying degrees at different levels. Pause may also be considered a prosodic device, but it obviously requires units larger than one word.

Many neuroscientists have studied the possible neural bases of production and the perception of prosody. The results may be summarized into four hypotheses:

1. The right hemisphere is dominant for all types of prosody.
2. The right hemisphere is dominant for affective (emotional) prosody, whereas the left hemisphere is dominant for linguistic prosody.
3. Duration, tone, and intensity are lateralized differently.
4. Prosody is a subcortical activity, not lateralized to either hemisphere.

Most authors agree that emotional tone is predominantly a right-hemisphere function and that linguistic tone is lateralized to the left hemisphere (Eysenck & Keane, 2000; Gandour et al., 2002, 2003; Gazzaniga et al., 2002; Mayer, Wildgruber, Riecker, & Dogil, 2002; Pinel, 2005), but there are results that lead to different conclusions (Baum & Pell, 1999; Mildner, 2004; Toepel & Alter, 2002; von Koss Torkildsen, 2002).

The tone may convey emotional information, but in tone languages (such as Thai or Chinese, or even in semitone languages such as Swedish or Croatian) has a phonological, or lexical function, which makes it part of linguistic prosody. It helps differentiate otherwise identical words. Hsieh, Gandour, Wong, and Hutchins (2000) used PET to record changes in cerebral blood flow while listening to Chinese monosyllabic morphemes and their low-pass filtered variants. Low-pass filtering removes all elements that contribute to intelligibility, leaving just the tone. This yields a nonlinguistic context that is used as a control stimulus in tests of distinguishing suprasegmental and nonlinguistic tone changes. Comparison of cerebral activity in native Chinese speakers and subjects whose native language was English, revealed differences in the areas participating in tasks involving discrimination of consonants, vowels, and tones. In native Chinese speakers, the left premotor cortex was activated in all tasks, whereas in native English speakers vowel discrimination activated the left frontal lobe, and tone discrimination activated the homotopic area in the right hemisphere. The left hemisphere was selectively involved in language functioning, regardless of the type of linguistic acoustic stimulus, and the right hemisphere was involved in processing prosody. The authors interpreted these results in support of the hypothesis that there are language-specific neural mechanisms. Furthermore, in the left frontal lobe executive processes activated more anterior regions and verbal working memory storage activated more posterior regions. Tong et al. (2005) concluded that perception of speech prosody involved widely distributed regions in both hemispheres.

Dichotic listening tests on healthy subjects showed that the two hemispheres cooperate in decoding linguistic prosodic information (see Baum & Pell, 1999 and von Koss Torkildsen, 2002 for reviews). In the tasks that required determining the place of accent in meaningful words, right-ear advantage was found, implying a more active left hemisphere. When the same words were low-pass filtered in order to eliminate phonemic information, left-ear advantage (i.e., right-hemisphere superiority) was found. When nonsensical words were presented, no ear advantage was found. These results point to the approximately equal activity of the two hemispheres when phonemic information is available but not relevant. Toepel and Alter (2002) had similar results. They found by ERP that tone, duration, and intensity are lateralized differently.

Moen (1993) used the dichotic listening method to study possible hemispheric asymmetry in healthy Norwegian subjects while they were detecting lexical differences based on tone. She reported greater activity in the left hemisphere than in the right. However, von Koss Torkildsen (2002) used the same method and language and found no significant interhemispheric differences in a similar task.

Bocker, Bastiaasen, Vroomen, Brunia, and de Gelder (1999) measured ERPs during a task of auditory distinction of two-syllable Dutch words with the stress on the first or the second syllable, and concluded that the negative peak at 325 ms after stimulus onset corresponds to processing of metric stress in speech signal. Greater activity was recorded for stimuli with stress on the second syllable (this accentual pattern is found in about 12% of Dutch words) than for those with stress on the first syllable (most Dutch words). The activity was also greater when forms with the stress on the second syllable were presented after a series of forms with the stress on the first syllable, as opposed to the instance when they were presented within a series of words with the stress on the second syllable. This is in line with other reports, according to which activity is higher when the stimulus is unexpected or less common (Gazzaniga et al., 2002).

Left-ear advantage (right hemisphere) was found for identification of intonation curves that correspond to statements, imperatives, conditionals, or interrogative sentences in English, even when the contours were superimposed on short nonsense syllables (Bradshaw & Nettleton, 1983). Zatorre (as cited in Kolb & Whishaw, 1996) believes that the right temporal lobe plays a special part in registering tone (regardless of its type, i.e., speech and music alike). In terms of speech, it would mean that tone as a prosodic element is represented in the right hemisphere (Herrmann et al., 2003).

Looking for a neural substrate of processing series of tones with respect to pitch and duration, Griffiths, Johnsrude, Dean, and Green (1999) found (using PET) in their right-handed musically untrained subjects bilateral activation for both types of analysis, with greater activation of the right hemisphere. The greatest activity was found in the cerebellum, and in the posterior superior temporal lobe and the inferior frontal lobe of the cerebrum.

Salmelin, Schnitzler, Schmitz, and Freund (2000) concluded on the basis of an MEG study that both cerebral hemispheres (i.e., the network comprising the left inferior frontal lobe and the right motor–premotor cortex) are important for merging linguistic and affective prosody with articulation during fluent speech.

Nakai et al. (2000) believe that working memory, selective attention, syntactic and semantic processing, as well as prosody, are organized as a universal system for auditory discrimination.

Pihan, Altenmüller, Hertrich, and Ackermann (2000) have shown by EEG measurements of electrical brain activity that during processing emotional (affective) prosody, cerebral hemispheres' functioning depends on the task and the type of auditory analysis required by the response. They presented their healthy subjects with pairs of sentences differing only with respect to emotional intensity. Differences in emotional intensity had been obtained by manipulating fundamental frequency or duration of accented syllables. When the subjects were asked to determine which of the two auditorily presented sentences expresses emotion more intensely, the right hemisphere was superior, with predominant activity at the frontal, central, temporal, and parietal points, regardless of emotion or whether the differences were obtained by manipulating tone or duration. When the subjects were asked to shadow the test sentences subvocally, activation patterns changed, depending on the manipulated feature. When the intersentence difference was based on fundamental frequency, the activity in the right fronto-temporal lobes decreased. On the other hand, when the difference was based on duration of accented syllables, the activity over left fronto-temporo-central regions increased. The authors attributed these differences to left-hemisphere speech perception mechanisms that are based in the subvocal repetition system, which is a part of the auditory control in the phonological loop. Although silent, subvocal repetition is still an articulatory activity, it establishes connections between the acoustic stimulus and planned verbal production. This in turn activates the appropriate neural network that facilitates constant control of speech production by comparing the produced signal with the planned one. In other words, the right hemisphere is only conditionally dominant—the actual lateralization pattern depends on whether the task is exclusively perceptual (right-lateralized activity) or perceptual and expressive (both hemispheres). Meyer, Steinhauer, Alter, Friederici, and von Cramon (2004) suggest a right fronto-lateral network for processing and a left fronto-lateral network for producing prosodic information.

Double dissociation between linguistic and prosodic levels of the speech message with respect to hemispheric dominance was found in patients with brain damage. Patients with left-hemisphere damage have difficulty understanding words, but no problems with interpreting emotional (affective) prosody. On the other hand, right hemisphere–damaged patients comprehend linguistically expressed meaning, but have great difficulty distinguishing among utterances on the basis of their affective (emotional) prosody (Gazzaniga et al., 2002). Similar results were obtained for recognition of faces: patients with injury to the amygdala or larger areas in the right hemisphere have difficulty in recognizing faces expressing fear.

Clinical studies of patients with head injury have shown that production and perception of prosody require intact parts of the right hemisphere that correspond to the standard speech-language areas in the left hemisphere. Brechmann and Scheich (2000) and Scheich, Ohl, and Brechmann (2002) revealed by fMRI that the right hemisphere is dominant in distinguishing the direction of frequency modulation (i.e., upward or downward pitch movement). Since pitch movement is one of the principal prosodic features, especially with respect to intonation, these results support the hypothesis about the importance (superiority) of the right hemisphere in prosodic aspects of speech.

Individuals with right-hemisphere damage have problems understanding and producing prosody (aprosodia). These two aspects need not be affected to the same degree. Disordered prosodic production is manifested as monotonous speech, with little or no variation in fundamental frequency, duration and accents, unnaturally equal pauses between words, and so forth. These patients seem depressed and their speech has a robot-like quality. They frequently accentuate the words exclusively by increasing intensity, without the accompanying changes in pitch and duration.

Disordered comprehension of prosody involves particularly emotional aspects—diminished reactions to paralinguistic information that reveals emotions (hand gestures, mimicking) and difficulties in perception of prosody, especially of pitch. Studies of prosody perception have revealed that different prosodic parameters may be affected selectively both after left- and right-hemisphere damage. The left hemisphere seems to be dominant for temporal features, such as sequence and duration. The right hemisphere seems to be dominant for spectral information (also dependent on time). Perception of the auditory stimulus frequency that bears information about pitch, may be more affected in right-hemisphere patients than duration, and it may be more important for distinguishing among different types of emotions (e.g., negative from positive).

Prosodic deficits are associated with different cortical and subcortical kinds of injury. Regardless of location, right-hemisphere damage may cause a group of disorders that include prosodic problems, but no firm connection was found between the injury location and the kind of prosodic disorder. It was found that the extent of injury was also important for the severity of communication disorders. Among the subcortical structures, the basal ganglia are particularly important with respect to their role in attention. Moreover, according to some authors, it is possible that prosody is in fact a subcortical activity, and therefore not lateralized (Baum & Pell, 1999).

Myers (1999) summarized characteristic deficits in linguistic and emotional (affective) prosody in patients suffering from right-hemisphere damage in terms of production and comprehension. Problems in production of linguistic prosody are manifested as too much reliance on intersyllabic pause and duration (when distinguishing nouns from other nouns or noun phrases); as slightly impaired use of emphatic stress on words in sentences, and as deficits in the use of fundamental frequency to distinguish sentence types. Problems in comprehension of linguistic prosody are manifested as difficulties in using stress patterns to distinguish parts of speech from one another, to determine whether two sentences are identical and to distinguish the correct use of linguistic prosody from its incorrect use. They may also be apparent in using sentence contour to determine its type (for instance to distinguish between declarative, imperative and interrogative sentences). Production of emotional (affective) prosody is characterized by flat, monotonous contours, by difficulties in matching prosodic contours and emotional content, and by reduced reliance on pitch variation while increasingly relying on semantic information to convey emotions. Comprehension of emotional prosody is characterized by reduced discrimination and identification of mood in neutral sentences outside of context, and by reduced ability to identify mood in sentences having meaning incongruent with prosodic contours.

Patients suffering from right-hemisphere damage have more pronounced disorders of affective than linguistic prosody, but poor affective prosody is not to be equated with lack of emotions—it is a manifestation of their inability to express emotions. The patients are frequently aware that their voice is not expressing adequately what they are feeling. The reverse is true as well. The problem is not in interpreting emotions: the patients are capable of comprehending different emotions that have been explicitly verbalized. Their problems lie in interpreting prosodic and paralinguistic information.

Inability to express and comprehend emotions is frequently extended to nonverbal communication. Such patients use hand gestures sparingly and mimic less, and they rely on these cues very little when trying to interpret the messages.

The most striking characteristic of prosodic production in right-hemisphere patients is insufficient use of intonation in speech. Their statements are unnaturally flat and monotonous and their interrogative sentences are characterized by unnaturally small variation in fundamental frequency that is typically the most straightforward indicator of sentence type. Difficulties with pitch are the most noticeable characteristic of their linguistic prosody comprehension as well. On the basis of her review of literature about clinical cases and healthy subjects Myers (1999) proposed that the source of the problem in prosodic comprehension might be at the perceptual level, with perception of pitch and other nontemporal spectral information bearing particular importance. She concluded that it might be possible that the problems of right hemisphere–damaged patients in prosodic production may be associated with their difficulties in pitch perception.

Since there is no definitive clinical evidence of neural networks that might be primarily involved in processing affective prosody, bilateral or subcortical mechanisms seem to be equally good candidates.

It may be concluded that laterality of particular functions is not based on the dichotomies such as verbal versus nonverbal or linguistic versus affective, but rather on the degree to which properties such as temporal sequence, timing, duration, or frequency are involved. The left hemisphere may be more involved when the material is more time-dependent or when sequential processing is required. The right hemisphere may be more active when the material is independent of temporal factors. Nontemporal features include spectral information, such as pitch and harmonic structure. Temporal features include sequencing, duration of elements, and pauses between them. Right-hemisphere patients have more problems solving tasks that involve spectral data, such as pitch distinction. On the other hand, left-hemisphere patients have significantly more problems in the perception of temporal patterns.

LEXICAL LEVEL AND MENTAL LEXICON

Devlin et al. (2000) compared the brain activity that was recorded by PET with the activity recorded by fMRI under identical testing conditions (during a semantic categorization task). PET revealed that, compared with a resting state, semantic categorization activated the medial part of the right cerebellum and three regions in the left cerebral hemisphere: Broca's area and further back well into the middle frontal gyrus, the posterior part of the middle and inferior temporal gyrus, as well as the antero-medial part of the temporal pole. fMRI revealed somewhat different results: activation was recorded in the frontal operculum, and spreading into Broca's area, in the homotopic area of the right hemisphere, on the medial surface of the left superior frontal gyrus, and in the right cerebellar hemisphere. The authors attributed the difference mainly to methodological artifacts.

During presentation of nouns, semantic attributes are activated automatically (in the temporal lobe) regardless of their relevance for the task at hand. The prefrontal cortex then selects the relevant information. Semantic tasks, such as generating semantically related words, activated the anterior cingulate gyrus (as recorded by PET)—similar to the inferior prefrontal cortex. Interestingly, injury to the cingulate gyrus did not result in any language disorder. That is why the cingulate gyrus is thought to play a role in coordination of activities of different attention systems, rather than being directly involved in semantic processing. For example, if the subjects are asked to generate verbs to given nouns over and over, the activity initially recorded in the cingulate gyrus will shift to the insula and the temporal lobe (Raichle, as cited in Gazzaniga, 2002). ERP recording has revealed the following course of events: 180 ms after target noun onset, activity in the cingulate gyrus occurs; 30 ms later there is activity in the left lateral prefrontal cortex; about 620 ms after stimulus onset, there is activation in the left posterior temporal lobe. A great amount of activity was recorded by ERP in the anterior cingulate gyrus when the subject made an error (manifested as error-related negativity—ERN) and in incongruent conditions on Stroop tests (incongruent color and word). These results point to the role of anterior cingulate in selection of appropriate elements from a semantic set (i.e., in disambiguation).

Gutbrod et al. (2000) found by fMRI that semantic processing (deciding whether a pair of visually presented words is synonymous or not) activates primarily the middle and superior temporal gyri and the anterior part of the inferior frontal gyrus—all in the left hemisphere.

Bokde, Tagamets, Friedman, and Horwitz (2000) found (also by fMRI) a strong functional association between the ventral part of the left inferior frontal gyrus and the left posterior regions in the occipital and temporal lobes during lexical, or semantic processing. On the other hand, they found a strong functional association between the posterior part of the left inferior frontal cortex and left posterior occipital and temporal areas during phonological processing (nonwords, letter series, and their comparison with words). Their results support earlier hypotheses that the ventral side of the left inferior frontal cortex is more specialized for semantic processing, whereas the dorsal part is responsible for phonological aspects.

Billingsley, McAndrews, Crawley, and Mikulis (2000) studied phonological and semantic components of reading in 20 epileptic patients and 10 control subjects. They tried to replicate an earlier study carried out on healthy subjects (Pugh, as cited in Billingsley et al., 2000) that had revealed relatively higher activation in frontal regions during phonological processing than during semantic processing, and higher activation in temporal regions during semantic processing than during phonological tasks. The phonological task involved determination of the rhyming status of visually presented pairs of words, and in the semantic task the subjects were asked to determine whether the pairs of visually presented words belonged to the same category. Their results only partly confirmed the results of Pugh et al.—the difference between the semantic and phonological processing was found only in the frontal lobe. The greatest activity was recorded in the left inferior frontal gyrus during phonological processing—significantly higher than during the semantic task. This was found in all subjects. Previously reported differences between the two types of processing were not confirmed for the temporal lobe. All epileptic patients (those with foci in the left and the right temporal lobe alike) exhibited higher activation in anterior regions (i.e., in the left frontal lobe) than healthy subjects. This is in agreement with the general tendency toward increased activity in the left frontal lobe in patients with damage to the posterior temporal regions.

Benefield et al. (2000) used fMRI to compare the activity of the middle frontal cortex during processing meaningful and meaningless linguistic elements. In the first type of task the subjects were asked to generate nonsense syllables with given initial or final consonants. In the second type, they were supposed to generate words that rhymed or list examples belonging to a given category. They found that the recall of existing lexical elements (meaningful words) involves the middle frontal cortex in both hemispheres (more in the left than in the right) and additionally activates the area anterior to the supplementary motor area (more in the left hemisphere in the rhyming task, i.e., during phonological processing; more in the right hemisphere or bilaterally in the category task, i.e., during semantic processing). Generating new phonological structures (nonsense syllables) was restricted to the left middle frontal cortex and elicited additional activity in the left supplementary motor area. Consistent with the authors' expectations, greater activity was recorded during processing meaningful elements than during processing of nonsensical ones. They conclude that the function of the middle frontal cortex is recall of existing representations and their retention in working memory.

The left and the right hemisphere seem to process semantic relations in different ways (Myers, 1999). The right hemisphere is more skillful in maintaining multiple meanings that are loosely related (i.e., with less semantic overlap). The left hemisphere is believed to focus on one meaning or on several meanings with considerable semantic overlap. The left hemisphere is involved in fine semantic encoding by rapid selection of one dominant meaning, repressing other, not so closely related meanings of the word. On the other hand, the right hemisphere is involved in rough semantic encoding during which it slowly produces multiple meanings that are weakly activated and loosely interrelated. For example, the word *dog* will quickly recall the concept of a four-legged hairy animal in the left hemisphere, whereas in the right hemisphere it will activate similar meanings (man's best friend) and related concepts (e.g., cat). Connotative and metaphorical meanings (man's best friend, faithful companion) are considered more weakly associated with the word than denotative or literal meanings. This type of research has shown that the right hemisphere is important for the types of isolated word processing (without context) in which alternate, less frequent, and less central word meanings are essential. Tests involving visual stimuli in healthy subjects have shown that priming facilitates access to less frequent or subordinate meanings of words that have been presented to the right hemisphere (left visual field). At the same time facilitation of the word's central meaning decreased. In other words, in a test situation that did not involve automatic processing, the right hemisphere reacted better to less familiar meanings of the word than the left. These results support the idea that right hemisphere lesions may disrupt processing of alternate and connotative meanings, but also suggest that we rely on semantic processing mediated by the right hemisphere when focused attention is required. In other words, the left hemisphere is dominant during automatic processing, when fast processing of familiar, denotative meanings is required. However, semantic information in the right hemisphere is probably activated only when controlled attention is required—in other words, when we are not happy with the central meaning of the word and have to make additional effort to access an alternate meaning instead. Clinical support was found in patients with left- and right-hemisphere injury. Namely, when given a choice between a denotative and connotative meaning of a word, left hemisphere–damaged patients (deficits in denotative aspects of meaning) regularly chose the connotative option, and right hemisphere–damaged patients (deficits in connotative aspects of meaning) more frequently chose the denotative variant. Under identical conditions healthy subjects chose one or the other alternative approximately equally.

It may be assumed that in healthy subjects, the two hemispheres cooperate during semantic processing so that both activate word meanings at the same time. The less selective right hemisphere elicits related meanings as well, which are, for a limited time, available to the faster, more selective left hemisphere in case additional explanation of the central meaning activated by the left hemisphere is needed.

This hypothesis is supported by the results of verbal fluency tests. In these tests subjects are typically asked to provide, in a limited amount of time (usually one minute) as many words according to some given criterion, such as words starting with the same letter, belonging to some category, and so on. In the first 30 seconds right hemisphere–damaged patients are no different from healthy subjects. However, after that, the number of their responses drops radically. Joanette, Goulet, and LeDorze (1988) propose that the initial production is the result of left-hemisphere functioning that automatically activates the most obvious and dominant members according to the given criterion. The differences start to emerge when it is necessary to access members of the category that are not so central to the given semantic field and whose retrieval requires conscious effort and/or sustained attention. In that case, the damaged right hemisphere cannot help the left.

The difference between the left and the right hemisphere in semantic processing with respect to activation and activated semantic concepts may be summarized as follows (Myers, 1999). Semantic concepts activated by the left hemisphere are typically familiar, dominant, closely interrelated, with substantial semantic overlap. Contrary to that, the semantic concepts activated by the right hemisphere are usually less familiar, connotative, alternate, loosely associated, with less semantic overlap. The left hemisphere is typically activated during automatic processing and is characterized by fast, intensive activation of dominant (central) meanings. On the other hand, the right hemisphere functions better under controlled processing conditions and is characterized by slower and weaker activation of alternate meanings.

Problems in semantic processing typical of right hemisphere–damaged patients may be manifested as:

1. Diminished capacity to provide appropriate category names for presented groups of objects (patients can name individual objects, e.g., *dog, cat, canary,* but are unable to associate them with the category *pets*).
2. Diminished capacity to determine whether pairs of objects are related (e.g., *tomato, potato*).
3. On tests of verbal fluency, compared with healthy controls:
   a. They produce more central (prototypical, dominant) items.
   b. They generate more items with common properties within the semantic category.
   c. They have more difficulties with goal-derived than with semantic categories (*things to take to the beach* vs. *beach towel, ball, sun lotion*).

Due to all this it is possible that they have more difficulties in using less central and less familiar meanings, in surpassing the closely related semantic categories, and that they have diminished capacity to solve lexical ambiguities (Myers, 1999).

Mental lexicon is the mental representation of the words any individual has at his/her disposal. Many neuroscientific and linguistic studies have addressed the organization of the mental lexicon with respect to various aspects of the word: meaning (semantics), form (morphology), rules for combination with other words (syntax), pronunciation (phonetics and phonology), spelling rules (orthography), and possible neural substrates. One of the central questions that such studies try to answer is: is there one mental lexicon for language production and one for perception, or is it all combined into one universal lexicon?

Since normal human communication is extremely fast (an adult native speaker of any given language can recognize and produce about three words per second), it is obvious that the mental lexicon must be organized so that it enables efficient and quick access to stored information. One type of organization can be quite reliably ruled out, and that is alphabetical. If the members of the mental lexicon were organized alphabetically, then the words starting with the initial and final letters of the alphabet would be retrieved faster than the ones starting with letters from the middle. More probably, the lexicon is organized like some sort of a network. Several features of the mental lexicon have been supported by empirical, experimental, and clinical evidence:

1. Mental lexicon is adaptable. We learn new words throughout our lives, but we also forget some of the words we have learned at some point and stopped using.
2. The words used more frequently are retrieved faster than the ones used less frequently.

3. Words that are pronounced similarly to many other words are retrieved more slowly than the ones whose pronunciation is unique or in some aspect special.
4. Semantically related words are stored closer to each other in the network. This was revealed by the effect of priming (a target word is recognized faster if the prime is a semantically related word); this is explained by the prime activating a set of expected words, and if the target word is part of that set it will take less time to respond to it than if it were not.

Typical semantic errors in brain-damaged patients support the notion of network organization:

1. Semantic paraphasias—within-category substitution of words (e.g., *snow* instead of *sleet*).
2. Difficulties in determining appropriate semantic categories—the patient does not know that *birch* belongs to *trees*.
3. Inappropriate use of superordinate terms—*bird* in response to the picture of a *pigeon*.

The first disorder is associated with Wernicke's aphasia and deep dyslexia, and the second two with progressive semantic dementia. Interestingly, some categories may be spared such semantic problems.

Word Recognition

Words are processed through three stages: lexical access, lexical selection, and lexical integration. Lexical access follows perceptual analysis of the input signal and is dependent on it. If the input is visual, such as in reading, the so-called dual route access is assumed (Colthart, as cited in Gazzaniga et al., 2002; Indefrey et al., 2000). One route is direct—from orthography to word form—and the other is indirect—mediated by phonological encoding. The latter is necessary if we are to explain reading of nonwords. Since nonwords do not have their representations in the lexicon, each letter must be converted into a phoneme and compared with the existing forms (representations). This route accounts for homophones as well. On the other hand, the direct route is necessary to enable reading words whose reading by means of phonological encoding would produce a nonsense word. The latter problem is more applicable to the languages that do not have close grapheme-to-phoneme mapping (e.g., English). In these languages direct mapping in irregular words would result in incorrect pronunciation (e.g., *have* would be pronounced as if it rhymed with *cave*). Pronunciation of such words has to be memorized, which in fact means that a direct connection between the perceived form and the form stored in the mental lexicon must be established.

The dual-route model is supported by evidence from patients suffering from acquired dyslexia. There are two types of such dyslexia: (a) patients suffering from phonological (deep) dyslexia cannot read nonsense words (nonexistent representation of such words in the lexicon, damaged indirect route), but have no difficulty reading irregular meaningful words, no matter how difficult they were (the words have their representations in the lexicon, intact direct route). They rely exclusively on the direct route and are therefore incapable of reading words that do not exist in their mental lexicon. They typically present with semantic paraphasias. Auditorily presented rhyming tests confirm that their phonological representations are intact; (b) patients suffering from surface dyslexia read all words using the indirect route (converting all individual graphemes into phonemes), which results in incorrect pronunciation of irregular words.

If the signals are acoustic, the temporal domain has to be considered as well. One of the best known models of speech recognition is the Cohort model (Marslen-Wilson & Tyler, 1980). The model is discussed in more detail in chapter 5. Binder et al. (as cited in Gazzaniga et al., 2002) used fMRI to determine brain areas that are activated during speech signal processing. Auditory data are processed in the auditory cortex first (Heschl gyrus), to be forwarded to the superior temporal gyrus. At this point there are no differences between speech and nonspeech signals. The difference emerges for the first time in the neighboring superior temporal sulcus, but at this level the lexico-semantic processing has not yet started. From here the information is transmitted to the middle and inferior temporal gyrus, where phonological and lexico-semantic processing takes place. The final analysis is carried out in the angular gyrus. Greater activity in the left hemisphere than in the right is usually recorded at the point where the phonological and lexico-semantic processing begins. In visually presented words, the initial processing is no different than processing of any visual stimuli, including nonlinguistic ones. It takes place in the primary and the secondary visual cortex in the occipital lobes of both hemispheres. Letter identification involves the occipito-temporal lobe (predominantly in the left hemisphere), but also the middle temporal gyrus—more so in words than in nonwords. During pronunciation, the left inferior frontal gyrus, including the ventral part of Broca's area, is activated.

Indefrey et al. (2000) used PET and ERP methods to study brain activity during access to German irregular words (meaningful words whose pronunciation cannot be predicted from their spelling), nonwords (meaningless words that are spelled in agreement with German orthography), and nonword–homophones (their written forms are meaningless, but they constitute meaningful German words when read out loud in agreement with German orthography) in 15 healthy native speakers of German. The subjects were asked to read visually presented words silently. The semantic status of the word (meaningful—meaningless) was found to be an important factor: irregular words and homophones resulted in increased blood flow in the left inferior frontal gyrus, contrary to nonwords. The differences between the two groups were manifested as selective activation in the posterior part of the superior and middle temporal gyri in both hemispheres for irregular words, whereas the homophones activated inferior parts of the occipital gyri, the left posterior fusiform gyrus, the left precentral gyrus, and the posterior part of the left inferior frontal gyrus (Broca's area). From these results the authors drew the following conclusions: (a) lexical access by means of visual input (direct route) involves posterior parts of both temporal lobes; (b) lexical access mediated by phonological encoding (indirect route) comprises a left-lateralized posterior-anterior loop that includes the fusiform gyrus, involved in sublexical grapheme processing (posterior part), and the inferior frontal gyrus, involved in phonological processing (anterior part); (c) regardless of the access route, the retrieved lexico-semantic information is further processed in the inferior part of the left prefrontal lobe.

PERCEPTUAL ANALYSIS OF LINGUISTIC INPUT

Linguistic input may be visual or auditory. Regardless of modality, the input signal proceeds through the prelexical level of visual or acoustic analysis. The result of such analysis is forwarded to the mental lexicon. If the stimulus was auditory, the input signal—a sound sequence—is converted into the phonological code (a phoneme sequence) in order to gain access to auditory word forms in the mental lexicon. If the stimulus was visual, the input signal—a letter sequence—may after identification be forwarded directly to the visual word form in the mental lexicon, or it may be converted into phonological units and proceed along the same path as the auditory signal. Lexical selection takes place at the mental lexicon level, and the selected word is the one that (best) matches the input signal. The selected word activates the lemma (grammatical data store) and finally the word meaning is retrieved. These stages underlie all language and speech models. Different alternatives propose a one-way process of speech and language comprehension (the so-called bottom-up processing) that typically proceeds as described above, or a process in which higher levels affect the functioning of lower levels by some sort of feedback (the so-called top-down processing). This brings us back to the familiar dispute between the advocates of modular models and supporters of interactive ones. Some models do not define the lemma level, but propose that word forms are in fact activation patterns that are widely dispersed (distributed networks).

On the basis of experiments, observations, and computer simulations Lieberman (1991) concluded that there is more than one lexicon in the brain, and that these lexicons are independent of neural mechanisms that control syntax and speech production. They are supposedly associative because they represent the storage of knowledge about the world accumulated by each individual through experience. Therefore, the words can be accessed semantically, phonetically, or by means of associations with previous experience. The mechanism of acquiring knowledge about the world is based on learning that takes place in neural networks in the brain. Many psycholinguistic models of the lexicon assume separate phonological, semantic, and orthographic information about words (Emmorey & Fromkin, 1988). Patients with brain damage that selectively affects access to one of these aspects are taken as evidence that supports this. Although knowledge about the world is not stored in a single location, its constituent parts are obviously connected. These connections are particularly close between the orthographic and the phonological representation— it was found that both these representations are automatically retrieved during recognition, regardless of the modality of word presentation. (By the way, studies have shown that words are retrieved fastest on the basis of their initial segments.) Connections within the lexicon are noticeable in morphology and semantics as well (Emmorey & Fromkin, 1988). Furthermore, Gazzaniga (1994) found that the isolated left hemisphere was entirely capable for normal comprehension of all aspects of language, whereas the right hemisphere linguistic capabilities were limited. In the rare right-handers who had language functions in the right hemisphere (as well), their lexicons were found to be organized in a different way. These observations are in agreement with the proposition that they reflect learning processes, and as such are more widely distributed in the cortex. Having said all this, it should be stressed that in the general population the lexicon seems to be left-lateralized. Its right-hemisphere counterparts seem to store information without any specific pattern or hierarchy. Faust and Lavidor (2003) found that during word recognition, the right hemisphere activates a broader range of related meanings than the left hemisphere, including alternate meanings of ambiguous words.

In healthy subjects, lexical decision tasks (e.g., deciding whether a word is meaningful or not) elicit marked left-lateralized activity, in the frontal language zone (Brodmann's areas 44, 45, and 47) and in the dorsal side of anterior cingulate (Brodmann's area 32) when tasks are more complex and related to a particular language (Specht et al., 2000a).

Isahai, Takeuchi, and Kuriki (2000) used MEG to study the activation sequence of different cerebral areas during generating nouns to visually presented hiragana symbols in six healthy right-handers. The first activity emerged around 100 ms after stimulus onset in both occipital lobes, mostly in the extrastriate areas (Brodmann's areas 18 and 19) and lasted until approximately 400th ms. About 200 ms after stimulus presentation, additional activity was recorded in the posterior part of the superior temporal gyrus in the superior temporal sulcus toward the Sylvian fissure in both hemispheres, with extended latencies until well into 700 ms (and longer in some subjects). Other authors have also reported these areas as active during language tasks and reading, with the somewhat shorter activity during reading. Activity at the junction of the left parietal and temporal lobe around the supramarginal gyrus with the latency between 230 and 715 ms was recorded in five out of the six subjects. Anterior activity, at the junction of the left anterior superior temporal lobe and the posterior inferior frontal lobe was found in two out of six subjects, with latencies between 455 and 720 ms. Since no activity in the latter two regions was recorded during reading, the authors concluded that they are involved in phonological manipulation and/or verbal working memory that is important for word construction.

In tasks of determining meanings of individual words (lexical) and meanings of words in a wider context (contextual) Homae, Hashimoto, Nakajima, Miyashita, and Sakai (2000) recorded by fMRI activity in four areas: in the primary and secondary auditory cortex (Brodmann's areas 41 and 42), in Wernicke's area (Brodmann's areas 42 and 22), in the angular and supramarginal gyri (Brodmann's areas 39 and 40) and in Broca's area (Brodmann's areas 44 and 45).

Activity was recorded in both hemispheres, with some differences in intensity dependent on modality (auditory vs. visual) and type of task (lexical vs. contextual). The left hemisphere was more active when the stimuli were auditory than when they were visual, and when the task was contextual rather than lexical. In the left Wernicke's area the activation was more marked in the contextual than in the lexical task only in the visual modality. Primary and secondary auditory cortex activity, as well as that recorded in Wernicke's area in the left hemisphere was similar in both types of task in the auditory modality. These results imply that different modalities have different input paths to Wernicke's area. On the other hand, in both modalities, activation in the regions of the supramarginal and angular gyri as well as in Broca's area in the left hemisphere was task dependent.

There is some disagreement among authors when it comes to recognition of isolated words in right hemisphere–damaged patients. Some found that the right hemisphere is generally not crucial for recognition of isolated words since this is a predominantly left-hemisphere activity. Others concluded that the importance of the right hemisphere becomes obvious when connotative meaning is required (Myers, 1999). Posner and Raichle (1997) recorded (by PET) activity in the frontal regions of the right hemisphere during recall of particular words.

WORD CATEGORIES

There is clinical evidence of the right-hemisphere contribution in processing high-frequency, concrete material (Bradshaw & Nettleton, 1983). Ely, Graves, and Potter (1989) found that the right hemisphere contributes to semantic processing of stimuli that may evoke multisensory and/or emotional percepts, and that it is to some extent (depending on the task) involved in all semantic processing. Easily imageable words are supposedly processed in the right hemisphere as opposed to the more abstract ones (e.g., *chair* vs. *destiny*). Similar results were reported for nouns versus function words (Coslett & Monsul, 1994).

Word recognition tests performed by means of the divided visual field technique revealed the differences between the hemispheres with respect to processing concrete and abstract words. Abstract words presented to the right visual field (left hemisphere) are typically recognized more frequently than those presented to the left visual field (right hemisphere). On the other hand, concrete words are recognized with approximately equal success regardless of the visual field. The results across authors and studies are not entirely consistent, but there is a trend toward less marked asymmetry for concrete than for abstract words. ERP and fMRI recordings have confirmed many of the trends obtained in behavioral studies (Eysenck & Keane, 2000). There is also evidence from deep dyslexics with relatively extensive damage to large areas in the left hemisphere: they have difficulty reading abstract, unimageable words, but are better at reading concrete, easily imageable ones. Some studies have shown that the differences are modality-dependent, and that they occur only in auditory tests (for a review see Eysenck & Keane, 2000). However, Kosslyn (as cited in Eysenck & Keane, 2000) cautions that the central problem is in the process of forming concepts, which was not addressed before. It seems that the left hemisphere plays a direct role in the formation of visual representations, but that the right hemisphere is also active, in a different way. In his PET studies he found differences in activity between the anterior and posterior parts of the visual cortex, depending on whether the subjects were asked to imagine small mental images (posterior parts) or large ones (anterior parts).

The left hemisphere processes abstract word representations that do not preserve particular input stimulus features, whereas the right hemisphere processes specific word forms. In other words, it seems that priming in the right but not in the left hemisphere is under the influence of the words studied.

Krause et al. (1999) found by PET that the important role in episodic memory, regardless of modality (visual, auditory) and word characteristics (abstract, imageable) is played by the *precuneus,* a part of the association multimodal area in the middle parietal lobe above the border with the occipital lobe.

Liotti, Woldorff, Perez, and Mayberg (2000) used the ERP technique to study the electrophysiological correlates of color–word interference in Stroop tests, on healthy subjects and three response modalities (loud verbal, silent verbal, manual). In all modalities the responses occurred between 350 and 500 ms after stimulus onset in the anterior cingulate, with manual responses eliciting activity in a somewhat wider area than the verbal ones. An additional late activity in the left temporoparietal region, occurring 500 to 800 ms after stimulus onset, regardless of response modality, was interpreted as a reflection of the need for additional processing of word meaning after the incongruity between color and word has been registered.

Tarkka (2000) found (by ERP) that aphasics suffering predominantly from the sensory (i.e., Wernicke) type of aphasia may perceive words, but exhibit no 400 ms negativity that is characteristic of semantic processing associated with deciding whether the second word of the presented pair belongs to the same category as the first one.

Studies of brain-damaged patients have revealed that different cognitive functions may be selectively impaired. For example, only one of the functions may be impaired, with others remaining intact: auditory/verbal working memory, phonological processing, grapheme-to-phoneme mapping, and semantic processing. Within semantic processing, further deficit "specializations" are possible: some patients are better at identifying inanimate objects than animate ones or food. Even more narrowly, some patients may have problems only with some semantic categories, such as fruits and vegetables, or tools, musical instruments, and so on. Such evidence suggests the probability of mental lexical organization in terms of categories, but it also points to the distinctions between processing pathways that are responsible for naming and those involved in name recognition.

The left dorsolateral prefrontal region is the area most reliably activated when deciding to which category individual visually presented stimuli belong (e.g., bugs, flowers, etc.). Other areas that may be activated, in order of likelihood, are: the left parietal lobe, the supplementary motor area, and the right inferior prefrontal region (Chee, Sriram, Lee, & Soon, 2000).

Functional neuroimaging techniques have shown that the occipital and temporal areas are activated differently for particular object categories. Gorno-Tempini, Cipolotti, and Price (2000) used the PET technique to study brain activation while: naming visually presented pictures of objects belonging to common, everyday categories (familiar faces, animals, body parts, geographical maps, colors, and man-made objects); categorizing the presented objects; and reading their names. Reading and naming in response to familiar faces, animals, and maps increased activity in the left extrastriate cortex (Brodmann's areas 18 and 19). Recognition of maps elicited additional activity in the right occipito-parietal and parahippocampal areas (Brodmann's areas 19, 7, and 30). In addition to the areas common to maps and animals, familiar faces elicited additional activation in the left antero-lateral temporal region (Brodmann's area 21). Body parts and man-made objects elicited activation in the postero-lateral part of the temporal lobe (Brodmann's areas 21 and 37). The authors attributed the activity in the extrastriate cortex—recorded during naming and reading names associated with familiar faces, animals and maps—to their greater visual complexity. Greater demands for spatial processing probably activate the right occipito-parietal and parahippocampal areas during map naming. In the left temporal lobe, naming familiar faces activates anterior regions that correspond to the recall of simple biographical data, whereas posterior regions are activated by objects and body parts whose naming is associated with knowledge about how they work.

Some brain-damaged patients are considerably better at identifying inanimate than animate objects. There are examples where the difference is as large as 90% correct for inanimate as opposed to only 6% correct for animate objects. On the basis of such cases we can draw inferences about the organization of the perceptual and semantic knowledge in the brain. Semantic knowledge is organized according to physical (visual semantic knowledge) and functional (functional semantic knowledge) object features. Injury will cause deficits in recognition of the category that has shared features, because knowledge about objects that belong to that category is stored and organized in the same or in the neighboring neuroanatomical substrate. The fact that there are considerably more reports of impaired capacity to identify animate objects than inanimate ones is explained by richer representation of the latter broad category. They may be experienced and perceived, which means that knowledge about them may be stored by multiple means—kinesthetically, by means of motor representations, and so forth. Due to these multiple representations it is more probable that after injury some of them will be preserved and available. This can best be illustrated by everyday situations when we cannot think of the name of a particular object, but are perfectly capable of demonstrating its use (which actually helps us remember the name). An interesting parallel may be found in dictionary definitions of animate and inanimate objects. The ratio of visual to functional descriptors is different depending on the category. In animate objects, the ratio is 7.7 (visual) to 1 (functional), whereas in inanimate ones it is 1.4 (visual) to 1 (functional; Gazzaniga et al., 2002).

Hiltunen, Rinne, Laine, Kaasinen, and Sipila (2000) confirmed that brain regions associated with processing of specific word categories are at least partially different. They studied seven healthy male subjects and used PET to record brain activity while the subjects were verbally providing the category to which the visually presented objects belonged. They found that the activated areas were dependent on whether the objects belonged to the categories referring to animals or to artifacts. Animals elicited increased activation in the right cingulate (Brodmann's area 9), in the right parahippocampal region (Brodmann's area 36), and in the left fusiform gyrus (Brodmann's area 37). The category of artifacts increased activation in the left prefrontal cortex (Brodmann's area 10) along the right cingulate gyrus. This difference between the activity in the left frontal regions for artifacts and bilateral medial temporal activation is in agreement with the previously noticed general distinction between anterior and posterior parts for artifacts (tools) and animals. The authors attributed the cingulate activity found in both categories to nonspecific attention mechanisms.

These conclusions have been tested on healthy subjects by means of PET and fMRI. It was confirmed that different neuronal circuits are involved in processing of animate stimuli and tools, and that they reflect the differences between perceptual and functional information. Martin et al. (as cited in Gazzaniga et al., 2002) got the following results: (a) when the tasks involved names or pictures of animals, the activated areas were the lateral part of the fusiform gyrus (on the ventral surface of the brain), the superior temporal gyrus, and the medial occipital lobe of the left hemisphere; (b) when the tasks included tools, the activated parts were the medial fusiform gyrus, the left middle temporal gyrus, and the left premotor area that is activated when one imagines moving one's hand.

Some word recognition models assume that word processing in different modalities and languages converges toward common brain systems associated with the semantic level of processing, and that localization of these systems varies with respect to semantic category. So, for example, words for tools are localized in an area different from that for fruits and vegetables. Le Clec et al. (2000) tested this hypothesis by means of fMRI on two word categories: numbers and body parts. They found higher activation in the left hemisphere (in the parietal and prefrontal area) for knowledge about body parts, and greater activation in the right parietal lobe for numerical concepts, regardless of presentation modality or language.

Damasio et al. (as cited in Gazzaniga et al., 2002) studied cerebral activation during naming familiar faces, animals, and tools, in patients with brain damage and healthy subjects. They got a remarkably clear picture of the representation of different categories in both groups of subjects. The regions of greatest activation during recall of names of famous individuals (on the basis of face recognition) were found in the left temporal pole. The anterior left inferior temporal lobe was found to be important for naming animals, and the left posterior inferior temporal lobe, including the junction between the parietal, occipital, and temporal lobes, was active during naming of tools. Damasio and coworkers point out that the differences are among lexical categories, and that the category-specific problems are restricted to the lexical level and do not include concepts. This may account for the absence of activation in the premotor areas that was characteristic of tools as conceptual categories. They add that conceptual networks, which involve several neuronal structures in both hemispheres, are connected with lexical networks in the left temporal lobe and that they probably contain specialized information about people, animals, and tools. Finally, lexical networks activate the phonological network from which the spoken word emerges as the final product.

As reported by Warrington et al. (as cited in Gazzaniga et al., 2002), some patients find it very difficult to point to and name pictures that refer to food and animate objects, whereas they effortlessly solve similar tasks involving tools. Others behave quite the opposite, although the latter are fewer. The members of the former group had an injury in the inferior and medial temporal cortex, most frequently in its anterior parts, in other words, close to the areas that are crucial for perception of objects based on visual stimuli (the so-called *what* pathway), and in the area of relay projections from the association cortex to the hippocampus that is important for long-term storage of information. The latter group is characterized by injuries to the left frontal and parietal regions that are close to or correspond to sensorimotor representations in general, including operations that may be performed with the presented tools. Therefore, they proposed a model of organization of semantic knowledge according to which biological categories are more dependent on physical characteristics and visual properties (i.e., how something looks), as opposed to the man-made objects that are identified on the basis of their functional characteristics (i.e., how something is used). Caramazza et al. (as cited in Gazzaniga et al., 2002) proposed a similar classification into animate and inanimate categories.

Hart, Sloan Berndt, and Caramazza (2000) presented a case of a 34-year-old right-handed man (M. D.) who suffered no aphasia after left-hemisphere damage, except immediately after injury. However, he consistently had serious difficulties in naming pictures and drawings of fruits and vegetables, and considerable problems in distinguishing between the two categories. The problems were not restricted to one modality: problems occurred regardless of whether testing was done with visual, auditory, or tactile stimuli. It might be inferred that the patient did not have the problem of accessing the semantic system but rather of selective damage to the semantic system itself. However, the same patient exhibited a remarkable ability to correctly categorize problematic concepts when appropriate words were presented instead of pictures, definitions, or actual objects that he was supposed to recognize by touch. The difference is obviously between lexical and semantic processing— with lexical processing intact, and semantic selectively impaired.

Grabowski, Damasio, and Tranel (2000) studied (by PET) brain activation in 10 healthy subjects during recall of names of well-known geographic locations and persons. They found that recall of proper names (places and persons, alike) involves the left temporal pole regardless of conceptual category, which is in agreement with the interpretation that its involvement is determined by a required level of specificity. Müller and Kutas (1996) found by ERP that proper names have the same latency but higher amplitude than common nouns. Moreover, the subject's own name elicited (in addition the N1 and P2 peaks) another response peaking at 400 ms after stimulus onset at the parieto-central electrodes and an even later response with the 500 to 800 ms latency at the left latero-frontal points.

Fujimoto, Miyatani, Oka, and Kiriki (2000) found (by ERP) that the strength of association between the prime and the target in a lexical decision task affects response times and temporal organization and pattern of the N400 wave: the words that are semantically more closely related with the prime elicit faster responses and higher amplitude. Conscious and unconscious semantic activations occur in similar locations in the brain, but have a different time course. (Unconscious semantic activation was achieved by visual presentation of masked words that the subject was unaware of during the test, but that affected the occurrence of the N400 wave, characteristic of semantic processing.) During unconscious processing, activity rapidly decreases within 200 ms after activation, whereas during conscious processing it increases steadily with time (Kiefer & Spitzer, 2000).

Stenberg, Lindgren, Johansson, Olsson, and Rosen (2000) also found (by ERP) that the words the subjects were unaware of (because they were masked during presentation) are processed semantically similarly to those that were identified consciously. They also found that neuronal populations that are recruited during subliminal lexical processing differ from those that are involved in supraliminal processing.

Wang et al. (2000b) recorded (by MEG) the differences in cerebral activity during coding (memorizing the size or meaning) words and pictures. They found that at the initial stage, pictures and words are processed in different systems, mainly in both lateral temporal lobes (words) and in both parietal lobes (pictures). However, at a later stage, they were processed in a common semantic system.

Thompson-Shill et al. (as cited in Gazzaniga et al., 2002) recorded activation of the left inferior frontal cortical regions during verb generation to given nouns, but also the activation in the temporal lobe, which they assigned the role of long-term store of semantic information.

Taylor, Meier, Brugger, and Weniger (2002) presented (visually) their subjects with pairs of words that were semantically related (categorically, idiomatically, or metaphorically) or unrelated. Overall, the results revealed right-visual-field advantage (left-hemisphere dominance) with respect to accuracy, and a trend toward right-visual-field advantage with respect to response time (shorter response times). An analysis of word pairs that were judged as semantically related by the subjects revealed interesting correlations between the type of association and functional cerebral asymmetry implied by visual field advantage. Namely, left-hemisphere dominance was found only for idiomatically related word pairs, whereas the right hemisphere capabilities matched those of the left in categorically and metaphorically related word pairs. These results support the notions that the idioms are treated as single lexical entries and that the right hemisphere is involved in processing metaphors as well as in processing general semantic relations. However, Rapp, Leube, Erb, Grodd, and Kircher (2004) did not find support for greater right-hemisphere involvement in processing metaphoric language: their fMRI study revealed greater left-hemisphere changes during reading metaphors. They suggest that previous results indicating right-hemisphere dominance in processing metaphors might reflect understanding of complex sentences.

Another interesting dissociation was reported by Kemmerer (2005). In addition to identifying the anterior left temporal lobe as being critical for proper nouns and the left inferior prefrontal/premotor region for verbs, he found that the same preposition is processed differently when it is used in the temporal sense than when used in a spatial context (*at 5 o'clock* vs. *at school*): patients with lesions in the supramarginal gyrus (involved in spatial processing) had problems with the latter meaning, but not with the former, whereas one patient with intact supramarginal gyrus had no such difficulties.

SENTENCE LEVEL: SEMANTICS AND SYNTAX

At the sentence level, right-ear advantage was found for nonsense words that have the morphological structure of meaningful English words (syntactically correct and presented with the correct intonation and stress; Bradshaw & Nettleton, 1983). Frackowiak (1994) found (by MRI) several foci of activity in the inferior temporal and parietal lobes and in the superior frontal lobe in his subjects while they were performing a semantic processing task.

Friederici, Pfeifer, and Hahne (1993) established (by ERP) that morphological, semantic and syntactic processes are separate not only along the temporal dimension, but also that these elements of language function are processed in different systems. Hagoort and Brown (1995) concluded that there are separate mechanisms for semantic and syntactic processing in the brain. Semantically unacceptable sentences produced a negative potential (N400) that was bilaterally distributed and the most prominent in posterior regions, whereas syntactically unacceptable sentences enhanced the negative response earlier (N125), in left anterior regions and elicited a negative response (N300–500) in the left temporal and parietal lobes. They also found that these effects occurred regardless of testing modality, in other words, whether the subjects read or heard the test sentences. The difference is that these effects start occurring earlier when the subjects read sentences. Holcomb and Anderson (1993) also found a common semantic system independent of modality. On the basis of their fMRI study of cortical organization of audiovisual sentence comprehension, Capek et al. (2004) also suggest that the left hemisphere may be biased to process language independently of the modality through which it is perceived. Constable et al. (2004) found some modality-specific sites (such as primary auditory cortex and superior temporal gyrus bilaterally for auditory modality, and several posterior sites, including the angular gyrus, supramarginal gyrus, and the fusiform gyrus in the left hemisphere for printed sentences) and some modality-independent regions (inferior frontal gyrus). Hagoort and Brown's results (1995) suggest that the same technique may be used to obtain effects sensitive to early phonological processing, which was addressed earlier by Molfese (1980). Similar results were reported by Neville et al. (as cited in Fromkin, 1995).

Benraiss, Haveman, Liegeois-Chauvel, and Besson (2000) found (by ERP) that words out of context elicit higher N400 amplitudes than the ones that are context-related, and that test words elicit smaller N400 waves if the preceding sentence was ambiguous.

Dien, Frishkoff, and Tucker (2000) used the same method to study the N3 component—negative polarity occurring before the most frequently mentioned N400 wave, which is also associated with semantic processing. On a large sample of subjects (78 students) they recorded electric brain activity while sentences were presented visually one word at a time, in which the last word varied with respect to the probability of occurrence and appropriateness within the given sentence context. They found that N3 was equally sensitive to the probability of occurrence and appropriateness of the test word, whereas N4 was more sensitive to appropriateness than to probability of occurrence, and it depended on word familiarity.

On semantic tasks in which the subjects are required to make a lexical decision (about word meaning), ERP studies revealed increased electrical brain activity about 400 ms after stimulus onset. This wave is usually called the N400 (occasionally N4), due to its negative polarity. Its amplitude is higher if test words are not in harmony with the preceding context, and the amplitude difference is called the N400 effect. In other words, this N400 effect reflects the level of lexical integration. In an identical experiment (where sentences were presented one word at a time on a computer screen) carried out by Kutas and Hillyard (as cited in Gazzaniga et al., 2002), words that were semantically related to the preceding context, but spelled in larger print, generated positivity. Other nonsemantic deviations did not elicit the N400 wave and it is therefore believed to be a feature of semantic processing. Moreover, it was found that it does depend on stimulus modality and that it occurs in different languages, including sign language used by congenitally deaf individuals. Frishkoff, Tucker, Davey, and Scherg (2004) and Palolahti, Leino, Jokela, Kopra, and Paavilainen (2005) reported on the basis of their ERP studies of sentence comprehension that left hemisphere activity preceded right hemisphere activity.

Lexical integration includes semantic and syntactic characteristics of the recognized word into the representation of the entire sentence or utterance and grasping of its sense in this wider context. Response-time measurements applied to the process of looking for a meaningful word within a nonsensical sentence have shown that syntactic analysis proceeds independently of semantics—response times are shorter if words are incorporated within a grammatical sentence than if they are embedded in an ungrammatical sentence (the differences are about 45 ms). This is explained by the concurrent activation of the word forms (lexemes) and their lemmas that contain information about syntactic properties of the words and their possible combinations (e.g., whether they are nouns or verbs; if they are verbs, whether they are transitive or intransitive, etc.). Each new word is defined in terms of its syntactic structure (parsing), and it is incorporated into an appropriate slot in the existing sentence.

Certain interpretations of sentences are preferred to others, which means that each sentence will be interpreted in a certain (preferred) way, and only if that interpretation proves to be incorrect, will it be changed. This approach of preferred interpretation satisfies the requirements of fast processing and it is based on two mechanisms: (a) the simplest possible structure (as few as possible syntactic nodes, i.e., minimally branching hierarchical tree); and (b) association of each upcoming word with the phrase that is being processed at the moment. If we adhere to these to mechanisms we take the path of least resistance. This is known as the *garden path approach*. Errors in interpretation can be corrected only when the entire semantic information becomes available (i.e., when we reach the end of the path). This is basically a modular model because syntactic analysis proceeds independently, and it does not predict a situation in which we can interpret the sentence differently based on what we know about individual words (e.g., their common combinations) even before we reach its end. According to more interactive models, other pieces of information, such as world knowledge or semantic information about a word, may keep one from taking the wrong path during processing. ERP studies support interactive models as being more similar to the actual language functioning. Namely, it was found that conceptual knowledge about the temporal sequence of events has considerable impact on sentence processing from its beginning (Gazzaniga et al., 2002).

Thierry, Cardebat, and Demonet (2000) found (by ERP) that syntactic analysis is incorporated into semantic processing. They demonstrated that semantic processing starts before (in their example before gender information) and lasts approximately 32 ms longer than syntactic processing. These results speak in favor of more-or-less independent and concurrent syntactic and semantic processing. The authors also conclude that perception of a word might be physiologically connected with its production (see chap. 1, this volume, for more detail).

Kuperberg et al. (2000) recorded (by fMRI) differences in activation during listening to sentences in which the last word was either semantically or syntactically incorrect, and concluded that the activity within the same neural network is different for semantic and syntactic data. In their 14 healthy subjects they recorded higher activation in semantically incorrect sentences than in syntactically anomalous ones in the left superior and middle temporal gyrus (Brodmann's areas 21 and 22) which corresponds to Wernicke's area, and in the inferior frontal gyrus (Brodmann's areas 47, 10, and 11). On the other hand, in the superior and inferior parietal gyrus, particularly in the right hemisphere, they recorded higher activation for syntactically incorrect sentences than for the semantically anomalous ones.

Friederici, Pfeifer, and Hahne (1999) compared (by means of ERP) subjects' reactions to the sentences in which the last verb was incongruent with the text in terms of semantics, syntax, or both. They found the N400 wave, characteristic of semantic processing, only in cases of exclusively semantic incongruity. When the incongruity was syntactic or semantic–syntactic, only the positive P600 was recorded. Besides, in both variants of semantic incongruity (exclusively semantic and syntactic–semantic) an additional late negativity around 700 ms after stimulus onset was found, which in examples of syntactic–semantic incongruity corresponded to the P600. The authors interpreted the absence of N400 in semantic-syntactic incongruity as the early effect of sentence structure information on the lexico-semantic integration.

Hagoort and Brown (2000a) studied (by means of ERP) the differences in processing syntactically anomalous sentences presented visually and auditorily.

In both modalities, 500 ms after onset of the word that eventually made the sentence incorrect the so-called syntactic positive shift (SPS) was recorded, which was manifested as positivity (P600). This shift consisted of two phases: early—approximately evenly distributed over anterior and posterior regions, and late—more noticeable posteriorly. According to the authors, the early phase corresponds to the complexity of structural integration, and the late phase reflects unsuccessful parsing and an attempt at repeated analysis. In some syntactic anomalies an early negativity was recorded over the left frontal lobe. By applying the same method to the comparison of semantic anomalies in the same two modalities (i.e., during reading and listening) the same authors (Hagoort & Brown, 2000b) found the N400 wave, with additional early negativity at 250 ms in the auditory modality. They explained this early negativity as a consequence of incongruity between word forms expected on the basis of context and the actual cohort of activated candidates that was generated on the basis of the speech signal.

The P600 wave (SPS), generally distributed over the parietal lobes and associated with syntactic anomalies regardless of modality (Hagoort & Brown, 1995; Hagoort & Kutas, 1995) has been found during reading syntactically correct sentences that at some point require revision of the initial (preferred) interpretation (see the so-called garden path sentences discussed previously).

Since the number of possible combinations (i.e., sentences that may be uttered or written) is limitless, it is quite obvious that there are no ready-made sentence representations, with the exception of idioms (Taylor, Meier, Brugger, & Weniger, 2002), and most probably proverbs, sayings, frequent quotations, and the like. However, the consequences of brain damage and neuroimaging studies of healthy subjects suggest that production or comprehension of sentence structure has neural substrates. For example, agrammatic aphasia, which may be manifested as Broca's aphasia with characteristic telegraphic speech, or as difficulties in understanding complex grammatical structures, may occur due to lesions in the area corresponding to Broca's center, but also in other areas of the left hemisphere as well. Caplan et al. (as cited in Gazzaniga et al., 2002) found (by means PET) increased activation in the general area of Broca's center during perception of complex syntactic structures. This activity in Broca's center was found in tasks that were not exclusively syntactic, but involved memorization, storage, and recall of word lists. It is, therefore, possible that Broca's area is important for working memory rather than for syntax (Gazzaniga et al., 2002). Except in Broca's area, activity elicited by syntactic tasks was recorded in the superior temporal gyrus, near Brodmann's area 22, and this area was shown to play an important role in aphasics as well. Some other authors, using similar tasks, found activation in Wernicke's center as well, but also in the homotopic areas of the right hemisphere.

Friederici, Wang, Hermann, Maess, and Oertel (2000) studied (by means of MEG) brain activity during assessment of syntactic correctness of acoustically presented sentences. Their results show that temporal regions, probably the *planum polare* and the fronto-lateral regions, are activated during early syntactic processing. Activation is bilateral, but it was found to be higher in the left than in the right hemisphere in four of their five subjects. The contribution of the temporal regions seems to be greater than that of the fronto-lateral ones.

The brain responds to the subject–predicate gender incongruity several hundred milliseconds after its onset. Demestre, Meltzer, Garcia-Albea, and Vigil (1999) recorded evoked potentials during auditory comprehension of grammatical and ungrammatical Spanish sentences, and found early negativity over anterior and central points, which was followed by positivity at central-parietal points when the sentences were ungrammatical.

Syntactic processing elicits early activity that, with respect to its polarity and latency, corresponds to the semantic N400 wave, but occurs at another location. As opposed to the N400 wave, this activity is recorded in frontal regions of the left hemisphere, due to which it was named left anterior negativity (LAN), or early left anterior negativity (ELAN). The activity was recorded during incorrect use of word types within a sentence (e.g., if an adjective is followed by a verb instead of a noun) and during morphosyntactic errors (e.g., use of an inappropriate suffix resulting in subject–predicate number incongruity; Gazzaniga et al., 2002).

Friederici et al. (1999) and Hahne and Friederici (1999) established that LAN reflects early, highly automatic activity (first parsing) and belongs to the process of determining sentence structure, whereas late positivity (P600) in parietal lobes reflects parsing that is under the subject's control (second parsing), and is associated with syntactic integration. Friederici and coworkers (Wang et al., 2000a) went on to study (by means of MEG) parts of the brain that are the most active during syntactic processes and which elicit this ELAN. Of their five healthy subjects, clear left-hemisphere dominance was found in all three male subjects and in one of the two female subjects. In the other female subject they found right-hemisphere lateralization (in spite of her right-handedness). Syntactic processes elicited increased activation in the *planum polare* in the temporal operculum and somewhat lower activation in the fronto-lateral regions in both hemispheres (Gazzaniga et al., 2002).

Knoesche, Maess, and Friederici (1999) studied (by means of MEG) activation in different brain areas during auditory presentation of syntactically correct and syntactically anomalous German sentences. Activity in the first 600 ms after syntactic error onset was the highest in the temporal lobe and in neighboring frontal and parietal areas of both hemispheres, with the statistically significant differences (compared with correct sentences) recorded in the frontal and temporal lobes. For latencies longer than 250 ms differences in activity were larger in the right hemisphere. The authors concluded that the asymmetrically increased activity in the right hemisphere, recorded during presentation of syntactically anomalous sentences, is the result of correction and reanalysis that go on in the right hemisphere leaving the left free to process subsequent stimuli.

Gutbrod et al. (2000) found (by means of fMRI) that syntactic processing elicits the greatest activity in the inferior frontal gyrus (i.e., in the dorsal part of Broca's area) and in the parieto-temporal regions of the left hemisphere.

During syntactic processing, Mayer et al. (2000) recorded (by means of fMRI) considerable activation of the traditional language areas in the left hemisphere (Wernicke's and Broca's), in the cerebellum, as well as bilateral activation in the dorso-lateral prefrontal cortex and anterior cingulate. Other authors before them had already suggested that the cerebellum might play a central role in the organization of speech and cognitive processes (Schmahmann, 1997; Ackermann & Hertrich, 2000; as cited in Mayer et al., 2000). Within the predominantly left-hemisphere activity during syntax generation at a sentence level, Haller, Radue, Erb, Grodd, and Kircher (2005) found (by means of event-related fMRI) significantly stronger left-dominant activation in Brodmann's area 45 compared to Brodmann's area 44. The dorso-lateral and the prefrontal cortex as well as the anterior cingulate gyrus are believed to be important areas within the entire network of grammatical encoding and verbal short-term memory (Deacon, as cited in Mayer et al., 2000).

Syntactic processing has traditionally been considered the most markedly left-lateralized language function. However, sentence comprehension may activate additional cortical regions that process not specifically linguistic information (Just, Newman, Keller, McEleney, & Carpenter, 2004). Difficulties in understanding complex syntactic structures in patients with right-hemisphere damage are most frequently explained by problems associated with activation and maintenance of attention that needs to be sustained for a longer time during processing of such complex structures.

DISCOURSE AND PRAGMATICS

Caplan, Dapretto, and Mazziotta (2000) have shown in fMRI studies of healthy subjects that different neural networks are involved in different aspects of discourse coherence. Logic is controlled by the left hemisphere, primarily by the middle and superior temporal gyrus, but also by the inferior frontal gyrus and anterior cingulate. A particularly high activation was recorded when the responses were illogical, whereas in logical ones it was somewhat more evenly distributed in both hemispheres. On the other hand, maintaining the topic of conversation is controlled by the right hemisphere, primarily by the inferior frontal gyrus, superior temporal gyrus, and the cerebellum. Responses that deviated from the topic increasingly activated precisely these areas. These results confirmed earlier observations of brain-injured patients. Faust, Barak, and Chiarello (2005) also found that the right hemisphere contributes to discourse comprehension by maintaining widespread meaning activation over an extended period of time, thus monitoring the coherence. Xu, Kemeny, Park, Frattali, and Braun (2005) found the right hemisphere to be increasingly active as contextual complexity increased.

Right hemisphere–damaged patients may have good language competence, but many of them have difficulties in extralinguistic forms of communication, which are very important in discourse. The problems may include insensitivity to cues that indicate communication context, speakers' intentions, and nuances in between-the-lines meanings. They manage to remember facts from the story they had just heard, but cannot connect the facts into a whole that would make the punch line. When these patients are asked to infer about what a picture they are viewing represents, they will describe the minutest details but will not be able to incorporate that description into a correct conclusion about the actual situation. Inference involves several (most frequently simultaneous) processes: noticing the details, selection of relevant details, connecting the relevant details with each other, and their association with previous experience and knowledge of the world. Right-hemisphere patients cannot distinguish relevant from irrelevant details, nor can they combine the observed details into a common macrostructure. The deficit is also noticeable when they are in the role of the speaker—they dwell too much on details and are incapable of conveying the main idea.

Right hemisphere–damaged patients have problems with alternate meanings of the word within discourse. This lack of flexibility prevents them from correctly resolving ambiguities and/or adjusting their initial attitudes and hypotheses. The problem may not necessarily be caused by the inability to activate alternate meanings (which is one of the important abilities of the intact right hemisphere), but also by the inability to suppress inappropriate meanings. It has been shown that healthy and brain-damaged subjects are capable of activating approximately equal numbers of alternate meanings. The difference was in the fact that after a time, the right hemisphere–damaged patients still kept all the activated meanings in their working memory, whereas the healthy subjects had suppressed the inappropriate ones (Tompkins, Lehman, Baumgaertner, Fossett, & Vance, 1996). This inability to suppress the unnecessary and/or inappropriate meanings may be manifested as too much reliance on the literal meaning of the idioms, inefficient discourse production, and rigidity in its production and perception, all of which has been found in the patient population. Grindrod and Baum (2003) found that both left- and right-hemisphere damage cause deficits in using local contextual information in the process of ambiguity resolution, but in different manners. Finally, be it slower activation or slower suppression, the result is little or no ability of right hemisphere–damaged patients to understand and use contextually appropriate meaning of a given concept during discourse.

Myers (1999) summarized discourse-level problems in patients with right-hemisphere damage with respect to discourse comprehension and discourse production. The most frequent discourse comprehension deficits are manifested as reduced sensitivity — to the gist of the narratives (regardless of modality of presentation); to intended and/or implied meanings; to new information, accompanied by the incapability of modifying one's approach; to emotional content, including sarcasm, irony, humor; to extra/paralinguistic information; to common knowledge; to conversational rules and conventions, and so forth. Discourse production deficits are manifested as impaired ability to produce macrostructure; reduced specificity, flexibility, and capacity to generate alternate meanings; and reduced use of conversational rules and conventions, etc. Coulson and Wu (2005) found (by a combination of priming and ERP) that the right hemisphere was more involved in processing joke-relevant information whereas the left hemisphere was more active during controlled retrieval in language comprehension.

If these difficulties occurred in all patients with right-hemisphere damage, without exception and to the same extent, it could be concluded that the right hemisphere is the seat of all these functions. However, not all right-hemisphere patients have problems with discourse, and among those who do, not all situations are equally problematic. When information is redundant or explicit, the problems will be less obvious. The deficits will emerge in more complex contexts, which makes it difficult to decide whether the disorders are caused by problems in sustaining or controlling attention or in specific cognitive deficits. On the other hand, discourse-level problems may occur in patients suffering from left prefrontal area damage or in those suffering from bilateral injuries to the same area, as well as in persons with damaged posterior cerebral areas. Obviously, the right hemisphere is more diffusely and less precisely organized than the left, and different right-hemisphere lesions may result in similar disorders, by the very fact that they affect larger, better interconnected, and less focally organized operational systems.

The most reliable correlation was found between diminished cognitive abilities and neglect; in other words, the degree of neglect seems to be the best predictor of how disordered cognitive functioning can be. This correlation is explained by the fact that neglect reflects reduced accessibility or impaired allocation of mental resources, which actually underlies the problems in solving more complex cognitive tasks, including the ones related to discourse. These patients have at their disposal fewer resources necessary for activation and maintenance (but apparently, for suppression as well—see previous discussion) of alternate meanings, disambiguation, revision of initial hypotheses, and generating secondary meanings required for conveying nonliteral meanings.

Kuperberg et al. (2000) used fMRI on healthy subjects to study neural activity during listening to correct spoken sentences and compared it with the activity recorded during listening to sentences that were pragmatically, semantically, or syntactically anomalous. All three contrasts revealed robust activation in the left inferior temporal and fusiform gyrus.

Kasher, Batori, Soroker, Graves, and Zaidel (1999) applied neuropsychological tests to individuals with left- and right-hemisphere injury and found that the elements of Grice's cooperative principle in communication (which is a part of his theory of conversational implicatures)—maxims of quality, quantity, relevance, and manner—are controlled by central processes rather than by separate modular systems, since no specific location that might be associated with implicatures was found.

Crinion and Price (2005) investigated (by means of fMRI) narrative speech activation in left-hemisphere stroke patients and normal controls. Their results support the role of the right temporal lobe in processing narrative speech and auditory sentence comprehension following left hemisphere aphasic stroke.

READING

Studies using PET and fMRI techniques have shown that written language relies on the same neural substrate at its input level as other visual stimuli. In other words, the first steps in visual processing of words will be identical to those in processing any other form; words will be analyzed one feature at a time (curvature and slant of the lines, etc.). Letters are recognized in the occipito-temporal regions of the left hemisphere, which is manifested as a large negative polarity occurring approximately 200 ms after beginning of presentation of a letter sequence (N200), but not during presentation of nonletters or faces. This area was activated regardless of the lexico-semantic characteristics of the words. Additional evidence in support of this is the fact that injury to this area caused the so-called *pure alexia* (i.e., a disorder characterized by the inability to read words) with otherwise intact language and visual nonlanguage functions (Gazzaniga et al., 2002).

When the task involves looking at two letters and deciding whether they are equal or different in appearance, phonetically or with respect to the category they belong to, the responses are faster if the letters are physically identical (AA) than when they are phonetically identical (Aa), and response times are the longest when they belong to the same category (vowels or consonants). The responses are considerably slower within the category of consonants than within the category of vowels. From these results Posner (1993) concluded that every, even the simplest, stimulus elicits several representations and that response time reveals order and/or amount of processing during activation. With letters as stimuli, physical representation is activated first, followed by phonetic, and finally by categorical.

Yamamoto, Kashikura, Kershaw, and Kanno (2000) asked their subjects to imagine capital letters A through J, and all the while they recorded their brain activity by means of fMRI. In all subjects, they found bilateral activation in premotor areas and the supplementary motor area, as well as in the posterior parietal lobe and in the cerebellum. Interestingly, they did not find activation of the primary visual area in all subjects, but only in three out of six. In the other three subjects the fusiform gyrus activity was recorded. On the basis of these results the authors proposed the possibility of two types of visual mental images, each with its neural substrate. Gutbrod et al. (2000) found by fMRI that letter naming activates the lateral part of the extrastriate occipital lobe and the posterior part of the temporal region in the left hemisphere, as well as the inferior frontal gyrus. This left extrastriate region reflects the basic visual processing of letters, whereas the posterior part of the temporal lobe is obviously the neural substrate of the orthographic aspect of the lexicon, containing all visual word forms. They proposed that the inferior parietal lobe plays a role in letter-to-phoneme mapping.

There is experimental evidence that letters are recognized more successfully (higher correct scores, shorter response times, higher certainty) if they are parts of meaningful words than if they are incorporated into a meaningless word or presented in isolation. This is referred to as the *word superiority effect*. This effect speaks in favor of the influence of higher levels on the lower ones and supports McClelland and Rumelhart's hypothesis (as cited in Gazzaniga et al., 2002) that word information present at higher levels can activate or inhibit activation of individual letters, and that words are most probably not perceived one letter at a time. But how and where are written words perceived?

Magnetic resonance and other neuroimaging methods have shown that patients suffering from reading disorders (alexia) typically have damage in the left hemisphere, in the area of the angular gyrus in the posterior parietal region (Eysenck & Keane, 2000).

Khateb et al. (1999) found (by ERP) that during reading, semantic and phonological processes activate identical general areas—in the left posterior temporal and anterior temporal region. Activation of the posterior region starts as early as 100 ms after stimulus onset, with the differences between the two types of processing emerging briefly between 280 and 380 ms after stimulus onset. After that the activated areas are the same, regardless of the type of processing. The authors concluded that the two processes overlap temporally and spatially during reading, and that the differences are to be attributed to later decision-making procedures.

Increasing word length increases the activity in the lingual and the fusiform gyrus (the two gyri at the junction of the occipital and temporal lobes), whereas the increase in visual contrast (i.e., separation of the figure from the background) increases activation in the fusiform gyrus and decreases activity in the lingual gyrus. This is explained by the differences between global and local processing. Word length increases the requirement for processing global forms. These results imply that the fusiform gyrus is responsible for local processing and the lingual gyrus for global (Mechelli, Humphreys, Mayall, Olson, & Price, 2000).

Eden, Brown, Jones, Given, and Zeffiro (2000) compared cerebral activation during phonological processing between good and poor readers. In good readers they recorded greater bilateral activation at the junction of the occipital and temporal lobes (Brodmann's area 37) than in poor readers. Comparable differences were recorded during visual processing of movements as well. In poor readers, processing of visually presented movements was associated with the activity in language regions: in the angular gyrus and the inferior frontal gyrus. This suggests that poor readers use these regions as compensatory mechanisms during reading. Based on a high correlation between success of letter recognition and activation of brain areas that belong to the speech sensorimotor system (areas deep within both central sulci; left supplementary motor area—Brodmann's area 6; right cerebellar hemisphere; motor areas of the right cingulate gyrus—Brodmann's areas 31/6; and the right inferior temporal lobe—Brodmann's areas 20/37), the same group of authors (Zeffiro, Eden, Jones, & Brown, 2000) concluded that reading probably depends on normal functioning of the system for motor control of articulation that is required for successful mapping of visual and auditory representations onto articulatory gestures.

Booth et al. (2000) used fMRI to study differences in activation of different brain areas in five children and four adults during various reading tasks. In both groups, similar neural networks were activated, which included extrastriate and fusiform areas in both hemispheres, as well as the traditional language areas in the left hemisphere (Wernicke's and Broca's). However, in adults they found greater activation in the bilateral fusiform gyri, and in children the activity was greater in Wernicke's area, in the superior parietal lobe, and in the cerebellum. These obviously developmental differences support the hypothesis that adults process words automatically in the fusiform gyrus, whereas children rely on attention (controlled by the superior parietal lobe) to integrate visual and language patterns in Wernicke's area.

WRITING

The process of writing proceeds through several stages: planning, sentence generation, and revision (usually in that order). On average, the planning stage takes about 30% of the time, sentence generation about 50%, and the revision stage the remaining 20%. More knowledgeable individuals write with less effort, but not necessarily better than those with less knowledge. Good writers use longer sentences (on average 11.2 words), or longer segments, than average writers (7.3 words). Skillful writers spend more time on text revision than average or poor writers, and their interventions are related to content rather than to individual words or phrases (Hayes & Flower, as cited in Eysenck & Keane, 2000).

Despite the importance of the planning and revision stages, the sentence generation stage has been the most extensively studied. Many authors agree that writing depends on internal speech to a great extent. This means that writers actually produce the words before they write them down. According to this hypothesis, writing would rely on the same neural structures that are involved in speech, in addition to those that are related to the actual motor activity associated with writing. Evidence can readily be found in healthy subjects who write orthographically incorrectly, but whose spelling reflects pronunciation (Levinthal & Hornung, 1992). Such examples are more easily found in languages with a low degree of grapheme-to-phoneme correspondence (e.g., English) than in those in which pronunciation and spelling are more similar (e.g., Croatian). Evidence from brain-damaged patients is contradictory. In some aphasics, in addition to speech, writing is completely or partially impaired as well; in others, writing is intact despite the practically nonexistent vocal and internal speech. Writing is most frequently impaired in persons suffering from jargon aphasia. Inability to auditorily process input stimuli is manifested, among other symptoms, as highly disordered writing, especially to dictation. Automatic writing, such as signing one's own name is usually preserved (Luria, 1976; Eysenck & Keane, 2000). All this points to the importance of the left hemisphere in writing. Gazzaniga (2000), however, reported cases of two split-brain patients whose right hemispheres could also partially control writing several months after surgery. In any case, many injuries to the language areas, and those associated with them, will result in some writing difficulties, due to the fact that the entire system responsible for writing is very complex and damage to any element may cause problems (Obler & Gjerlow, 1999). Henderson et al. (as cited in Obler & Gjerlow, 1999) reported on writing deficits in Alzheimer's patients: their phoneme-to-grapheme matching ability (the language studied was English) remained intact longer than memory for words that are spelled irregularly and whose graphic form has to be learned and cannot be deduced from pronunciation. Their spelling errors reveal this difference (spelling *floor* as *flore*). Writing disorders—agraphia and dysgraphia—are discussed at the end of this chapter.

Ellis and Young (as cited in Eysenck & Keane, 2000) propose that, similar to reading, writing can be accomplished in two ways. Writing of familiar words relies on the part of the word store (lexicon) that contains data about written forms of familiar words. They call it the *graphemic output lexicon*. Access to this part of the lexicon is possible through the semantic system (which contains word meanings) or through the phonological system (which contains spoken word forms), which they refer to as the *phonological output lexicon*. In healthy individuals both routes are accessible and open. Writing of unfamiliar and meaningless words may, obviously, be accomplished only through a direct phoneme–grapheme association because these words do not exist in the semantic system. Taken together, reading and writing assume four parts of the lexicon: visual and auditory input (that are used during reading) and phonological and graphemic output (that are used during writing).

CALCULATION

Xu, Yamaguchi, Kobayashi, Yamashita, and Takahashi (2000) used fMRI to study brain activity during addition and subtraction in healthy right-handers. They tested the earlier neuroimaging results that suggested the left inferior parietal lobe is involved with solving mathematical problems. Their data reveal great intersubject variability with respect to particularly active regions. All the subjects had in common considerable activity in the left cerebral hemisphere, particularly in the parietal lobe (Brodmann's areas 7 and 40) and in the prefrontal cortex (Brodmann's areas 6 and 8), as well as in the right cerebellar hemisphere. In some subjects, activity was recorded in homotopic areas of the right hemisphere and the left temporal lobe (Brodmann's areas 21, 22 and 37). Differences between subtraction and addition were manifested primarily as lower intensity of activation in these areas (especially in the parietal regions). In other words, activity was recorded in fewer subjects during addition (particularly in the prefrontal regions and the cerebellum). This smaller degree of activity during addition than during subtraction may be explained by the fact that addition is obviously easier than subtraction and accordingly, requires fewer resources. Response time measurements during arithmetic operations (Mildner, 2001) did not reveal significant functional cerebral asymmetry, but there was a trend toward left lateralization (laterality index equaled 5.66). Judging by response time values, of the four basic arithmetic operations, addition was the easiest, followed by multiplication and division, with subtraction being the most difficult.

Varley, Klessinger, Romanowski, and Siegal (2005) offer evidence that numerical reasoning and language are functionally and neuroanatomically independent in adult humans. They tested three aphasic patients suffering from diffuse brain damage to the perisylvian language area, who were incapable of understanding or producing grammatically correct language, with mathematical problems that required procedures computationally equivalent to the linguistic grammatical problems (e.g., embedding). All three patients were successful at the mathematical tasks. The results shed new light on many hypotheses and theories addressing the relationship between language and thought, and among various faculties (Marsh & Maki, 1976). They are also evidence in support of modularity of the human mind.

IS SPEECH SPECIAL?

Some of the studies of differences in functional cerebral asymmetry for various types of stimuli propose two basic groups of hypotheses: those that focus on stimuli (cue-dependent) and those that focus on tasks (task-dependent). According to the first group, the left hemisphere is dominant for complex auditory stimuli, language/speech, and nonlanguage alike. According to the second group, there are specific neural mechanisms that are activated exclusively by speech or speech-related tasks. Obviously, the decades-long discussion on whether speech is special was expanded to include the realm of functional cerebral asymmetry.

Kimura (1973a, 1975, 1979) proposed that, in spite of speech being the best known and most highly lateralized ability of the human left hemisphere, it does not mean that the left hemisphere is specialized for speech as such. Rather, it is specialized for control of fine motor movements of which speech is only one, albeit exceptionally important, example. Kimura offered two major pieces of evidence in support of her theory. First, left-hemisphere injuries selectively impair voluntary oral movements, be they speech related or not. Second, the degree of impairment of voluntary nonspeech facial movements caused by left-hemisphere injuries is in high positive correlation with the severity of aphasia resulting from them. She also showed (Kimura, 1973c) that a greater degree of bilateral representation of speech characteristic of left-handers is accompanied by more gesturing with both hands, as opposed to the right-handers who gesticulate less and mainly with the right hand. Kimura believes that verbal communication developed from communication that used to be carried out primarily by means of gestures with a few vocal components into one that is primarily vocal with some gestural components. This view has been recently supported by the mirror-neuron studies (Rizzolatti & Arbib, 1998; Rizzolatti & Craighero, 2004).

Basili, Diggs, and Rao (1980) also showed that right-hemisphere contribution to speech perception should not be underestimated. They, too, found that speech-like stimuli (backward speech, incomprehensible babble, etc.), albeit unintelligible, is analyzed primarily in the same hemisphere (i.e., left) as the comprehensible speech stimulus.

Advocates of the theory that speech perception is not a special kind of perception but that all aspects of speech that used to be thought specific are present in music as well, propose that speech analysis in the left hemisphere is only a part of the much wider system for segmenting sequential acoustic input (Bradshaw & Nettleton, 1983).

Eulitz, Eulitz, and Elbert (1999) found, by means of MEG and EEG, neuroanatomic differences between verbal and nonverbal tasks, but they were not systematic or consistent enough to allow precise determination of the structures that were predominantly active in one or the other type of tasks.

Many studies have shown right-hemisphere dominance for singing (Epstein, as cited in Riecker, Ackermann, Wildgruber, & Grodd, 2000). Dronkers (1996) reported that anterior insula was the only structure active in singing and speech. Riecker et al. (2000) used fMRI to study the differences in the activation of anterior insula while listing months of the year (automatic speech) and "singing" Mozart's *Ein kleines Nachtmusik* using just the syllable *la*. Their results reveal opposite lateralization of automatic speech (left anterior insula) and singing (right anterior insula). The authors concluded that insula is important for temporal organization in general, which is manifested as timing of speech segments or as temporal organization of melodic sequences.

Even very young babies (one month) are capable of distinguishing sound categories (e.g., /p/ vs. /b/; Dehaene-Lambertz & Baillet, 1998; Molfese, Fonaryova Key, Maguire, Dove, & Molfese, 2005). Although such results used to be taken as evidence of innate speech ability for perceptual phoneme categorization, it was found that children are just as good at distinguishing among nonspeech sounds, but also that this capacity was characteristic of other mammals as well. By their sixth month of life, babies learn to categorize not just sounds of their mother tongue, but also normalize across different speakers, sound contexts, and prosodic features. Cross-linguistic studies of speech acquisition revealed that children exhibit selective sensitivity to their mother's voice and to the sounds of their mother tongue, which implies the influence of prenatal auditory experience (review in Kuhl, 2004).

Shtyrov et al. (2000a, 2000b) looked (by MEG) for a possible neural mechanism that would be speech-specific. The stimuli they used were speech (irregular alternating syllables /ka/ and /pa/) and nonspeech, with speech-like complex rapid and slow acoustic changes. They observed MMN patterns. In all test conditions, the negativity corresponded to the activity in the auditory cortex, but its distribution was different on two kinds of tasks. For syllables it was significantly greater in the left than in the right hemisphere, whereas for rapid complex nonspeech sounds there were no interhemispheric differences. On the other hand, when the stimuli were slow complex nonspeech stimuli, a significantly higher activity was recorded in the right than in the left hemisphere. This would suggest that the left hemisphere is not dominant for all acoustic changes (as proposed by some authors; Bradshaw & Nettleton, 1983). Rather, it would imply the existence of a speech-specific mechanism, or representation, and something like a long-term acoustic memory for speech sounds lateralized to the left hemisphere, which develops on the basis of previous experience. The differences in representations of rapid and slow nonspeech changes are comparable with the hypotheses of Ivry and Robertson (1999) about left-hemisphere dominance for high-frequency (i.e., fast) changes, and right-hemisphere dominance for low-frequency (i.e., slow) changes.

Boulanouar et al. (2000) found (by fMRI) that listening to tones increases activation of the left superior temporal gyrus, whereas listening to phonological changes activates the left supramarginal gyrus.

Binder et al. (as cited in Gazzaniga et al., 2002) compared activity in different brain areas during listening to noise, frequency-modulated tones, and speech sounds (backward speech, nonsense words, meaningful words). Compared with noise, frequency-modulated tones elicited greater bilateral activation in posterior parts of the superior temporal sulci. Compared with tones, speech sounds activated more ventrolateral areas—in the superior temporal sulcus and around it. The fact that no differences in activation were recorded between words and nonwords lead them to the conclusion that these areas are probably not the seat of lexico-semantic levels of word processing. Other studies have also shown that the areas involved in processing of lexico-semantic data are located more in the left hemisphere and that they are positioned more ventrally than the areas that are active during speech perception in general.

Horwitz, Jeffries, and Braun (2000) used PET to study the connections of speech areas with the neighboring nonspeech motor and auditory regions. Their 20 healthy right-handers were presented with four tasks: (a) tell about an easily imageable event; (b) generate nonsense syllables and phonemes of complex intonation contours; (c) recite the lyrics of a familiar song; and (d) generate nonlanguage sounds with their articulators (larynx and mouth articulators). The closest and the widest functional connections among several areas were found in task (a)—during storytelling. Broca's area (Brodmann's area 44, i.e., 6 and 45) was connected with Wernicke's area (Brodmann's areas 22 and 39), with the inferior parietal lobe (Brodmann's area 40), with the middle and inferior temporal lobe (Brodmann's areas 21 and 20), and with the visual areas in the occipital lobe (Brodmann's areas 18 and 19). Most of these functional connections were not found in conditions (b) or (d). The activity recorded in the left middle and inferior temporal lobe during storytelling is attributed to the stored semantic representations. These results point to a marked interaction within the left perisylvian regions during spontaneous speech production, but not on tasks that require similar but nonspeech muscle movements and vocalizations. During automatic speech—test condition (c)—functional connections were weaker. Although some of the observed regions were activated during nonlanguage tasks, the authors believe that functional connections, rather than selective activation of particular areas, are indicative of brain areas that are crucial for language.

Weniger, Crelier, Alkadhi, and Kollias (2000) compared brain activity (by means of fMRI) during visually presented language and nonlanguage tasks. They found that the language task, as opposed to the nonlanguage one, activated several areas of the dominant (left) hemisphere in healthy subjects, regardless of gender: the middle and inferior frontal gyrus, the superior parietal lobe, the middle temporal lobe, and the precuneus. Bilateral activation was found in the lingual and fusiform gyri (two small gyri at the medial and inferior surface of the occipital-temporal lobe junction).

Gros et al. (2000) studied the influence of language context on phoneme and grapheme processing and recorded brain activity by means of fMRI. The stimulus was the form O that could be perceived as a circle or a letter. Activation was recorded only in the left hemisphere (Brodmann's area 37) irrespective of whether the stimulus was presented in the context of other forms (nonlanguage) or other letters (language). Compared with the language context, the nonlanguage one elicited an even higher signal amplitude and a larger activated surface than other forms, such as the nonlanguage signal that evoked bilateral activation in occipito-temporal regions (Brodmann's areas 18, 19, and 37). This asymmetry reflects the fact that an ambiguous symbol is primarily processed as a letter. It confirms earlier results of the same group of authors obtained by means of the ERP technique, indicating cross-modal specialization of the association cortex in the posterior part of the left hemisphere for perceptual processing of language stimuli (Celsis, as cited in Gros et al., 2000). Hauser, Chomsky, and Fitch (2002) divided human language abilities into faculties in the broad sense and faculties in the narrow sense: the former are shared with nonhuman animals, but the latter are human-specific. Remez (2005) argues that perceptual organization of speech cannot be reduced to the general principles of auditory perceptual organization, and Rosenblum (2005) concludes that research aimed at proving that speech is special may eventually lead to parallels in nonspeech perception. Gentner and Ball (2005) believe that human language processing exceeds perceptual and cognitive abilities of other species, but also that it is highly constrained, and that the constraints are shared with other organisms.

The discussions about the issue of whether speech processing is a special function of the brain, specific to humans, have not produced a final answer, but clinicians tend to classify stimuli as verbal versus nonverbal more than neuropsychologists. In terms of sequencing, they claim that left-hemisphere damage affects verbal sequencing, and right-hemisphere damage impairs nonverbal sequencing. The question of whether linguistic specialization precedes early cognitive segmental-analytical capabilities or is determined by them has not yet been answered, even by the most fervent advocates of such distinctions.

LANGUAGE SPECIFICITIES

Many studies have shown that language specificities, such as alphabet (e.g., ideographic vs. syllabic or phonemic), orientation during reading and writing (e.g., left-to-right vs. right-to-left), the role of tone (e.g., phonemic vs. prosodic), among others, may affect their cerebral representation.

Xiong et al. (2000) studied language-processing strategies and corresponding neural substrates in native speakers of English and Chinese, by means of PET and MRI. Native Chinese speakers, who had started learning English after 9 years of age, exhibited activation in identical language and motor areas on tests with Chinese material (generating verbs to given ideographic symbols) and on tests with English material (generating verbs to visually presented English nouns): in the supplementary motor area (Brodmann's area 6), in Brodmann's areas 44, 45, 47 and 37, as well as in visual areas (Brodmann's areas 17, 18, and 19), all predominantly in the left hemisphere. In addition to these areas, strong activation was recorded on both types of tasks, in left middle frontal gyri (Brodmann's areas 9 and 46), that are believed to mediate in spatial working memory. In native English speakers no activation was found in the spatial regions. When the results of native Chinese speakers on Chinese tests are analyzed separately, a high correlation is found with the activity in the superior parietal lobe (Brodmann's area 7) that is a part of the *what* pathway (i.e., in the area where information about the position of an object in space with respect to the observer is processed). This correlation is explained by the nature of the Chinese ideographic script—its spatial configuration is one of its properties. These revealing results suggest that the language-processing strategy adopted in the process of acquiring one's native language is transferred to languages learned later.

Pu et al. (2000) found (by means of fMRI), in their Chinese subjects who had learned English between the ages of 8 and 19, greater activity in the region of the left middle to inferior frontal lobe than in the right hemisphere, while generating Chinese and English words to visually presented tasks. The difference between languages was manifested as a significantly smaller activated area during solving tasks in Chinese than in English.

Liu et al. (2000) tested their 10 healthy native speakers of Chinese with visually presented semantically indeterminate Chinese symbols to which they were supposed to generate related words. Brain activity was recorded by fMRI. There was marked activation between the left middle and inferior prefrontal gyri. Additional activation was found in visual areas, in the temporal lobe in motor areas, and in several other areas. Left lateralization in the prefrontal area was recorded in all subjects. Interestingly, no activity was recorded in the parietal lobe.

Zhang, Ma, Li, and Weng (2000) compared the brain activity (recorded by fMRI) of their eight healthy subjects during subvocal reading of a common Chinese symbol and an Arabic numeral. Both tasks activated similar regions, but the area activated while reading the Chinese symbol was larger. The activated regions included prefrontal (Brodmann's areas 9, 10, and 46), temporal (Brodmann's areas 22, 37, and 39), and occipital lobes (Brodmann's areas 18 and 19). Reading the numeral additionally activated Brodmann's area 40. Activation of identical areas was attributed to the fact that both the Chinese symbol and the Arabic numeral may be considered ideograms, which means that they can be processed in the same way. The larger area activated while reading the Chinese symbol is explained by the multiplicity of its meanings as opposed to the numeral.

Tan et al. (2000) also used fMRI to record brain activity in six healthy adults, native Chinese speakers, while they were generating words to visually presented undefined Chinese symbols, to unambiguous symbols, and to words that consisted of two symbols. They found pronounced left-hemisphere dominance on all tasks, with the greatest activation in the frontal lobe, although there were traces of activity in other regions as well, and in the homotopic areas in the right hemisphere (e.g., Brodmann's areas 9 and 37 in the left frontal and temporal lobes, Brodmann's areas 3 and 1 in the parietal lobe, and Brodmann's areas 17 and 18 in the occipital lobe of the right hemisphere). Their results did not confirm the difference between symbols and words, but the total activated area in the left frontal lobe recorded during processing undefined symbols and words consisting of two symbols was larger than that activated during processing unambiguous symbols. These results suggest (again) that more laborious recall of symbols and words increases cortical activations, just as Pu et al. (2000) have shown that a task in a foreign language elicits activation over a larger area.

Kim et al. (2000b) used fMRI to study brain activity in 14 healthy right-handers while they were generating verbs to visually and auditorily presented Korean nouns. The areas that were activated regardless of modality were the left inferior frontal gyrus, left lateral premotor areas, and supplementary motor areas in both hemispheres. During visual presentation, both occipital lobes were active (lateral parts), but greater activation was recorded in the left hemisphere. There was also activity in the left parietal lobe. During auditory presentation, superior and middle temporal gyri were activated in both hemispheres, with some leftward asymmetry, but there was no parietal activation. Involvement of the parietal lobe in the visual, but not in the auditory modality, is explained by the requirements for spatial processing during reading Korean script, similarly to Chinese examples.

Gandour et al. (2002, 2003) carried out a cross-linguistic fMRI study of spectral and temporal cues underlying phonological processing. Their Thai and Chinese subjects were asked to perform discrimination judgments of pitch and timing patterns in auditory stimuli under speech and nonspeech conditions. They concluded that hemispheric specialization is sensitive to language-specific factors because both groups exhibited similar frontoparietal activation patterns in the nonspeech condition, but in the speech condition only the Thai group showed increased activation in the left inferior prefrontal cortex.

These were just a few examples of different functioning of language neural networks affected by language and language-related modality specificities.

BILINGUALISM

As a topic of special interest for psycholinguistics, language acquisition and learning, but also cognitive science in general, bilingualism has attracted a great deal of attention by linguists, psychologists, neuroscientists, and speech and language therapists. Volumes have been written on the advantages and disadvantages of bilingualism in the mental and speech development of children, about different types of bilingualism, and about what makes a real bilingual, how to become a bilingual, about relationships between a bilingual's languages, about the critical age after which a foreign language cannot be mastered with native-like competence, and other related issues (Albert & Obler, 1978; Fabbro, 1999, 2001a, 2001b; Galloway, 1982; Grainger & Dijkstra, 1992; Harris, 1992; Paradis, 2004; Romaine, 1989).

Some of these aspects are addressed in this section. Before going on to the discussion about the neurolinguistic aspects of bilingualism, the term itself should be defined. I tend to agree with Grosjean's definition (1992, 1997) that determines bilingualism as use of different languages or dialects in different domains or situations for different purposes and with different interlocutors. Such a broad definition obviously refers to persons who have equal mastery of two languages or dialects as well as those who use languages at different levels of competence—such as those who use English in everyday conversation with their family and friends and can equally successfully read German scientific texts, but cannot participate in a conversation in German. These two types of bilingualism are covered by the terms *balanced bilinguals* (those with equal competence in both languages or dialects) and *dominant bilinguals* (those who are better in one language than the other). Accordingly, someone may become bilingual at any time—if they can master some level of communicative competence, even if only in some forms of language functioning (e.g., reading or writing). Since such communicative competence may be acquired at ages older than the traditional critical periods, bilinguals may be classified as early, late, or adults, if they started learning the second language before age 6, after age 6, or after puberty, respectively (Paradis, 2004).

For lack of a better classification of bilinguals according to their interlanguage relationships, we usually talk about three types: compound or compact, coordinate and subordinate. Compound bilinguals are those who have mastered both languages simultaneously by age 6 (usually in a bilingual family, where the two parents speak different languages). These bilinguals have one set of concepts that can be expressed by words in one or the other language. Coordinate bilinguals have learned the second language before puberty within or outside the family. They have two sets of lexical concepts, and the words belonging to the two languages are stored separately. Subordinate bilinguals have acquired their first language as their mother tongue and the second language by means of the first one. They have lexical concepts only in their mother tongue and generate words in the second language by translation from the first. Obviously, few bilinguals can be clearly described as belonging to one of these categories. It is particularly difficult to draw the line between the coordinate and subordinate bilinguals. Even in the case of compound bilinguals the two languages are frequently not quite equal. Formal education is usually offered (or predominant) in one language, they socialize with friends who are mostly monolingual or prefer one language, and so on. From informal reports of bilingual children's parents it can be inferred that despite the consistent application of the one-parent-one-language principle at home, each subsequent child increasingly uses the language of the environment. The result is weakening of the "compactness" at the expense of the language not used in school or among peers.

One of the models that take into consideration interlanguage relationships is de Bot's model of language organization in bilinguals (1992). It is based on Levelt's monolingual model (1989; Levelt, Roelofs, & Meyer, 1999), which is discussed in more detail in chapter 5. De Bot's model consists of three subsystems of language: production, comprehension subsystem, and the lexicon (which is involved in production and comprehension). The three production subsystems are the conceptualizer, the formulator, and the articulator. The conceptualizer is the preverbal stage—it contains concepts or information that may be expressed by words in any language. The formulator corresponds to Levelt's level of lexical selection and subsequent stages. In the formulator, appropriate lexical units are selected and grammatical and phonological rules are applied. At this level, the bilinguals differ from each other depending, among other factors, on the age and method of language learning, competence, and use. The articulator corresponds to Levelt's level of transformation of phonetic articulatory programs into articulation. At this level the selected language is finally verbalized by transforming sequences of syllables into articulatory gestures. It is probable that the two languages are activated simultaneously at all levels, except at the last one (articulation), where the unselected language is inhibited (for discussion see Fabbro, 1999).

Costa, Miozzo, and Caramazza (1999) studied lexical selection in Spanish–Catalan bilinguals and concluded that there is a parallel semantic activation of lexicons of both languages, enabled lexical access in the unselected lexicon, and a nonlexical mechanism of activation of phonological units of the written word.

The interest in cerebral representation of language functions in general was paralleled by the interest in neurolinguistic organization of bilinguals. Naturally, neurolinguistic aspects of bilingualism involve additional factors that may play an important role in representations of the two languages: gender, preferred hand, age at the beginning of learning, order of learning/acquisition, methods and strategies, frequency and circumstances of use, competence, language specificities, and so forth (Fabbro 2001a, b; Hoosain, 1991; Keatley, 1992; Kroll & Sholl, 1992; Lubow, Tsal, Mirkin, & Mazliah, 1994; Magiste, 1987; 1992; Obler, Zatorre, Galloway & Vaid, 1982; Perani et al., 1996; Sussman, Franklin & Simon, 1982; Tamamaki, 1993; Vaid, 1983; Votaw, 1992; Wuillemin, Richardson & Lynch, 1994; 1998; Yokoyama et al., 2006).

Paradis (1994) believes that bilinguals have their two languages stored in separate memory systems. The first language (L1) is stored in nondeclarative memory by means of implicit strategies, contrary to the second language (L2), which involves mental translation processes and explicit learning of grammar, and is stored in the explicit (semantic, episodic, autobiographical) memory. L1 is represented in the basal ganglia, cerebellum, and in various cerebral areas, whereas L2 is represented more diffusely in the cerebral cortex. Accordingly, acquisition and learning activate different brain structures: acquisition involves emotional systems as well as cortical and subcortical structures, whereas learning goes on mainly in the cerebral cortex. Acquisition, typically associated with L1, proceeds naturally in an informal setting; learning takes place in an institutional environment by means of formal methods and rules.

As a result of his extensive studies of bilinguals with disordered language functions (aphasics) Paradis wrote the following five hypotheses about the representation of their languages:

1. Extended system hypothesis—the languages are undifferentiated; elements of the two languages are processed as allo-elements.
2. Dual system hypothesis—each language is represented independently in separate circuits.
3. Tripartite system hypothesis—items that are identical in both languages are represented in a single underlying neural substrate; those that are different each have their own separate representation.
4. Context of acquisition hypothesis—languages that are acquired in different contexts are neurofunctionally more separately represented than those acquired in the same context.
5. Subsystem hypothesis—bilinguals have two subsets of neural connections, one for each language, within the same cognitive system (the language system).

De Bot's model of language production in bilinguals includes the question of neural substrate of his three subsystems. The general conceptualizer, which is not language-specific, is supposedly represented in the most anterior regions of the left hemisphere. The formulator is probably represented in common cortico-subcortical structures, and different languages are realized by different neurofunctional mechanisms. Syntax (grammar) and phonology of the two languages are probably separate in late bilinguals. According to de Bot, in balanced bilinguals, the lexicon is probably represented in common neural structures located in the parieto-temporal areas. De Bot believes that late bilinguals differ from the early ones in the organization of syllabic and prosodic aspects of articulators so that late bilinguals have independent stores for each language, whereas early bilinguals have a common store for all elements of the two languages.

Cases of a Dutch–English male right-handed bilingual and a Spanish–English left-handed bilingual have revealed common centers for the two languages but also areas that were variably inhibited in the two languages (Ojemann & Whitaker, 1978). Some earlier studies have pointed to the possibility that L2 may be more diffusely represented in the left hemisphere, but subsequent tests suggested otherwise (for reviews see Albert & Obler, 1978; Fabbro, 1999, 2001a, 2001b; Paradis, 2004; Zatorre, 1989).

Interesting results of fMRI studies of brain activity in bilinguals were reported by Kim, Relkin, Lee, and Hirsch (1997). They found that the spatial pattern of activation in Broca's area for the two languages (French and English) in early bilinguals differs from that found in late bilinguals: in early bilinguals the two languages were represented in overlapping areas, whereas in late bilinguals the representations were separate. On the other hand, there were no differences between early and late bilinguals with respect to the representation of their languages in Wernicke's area.

In spite of their great number, cases of differential recovery from aphasia in bilinguals and polyglots have not provided us with final answers about neurolinguistic organization of bilinguals (for reviews see Fabbro, 1999, 2001a, 2001b; Gitterman & Sies, 1990, 1992; Paradis, 2004). Aphasia in bilinguals may be manifested as an imbalance between activation and inhibition of L1 and L2, as problems with switching between the languages or as pathological fixation on just one of the languages. In all of these cases both languages are preserved, but conscious selection is difficult or impossible. Different patients recover in different ways and at a different rate for as yet unknown reasons. There have been attempts to explain the differences by the influence of numerous factors, such as language that was spoken at the moment of damage, language familiarity or competence, order of acquisition, modality of acquisition/learning (spoken or written), and many psychological factors as well (Fabbro, 2001a; Paradis, 1995; 2004; Van Lieshout, Renier, Eling & de Bot, 1990; Watamori & Sasanuma, 1978). It was found that, at least in some cases, the disordered language was not completely lost, but merely inhibited. Parallel recovery from aphasias, found in about 40% of patients, supports the hypothesis that both languages are organized in the same areas. On the other hand, selective aphasia that affects only one language, leaving the other intact, is taken as evidence of functional separation of languages, although the languages may not be represented in different areas. Cases of alternate antagonism, in which languages recover alternately, one at the expense of the other, speak in favor of independent mental systems in the two hemispheres. Some clinical cases of pathological switching and mixing of languages show that the mechanisms for language selection and interlanguage switching are located in the right hemisphere, although there are cases of left-hemisphere damage with identical consequences (Paradis, 1995). Hernandez, Martinez, Wong, Frank, and Buxton (2000) found (by means of fMRI applied during a naming task) such a switching mechanism involves Broca's area, the supramarginal gyrus, and the anterior cingulate gyrus, without differences in the representation of L1 and L2. Proverbio, Leoni, and Zani (2004) recorded (by ERP) the first effect of lexical switching and code switching in their simultaneous interpreters between 140 and 200 ms at left anterior sites. In the final analysis, it is not entirely clear whether such a neuroanatomical center for activation and inhibition of languages actually exists in bilinguals.

It is highly probable, however, that bilinguals do not have any special mechanisms that would be absent in monolinguals. In other words, the differences in brain organization are quantitative rather than qualitative. For example, the code-switching mechanism that is frequently the object of discussions on bilingualism (Macnamara & Kushnir, 1971) exists in monolinguals as well. It is manifested as the ability to switch between formal and colloquial speech, depending on the situation and the interlocutors. Both languages of bilinguals are susceptible to left-hemisphere damage just as the one language in monolinguals. Minkowski and Paradis (Fabbro, 1999; Paradis, 2004) concluded that the differences between the languages are physiological rather than anatomic—the same centers are involved, but the same active elements are combined in different ways. That view is in agreement with language functioning seen as a neural network. Within such a model it may be said that the two languages are supported by different circuits located in the same language areas. These are macroanatomically identical, but microanatomically different neuronal assemblies.

Among healthy subjects, simultaneous interpreters are a particularly interesting group to study organization of the two languages (Fabbro, 1999; Green, Nicholson, Vaid, & White, 1990; Malakoff, 1992; Proverbio et al., 2004). It is most probable that both hemispheres are used very actively during interpreting. The left hemisphere is supposedly preoccupied with recognition of the original message, interpreting, and speech production (of the new message as a translation), whereas the primary role of the right hemisphere is control of attention and monitoring of nonverbal, emotional, and pragmatic features of the message, the speaker, and the wider context in other words of overall communication. Experienced simultaneous interpreters rely on nonverbal contextual signs a great deal, including body posture, gesturing, mimicking, and tone of voice, because these supply valuable information that supplement and help anticipate verbal content. Obviously, while interpreting, both languages have to be activated simultaneously, but probably not to the same degree at all times. The unselected language (i.e., the language of the source message) is not entirely inhibited—its activation threshold is temporarily raised to prevent self-activation, but not so much to disable comprehension and interpreting. The more frequent the use of both languages, the lower the threshold. It is reasonable to assume that the two languages are separable within one speaker, and that comprehension is separable from production: otherwise interpreters would not be able to listen to the message in one language and talk in the other at the same time. It should be stressed, however, that translation skill is separable from bilingual competence; balanced bilinguals do not necessarily make good simultaneous interpreters.

Besides the effects of the above factors, it is possible that the two languages of a bilingual are represented differently at various levels (e.g., at the biochemical, anatomic, neurofunctional, psychological, or linguistic). These differences may account for the disagreements among different authors, because the studies may not tap into identical levels.

In the past several decades, many studies have addressed the issue of possible different lateralization of language functions in bilinguals, mostly by analyzing the accuracy of responses and response times. Three main hypotheses have emerged: (a) the left hemisphere is dominant for both languages; (b) L1 and L2 are lateralized differently—L1 to the left and L2 to the right—and the differences are influenced by many factors (age, competence, methods of acquisition, etc.); (c) neither language of the bilingual is as clearly lateralized as the one language in monolinguals.

Some tests with monolinguals have exhibited greater activation of the left frontal lobe during processing of grammatical (closed-class) words, as opposed to greater activation of more posterior left-hemisphere regions during processing lexical (open-class) words. Differences between the two classes of words were also found in the left temporal areas with open-class words, but not closed-class ones eliciting a theta power increase in an EEG study (Bastiaansen, Van der Linden, Ter Keurs, Dijkstra, & Hagoort, 2005). Absence of clear activation in the left anterior regions during syntactic processing in late bilinguals has been taken as evidence that some other cerebral structures are responsible for the organization of L2 grammatical aspects. Neville, Mills, and Lawson (1992) reported on an ERP study of early and late bilinguals, in which they looked for differences in cortical representation of the two languages as a function of age of acquisition/learning. In their early bilinguals, they found activation for the closed-class words of both languages in the left frontal lobe, and activation for the open-class words in postrolandic cortical structures. In their late bilinguals (who started learning L2 when they were 7) they found that closed-class words of L2 were represented together with open-class words in postrolandic areas.

Listening to stories in L1 (French) and L2 (English) revealed different activation of the two hemispheres. Greater right-hemisphere activation was found for L2 than for L1 in moderately fluent bilinguals who had started learning L2 at age 7 (Dehaene et al., 1997). Proverbio et al. (2004) found in their ERP study of simultaneous interpreters that the difference in L1/L2 processing was not related to a difference in proficiency, but to the later acquisition of L2 compared to L1, which resulted in different functional organization (lesser degree of hemispheric lateralization for L2 than for L1).

Newman et al. (1998) looked at age of acquisition as a possible factor influencing cerebral representation of sign language in native and late (age 15) signers of American Sign Language (ASL) who also used verbal English. Their fMRI study revealed that in native signers verbal English was represented in the left hemisphere, whereas ASL was bilaterally represented. In late signers verbal English and ASL had similar representation.

Chee, Tan, and Thiel (1999) found no differences between early and late Mandarin–English bilinguals in cerebral representation (recorded by fMRI) of their L1 and L2. They found common macroscopic areas to be active during L1 and L2 processing and concluded that the two languages shared one store.

Barkat-Defradas and Denolin found no significant differences in cerebral representation of vernacular Moroccan Arabic (L1) and Classical Arabic (L2) in their late (started learning L2 around age 7), highly proficient bilinguals. Klein, Milner, Zatorre, Zhao, and Nikelski (1999) found no differences between language representation (recorded by PET) of Chinese (L1) and English (L2) during Chinese–English verb generation in their late bilinguals who use both languages in everyday life. Both languages evoked primarily left-hemisphere activity.

Perani et al. (1998) reexamined their earlier PET data involving auditory processing of stories (Perani et al., 1996) and applied some additional tests, and came to the conclusion that it was proficiency rather than age of acquisition that affects L2 representation. In their highly proficient early and late acquirers of L2 there were no differences between L1 and L2 representation, contrary to low-proficiency late acquirers in whom they found that L1 activated temporal and temporo-parietal areas more than L2.

ERP studies of 20-month-old babies revealed that lateralization is correlated with the number of words in their repertoire, not their age. Namely, children with rich vocabulary had left-lateralized brain activity while listening to words, whereas those with a relatively smaller vocabulary exhibited bilateral activation in identical conditions (Gazzaniga et al., 2002). Weber-Fox, Davis, and Cuadrado (2003) found language proficiency to be an important factor in monolinguals' language processing as well. Their ERP study revealed that adults with high-language proficiency (compared to those with normal proficiency) exhibit slightly faster lexical access over left anterior brain regions for closed class items, and a reduced reliance on contextual information available in sentences. This may be observed in the context of L2 competence influence on language laterality as well.

Pouratian et al. (2000) found (by means of optical imaging) in a balanced English–Spanish bilingual cortical areas that are common to both languages (the superior temporal sulcus, superior and middle temporal gyri and parts of the supramarginal gyrus) and those that were language-specific (in the supramarginal and precentral gyri). The authors concluded that the common areas are important for general language processing and are, therefore, not language-specific. Such functional distinction between common and language-specific areas of activation does not depend on age of acquisition or level of competence of L2.

Rodriguez-Fornells et al. (2005) found phonological interference in bilinguals' performance (compared with monolingual controls) and located the control of this interference (on the basis of ERP and fMRI results) in the left middle prefrontal cortex, which is one of the brain areas that is not language-specific.

Coutin-Churchman and Pietrosemoli (2002) conducted an ERP study of L1 and L2 cerebral representation in two groups of adults. The subjects in one group spoke Spanish as their L1. The subjects in the other group spoke Spanish as L2 (the group was heterogeneous with respect to their L1s). They found that native speakers of Spanish exhibited left-hemisphere activation, whereas subjects who spoke Spanish as L2 (and had learned it as adults) exhibited right-hemisphere activation.

The Croatian (L1)–English (L2) pair of languages has been examined for possible differences in lateralization, by means of behavioral studies on female right-handed late unbalanced bilinguals. The tests included several variations of: dichotic listening tests (Mildner, 1996; Mildner & Rukavina, 1996a; Mildner, 1999; Mildner & Golubić, 2003); rhyme tests (Mildner & Rukavina, 1994; 1996b; Mildner & Ratković, 1997); English–Croatian translations (Horga, 2002b); and tests involving concurrent activities (motor and verbal; Mildner, 2000). On all of them right-ear advantage was found for L1 and a trend toward left-ear advantage (i.e., right-hemisphere dominance) for L2, but no significant differences. Another common feature of all these tests was great variability among subjects and less marked left-hemisphere dominance than reported in literature on monolinguals (Albert & Obler, 1978; Gordon, 1980; Mildner, 1996; Obler & Gjerlow, 1999). On the contrary, on a comparable sample, a statistically significant difference was found between the two languages in preferring the left or the right hemispace (Mildner, 2002). The activation-orienting hypothesis tested on the same sample and with identical stimuli (simultaneous auditory commands to be executed with the right or the left hand) was confirmed for L1 but not for L2, which would again suggest more diffuse representation of L2 than L1 (Mildner, Stanković, & Petković, 2005).

Paradis (2004) has compiled an excellent volume dealing with all the issues touched upon in this section. He proposes a neurolinguistic theory of bilingualism according to which all speakers, be they monolingual or bilingual, rely on four mechanisms in verbal communication: implicit linguistic competence, metalinguistic knowledge, pragmatics, and affect. The extent to which each of them is used may vary under the influence of many factors (e.g., competence, formality of the situation, etc.). His central message is that "… there is no mechanism at work in the bilingual speaker's brain that is not also operative … in the unilingual brain" (p. 229).

SPEECH AND LANGUAGE DISORDERS

It should be kept in mind that functional disorders after damage to any restricted area in the brain are more quantitative than qualitative. In other words, the consequences are more dependent on the amount of affected tissue than on the location per se. Symptoms of disordered function may occur even if specific cytoarchitectonic or functional cortical areas have not been directly affected: they may emerge if the connections between them have been damaged (see chap. 5, this volume). In any case, it has been found that cortical areas do not function optimally if they are not connected (Kolb & Whishaw, 1996).

Luria (1982) has warned that connecting consequences of brain injury with the functioning of the intact brain is flawed, but at the time, it was the practical way to study language behavior. Caution should be exercised when looking for a neurological substrate of language on the basis of brain injury, particularly if damage is extensive. In such cases, substantial reorganization of cognitive functioning is possible, which does not correspond to the functioning of the intact brain, and makes inferences invalid. For example, aphasia literature has revealed low correlations between specific language difficulties and place of injury (Hagoort & Kutas, 1995). What we can infer from them, as indeed from any speech and language problems caused by central nervous system disorders, is that there have been changes in the timing and planning of language-relevant processes. It is, therefore, important that research techniques, whether they be applied on patients or healthy subjects, have good temporal resolution (e.g., ERP).

Representation of speech and language functions different than in a healthy population does not occur only in brain-damaged patients. Serious hearing impairment, particularly if congenital or occurring at a very early postnatal age, may cause different cortical representation.

When subjects with intact hearing are silently lipreading, considerable activation occurs in their middle and superior temporal gyri of both hemispheres (Brodmann's areas 42 and 22), which corresponds to the secondary auditory area and the area traditionally associated with speech perception. There is also activity in the right transverse temporal gyrus (Brodmann's area 41). In congenitally deaf individuals, the same task activates the temporal lobe to a lesser extent, and that activation is not as strictly or as consistently localized. Deaf individuals have exhibited increased activation in lower regions of the temporal lobe (including the middle and the inferior temporal lobe) (Brodmann's areas 20 and 21) and/or more anteriorly or posteriorly in the superior temporal lobe (MacSweeney et al., 2000).

In any case, it is very important that despite the disabled auditory input there is activation in the appropriate regions as if there were no hearing impairment. This fact makes clearer many principles and results of Guberina's Verbotonal theory and method of rehabilitation of the hearing impaired (Boroković, 2004; Guberina, 1992–1993; Pansini, 1995, 2002; Pozojević-Trivanović, 1984).

People suffering from central deafness cannot understand words, but they are capable of repeating them or writing dictation, which shows that they are able to access the stored auditory representations of word forms. Their access to semantic information in the visual modality is intact, which suggests that in such cases damage may be caused by injury to connections between the relatively intact system that manipulates acoustic-phonological properties of spoken words and the relatively intact semantic system. However, such cases are very rare. Auditory verbal agnosia affects speech perception with impaired repetition, and it is associated with disruption of subcortical projections to the primary auditory cortex.

Aphasia

Aphasia is a disorder of language perception and/or production that occurs as a consequence of brain damage. Aphasias are generally classified on the basis of three main criteria: spontaneous speech, comprehension of auditorily presented speech, and verbal repetition. The term is used for adults who suffered brain injury and consequently lost what had been normal language functioning. A milder form of aphasia is called dysphasia. The term *developmental sensory dysphasia* is more commonly used for children younger than 10 who have failed to develop normal language.

Records of aphasic disorders date back to ancient Egypt, 4000 to 5000 years ago. In the sense that we refer to it at present, it was first described by Broca in 1861, who reported that one of his patients had suffered a head trauma and could only produce, besides a few swear words, one word—*tan* (he was frequently referred to by that name, although his actual name was Laborgne). When the patient died, the autopsy revealed injury in the posterior part of the left inferior frontal gyrus, immediately anterior to the primary motor cortex responsible for muscles involved in speech (lips, tongue, jaw, palate, vocal folds, diaphragm), without paralysis to the muscles themselves. The area was named Broca's area or center for speech production, and the aphasia is known as Broca's aphasia. It is a motor (expressive) type of aphasia. The patients typically exhibit good speech comprehension (albeit not as intact as it used to be thought—the comprehension of complex syntactic structures is impaired). They comprehend the sentence by inferring about its meaning on the basis of the major lexical units (nouns, verbs, etc.) independent of syntactic structure. The fact that injuries to that area impair grammatical processing in speech production and in speech perception suggests that neuronal circuits in that region are responsible for completing the whole on the basis of constituent parts of the sentence (Damasio & Damasio, 1992). They produce little speech, slowly, nonfluently, with great effort and poor articulation. Their speech is telegraphic and ungrammatical: auxiliaries, suffixes, conjunctions, and articles are usually omitted and patients rely mostly on nouns and, to a lesser extent, on verbs, which suggests that these two parts of speech are represented in different areas. Some patients' speech is spared and they retain idioms and proverbs, and can recite text segments they had previously learned by heart. Singing may also be intact. The example of a patient who could not read aloud the sentence *"To be or not to be"* but had no difficulty with *"Two bee oar knot two bee"* although they are pronounced identically, indicates that these aphasics have problems with meaning as well, not just with speech production (Kalat, 1995). They frequently overuse empty words like *this, thing,* and so on. Their naming ability is poor, but it improves when prompted (which indicates that the deficit is not limited to articulation). Consonants are more difficult than vowels, as are long words compared with short ones. Frequent phonemic paraphasias are taken as evidence of breakdown in the organization of the processor that encodes phonological units. If the injury is restricted to the very small area around Broca's center, aphasia is transitory. More permanent motor aphasias are caused by more extensive injuries that involve areas outside of Broca's center (e.g., the insula), particularly more anterior regions and/or go deeper involving the thalamus and basal ganglia. It has been found that deficits are not language related, but are a part of a wider motor problem. Dysarthria and apraxia of speech frequently co-occur with aphasia (Gazzaniga et al. 2002).

Sensory (receptive, jargon) *aphasia* is also called Wernicke's aphasia, after the physician who described it in 1874. It occurs as a consequence of damage to the posterior part of the superior temporal gyrus, the first temporal gyrus at the temporo-parietal junction in the left hemisphere, along the Heschl's gyrus containing the primary auditory zones. This type of aphasia is characterized by poor comprehension of spoken and written language. Auditory comprehension is unsuccessful because normal acoustic analysis of forms reaching the patient is impaired at its very beginning, rather than, as used to be traditionally thought, because of damage to the word-meaning store (Damasio & Damasio, 1992). The utterances are typically fluent, fast, effortless, mostly syntactically and prosodically well formed, but totally meaningless. There may be substitutions of more general terms for the specific ones (e.g., *animal* instead of *horse*), semantic paraphasias (e.g., *telescope* for *glasses*), poor object naming, and seriously deficient ability to repeat and read. Articulation is relatively intact. On the basis of that it may be inferred that temporal lobe damage affects verbal memory, not phonological, syntactic or articulatory mechanisms, as is the case with frontal lobe injuries. Nevertheless, there are cases of syntactic and lexical impairments (Blumstein, 1988). Dimond (1980) claims that Wernicke's area extends further back (occipitally) and upward (parietally) than originally thought. These claims are consistent with the propositions of the parietal hypothesis of language organization in the brain (Deane, 1992; for more details see chap. 5, this volume). Interestingly, severity of Broca's aphasia varies more than that of Wernicke's (Kolb & Whishaw, 1996). Severe and permanent Wernicke's aphasia occurs after injuries that, in addition to Wernicke's area, involve surrounding cortical tissue and/or the white matter underneath. Injuries restricted to Wernicke's area result in transient aphasia of Wernicke type (Dronkers, 1996).

Wernicke also proposed the possibility of *conduction aphasia,* typical of patients who have suffered injury to the connections between the two centers for speech production and perception. The most frequently found culprits in the literature are injuries to insula and the *fasciculus arcuatus.* This type of aphasia is manifested as the inability to repeat aloud what the patient heard. Comprehension of written or spoken material is intact, but the patients have great difficulty naming objects. They have difficulties in producing spontaneous speech and they are incapable of acting on verbal commands. They can register their own errors, but are unable to correct them. Dimond (1980) claims that the thalamus is involved in the integration of input (receptive) and output (expressive, motor) speech. He also believes that the general area of *fasciculus arcuatus* is actually the seat of the mental lexicon, which would make it readily available to the centers for speech production and perception.

Transcortical sensory aphasia occurs in patients with injuries to the areas of the supramarginal and angular gyri. The patients are capable of repeating what they heard, of writing dictation, and of correcting grammatical errors in the expressions they heard, but they do not understand speech, regardless of modality. These symptoms are generally explained by the loss of access to semantic data without the loss of syntactic or phonological abilities. It could, therefore, be inferred that what is affected is the perceptual representational system that contains separate information about word form and their semantic information (Gazzaniga et al., 2002).

Transcortical motor aphasia occurs as a consequence of a break in the connections between Broca's area and the rest of the frontal lobe. The principal feature of this type of aphasia is the lack of the will to speak, with intact ability to understand and repeat the speech of others. In extreme cases this may result in echolalia. The patients speak unwillingly and have great difficulty finding the right words, but articulation is relatively good. The sentences are simple and comprise mostly nouns.

Global aphasia is a severe language disorder in all its aspects, because it is caused primarily by left-hemisphere damage. Injuries that may cause such a loss of speech and language abilities occur, in addition to the anterior and posterior cerebral regions, in a great portion of the subcortical white matter. The patient does not understand speech, cannot speak, and aphasic symptoms are usually accompanied by alexia, agraphia, and acalculia. Milder forms of global aphasia may be manifested as sensorimotor aphasia—to some extent as impaired speech and language comprehension and expression.

Primary progressive aphasia is a degenerative neurological impairment causing progressive and selective disruption of language. In such patients Gitelman et al. (2000) found by fMRI applied during phonological and semantic tasks (determining whether the two visually presented words are homonyms and determining whether the two visually presented words are synonymous, respectively), in addition to the activation in Broca's area (recorded in healthy subjects as well), activation of surrounding dorso-lateral regions. This wider activation was attributed to the inefficiency of the frontal component of the language network, because these were patients suffering from aphasia of the predominantly nonfluent type. Contrary to them, in healthy subjects greater activation was recorded in the parieto-temporal association cortex, and in the inferior frontal cortex, which they attributed to better access to various language associations. According to the previously mentioned authors, additional activation of the frontal cortex in aphasics probably reflects the process of compensation or reorganization within the language network.

Anomia is a condition occurring as a consequence of brain damage, when patients are incapable of naming objects and notions. The ability to describe the object's function and appearance is frequently preserved. Comprehension and speech are intact. Anomia may be restricted to particular categories. It is manifested as the inability to name objects belonging to a category, in spite of the intact access to semantic data about them. For example, there may be anomia for inanimate objects, without anomia for other categories. Other terms used for this type of aphasia are amnestic or nominal aphasia (Brinar, Brzović, & Zurak, 1999).

PET studies revealed in all aphasics, regardless of the aphasia type, diminished glucose intake in the parieto-temporal area. However, it should be stressed here that anatomic damage did not correspond closely to the areas of decreased glucose consumption; even cerebral areas that had suffered no anatomic damage were found to have decreased metabolism (e.g., supramarginal and angular gyri). It has been shown that the correlation is higher between aphasic symptoms and metabolism than between the symptoms and damage (Gazzaniga et al., 2002).

RECOVERY OF LANGUAGE FUNCTIONS: FUNCTIONAL CEREBRAL REORGANIZATION

Kim, Kim, Hong, Parrish, and Kim (2000a) found, in their right-handed male patients recovering from aphasia, greater activation of the right frontal lobes than of the left. However, in different patients different areas were active. In two of them, the area homotopic to Broca's area (inferior frontal gyrus) was activated. In one there was bilateral activation of the frontal lobes. One of them exhibited no activation in the inferior frontal gyrus, but rather in the right prefrontal area of the middle frontal gyrus. Obviously, the results suggest different mechanisms of cortical reorganization of language functions during recovery from aphasia in the course of long-term rehabilitation.

On various language tasks, patients with anterior injuries behaved differently from those with more posterior injuries in the left hemisphere. All posterior damage patients exhibited significant activation of the left frontal cortex (Brodmann's areas 44, 45, 46, and 47), whereas most patients with damage to those areas exhibited activation of homotopic areas in the right hemisphere. In some patients there were no task-dependent activation differences, and in one there was activation of the left hemisphere immediately next to the damaged location. Contrary to healthy subjects in whom different areas in the left hemisphere are activated depending on the type of language task, in these patients Specht et al. (2000a) recorded less pronounced sensitivity to the type of activity associated with different language tasks.

Duffau, Capelle, Lopes, Faillot, and Bitar (2000) and Duffau and Capelle (2000) performed several cortical stimulation studies in patients suffering from different injuries and conditions in order to shed some light on functional reorganization of language functions. They found that slow progressing damage (e.g., a slowly growing tumor) may elicit local functional reorganization and enable preservation of language functions. Such reorganization is not possible in all regions of the brain: it was found in cases of glioma in Broca's center, but not when the tumor was located in the insula. They raised the issue of whether this selective reorganization capacity possibly reflected some hierarchical organization of language areas, due to which the capacity might depend on the importance of the location in the hierarchy. Some language areas may keep their key role and remain active despite the tumor progression. Surgery itself may stimulate reorganization and cause changes in synaptic efficiency or in the properties of the relevant neural network, by changing the values of weights and/or by activating latent networks. Duffau et al. (2000) proposed that this reflected the importance of these regions in the hierarchy of language functioning, according to which the less important structures can be replaced by others, but the essential ones cannot. According to their proposition, the insula in the dominant hemisphere is more important for language processing than the fronto-opercular region. However, the arguments may be interpreted differently. Would it not be equally possible and, indeed probable, that the brain provided the possibility of reorganization, namely, a substitution of structures, essential for some (in this case language) function? In this case the reorganization capacity would imply the importance of a region for the particular function.

Kiviniemi et al. (2000) found (by MEG) that rehabilitation of anomic patients has, in addition to the direct benefits (in naming tasks, the patients are more successful in recalling practiced words), some indirect effects as well: semantic activation extends to the entire lexical system, with the greatest benefit for the words that are semantically related to the practiced ones. The neural substrate of these changes has been found in the inferior part of the left parietal lobe, in the supramarginal gyrus or near it, and it is manifested as 400 to 500 ms latency. In other words, the improvement is not achieved by the intact right hemisphere taking over, but rather by reestablishment of cerebral activity in the partly damaged region of the left hemisphere (that was related to the phonological store and encoding).

Bellman Thiran et al. (2002) reported on a patient suffering from progressive aphasia caused by the atrophy of the left temporal lobe. They used fMRI to record her brain activity during various language tasks over a longer time period. They too found reorganization primarily in the damaged left hemisphere, with increasingly bilateral reorganization of specialized networks.

In the attempts to define the neurobiological substrate of speech on the basis of damage data, two key issues have been raised: (a) Do speech production and perception deficits reflect selective damage to sound characteristics of speech and their representations, or to impaired processes involved in access to these representations? (b) Do speech production and perception deficits reflect impairments that are primarily phonological but influence structural properties of language? Or, are they primarily phonetic and influence the articulatory application in language production and acoustic decoding in speech perception? Blumstein (1995) compared the speech production and perception errors in aphasics and concluded that they both indicate that the problems reflect impaired processes involved in the access to sound structure, rather than selective damage to sound features of speech or their representations. Speech production deficits occur at the phonological level, reflecting the impaired selection or access, but also at the phonetic level, reflecting the deficits in articulatory implementation, particularly in timing of transition from one articulator to the next. Phonological disorders occur regardless of the place of injury, whereas phonetic disorders are a consequence of damage to specific neuroanatomic structures. Speech perception deficits reflect erroneous perception of phonetic features, not impaired isolation of acoustic parameters associated with these features. Despite the injury, the language-specific phonological and phonotactic syllable-forming rules are preserved. The errors are most frequently found between phonemes that differ along a single distinctive feature (e.g., /p/ vs. /t/) and they are more frequent with respect to place of articulation than voicing (Blumstein, 1988). The most resistant is the opposition vowel-consonant, followed by the oral-nasal distinction (Vuletić, 1993).

On the basis of her studies of phonemic paraphasias in Wernicke, Broca, and conduction aphasics, Kean (1995) concluded that there were three levels of representation of morphemes, or words: basic, lexical, and surface. At the first levels the segments differ in (minimal) distinctive features necessary to be unambiguously defined. At the second level, the sequences are syllabified in agreement with the language-specific algorithm, and feature matrices are determined by redundancy rules. At the third level, each segment is associated with complete matrices of distinctive features. In Wernicke aphasics the access to the first level is disabled, and in Broca aphasics the third level and movement planning are impaired. In conduction aphasia the first and the second level are affected, with more strongly marked characteristics being replaced with the less marked ones. According to Kean, not all paraphasic errors can be explained as replacement of a marked feature by an unmarked one—this is true only of conduction aphasia.

Another question is whether language comprehension problems in aphasics are created by the loss of language knowledge, or by impaired processing of representations. Similar to the speech proper, it is believed today (contrary to earlier authors) that the problems lie in processing, not in actual loss of data. If representations were in fact lost, no task could tap into that knowledge. However, Broca aphasics, for example, have great difficulty in recognizing correct grammatical sentence structure in some tasks, but in others they may distinguish grammatically correct from grammatically incorrect sentences, even when presented with syntactically very complex structures. In other words, their syntactic knowledge is preserved, but not the processes that are necessary to manipulate it. Wernicke aphasics have intact lexico-semantic knowledge, but not all the procedures that are involved in recall and/or processing of that knowledge. It is possible that in both cases the underlying problem is in the necessary speed of language processing that the damaged brain can no longer achieve. The next logical question is related to the stage at which these disorders occur. It seems that lexical integration is more likely a culprit than lexical access: the aphasics are not fast enough at integrating the words in the existing context. In other words, they are incapable of selecting quickly enough the meaning of the word that is most appropriate for the actual communicative situation (Gazzaniga et al., 2002).

Although aphasia used to be considered speech pathology, it turned out to be a language rather than speech disorder. A general conclusion has been that, regardless of the sensory channel through which the language information is conducted, the left hemisphere is the seat of language functioning. Aphasic difficulties identical to those found in hearing patients were found subsequent to left-hemisphere injury in hearing-impaired patients who use sign language. Moreover, these subjects exhibit considerably impaired sign language, but they can correctly process nonlanguage visual-spatial relations. Similar to hearing individuals, congenitally deaf subjects exhibit right visual field advantage for printed words. They also exhibit right visual field advantage for hand signs that have some meaning in sign language, and left visual field advantage for shapes and hand movements that are illegal in sign language. In other words, the left hemisphere is not dominant for speech, but for a cognitive system on which speech and sign language are based. It may be inferred that hearing and speech are not a prerequisite for the development of hemispheric specialization for language. Consequently, left-hemisphere specialization for language acquisition is not a result of its fine auditory analysis abilities, but rather of its capacity for language analysis (Fromkin, 1995). Another support for lateralization of language as a symbolic communication system (without the need for oral speech) is provided by the occurrence of the so-called N400 effect (a negative peak occurring approximately 400 ms after the stimulus onset in test but not in control stimuli) in sign language as well (Hagoort & Brown, 1995).

AGRAPHIA AND ALEXIA

Agraphia is a writing disorder that occurs after damage to the angular gyrus in the inferior part of the left parietal lobe, at the junction of the temporal, parietal and the occipital lobes. Comparisons of Japanese scripts *kana* (each sign represents a syllable) and *kanji* (ideographic) reveal that the two systems (phonological and semantic) function independently and that each of these two types of processing proceeds in a different place. It seems that the phonological aspect of reading is represented in the left hemisphere, whereas the right hemisphere probably kept the ability to obtain direct semantic information from the written word, independent of the phonological (grapheme-to-phoneme) encoding. Paragraphias (grapheme substitutions) generally correspond to paraphasias that occur in speech (Vuletić, 1993).

Alexia is total loss of the ability to read, most frequently due to damage in the left occipital lobe and part of the corpus callosum that would otherwise connect the spared right occipital lobe with the angular gyrus. In 1892 Dejerine noticed that alexia (and agraphia) is a consequence of damage to pathways that connect the visual cortex with the left angular gyrus (a region in the left temporal and parietal lobe immediately posterior to Wernicke's area). Based on that, he concluded that the left angular gyrus is responsible for understanding verbal visual information that is obtained directly from the neighboring left visual cortex and indirectly from the right visual cortex via the corpus callosum. In cases of pure alexia (without agraphia) patients have no problems in writing, but they cannot read what they have written. Literal alexia is a disorder that prevents the patients from reading individual letters, but they can read whole words, especially if they are frequent and concrete nouns. Infrequent, abstract, and function words present great difficulties, as do the meaningless words. Cases of verbal alexia present the opposite picture: patients can read letter by letter, and connect what they have read into whole words (even when they are meaningless), but they cannot understand whole words. The disorder affects all word classes and word length has significant influence on the time necessary to read the word. The disorder is usually a consequence of cortical damage in the left occipital lobe. It used to be believed that it was a disorder in the system of word forms that supported whole-word reading, but studies have shown that at least some people who read letter by letter have the system of word forms intact. One and the same patient may exhibit signs of both types of alexia (Vuletić, 1993). Subsequent to damage to the angular gyrus, patients are incapable of reading or writing, and they have mild aphasic symptoms (alexia with agraphia).

Dysgraphia is a writing deficit that is considered a developmental disorder in children and a milder form of agraphia when occurring in adults after insult or some other type of brain damage. There are several kinds of dysgraphia. Patients suffering from phonological dysgraphia cannot establish the relationship between graphemes and phonemes, which means that they are incapable of writing unknown and nonsense words, but are perfectly able to write familiar words whose written forms are stored in their graphemic output lexicon. When writing, patients with deep dysgraphia make semantic errors that reflect damage to the semantic system. For example, they might write *sun* although the word that they heard was *sky,* or they will respond to the picture of a hairbrush by saying *comb* and writing *hair.* Surface dysgraphia is a writing disorder in which incorrectly written words sound like the target word, and writing of regular words is superior to writing irregular ones (that are stored in their written form in the lexicon), although the ability to write irregular words is not entirely lost. Patients suffering from surface dysgraphia cannot write capital letters as small (e.g., seeing B and writing b; Eysenck & Keane, 2000).

Vlachos and Karapetsas (2002) have shown that short-latency visual-evoked potentials may provide data on the children who are at risk for dysgraphia, even when the usual psychological testing has revealed no differences between them and children who have no writing difficulties. In their studies they found significant differences in the P100 latencies between dysgraphic children and those with no writing difficulties.

One of the relatively frequent and widely studied reading disorders is *dyslexia.* It is usually classified along two criteria: with respect to onset it can be acquired or developmental, and with respect to type it can be deep or surface. Acquired dyslexia is usually a consequence of brain injury in individuals who had already mastered reading, and the symptoms are not as severe as in alexia. Developmental dyslexia is probably the most frequent kind of dyslexia. It is associated with the difficulties in mastering reading without noticeable brain injury. In deep dyslexia the reading of unknown or nonsense words is impaired, because the patients are incapable of decoding presented stimuli. Semantic paraphasias are frequent: e.g., the word *missile* will be read as *rocket.* Surface dyslexia is manifested as the inability to read whole words, with intact phonological decoding of presented words. In other words, in a language that does not have a close phoneme-to-grapheme correspondence, such as English, the patients will be able to read words that are spelled regularly, even nonsense words, but will be incapable of reading those whose spelling must be learned and is stored as a written form in the lexicon (e.g., *yacht*).

Developmental dyslexia is usually associated with abnormalities in the processing of short latency sounds, implicating subcortical structures. Regions of focal cortical dysplasias and changes in the structure and cells of the thalamus have been found in brains of dyslexics. Galaburda (2002) concluded that developmental dyslexia may be caused by early cortical injury that creates deficits in the processing of short-latency auditory data.

Leppaenen, Pihko, Eklund, and Lygtinen (1999) have shown (by ERP) that babies that are considered to be highly at risk with respect to the probability of genetic developmental dyslexia process duration of speech and auditory stimuli differently than control babies. Khan, Frisk, and Taylor (1999) also found differences in the use of cortical resources between very low-birth-weight children and the control group. The differences persist as late as ages 8 to 10. On the basis of their extensive fMRI study (70 children with developmental dyslexia and 74 children with no reading deficits), Shaywitz et al. (2000) revealed some interesting differences between the two groups of children. On the tasks that require decoding (estimation of rhyming status of pairs of nonsense words or determination of semantic category), a significantly higher activation in the dorsal parts of the parieto-temporal regions and in ventral parts of the occipito-temporal regions was found in control subjects, compared with the dyslexic ones. This is in agreement with earlier results for adults. The differences between the two groups of children were also found in the activity of the inferior frontal gyrus and the supplementary motor area. Reading success was positively correlated with the activation in posterior regions, particularly in the left occipito-temporal area. Furthermore, contrary to the controls, in whom activation of the inferior frontal gyrus during the assessment of the rhyming status of nonsense words (phonological task) did not depend on age, in dyslexic children the activation increased with age, indicating that Broca's area may have an increasingly important role. The authors concluded that the dysfunction recorded in the posterior parts of the left hemisphere that are responsible for reading exists at the very beginnings of mastering reading. Activation of anterior regions is age related in dyslexics, with older children relying more on the inferior frontal gyrus, which is probably a compensation for the disordered posterior function.

It is believed that the kinds of dyslexia associated with difficulties in auditory comprehension are caused by competition between ipsilateral and contralateral pathways for left-hemisphere resources and allocation of attention. McColl and Moncrieff (2000) studied, by means of fMRI, patterns of brain activation during a language task presented in the form of dichotic listening with controlled direction of attention in dyslexic and control children. Their most important result is the decreased level of activity in the children who exhibit strong advantage of the contralateral pathway, and this difference is considered to be a manifestation of decreased attention resources. They found no differences in laterality of language functions between their two groups of children.

Helenius et al. (2000) used MEG to study whether the same cerebral areas are involved in comprehension of reading text in adults suffering from developmental dyslexia and in healthy subjects. The sentences were presented visually, one at a time. With respect to preceding context, the last word in each test sentence could be: (a) expected; (b) semantically appropriate but unexpected; (c) semantically anomalous but composed of the same letters as the expected word; or (d) semantically and orthographically inappropriate for the current sentence context. In both groups of subjects, all examples, except the first one, elicited powerful cortical responses, consistently localized in the left superior temporal lobe, with occasional additional points of activation in more posterior parietal and temporal regions in the right hemisphere as well. In other words, there were no statistically significant differences in spatial distribution of semantic processing. Intergroup differences were expressed in timing and power of activation in several ways. Activity resulting from the analysis of semantic acceptability of the test word with respect to sentence context started about 100 ms later in dyslexics than in control subjects. The authors explained this by the dyslexics' impaired presemantic stages of processing. Also, the dyslexics' neural responses were significantly weaker, indicating smaller or more weakly synchronized neuronal groups, activated during comprehension of the reading text. The difference that perhaps best reveals different reading strategies of dyslexics and control subjects was found in responses to the third and fourth type of test words—(c) and (d). Contrary to the control group, significantly lower activity was elicited in dyslexics when the test word was semantically anomalous but beginning with letters that corresponded to the expected word (c) than when the test word was neither semantically nor orthographically appropriate (d). On the basis of these results it may be concluded that control subjects perceive words as wholes, whereas dyslexics rely on sublexical word recognition, causing them to incorrectly perceive words with correct (expected) beginnings as expected words.

McCrory, Frith, Brunswick, and Price (2000) compared (by means of PET) the brain activity of dyslexics and controls during repetition of meaningful words, nonwords, and at rest. In both groups repetition of speech stimuli elicited widely distributed bilateral activation in the areas associated with auditory speech processing, regardless of the type of stimuli (meaningful or nonsense). However, in the group of dyslexics they recorded lower activation in the superior temporal and postcentral gyrus of the right hemisphere and in the left cerebellar hemisphere than in the control group. Especially the right Brodmann's area 22 was less activated in each dyslexic than in any of the individual controls. This difference seems to be characteristic of repetition of auditorily presented words, because it has not been found in any of the earlier studies in which the same test material was read, rather than repeated. This led the authors to conclude that developmental dyslexia is a functional rather than a structural disorder.

Boulanouar et al. (2000) found (by fMRI) that listening to tones increases activity in the left superior temporal gyrus and that detection of phonological changes activates the left supramarginal gyrus. During listening to syllables there was bilateral activation of the superior temporal gyrus (as opposed to dyslexics, in whom the activation was found in the middle temporal gyrus). Another difference was noticed between control subjects and dyslexics: when /pa/ syllables were included among /ta/ syllables, the left supramarginal gyrus was activated in control subjects, which was not the case with dyslexics. On the other hand, in both groups the number of deviant /pa/ syllables was directly correlated with the extent of activation of the primary auditory cortex. Alonso-Bua, Diaz, and Ferraces (2006) found evidence of the existence of a preattentional auditory deficit underlying phonological processing in children with reading difficulties, and pointed to important differences between the various stages of automatic information processing in good and poor readers.

Although it is assumed that in deep dyslexics (subsequent to left-hemisphere injury) the recognition of written words and their lexico-semantic analysis is controlled by the intact right hemisphere, Laine, Salmelin, Helenius, and Martilla (2000) found in their one deep dyslexic, as in most control subjects reported in other studies, activation in the superior part of the left temporal lobe while reading isolated words and in reactions to sentence-final semantic anomalies. They monitored (by means of MEG) their patient, and continuous testing revealed that, with time, differences in activation occur in the damaged left hemisphere, despite the unchanged behavior.

MOTOR SPEECH DISORDERS

Contrary to aphasias, which are manifested through speech, but are in fact language disorders, motor speech disorders reflect impaired control at some level of the speech mechanism, occurring as a consequence of damage to or dysfunction of the nervous system structures that are in charge of that particular mechanism. The most frequent kinds are stuttering, dysarthria, and apraxia of speech, which may accompany neurological diseases or conditions such as Parkinson's disease, traumatic brain injury, amyotrophic lateral sclerosis, multiple sclerosis, stroke, and so on.

Patients with motor speech disorders frequently suffer from disorders of rate of speech. This is important to keep in mind during studies, because speech comprehension in the observed patients may considerably depend on the rate of speech required in laboratory conditions. Disordered laryngeal function is one of the characteristics of speech motor disorders. It may be manifested as altered voice quality (hoarseness), as problems in pitch control (tremor), as incorrect segmentation of voicing (short voiceless intervals, e.g., breaks of voice—or the inability to stop voicing) and "unnaturalness." Common articulatory features of patients suffering from motor speech disorders are decreased movement and speed, but also poorer coordination, resulting in poor intelligibility of their speech. One of the consequences of the reduced movement range and articulatory rate is inappropriate articulation of stops and their substitution with fricatives, because the subjects are incapable of completing the movement that would enable complete stop articulation, or completion of closure in the appropriate place of articulation (Eysenck & Keane, 2000; Horga, 1996; Kent & Tjaden, 1997).

Dysarthria

Dysarthria is a condition caused by brain damage, manifested as severe motor disorder due to decrease or loss of control over articulator muscles. For a disorder to qualify as dysarthria it has to affect speech production, not just the structures of the speech mechanism. Weismer (1997) advocates the stand that dysarthria should include even speech production deficits that have no bearing on patients' intelligibility, but can only be discovered by acoustic analysis of their utterances. The typical classification includes the following types of dysarthria (Judaš & Kostović, 1997):

1. Flaccid—injury to the motor neurons of cranial nerves V, VII, IX–XII, in the nuclei of the ventral horn of the spinal cord that serve head, neck, and respiratory system muscles, in the nerves between motor neurons and periphery, on the border with muscle fibers, or a combination of these locations. The consequences of such injuries is muscle paralysis or weakness, which is, due to decreased tone of laryngeal muscles, manifested in speech as disorders of phonation, resonance, and prosody.
2. Spastic—the injury is located above the level of cranial nerves, in the area of corticobulbar and/or corticospinal tracts. The consequence is hypertonicity, which is, due to increased tone of laryngeal muscles, manifested in speech as hoarse and tense voice, monotonous prosody, strong and unchangeable accent, slow speech, nasality, distorted vowels, and imprecise consonants.
3. Ataxic—the injury is located in the cerebellum or in pathways leading to it. The consequences are poor control of the range and force of movement, inability to produce precise movements, disintegration of complex movements into simple constituents, slowness of movements, hypotonia, and difficulties in alternating agonistic and antagonistic muscles. It is manifested in speech as articulatory imprecision (distorted vowels and imprecise consonants), overstressing, and prolonged sounds.
4. Hypokinetic—usually accompanies Parkinson's or similar diseases, the injury is located in *substantia nigra* (in the midbrain), where the neurotransmitter dopamine is normally produced, which decreases its influence on basal ganglia cells. Consequences of such neurotransmitter disbalance are difficulties in initiating movements and their small range. Such numerous rapid micromovements are manifested in speech as variable rate of speech, decreased stress, short bursts of speech, and imprecise consonants.
5. Hyperkinetic—the injury is located in the extrapyramidal tract and causes uncontrollable involuntary movements. It is manifested in speech as prosodic disorders: poor or exaggerated prosody, articulatory imprecision, tense voice, and poor resonances.

APRAXIA OF SPEECH

Apraxia of speech is a motor speech disorder that is not a consequence of paralysis, weakness, incoordination and/or involuntary movements. It is believed that it affects motor programming, because patients have problems initiating the utterance, they take a long time to find appropriate articulatory positions and their speech is affected by phonetic complexity and length of utterance. They frequently have injuries in Broca's area, in *capsula interna* or in the thalamus, which causes aphasic deficits together with apraxia of speech. With time, aphasic symptoms decrease and apraxia remains the dominant disorder. Pure apraxia is not accompanied by aphasia, and such cases are frequently indistinguishable from dysarthria.

Great intersubject variability makes group studies unreliable. Case studies are, therefore, more informative (see also chap. 4 for a discussion of group and case studies). Or possibly it is helpful to group subjects with respect to their speech verbal behavior rather than with respect to the neuropathology that caused the motor disorder. A more detailed review of motor speech disorders and a summary of articulatory difficulties were given by Weismer (1997).

STUTTERING

On the basis of PET results, Fox et al. (2000) concluded that cerebral correlates of stuttering are the speech-motor areas of the nondominant (usually right) hemisphere and the nondominant (usually left) cerebellar hemisphere. Apart from the atypical right hemisphere activation in stutterers mentioned elsewhere in the literature, Fox and colleagues draw attention to the cerebellum. The degree of stuttering was positively correlated with the activity of the right cerebral hemisphere and the left cerebellar hemisphere, and fluency was positively correlated with the pattern typical of healthy right-handers: the more fluent syllable pronunciation, the greater the activity of the left cerebral and the right cerebellar hemisphere. Homotopic areas of both hemispheres were active: the areas where mouth muscles are represented in the motor cortex, supplementary motor area, inferior lateral premotor cortex (Broca's area), anterior insula, and the cerebellum. This was true of all subjects, with opposite laterality in stutterers and controls. They also claim that stutterers have problems with auditory processing, not just motor performance.

De Nil, Kroll, Kapur, and Houle (2000) also showed that stuttering was correlated with atypical lateralization of language processes. The results of their PET measurements show that reading of individual words aloud activates cortical and subcortical structures in both hemispheres, but that compared with the control (nonverbal) task, stutterers exhibit greater right-hemisphere activation when controls exhibit greater left-hemisphere activity. During silent reading there was increased activation of the left anterior cingulate in stutterers but not in controls. The authors explained this difference by cognitive anticipatory reactions in stutterers, because the activated area is responsible for selective attention and practicing articulation without actual speech.

Tandon et al. (2000) talk about several abnormally activated cerebral areas in stutterers: the right supplementary motor area and insula, the *claustrum* (groups of neurons in the white matter that constitute basal ganglia), and the lateral part of the thalamus in the left hemisphere. Abnormally low activity was found in Brodmann's areas 22 and 47 in the left hemisphere, which correspond to the posterior temporal lobe and inferior frontal lobe.

Salmelin, Schnitzler, Schmitz, and Freund (2000) studied (by MEG) the temporal sequence of cerebral activation during reading common nouns seven to eight letters long. In controls, approximately 400 ms after presentation of the word there was activation in the left inferior frontal lobe (region of articulatory programming), followed by activation in the lateral part of the central sulcus and the dorsal premotor cortex (region of preparation for motor execution/performance). In stutterers, the order of activation was reversed: there was activity in the left motor cortex before activity in the inferior frontal lobe—as if they start speaking before they knew how to. The authors also found that the neighboring representations of mouth and hand were not entirely functionally separate during speech production in stutterers, because the suppression of the slow motor cortical rhythm associated with fluent speech is not restricted to mouth representation, but extends to hand representation as well. Contrary to fluent speakers, this was found in the right hemisphere of the stutterers. Furthermore, they concluded that the network comprising the left inferior frontal lobe and the right motor–premotor cortex is partially functionally damaged in stutterers.

OTHER CAUSES OF SPEECH AND LANGUAGE DISORDERS

SCHIZOPHRENIA

In their ERP study of healthy and schizophrenic subjects Bruder et al. (1999) found differences in functional cerebral asymmetry between the two groups on a dichotic listening test involving perception of CV syllables. In healthy subjects, 200 ms after stimulus onset (N200) they recorded greater activity over parieto-temporal points in the left than in the right hemisphere. The patients exhibited no right-ear advantage. Their results confirmed earlier reports of decreased or nonexistent left-hemisphere superiority for syllable or word perception in schizophrenics. Similar results were reported by Walter et al. (2000) who used fMRI.

Shergill, Brammer, Williams, Murray, and McGuire (2000) recorded brain activity of their schizophrenic patients while they were having auditory hallucinations and during periods without hallucinations, and found a widely distributed network of cortical and subcortical areas: the inferior frontal lobe and insula, the anterior cingulate, the bilateral temporal lobe (with greater right-hemisphere activation), the right thalamus and inferior colliculus, as well as the left hippocampus and surrounding areas.

Kircher et al. (2000) found in their schizophrenic patients during production of neologisms activation in the anterior cingulate (Brodmann's area 32), left posterior middle temporal gyrus (Brodmann's areas 21/37), and the right posterior cerebellum. Obviously, production of neologisms involves only some of the areas otherwise included in word generation (e.g., the anterior cingulate gyrus), but also higher than normal right-hemisphere activation. They attributed the activation of the right temporal lobe to the activation of too wide a semantic field.

Epilepsy and Tumors

Localization of language functions in epileptics' brains is much more variable than in healthy subjects. In all of their patients, Carpentier et al. (2000b) found activation of homotopic language areas in the right hemisphere reflecting language plasticity, although there were no anatomic changes in the classical language areas. It seems that disordered electrical brain activity, which is characteristic of epilepsy, affects normal functioning of language neural networks, and, in order to bypass that noise, the brain undergoes functional reorganization. These epileptic foci are called the nociferous cortex, and they disrupt normal functioning of the surrounding cortical regions, forcing the more distant areas to take over the function. Azari et al. (1999) also found reorganization of language areas in temporal lobe epileptics, which created problems in processing verbal data.

There are examples of normal language function lateralization. Moeller et al. (2000) found (by means of MEG) clear left-lateralization of language functions during silent reading and silent object naming. They located Wernicke's center in the posterior part of the left superior temporal gyrus in all of their 26 patients with a brain tumor or epilepsy; they located Broca's center in the left inferior frontal gyrus in 77% of the same subjects. Direct cortical electrical stimulation confirmed MEG results in three patients in whom it was applied.

In their fMRI study of 17 patients suffering from temporal lobe epilepsy, Baciu et al. (2000) found left-hemisphere dominance in tasks of determining rhyming status of visually presented pairs of words. Activation was recorded in the inferior frontal gyrus (Broca's area), the posterior part of the superior temporal gyrus (Wernicke's area), the inferior temporal lobe, the prefrontal gyrus, the premotor cortex, the inferior temporal gyrus, and the anterior and posterior cingulate gyrus. The dominance was assessed on the basis of asymmetric responses in the first five of the above-mentioned activated areas. In 11 patients these results have been confirmed by more invasive techniques.

It seems that the left hemisphere cannot be prevented from automatic speech processing. Therefore, it is not surprising that better results of speech and language functions may be obtained if the left hemisphere is removed completely, rather than keeping it together with its inhibitory, but inappropriate, activity that prevents the right hemisphere from taking over. This conclusion was reached by Feindel (1994) pertaining to epileptics: epileptic tissue causes impairment of language functions, and removal of this abnormal tissue stopped epileptic seizures and improved language functions. In any case, only one hemisphere may be dominant for language—not so much because of semantics or syntax, but primarily due to the nature of speech. Very rapid synergic movements of speech muscles cannot be controlled from two places at the same time—one hemisphere has to control organs in the body midline (Gazzaniga, 1994). It has been discussed above why this one hemisphere is usually the left, and in what cases the role is taken over by the right hemisphere.

Right-Hemisphere Damage

Right-hemisphere damage generally does not cause obvious aphasic symptoms. However, more sensitive tests have revealed mild language deficits—particularly with respect to abstract notions or abstract words that are typically missing in sentence completion tests. Problems were also found in learning new language material, articulation, metaphor comprehension, responses to complex utterance of unusual syntax, word finding, and verbal creativity, as well as in writing familiar automatic phrases. Boatman (2000) found in two girls (9 and 10 years old) that speech perception after right hemispherectomy is intact in optimal conditions and on simple tasks; however, in difficult listening conditions and on more challenging tasks she found that speech comprehension without the right hemisphere is difficult. The speech of right hemisphere–injured patients is frequently monotonous, which implies prosodic abnormalities that include fundamental frequency. Timing and temporal control of speech course, duration of words, pauses, and so forth, are impaired to a lesser extent. Fluency may be impaired after damage to the orbito-frontal region (Kolb & Whishaw, 1996). Furthermore, although right-hemisphere-damaged patients at first glance seem to have intact language, it has been found that the right hemisphere is superior to the left in processing words from the same semantic category, but without relations by association (e.g., *cat–cow*; Gazzaniga et al., 2002).

The primary contribution of the right hemisphere to normal language processing is at the level of pragmatics (Blumstein, 1988). Patients with severe right-hemisphere damage frequently exhibit difficulties in integrating facts represented in individual propositions into a larger coherent set. For example, while they are trying to remember details of a story, they are incapable of inferring about what is likely to happen, nor can they grasp the moral of the story. Obviously, normal language functioning requires that both hemispheres work together.

Problems occur at the level of nonverbal and verbal communication of emotions. Reliance on body posture, facial expressions, and hand gestures of interlocutors is decreased. Some patients base their recognition of persons on clothes, hairdo, and voice pitch more than on the face. In recognizing moods that the interlocutors wish to convey by nonverbal means, these individuals frequently rely on entirely different cues than do the controls. Accordingly, their facial expressions during recall or observation of some emotionally intense events are much poorer than those of the healthy subjects. In natural conversational situations recorded without the participants' knowledge and with familiar interlocutors, such patients use significantly fewer facial expressions that are common in social interaction (e.g., smiling). At the verbal level, the disorders are manifested as difficulties in identification of emotions in phrases and sentences, even in sentences in which emotions are clearly stated. On the other hand, there were no problems in utterances without explicitly emotionally colored words, but in which the type of emotions had to be inferred from context. The authors concluded that the right hemisphere is the seat of some lexico-semantic representations of emotional expressions, and that right-hemisphere damage prevents access to these representations and/or their activation, but not their content. To a great extent the success of understanding emotions (e.g., expressed in a series of cartoons) depends on the amount of cognitive effort necessary to describe the cartoons. This again stresses the issue of allocating and maintaining attention, which was found to be crucial in right hemisphere–damaged patients, and that apparently constitutes most disorders of right-hemisphere speech and language functioning. Other verbal problems noticed in right hemisphere–damaged patients include decreased recall of emotionally loaded stories (as opposed to the neutral ones with respect to which the patients are no different than controls). On the other hand, thrillers were as easily remembered by right hemisphere–damaged patients as by healthy controls. However, boring stories were much better remembered by controls. The marked positive influence of thrill effects on the success of recall in right hemisphere–damaged patients as compared with controls is explained by their otherwise decreased arousal level. In other words, it was necessary to make the story more interesting in order to reach their arousal threshold, than was the case in controls. The decreased arousal level contributes to decreased ability to understand humor and laughter in general. Poorly expressed emotional content is manifested as decreased use of emotional words during descriptions or retelling of some emotionally colored pictures and events. In this respect, right hemisphere–damaged patients differ significantly from controls or left hemisphere–damaged patients. On neutral tasks their results were comparable with those of the other two groups. It is important to keep in mind that right hemisphere–damaged patients feel the emotional content equally intensely, but are incapable of expressing it. In other words, their capacity to feel and experience emotions is intact, only their ability to comprehend and express has been impaired, with the exception of patients who have other psychological problems (depression, confusion, etc.; Eysenck & Keane, 2000; Gazzaniga et al., 2002; Myers, 1999).

Right-hemisphere damage may affect general communication abilities without impairing language functions. On the other hand, just as not all left hemisphere–damaged people suffer from aphasias, so cognitive or communication disorders are not necessarily a consequence of right-hemisphere damage.

Epilogue

Speech and language functions, especially their representation in the brain, have always been among the central issues studied by neuroscientists, and there is no reason to believe this will not continue to be so in the future. In the past several decades we have seen the coming together of the "hard" sciences, such as neurology, molecular biology, biochemistry, physiology, and physics with the fields such as psychology, linguistics, and phonetics and speech communication. This welcome trend is manifested not just in the emergence of new terms (e.g., neurolinguistics, biopsychology, cognitive neuroscience, etc.) but, what is more important, in increasing interest, understanding, appreciation, and cooperation among scientists of various research disciplines. Many early hypotheses, theories, and models have been reexamined and tested on different material and by different methods, and new ones are being proposed regularly. Some have stood the test of time and advancement of science in general; others have been revised or discarded completely. This is very exciting, and it is what research is all about. A possible risk is that we might get so impressed and carried away by new methods and techniques offering a wealth of possibilities that we spend too much time looking at the trees instead of trying to understand the forest. Hopefully, interdisciplinary texts like this one are helpful in relating individual and widely dispersed facts and results and putting them into perspective.

Although speech and language are primarily left-hemisphere activities, they need the right hemisphere to proceed optimally, and numerous studies have shown that many speech and language functions are seriously impaired without the involvement of the right hemisphere. They are equally difficult if not entirely impossible without subcortical and peripheral structures. Speech and language are in their own way just as much a living system as the brain, and the beauty of it is that we can use one to explore and explain the other.

Glossary

Absolute limen (threshold) The lowest level of intensity, or other stimulus feature, that can be detected 50% of the time (threshold).

Absolute pitch Ability to identify and/or sing a particular tone (frequency) without a referent tone.

Acalculia Inability to do mathematical calculations; a type of agnosia and apraxia related to numeric symbols. A milder form is called dyscalculia and it is manifested as difficulties in performing mathematical operations.

Achromatopsia Inability to recognize colors. Perception of patterns and movements is relatively intact.

Acquisition (a) The first step in the encoding stage of learning during which input data are registered by sensory organs and subjected to sensory analysis. (b) The term language "acquisition" rather than language "learning" is used when referring to the adoption of the first language (mother tongue), which is acquired automatically, implicitly, and typically in informal situations.

Action potential Propagation of the nerve impulse through a neuron. Action potential occurs at the axon hillock as a consequence of some stimulus. It is, in fact, an instantaneous depolarization from approximately –70mV to about +50mV. Action potential is based on the change in the permeability of the cell membrane to potassium and sodium ions.

Acute In phonology, one of the distinctive features that is important for distinguishing among sounds by their place of articulation. Acoustic energy is concentrated in higher frequencies and articulation is in the central part of the mouth cavity. Front vowels, e.g., /i/, and alveolar, dental and palatal consonants (e.g., /t/) are [+acute]. Back vowels (e.g., /u/), and labial and velar consonants (e.g., /p/, /k/) are [–acute]. Opposite: grave. See also **Distinctive features**.

Afferent nerves Neural fibers that transmit stimulus information to the central nervous system from some other part of the nervous system or from a sensory organ.

Afferent pathway A bundle of axons of afferent nerves.

Aggregation of neurons A phase in the formation of the nervous system that partly overlaps with the migration phase. During this phase nerve cells are selectively grouped into major cell assemblies or layers in the nervous system. Larger structures are formed in this way.

Agnosia Inability to structure, i.e., recognize sensory information, with intact sensation. It occurs as a consequence of damage to secondary sensory areas in the brain. There are different types of agnosia: see anosognosia, apperceptive agnosia, associative agnosia, asomatognosia, astereognosia, auditory (acoustic) agnosia, visual (optic) agnosia.

Agrammatism A condition in which grammatical structure is impaired in speech production (expressive agrammatism) or in speech perception (receptive agrammatism). In expressive agrammatism, many grammatical words and suffixes are omitted.

Agraphia The inability to write caused by brain damage in the frontal lobe in the area between Broca's area and the cortical motor representation of hand muscles. See also **Dysgraphia**.

Akinetopsia Inability to perceive moving objects, with intact perception of immobile objects.

Alexia Condition in which the ability to read is impaired, with intact speech comprehension and nonverbal visual perception, i.e., object recognition resulting from neural damage, typically in the parieto-occipital areas of the language-dominant (usually left) hemisphere. Analytical processing is impaired. A milder form of the disorder is called dyslexia. See also **Developmental dyslexia**.

Allocentric encoding of space Processing of spatial information with respect to some point in space—e.g., the selection of the object (among several available) that is the closest to some other object. Opposite: egocentric encoding of space.

Alphabet A type of script in which each symbol represents one letter (grapheme), which more or less corresponds to one phoneme. With respect to correspondence between letters and sounds we usually talk of shallow orthography (e.g., Croatian), with high degree of letter-to-sound correspondence and deep orthography, with a low degree of correspondence (e.g., English).

Alzheimer's disease A type of dementia resulting from, among other causes, progressive deterioration of nerve cells in the brain. It has a strong genetic component. The abbreviations DAT (dementia of Alzheimer type) and AD are also frequently used in literature.

Amnesia Difficulties in memory as a consequence of brain damage, illness, or psychological trauma. It may involve loss of already existing knowledge (retrograde amnesia), inability to acquire new information (anterograde amnesia), or both.

Ampulla A wider part of the semicircular canal in the vestibular organ in the inner ear where the receptor cells are located.

Amusia Impaired auditory recognition of music and musical expression.

Amygdala A small almond-shaped group of neurons in the medial part of the temporal lobe immediately next to the anterior part of the hippocampus in both hemispheres. It is involved primarily in processing negative emotions (e.g., fear), but is also active, to a smaller extent, in responses to positive and neutral stimuli. It plays an important role in emotional learning and memory.

Analytic processing Processing of stimuli and other data that relies on individual parts, rather than on the whole. Opposite: holistic processing.

Anarthria A condition occurring after central or peripheral paresis or paralysis of speech musculature, difficult coordination, or hyperkinesia, due to which the patients are incapable of speaking in spite of intact language competence.

Angular gyrus (gyrus angularis) A gyrus at the junction of the temporal and parietal lobes, immediately posterior to Wernicke's area. It is believed that this gyrus in the language-dominant hemisphere (typically left) is involved in reading and arithmetic. It corresponds to Brodmann's area 39.

Anomia After brain damage, condition resulting in the patient being incapable of naming objects and concepts. The ability to describe the function and appearance of the object is frequently preserved. Comprehension and production of speech are intact. Anomia may be limited to particular categories. In such cases it is manifested as the inability to name objects belonging to a specific category. For example, the patient may be anomic for inanimate objects, without anomia for other categories. It is sometimes referred to as amnesic or nominal aphasia.

Anosognosia Inability or refusal to acknowledge suffering from an illness or disorder, inability to recognize one's own symptoms; it may be accompanied by contralateral neglect. It usually occurs as a consequence of parietal lobe damage (most frequently in the right hemisphere).

Anoxia Oxygen deprivation.

Anterior Used to describe the position or direction of various structures in vertebrates that is toward the front, toward the nose (see also rostral). Opposite: posterior, caudal.

Anterograde amnesia Decreased ability to memorize data (acquire new knowledge) after onset of amnesia, i.e., after brain damage that caused it. Opposite: retrograde amnesia.

Anvil (*incus*) One of the three ossicles in the middle ear. It is located between the hammer (*malleus*) and the stirrup (*stapes*).

Apex Tip. The term may refer to (a) the tip of the tongue: sounds produced with the tip of the tongue are called apical sounds; or (b) the tip of the cochlea, i.e., the part that is the farthest away from the point at which the plate of the stapes closes the oval window.

Aphasia A disorder of language production and/or perception caused by brain damage. Primary aphasia is a pure language disorder. Secondary aphasia is a consequence of disordered memory, attention, or perception (see also Broca's aphasia, global aphasia, conduction aphasia, transcortical aphasia, Wernicke's aphasia).

Aphemia The term Broca used for aphasia.

Aphonia Phonation disorder resulting in a whisper-like voice.

Apoptosis Programmed death of nerve cells. The neurons that have not established or have lost communication with other neurons die, as do the cells that for some reason are no longer able to function normally (e.g., due to illness).

Apperceptive agnosia A type of visual agnosia in which the patient can recognize an object only from the familiar angle; if the position of the object is changed or the object is not clearly visible, the recognition is unsuccessful.

Apraxia A consequence of brain damage that is manifested as the inability to combine movements into complex activities, with intact ability to perform simple movements. Parietal lobe lesions usually cause ideational apraxia, whereas damage to secondary motor areas cause motor apraxia. See also apraxia of speech, construction apraxia, oral apraxia.

Apraxia of speech Difficulties in producing speech due to the inability to program articulatory movements. See also **Apraxia**.

Aprosodia Disordered comprehension and production of prosody and emotional gesticulation accompanying speech. Most frequently, it occurs as a consequence of damage in the language-nondominant (typically right) hemisphere.

Asomatognosia Loss of awareness about one's own body, resulting from brain damage. It is usually unilateral.

Association cortex Part of the cerebral cortex that receives information from several different sensory modalities. Information arriving from secondary areas is integrated and combined with affective data. In other words, new information is interpreted in reference to earlier experiences and existing knowledge.

Association fibers Myelinated axons of neurons that connect parts of the cerebral cortex within the same hemisphere.

Associative agnosia A type of visual agnosia in which the patient is capable of recognizing an object, but is unable to associate it with the existing knowledge about that or another similar object.

Associative learning Type of learning during which the organism learns about relationships among different stimuli or about the relationship between the stimulus and his/her own actions.

Astereognosia (tactile agnosia) Inability to recognize objects by touch, most frequently caused by parietal lobe lesions.

Ataxia Loss of motor coordination manifested as falling or staggering to one side.

Attention Directing (on purpose or reflexively) of psychic and psychomotor activity toward specific data or stimuli. See also **Selective attention**.

Auditory (acoustic, phonological) agnosia A condition in which perception of unknown and nonsense words is impaired, with intact recognition of familiar words.

Auditory pathway A group of neural structures that connect the peripheral part of the auditory sensory system and the auditory cortex.

Autobiographic memory Memory for events from one's own life.

Autonomic (visceral) nervous system Part of the peripheral nervous system that regulates internal processes (e.g., blood pressure, cardiac rhythm, digestion) and enables homeostasis (optimal condition and operation of the organism). Its afferent nerves transmit impulses from the internal organs to the central nervous system, and its efferent nerves transmit motor stimuli from the central nervous system to internal organs. Efferent nerves that exit the lumbal and the thoracic parts of the spinal cord make the sympathetic system, and those exiting the brain and the sacral parts of the spinal cord make the parasympathetic system. These two systems have antagonistic effects; activation of the sympathetic system causes a more rapid heartbeat and breathing and elevated blood pressure, as well as increased secretion of adrenalin and inhibition of the digestive system. This activity is associated with strong emotions. The work of the autonomic system is primarily controlled by the hypothalamus.

Autotopagnosia Inability to orient oneself with respect to parts of one's own body. The patient is incapable of orienting or recognizing what is left and what is right. The condition occurs as a result of brain damage near the angular gyrus (most frequently in the right hemisphere).

Axon The long process that extends from the cell body, by means of which stimuli are transferred to other neurons. It begins at the axon hillock and ends with terminal nodes at the presynaptic axon terminal.

Axon hillock The part of the nerve cell in which cell body and axon merge. This is where action potential is formed.

Back propagation A learning mechanism based on the comparison of actual responses with the correct ones. The term is mostly associated with neural network models.

Basal end Part of the cochlea that is closest to the oval window.

Basal ganglia A group of nuclei composed of gray matter deep within the cerebrum. They are interrelated with the cortex, thalamus, reticular formation, and parts of the midbrain and the spinal cord. The nuclei are involved in motor control and learning. The best known disorders associated with basal ganglia damage are Huntington's and Parkinson's disease.

Basilar membrane Part of the cochlea; a membrane on which auditory receptor cells are situated (organ of Corti).

Behaviorism A school of psychological thought that analyzes people by studying their behavior; environment and learning are believed to be principal factors of mental development.

Blood-brain barrier A barrier between the blood vessels in the brain and the tissues of the brain that protects the neurons in the brain from unwanted substances in the blood; it is based on the special structure of cerebral blood vessels.

BOLD (blood oxygenation level dependent) effect Effect dependent on blood oxygen level; measured by fMRI.

Bottom-up processing Processing of stimuli that is directly affected by environmental stimuli; the processing is instigated by an external stimulus (data-driven processing). Opposite: top-down.

Bradykinesia Pathologically slow or stiff movements. The causes may be organic or functional. The disorder is most frequently associated with Parkinson's disease.

Brain (encephalon) Part of the central nervous system. The main parts are brain stem, cerebellum, midbrain, and cerebrum.

Brain stem (truncus cerebri) Connects the brain with the spinal cord; it has functions of its own, primarily reflex actions that are crucial for life support (e.g., breathing). Afferent and efferent pathways run through the brain stem.

Broca's aphasia Traditionally this term refers to the speech and language disorder caused by lesions in the frontal lobe, in the area roughly corresponding to Broca's area. The disorder is characterized by difficulties in speech production with relatively intact speech perception. This type of aphasia is therefore also commonly referred to as motor, nonfluent, or expressive aphasia. It has been found, however, that patients suffer from difficulties in comprehension of grammatically more complex utterances as well.

Broca's area Part of the inferior prefrontal cortex of the language-dominant hemisphere that has been traditionally considered a center of speech production. It corresponds to Brodmann's areas 44 and 45. The area is named after the physician who was among the first to describe the problems in speech production and relate them to lesions in that particular part of the brain.

Brodmann's areas Parts of the cerebral cortex denoted by numbers 1 through 52 differing in cytoarchitectural structure. Some areas have special functions (e.g., Brodmann's area 17 is the primary visual cortex), whereas in some other functions multiple fields are involved. The descriptions were done by K. Brodmann at the beginning of the 20th century, hence the name. See also **Cytoarchitecture**.

Callosotomy Partial or complete cutting of the corpus callosum. See also **Commissurotomy**.

Cascade models Similar to modular models. They involve different, but interconnected neural modules, each of which is responsible for a different level of processing information about the word or some other information.

Case study Method of study that includes collection of data, testing, and analysis of behavior of individual subjects.

Categorical speech perception Classification of speech sounds as belonging to specific phoneme categories in an all-or-none manner.

Caudal Toward the back or tail. Opposite: rostral. See also **Posterior**.

Cell body (soma) Body of a neuron. It consists of a nucleus, mitochondria, endoplasmic reticulum, ribosomes, and Golgi apparatus, all suspended in cytoplasm (intracellular fluid), and enveloped by a semipermeable cell membrane. The cell body is the center of metabolic activity of the neuron. Extending from the cell body are dendrites and the axon.

Central executive A component of the working memory of limited capacity and modality-independent. It regulates and controls attention and it is superordinate to two active systems: the phonological (articulatory) loop and the visuospatial sketchpad.

Central nervous system Part of the nervous system contained within the spinal column and the skull, comprising the spinal cord and the brain. Opposite: peripheral nervous system.

Central sulcus A deep groove that separates the frontal and parietal lobes. It is one of the major sulci on the lateral side of the brain. Immediately anterior to it is the precentral gyrus with the primary motor cortex, and immediately posterior to it there is the postcentral gyrus, with the primary somatosensory cortex. Also referred to as Rolandic fissure.

Cerebellum (little cerebrum). A part of the brain located between the cerebrum and the brain stem at the level of the pons. It has a highly convoluted three-layered cortex, subcortical white matter, and subcortical nuclei. Morphologically it is divided into two hemispheres and the medial part (*vermis*). Input data are integrated and processed here before being transmitted to other brain areas. It coordinates and smooths muscle activity, and together with the vestibular system coordinates head movements and body posture with other activities.

Cerebrospinal fluid A clear fluid that fills the cavities (ventricular system) of the central nervous system; it has a protective role.

Cerebrovascular insult (CVI) Stroke.

Cerebrum The largest part of the brain involved in complex processes (e.g., learning, perception, planning).

Cingulate cortex (cortex cinguli) Cortex of the cingulate gyrus that surrounds the corpus callosum. The anterior cingulate, located under the frontal lobe connects that lobe with the limbic system and it is important for different executive functions (e.g., response monitoring, error detection and directing attention).

Cingulate gyrus (gyrus cinguli) Part of the cerebrum immediately above the corpus callosum. It is part of the limbic system.

Co-articulation Influence of one speech segment on another during speech production.

Cochlea Part of the inner ear that houses hearing cells (auditory receptor cells). Here, mechanical energy is transformed into nerve impulses that are transmitted to the brain via the auditory pathway.

Cocktail-party effect A phenomenon commonly observed in noisy environments, illustrated for example, by the ability to pick out a particular conversation at a party where many simultaneous conversations are taking place, while at the same time monitoring all others. See also **Selective attention**.

Cognitive neuropsychology For the most part involves the study of cognitive functioning in brain-damaged patients with the purpose of understanding normal cognitive operations.

Cognitive neuroscience Study of the functioning of the human brain; involves use of various methods that enable registering and imaging of brain activity.

Cognitive psychology Branch of psychology that deals with internal representations of the external world in the human mind. It involves study of mental processes related to perception, attention, learning, and problem solving.

Cognitive science The multi- and interdisciplinary study of cognitive processes (artificial intelligence, linguistics, psychology, neurology, and information science), which involves designing computer models of human cognitive functioning.

Cohort The term originally referred to a Roman infantry unit of 300 to 600 people; metaphorically it refers to a tightly connected group of people. In linguistics, the term was introduced in the Cohort theory (Marslen-Wilson, 1980), and it refers to all words in a person's mental lexicon that are activated at a particular moment in word or sentence processing, and that participate in subsequent phases of language processing. The processing of speech data starts when the listener hears the first sound or phoneme. An example of a cohort is all words starting with the phoneme /p/ that are activated when this phoneme is presented as a stimulus in a test (initial cohort). Addition of the subsequent phoneme, e.g., /a/, decreases the number of members in the cohort because all members that do not share that particular combination of phonemes are eliminated, and so on. As the amount of perceptual data increases (i.e., more and more phonemes are added on), the number of active representations decreases until the moment when the input signal (perceived word) matches one representation. In other words, a larger context decreases the size of the cohort, because other acoustic and phonetic data, as well as higher-level expectations become active. A modified cohort model predicts activation of all word forms that even partly match the input word, not only those that have the same initial phoneme (Norris et al., 1995; as cited in Gazzaniga et al., 2002).

Cohort theory See **Cohort**.

Colliculus inferior Largest subcortical auditory structure It is located in the midbrain and is an obligatory relay in the ascending auditory pathway.

Columnar organization Functional organization of the cerebral cortex into columns of neurons, perpendicular to the cortical surface, which share a common function.

Coma Unconscious state when the patient is unresponsive to external or internal stimuli.

Commissural fibers Myelinated axons of neurons that connect the two hemispheres. The largest commissure is the corpus callosum, but the hemispheres are connected with other commissures: the anterior commissure, posterior commissure, hippocampal commissure, massa intermedia; the left and the right auditory pathways are connected via the Probst commissure; the left and the right visual pathways are connected via the optic chiasm.

Commissure See **Commissural fibers**.

Commissurotomy Partial or complete disconnection of the left and the right hemispheres. It is usually done in the corpus callosum, but it may involve cutting one or all of the other commissures (e.g., anterior commissure, posterior commissure, massa intermedia), in which case the connections between the subcortical structures of the two hemispheres are cut as well.

Compact One of the distinctive features that is important for distinguishing phonemes on the basis of place of articulation. Open vowels (e.g., /a/) and central and back consonants (e.g., /t ʃ/, /k/) are compact. Opposite: diffuse. See also **Distinctive feature**.

Competence Basic ability that may be realized by performance. It is based on the idea that everyone has an internal set of language rules, even when their application does not yield a perfect result. For example, a person may have language competence that, for some reason, cannot be realized in speech.

Conditioned reflex (response) Behavior that was generated by classical or operant (instrumental) conditioning.

Conditioning Type of learning in which an otherwise neutral stimulus (that does not evoke a response on its own) when paired with an unconditioned stimulus (that always evokes a response) becomes excitatory or inhibitory (i.e., conditioned stimulus). This is known as classical (Pavlov's) conditioning. In it the response is evoked and established passively, as a reflex reaction to exogenous stimuli. Contrary to that, in operant (instrumental) conditioning the organism is active. In this type of learning the probability of occurrence of a particular response is based on the consequences that response has on the organism (Zarevski, 1994, p. 123). Reinforcement is a key element of operant conditioning. Both types of conditioning are simple forms of associative learning: in the first type we learn to predict relations between two events, and in the second, we learn about the relationship between our own behavior and consequences it will cause.

Conduction aphasia Type of aphasia occurring after lesions in the insula or in the arcuate fasciculus, a part of the brain that connects Broca's and Wernicke's areas. Patients usually have no difficulties with spontaneous speech or with speech comprehension, but are unable to repeat the words they heard. This is a subcortical type of aphasia, characterized by logorrhea and paraphasias.

Cones Photoreceptors specialized for the perception of color and high visual acuity. Most densely located in the fovea of the retina. See also **Rods**.

Connectionist models Computer models that rely on an analogy to neurons: they use basic units or nodes that are interconnected into networks. Each network has several structures (layers): input, hidden, and output. The principal characteristic of these models is that they propose that everything is connected, that processes go on in parallel, and that there is feedback between layers (contrary to localistic and modular models). See also **Neural networks**.

Consolidation The second step in the encoding stage of learning, occurring after acquisition.

Construction apraxia A disorder occurring after injury in the right posterior parietal lobe at the junction with the occipital lobe, in which the patients are unable to (re)construct a whole object from its parts or are incapable of copying even the simplest shapes.

Contralateral Relating to the opposite side. Opposite: ipsilateral.

Converging evidence Similar results obtained by different research methods, which point to the same conclusion. For example, studying a problem by means of methods that have good temporal resolution (e.g., ERP) combined with those that have good spatial resolution (e.g., fMRI) and obtaining identical results.

Cornea The transparent surface of the eyeball (in front of the lens).

Coronal section (plane) A section that exposes brain structures as they would be seen from the front; hence also the synonymous term, frontal plane.

Corpus callosum The largest commissure in the brain that connects the left and the right hemisphere.

Corpus geniculatum laterale (lateral geniculate body) Part of the visual pathway that runs through the thalamus.

Corpus geniculatum mediale (medial geniculate body) Part of the auditory pathway that runs through the thalamus.

Cranial nerves (nervi craniales) Twelve pairs of peripheral nerves that transmit sensory information from the face and the head as well as commands for motor control of the movements of the face and head; in other words, they have sensory, motor, and combined functions.

Critical period A period during which the nervous system is particularly susceptible to external influences and learns most efficiently. There are several critical periods in each individual's life, and their onset corresponds to particular phases of the nervous system development. It is also associated with the acquisition and learning of the first and second languages.

CT/CAT Computerized axial tomography.

Cupular organ Part of the vestibular organ in the inner ear consisting of semicircular canals that processes angular accelerations. The receptors (hair cells) are embedded in the gelatinous structure called cupulae.

Cytoarchitecture Cell architecture; differentiation of cells on the basis of their structure, density, and laminar organization. Cytoarchitectonic brain maps are obtained by grouping the cells of an identical or similar structure. See also **Brodmann's areas**.

DAT Dementia of Alzheimer Type; another term for Alzheimer's disease.

dB Decibel (one tenth of a Bell); the most frequent unit of sound intensity used in acoustics. It is, in fact, the difference between the actually measured sound level and a referent value, or a difference between any two sounds. A 1,000 Hz sound of the intensity sufficient to reach the absolute hearing threshold in an average healthy young person is taken as referent. That sound's physically measurable value is 10^{-12} W/m^2 (power/intensity–I_r), i.e., 20 µPa (pressure–p_r), which corresponds to 0 dB. The linear decibel scale corresponds to the logarithmic scale of physical values of power/intensity and pressure. Intensity level of a sound of intensity I equals 10 $\log_{10}$ (I/I_r) dB. Sound pressure is calculated by a similar formula—(20 $\log_{10}$ (p/p_r) dB)—but instead of being multiplied by 10 the result is multiplied by 20, because power is proportional to the square of pressure. The range between absolute threshold (limen) and the threshold of discomfort or pain is approximately 120 to 140 dB, i.e., between 10^{12} and 10^{14} times. The intensity of a whisper is about 30 to 35 dB, of quiet conversation about 50 dB, and of loud speech between 70 and 75 dB.

Declarative memory/knowledge (explicit, direct) Refers to knowledge of facts. It is studied in laboratory conditions of intentional learning in which the subjects are required to remember, recognize, and reproduce particular facts. It involves episodic and semantic memory. Opposite: nondeclarative/implicit/indirect memory.

Deductive reasoning Part of the process of forming ideas and solving problems. On the basis of general principles, inferences are drawn about the individual and particular. Opposite: inductive reasoning.

Deep dysgraphia A disorder associated with semantic errors in writing; nonwords (nonsense words) are spelled incorrectly. Opposite: surface dysgraphia. See also **Phonological dysgraphia**.

Deep dyslexia A disorder manifested as impaired reading of unfamiliar words with semantic paraphasias (reading errors): e.g., telescope instead of binoculars; due to impaired nonlexical procedure and intact lexical procedure in reading. Opposite: surface dyslexia.

Deep dysphasia A condition in which the ability to repeat heard nonwords is impaired; there are also semantic errors in repeating heard meaningful words.

Dendrite A short process on the cell body by means of which the cell receives most of the stimuli from other neurons. Dendritic spines, tiny growths on dendrites, increase the richness of connections among neurons.

Depolarization Decrease in membrane potential.

Detection A form of perceptual response, by which the existence of a stimulus is registered. See also **Discrimination**, **Identification**.

Developmental dyslexia Difficulties in reading that occur in childhood and are not caused by brain injury. It occurs more frequently in boys and in left-handers than in girls or right-handers. Other cognitive abilities are normal or even above average.

Dichotic listening One of behavioral methods of studying cerebral lateralization of speech and language functions by simultaneous presentation of different auditory stimuli to the left and the right ear.

Dichotomy Division of a continuum into two categories—e.g., verbal versus nonverbal functioning or global versus local representation of data.

Diencephalon Part of the brain wedged between the brain stem and the cerebral hemispheres. Includes the thalamus and hypothalamus.

Difference limen (threshold) The smallest difference in intensity (or some other stimulus feature) of two stimuli, which is sufficient and necessary to distinguish between sensations elicited by these two stimuli.

Differentiation of neurons A phase in the development of the nervous system that occurs after the aggregation phase. It involves the development of cell body, axon, and dendrites, as well as the establishment of neurotransmitter specificity and synaptogenesis.

Diffuse One of distinctive features that is important in distinguishing sounds on the basis of place of articulation. Close vowels (e.g., /i/, /u/) and front consonants (e.g., /m/, /p/) are diffuse. Opposite: compact. See also **Distinctive features**.

Direct memory See **Declarative memory**.

Discourse Connected text or speech, longer than a sentence.

Discrimination A form of perceptual response by which two stimuli are differentiated. See also **Identification, Detection**.

Dissociation A situation when a person exhibits impaired function or behavior A, with intact function or behavior B. It is taken as evidence that the two functions or behaviors are organized or represented in independent parts of the brain. See also **Double dissociation**.

Distal Away from a referent point. Opposite: proximal.

Distinctive feature Linguistic term referring to the smallest feature that distinguishes phonemes. Each phoneme may be described by a series of distinctive features with only one of them sufficient to distinguish it from other phonemes. For example, in English and many other languages, the phonemes /t/ and /d/ differ in the feature [± voiced]. See also **Acute, Diffuse, Grave, Compact**.

Distractor In multiple-choice tests these are the wrong answers. More generally, it is any stimulus that averts the attention from the main task.

Divided attention A situation where two tasks are performed simultaneously and they both require attention.

Divided visual field technique A method of studying cerebral functional asymmetry by briefly presenting visual test stimuli to the left or the right of the fixation point. See also **Visual field advantage**.

DNA Deoxyribonucleic acid.

Dominant hemisphere Hemisphere that is more active while performing a function. Left hemisphere used to be referred to as the dominant hemisphere, as opposed to the nondominant right, because it was believed that all cognitive functions are controlled by the left hemisphere. That belief was supported by overwhelming evidence of left-hemisphere dominance for speech and language functions.

Dorsal In descriptions of locations of structures in vertebrates, denoting direction or position toward the back or top of the head. In primates, due to their upright posture, the term *superior* is more frequently used to refer to the position or direction toward the top of the head. Opposite: ventral, i.e., inferior.

Dorsal path See **What–where dichotomy**.

Double dissociation The phenomenon that some individuals (typically after brain damage) do well on certain types of tasks but not on others, whereas other individuals behave exactly opposite. For example, double dissociation was found between alexia and prosopagnosia: patients who suffered from one deficit did not suffer from the other. Each of the groups of patients differed by dissociation from the control group. Such cases provide evidence for selective deficits, i.e., confirm that two activities have separate neural substrates; in other words, the processes and systems underlying one activity are not characteristic of the other. See also **Dissociation**.

Dualism A philosophical approach according to which the brain and mind are separate.

Dysarthria A serious motor speech disorder caused by decreased or nonexistent control over articulator muscles or due to their illness.

Dysgraphia A learning disorder related to writing. It is manifested as poor writing skills in children of at least average intelligence, without noticeable neurological and/or perceptual or motor disorders. Depending on difficulties it can be deep dysgraphia or surface dysgraphia.

Dyslalia A developmental speech anomaly that is manifested as erroneous pronunciation or sound substitution.

Dyslexia A milder form of alexia. Most frequently it refers to reading difficulties that are commonly developmental, not caused by visual, motor, or intellectual deficits. It is manifested as deep dyslexia or surface dyslexia. See also **Developmental dyslexia**.

Dysphasia A milder form of speech and language perception and/or production disorder caused by brain damage in adults. In children, the term *developmental sensory dysphasia* is used even in the absence of apparent brain damage. See also **Aphasia**.

Dysphonia Disorder of phonation manifested as hoarse voice.

Ear advantage The phenomenon that the auditory stimuli presented to one ear are responded to faster and more accurately than those presented to the other ear. It is taken as an indicator of superiority of the contralateral cerebral hemisphere for the particular task. It is usually measured by the method of dichotic listening. The conventional abbreviations are LEA for left ear advantage and REA for right ear advantage.

Echoic store (memory) A type of sensory store for auditory stimuli. In this store the stimuli are kept very briefly: from several tens of milliseconds to a maximum of two seconds. See also **Iconic store, Haptic store**.

Echolalia Pathological repetition of words or sentences said by the interlocutor.

Ectoderm The outer layer of embryonic cells; the neural plate is formed from its dorsal part, and subsequently the nervous system and the epidermis. See also **Endoderm** and **Mesoderm**.

EEG Electroencephalography; one of the methods of recording electrical brain activity.

Effector Executive unit (muscle or gland) where the efferent pathway ends, which acts on the basis of the impulses or reacts to environmental influences (e.g., foot, hand).

Efferent nerves Neurons that transmit impulses from the central nervous system to some other part of the nervous system or to an effector.

Efferent pathway A bundle of axons of efferent neurons. See also **Afferent pathway**.

Egocentric encoding of space Processing spatial information with respect to the observer's position; e.g., selection of an object (from among several available objects) that is the closest to the observer. Opposite: allocentric encoding of space.

ELAN Early left-lateralized/left anterior negativity. See also **LAN**.

Emphatic stress Sentence or word stress that is realized by greater intensity.

Empiricism The idea that all knowledge originates in sensory experience.

Encoding Processing of input information. It is the first phase in the learning process during which the material is presented and processed. Encoding proceeds in two steps: acquisition and consolidation.

Endoderm The innermost layer of embryonic cells. See also **Ectoderm** and **Mesoderm**.

Endolymph Potassium-rich fluid in the membranous labyrinth of the inner ear (fills the cochlear duct of the auditory portion and the semicircular canals of the vestibular portion). The cilia of the hair cells are immersed in it.

Engram Permanent change in the neural structures occurring as a result of learning; a kind of a brain record.

Epiglottis (cartilago epiglottidis) An elastic cartilage in the front part of the larynx that can close the entrance into the larynx.

Epilepsy A neurological condition characterized by spontaneous, repeated disorders in motor, sensory, and neurovegetative functions, occasionally accompanied by loss of consciousness. The seizures are caused by abnormally increased electrical activity of the brain in groups of neurons, the so-called epileptic foci.

Episodic memory Memory for events that occurred in a specific place and time. This type of memory is associated with personal experience—some facts are remembered together with the situation in which they were encountered and learned. It is a part of declarative long-term memory. Opposite: semantic memory.

ERN Error-related negativity; a negative wave recorded by ERP, which is a reaction to the error made in one's response; it corresponds to greater activation of the anterior cingulate gyrus. The amplitude of the wave is directly proportional to the gravity of the error. There is no response if the subject is unaware of the error.

ERP Event-related potentials. One of the methods of measuring electrical brain activity during a task. Early evoked potentials are a reflection of activity in the brain stem, and they are one of the methods of examining sensory pathways (e.g., auditory pathways).

Ethology The study of animal behavior.

Excitation Stimulation, arousal. Excitatory postsynaptic potential (EPSP) depolarizes the cell and increases the likelihood of action potential occurring in the postsynaptic neuron. Opposite: inhibition.

Executive functions Planning, initiating, assessing possibilities and options, making action plans, modifying actions on the basis of feedback, monitoring responses and error detection, all directed toward a set goal. All these activities require conscious manipulation of information and are the highest level of cognitive functioning. All these functions are associated with frontal lobes. In working memory, we talk of the central executive.

Explicit memory Type of memory that involves conscious recall; memory for facts and/or specific events. Opposite: implicit memory.

Extinction A milder form of neurological disorder associated with direction of attention. The patients are capable of responding to stimuli occurring on either side, but when presented with two simultaneous stimuli, they do not pay attention to the stimulus on the side opposite to the side of brain injury—simultanagnosia. According to Zarevski (1994, p. 281) extinction is a gradual decrease in the intensity of conditioned response due to the cessation of co-occurrence of the conditioned and the unconditioned stimuli in classical conditioning, i.e., less and less frequent occurrence of the instrumental response that is not accompanied by positive reinforcement.

Extrastriate area Secondary visual area located in the occipital lobes; corresponds to Brodmann's areas 18 and 19.

Facilitation Making something easier. In neural transmission, the term refers to the phenomenon that a neuron's threshold of excitability is lowered: (a) due to the action of other neurons with which the facilitated neuron is connected, or (b) due to a preceding action potential. See also **Excitation**, **Inhibition**.

Fasciculus arcuatus A tract in cerebral white matter that connects Broca's and Wernicke's areas. Lesions in this tract typically result in conduction aphasia.

Fechner's law Defines the relation between stimulus intensity and sensation intensity. The intensity of sensation is the function of the logarithm of stimulus intensity. It is expressed with the formula:

$$\psi = k \log S$$

where ψ = intensity of sensation, k = constant and S = stimulus.

In other words, while the sensation intensity increases in arithmetic progression, stimulus intensity increases in geometric progression.

Feedback The process by means of which the sender of a message gets information from the receiver, which enables him to test the efficacy of communication.

Filter A device that selectively passes certain frequencies. It is typically an electronic device that may be set in terms of filtering conditions: frequencies and attenuation slope. Depending on which frequencies are passed or attenuated, we talk of low-pass filters (that attenuate all frequencies above a certain cut-off frequency), high-pass filters (that attenuate all frequencies below a certain cut-off frequency), or band-pass filters that attenuate frequencies below and above certain cut-off frequencies. Attenuation slope is expressed as decibels per octave (the higher the number the steeper the attenuation slope, i.e., the greater the difference in intensity between the cut-off frequency and the frequency one octave higher or lower). In speech production, according to the generally accepted source-filter theory, the sound produced in the larynx during the phonation phase (= source) reaches the system of filters consisting of articulators and supraglottal cavities, where it gets its final form and content.

Fissure A deep furrow in the cortex.

fMRI Functional magnetic resonance imaging; one of the most widely used neuroimaging methods.

fNIRS Functional near infrared spectroscopy; one of the methods of measuring cerebral blood flow.

Formant Concentration of acoustic energy in the speech signal that can be clearly detected on the spectrogram. It depends on the resonators in the vocal tract, through which the air flow passes during speech. On the basis of formant positions and their relationships (particularly of the first and the second formant) vowels and similar sounds are best differentiated, but also the transitions to other sounds. The formants are typically marked as F1, F2 and so on from the first formant toward the higher formants. F0 refers to the fundamental frequency. Formant values are expressed in hertz (Hz).

Fovea Part of the retina densely covered with cones and containing few rods. It is specialized for high visual acuity.

Frequency encoding Neural encoding based on the frequency and specific timing of action potentials in individual neurons. Stronger stimuli elicit more numerous and more frequent action potentials.

Frontal lobe (lobus frontalis) Part of the cerebrum anterior to the central sulcus (Rolandic fissure) and dorsal to the lateral (Sylvian) fissure. The two major parts of the frontal lobe are the motor and prefrontal cortex.

Frontal section (plane) See **Coronal section**.

fTCD Functional Transcranial Doppler Ultrasonography. One of the methods of measuring event-related cerebral blood flow.

Functional asymmetry The fact that the two cerebral hemispheres are not equally active during various functions.

Functional reorganization Changes in cerebral representation of a function or a sensation as a consequence of lesion, practice, or normal aging.

Fundamental frequency Frequency of the tone produced by a person's vocal tract by means of vocal fold vibration. In men, the fundamental frequency is approximately 120 Hz, in women 220 Hz, and in 10-year-old children about 330 Hz. During a typical conversation the male voice ranges between 50 and 250 Hz, and the women's between 120 and 480 Hz (Laver, 1994).

Fusiform gyrus (gyrus fusiformis) One of the gyri at the junction of the occipital and temporal lobes (in the medial and ventral regions). Corresponds to Brodmann's area 37. Its activity is associated with observing human faces. Lesions in this gyrus cause prosopagnosia.

Ganglion Collections of cells in the peripheral nervous system. For example, in the auditory system there is the spiral ganglion, a group of cells in the inner ear. This is where the first neuron of the auditory pathway starts; it is directly connected with the receptors in the organ of Corti. See also **Basal ganglia**.

Gestalt (from the German *Gestalt* meaning configuration, integral structure, form): A structural combination of particular features that is not a simple sum of constituent parts, but has properties of its own.

Glia Neuroglial cells (from the Greek word for glue: *neuroglia* means nerve glue); support (nonneuronal) cells that do not conduct impulses. Their name originated in the belief that they keep the neurons together.

Glioma Type of tumor that grows on glial cells.

Global aphasia A severe disorder of speech and language functions caused by extensive lesions in the language-dominant hemisphere. Lesions that can result in such deficits include, in addition to the anterior and posterior parts of the cerebral cortex, a large portion of the subcortical white matter. Aphasic symptoms are typically accompanied by alexia, agraphia, and acalculia. The term *sensorimotor aphasia* is also used.

Grammar A set of rules that describe a language, with the help of which it is possible to produce any and all correct utterances in a particular language. Frequently equated with syntax.

Grammatical word Mostly unchangeable parts of speech like articles, prepositions or conjunctions, whose main role is to mark grammatical relations. Also called closed-class words and function words. Opposite: lexical word.

Grapheme The smallest distinctive unit of the alphabet. See also **Phoneme**.

Grave One of the distinctive features, which is used to distinguish sounds according to place of articulation. Acoustic energy is concentrated in lower frequencies and articulation in peripheral points of the oral cavity. Back vowels (e.g., /u/) and labial and velar consonants (e.g., /p/, /k/) are [+grave]. Front vowels (e.g., /I/) and dental, alveolar, and palatal consonants (e.g., /t/, /s/) are [–grave]. Opposite: acute. See also **Distinctive features**.

Gray matter Parts of the nervous system (e.g., the cerebral cortex, basal ganglia, and thalamic nuclei) that consist mainly of cell bodies that are responsible for their gray color, as opposed to white matter.

Grice's principle of cooperation Comprises four conversational maxims as prerequisites of successful communication: (a) maxim of quality—do not say what you know to be untrue and do not say what you have insufficient proof of; (b) maxim of quantity—make your contribution as informative as needed in a given moment and do not offer more information than is necessary; (c) maxim of relevance—make your contribution relevant; and (d) maxim of manner—avoid ambiguities, be brief, and be organized (Levinson, 1983).

Gyrus A ridge or bulge on the surface of the cortex formed by folding; gyri alternate with sulci or fissures.

Gyrus angularis See **Angular gyrus**.

Habituation Getting used to a stimulus; weakening of the organism's response to the repeated and harmless or insignificant stimulus. The response decreases with repeated stimulus presentations. With sensitization, one of the types of nonassociative learning.

Hallucination Sensory experience similar to perception that occurs without the actual stimulus.

Hammer (malleus) One of the three ossicles in the middle ear: laterally, it grows into the tympanic membrane, and on its medial side it is connected to another ossicle—the anvil (*incus*).

Haptic store (memory) Type of sensory store for tactile stimuli. In this store the stimuli are kept very briefly. See also **Iconic store**, **Echoic store**.

Harmonic Integral multiple of the fundamental frequency. For example, if the fundamental frequency is 100 Hz (first harmonic), the second harmonic will have the frequency of 200 Hz, the third 300 Hz and so on.

Hebbian synapse (learning) Named after Canadian psychologist Donald O. Hebb. Each repeated stimulation contributes to the development of a structure consisting of neurons capable of acting together as a closed system. This structure is diffuse: neurons of the cell assembly are probably not located in the same place, but rather spread over the entire brain. Neurons in the cell assembly act together due to changes in the connections among them—the synapses. During learning, the combination of cells into an assembly makes the connections stronger, which makes even a weak signal from one neuron sufficient to activate another and so on. As a result, firing of one cell within the assembly triggers firing of all other elements of the same assembly. Mental representations of perceptual experiences are built on the basis of the activity of several such cell assemblies that are hierarchically structured and may be compared with a network.

Hemiparesis Partial loss of voluntary motor control (muscle weakness) of one side of the body.

Hemiplegia Paralysis of one side of the body. It is usually a consequence of lesions in the motor cortex or in descending motor pathways.

Hemisphere Left or right half of the brain.

Hemispherectomy Surgical removal of one cerebral hemisphere.

Heschl gyrus Gyrus in the lateral (Sylvian) fissure in the temporal lobe, just anterior to the *planum temporale*. It seats the primary auditory area.

Hierarchical models Models based on the principle of hierarchical organization of sensory systems. The complexity of coding increases with proximity to the cortex. According to traditional models, the final destination of sensations are vaguely defined and insufficiently understood brain areas that are referred to as the association cortex. It is assumed that hierarchical phases are closely connected. Basically, the models start from the premise that each level analyzes the input arriving from the preceding level and thus adds to the complexity of the analysis.

Hierarchical structure Organization of neuronal connections in which the receptors project onto first-order neurons in the central nervous system; these project onto second-order neurons, and so on, toward the cerebral cortex. It is based on the idea of different functional levels (hence, hierarchical models).

Hippocampal commissure A bundle of axons that connect the hippocampus in the left hemisphere with the one in the right.

Hippocampus Part of the limbic system in the medial temporal lobe, which plays a particularly important role in learning and memory. It is located between the thalamus and the cerebral cortex.

Hiragana Japanese syllabic writing system (a type of *kana* script) that enables marking grammatical forms, which is not possible by the *kanji* script. Adverbs and most adjectives, as well as frequent phrases, are written in *hiragana* rather than *kanji* and *hiragana* is frequently combined with kanji to indicate grammatical functions. See also ***Katakana*** and ***Kanji***.

Holistic processing Processing of stimuli or other data as a whole, rather than relying on individual parts or properties. Opposite: analytic processing.

Homology Structures, genes, or behaviors in different species that share a common ancestor (e.g., a bat's wing and a human arm are homologous structures). In the brain, for example, the primary visual cortex in a monkey is homologous to the primary visual cortex in a human. However, homologous structures do not necessarily have identical functions.

Homophones Words that sound the same but have different meanings (e.g., the English words *meat* and *meet*).

Homotopic areas Areas that occupy corresponding positions in the left and the right hemisphere.

Homunculus Little man. An illustration of sensory and motor functions in the primary somatosensory or motor cortex in the form of a little man.

Huntington's disease Genetic degenerative disorder in the basal ganglia that is manifested as clumsiness and involuntary movements of the head and body, often accompanied with cognitive deficits.

Hyperkinesia Pathologically excessive movement.

Hyperpolarization Increase of the membrane potential—the value becomes more negative.

Hypokinesia Reduced amount of movement.

Hypothalamus Part of the midbrain. Hypothalamus comprises several nuclei and its principal functions are regulation of body temperature, blood pressure, hunger, and thirst. It is also involved in the regulation of emotions and pituitary function. There is evidence of its role in cognitive processes as well.

Hz Hertz. Unit of tone frequency typically used to express pitch. Sometimes expressed as cycles per second.

Iconic store (memory) Type of sensory store for visual stimuli. In this store the stimuli are kept very briefly (about 30 seconds). See also **Haptic store**, **Echoic store**.

Ideational apraxia Inability to perform complex movements due to deficits in the programs for their performance, i.e., due to impaired knowledge about the intent of an action; for example, patients are incapable of demonstrating the use of an object or understanding its use, but are able to carry out the required movements upon request. It is also referred to as sensory apraxia. It is most frequently caused by diffuse bilateral parietal lesions.

Identification A form of perceptual response by which the stimuli are recognized and named. See also **Detection**, **Discrimination**.

Ideographic script Type of script (sometimes referred to as logographic) in which the symbols represent morphemes rather than phonemes (e.g., Chinese). See also *Kanji*.

Ideomotor (ideokinetic) apraxia Inability to execute the desired action. The patients know the use of an object and how it should be applied, but are incapable of putting their knowledge into action. Caused by the disconnection between the center where the movement is planned and the executive motor part.

Implicature The term introduced by H. P. Grice that is used in studying conversational structure. Conversational implicature refers to implications that may be drawn from utterances on the basis of cooperative principles that underlie efficient and acceptable conversation. See also **Grice's principle of cooperation**.

Implicit learning Learning of complex information without the ability to consciously remember learned material.

Implicit memory Type of memory that does not depend on conscious recall. Opposite: explicit memory.

Impulse See **Action potential**.

Incus See **Anvil**.

Indirect memory See **Nondeclarative memory**.

Inductive reasoning Part of the process of forming ideas and solving problems. Generalizations are made on the basis of examples and individual cases. Opposite: deductive reasoning.

Inference Interpretation based on earlier explanations and beliefs.

Inferior Below something else; when used in describing positions of various brain structures in primates it refers to the position below or direction downward from another structure. Opposite: superior. See also **Ventral**.

Inhibition Slowing down or preventing a process from happening. Inhibitory postsynaptic potential (IPSP) decreases the probability of action potential in the postsynaptic neuron. Opposite: excitation, facilitation.

Innervate Establish synaptic connections with the target.

Insula The "island" lobe that got its name because it is separated from the surrounding area with a circular sulcus. Positioned deep within the lateral fissure, covered by parts of the temporal, parietal, and frontal lobes, the so-called *opercula* (lids). The opercula are named after the lobes they belong to: frontal operculum (*operculum frontale*), fronto-parietal operculum (*operculum frontoparietale*), and temporal operculum (*operculum temporale*). Sometimes referred to as the fifth lobe.

Integrative agnosia Difficulties in object recognition due to the inability to group and integrate parts into a whole.

Interference Two or more processes affecting each other so that the effectiveness of at least one of them (and sometimes of both) is decreased.

Interneurons Neurons between two other neurons, which receive information from them and transmit it to motor neurons or to other interneurons.

Interpreter A left-hemisphere system that supposedly tries to explain external and internal events in order to react appropriately.

Ions Positively or negatively charged particles.

Ipsilateral Relating to the same side. Opposite: contralateral.

Isomorphism Assumption that the organization of the mind matches that of the brain.

Jargon aphasia A language disorder caused by brain lesions; speech is relatively grammatical, but the patients have great word-finding difficulties.

JND Just Noticeable Difference: The minimal difference between two stimuli necessary to distinguish them 50% of the time. See also **Weber's law**.

Kanji Chinese script used in Japanese. It is an ideographic system in which each symbol represents a term. It is typically used for writing nouns, verb roots, and adjectives. Since it does not provide grammatical markers, these are expressed by adding *hiragana* symbols. See also *Hiragana* and *Katakana*.

Katakana A type of Japanese syllabic script written in columns from top to bottom. The symbols are square. This type of script is most frequently used for foreign words, telegrams, advertisements, and sometimes in children's books. See also *Hiragana* and *Kanji*.

Kinesthetic sensations Sensations of rotation, effort, force, weight, movement, and limb positions resulting from stimulation of proprioceptors.

L1 A frequent abbreviation for the first language or mother tongue, as opposed to the second or foreign language (L2).

L2 A frequent abbreviation for the second or foreign language, as opposed to the first language or mother tongue (L1).

Labyrinth A common name for the auditory and vestibular parts of the inner ear. In a bony capsule (osseous labyrinth), separated from it by the fluid perilymph and membranes there is the membranous labyrinth with auditory and vestibular receptors.

Laminar structure A kind of layered structure characteristic of the cerebral cortex, hippocampus, spinal cord, and the cerebellum.

LAN Left Anterior Negativity. A negative wave recorded by means of ERP over frontal regions of the left hemisphere. It is associated with syntactic processing, and it occurs in cases of incongruent word types or morphosyntactic errors. It is sometimes called early left anterior negativity (ELAN) because it occurs early, i.e., before the positive P600 wave that is also associated with syntactic processing.

Language acquisition This term is commonly used for the process of mastering the first language or mother tongue that is adopted automatically, implicitly, and typically in informal situations, as opposed to language learning that is related to the second or foreign language.

Language learning This term is commonly used for the process of mastering the second or foreign language that is adopted in a planned, explicit, and primarily formal manner and conditions, as opposed to language acquisition that is related to the first language (mother tongue).

Latency Time elapsed between stimulus onset and the beginning of response or sensation.

Lateral Designating the position of a structure or direction away from the midline toward the sides. Opposite: medial.

Lateral (Sylvian) fissure The furrow that separates the temporal from the frontal and parietal lobes.

Lateral inhibition Limiting the activity of one neuron by the activity of another; one of the key mechanisms in neural functioning.

Laterality index One of indirect behavioral measures of functional cerebral asymmetry. Several formulas have been suggested, but the most frequently used is:

$$LI = (R - L) / (R + L) * 100$$

R denotes responses to stimuli presented to the right ear and L to the left. Bradshaw and Nettleton (1983) suggested a two-way laterality coefficient (i.e., two formulas) that depending on overall success take into account only correct answers or both correct and incorrect ones. If overall success is less than 50%, the following formula should be used:

$$LI = (R_c - L_c) / (R_c + L_c) * 100.$$

If it is greater than 50%, they suggest the following formula:

$$LI = (R_c - L_c) / (R_e + L_e) * 100$$

Subscripts c and e stand for correct and erroneous responses, respectively. Obviously, positive values indicate right-ear advantage (i.e., left-hemisphere dominance), negative values indicate left-ear advantage (i.e., right-hemisphere dominance), and in cases of no ear advantage (i.e., symmetrical functioning), the laterality index value will be zero. Other ways

of measuring functional asymmetry in behavioral tests have been suggested as well (e.g., Repp, 1977; Mildner, 1996).

Lateralization of functions The phenomenon that different functions are represented exclusively or primarily in one cerebral hemisphere.

Learning A process of adopting information and skills. It proceeds through several stages. Encoding, during which the material is presented and processed, consists of two steps: first, the input data are registered by sensory
organs and subjected to sensory analysis (acquisition), and then they are
consolidated. The second stage is storage, during which some of the available information is stored in the memory system. During the third stage
(retrieval) the stored material is retrieved from memory in the form of a
conscious representation, recognition, or as some form of learned behavior. The result of learning is memory.

Lemma A canonical form of changeable parts of speech (e.g., infinitive for verbs,
masculine singular for adjectives).

Lemniscus Axonal tract in the brainstem by means of which the mechano-sen-
sory data are relayed to the thalamus.

Lexeme The smallest distinctive unit of meaning.

Lexical access Accessing the words in the (mental) lexicon during which perceptual stimuli activate information (e.g., semantic, syntactic) about words.
Followed by selection of one of the activated forms that best matches the
stimulus (lexical selection).

Lexical decision Decision on whether a given series of graphemes or phonemes
constitutes a word.

Lexical procedure (in reading) The kind of reading that is based on learned
pronunciation of written words. It usually refers to the irregularly spelled
words, i.e., those whose pronunciation cannot be predicted from the general rules of pronunciation. The procedure is characteristic in languages in
which the grapheme-to-phoneme correspondence (matching) is low (e.g.,
English), as opposed to languages where that correspondence is very high
(e.g., Croatian). It is also referred to as direct procedure because the path
from grapheme to the term is direct, bypassing the phonological loop.
Deficits in this procedure result in surface dyslexia. Opposite: nonlexical
procedure.

Lexical selection Selection of one among the activated word forms that best corresponds to the sensory input, which is part of lexical access.

Lexical word A part of speech that has semantic content, such as nouns, verbs,
adjectives. Also referred to as open-class words. Opposite: grammatical
word.

Lexicon A store of detailed information about words, including data about
orthography, phonology, semantics, syntax, and morphology. See also
Mental lexicon.

Limbic system A set of nuclei and neural pathways along the corpus callosum that processes and controls emotions, as well as the endocrine and

autonomic systems. Its most important parts are the cingulate gyrus, hippocampus, and amygdala.

Lingual gyrus (gyrus lingualis) One of the gyri at the junction between the occipital and temporal lobes in the medial and ventral surface. See also **Fusiform gyrus**.

Liquor See **Cerebrospinal fluid**.

Lobe A major division of the cerebral cortex. Most frequently we talk of the four lobes: frontal, parietal, temporal, and occipital. Some other structures have been called lobes in the literature (e.g., insula is the fifth lobe; limbic system is the limbic lobe).

Lobectomy Surgical removal of a lobe or its part.

Lobotomy Surgical severing of connections between the prefrontal cortex and the rest of the brain. Around the middle of the 20th century it used to a popular method for treatment of depression, schizophrenia, and other psychiatric disorders.

Lobulus A small lobe.

Localistic models Models that assume that each function or behavior is represented in a specific and strictly localized place in the brain, as opposed to connectionist models.

Localization of functions Representation of a function or its control in a distinct region or location in the brain.

Logographic script See **Ideographic script**.

Logorrhea Pathological talkativeness.

Longitudinal fissure (fissura longitudinalis cerebri) A deep groove that separates the two cerebral hemispheres.

Malleus See **Hammer**.

Map An organized projection of axons from one part of the nervous system into another, which reflects organization of the body or some function.

Mechanoreceptors Receptors specialized for mechanical stimuli.

Medial Designating the position of a structure or direction toward the midline. Opposite: lateral.

Medulla (medulla oblongata) The most caudal portion of the brainstem connecting it with the spinal cord (*medulla spinalis*). Its nuclei relay somatosensory information from the spinal cord to the brain as well as motor commands to the spinal cord.

Medulla oblongata See **Medulla**.

MEG Magnetoencephalography. One of the methods of measuring brain activity.

Membrane potential See **Resting potential**.

Memory The result of learning (acquisition), storing, and recall of information.

Mental lexicon Mental store of words that contains information about their meaning (semantics), rules for formation and use (morphology and syntax), and data about spelling and reading (orthography, phonetics, phonology). The actual organization of the mental lexicon is still the subject of debate by many cognitive linguists and neuroscientists.

Mental representation The result of interaction between a perceptive mechanism and the perceived object, affected by the characteristics of both.

Mesoderm The middle layer of embryonic cells. They eventually develop into muscles, skeletal, and connective tissue (among other structures). See also **Ectoderm** and **Endoderm**.

Midbrain (mesencephalon) The most rostral part of the brainstem.

Middle ear Part of the peripheral auditory system positioned between the external ear (from which it is separated by the tympanic membrane) and the inner ear (located in the bony labyrinth). Its primary role is to match the low-impedance airborne sounds to the higher-impedance fluid of the inner ear. This is achieved by means of two mechanical processes: (a) the lever action of the three ossicles; and (b) the difference in area between the tympanic membrane and the oval window (i.e., plate of the stapes).

Migration of neurons Movement of neurons from the point of their formation to their final destination that they will occupy in the mature system. Migration proceeds in the inside-out manner, which means that the neurons that start migrating later must pass through all the existing layers. The migration phase is preceded by the proliferation phase.

MMN Mismatch Negativity. A negative wave computed from the electric activity of the brain when the subject registers a change. It can be measured by ERP, MEG or some other method. It comprises two components: the one generated over the temporal lobe, which reflects automatic discrimination, and the one generated over the frontal lobes, which is attributed to attention changes. The MMN may be electric or magnetic (MMNm).

Modality Type of sensory experience (visual, auditory, gustatory, somatosensory, and olfactory).

Modular models Models that propose that the brain is organized as a set of mostly independent modules, each of which is responsible for some function. Only a finished output from one module (process) may serve as input to another module. Contrary to connectionist models, no feedback is posited.

Morpheme The smallest distinctive unit in grammar. Morphemes may be free (individual words) or bound (e.g., affixes).

Morphology Study of forms and structures. It may refer to natural organisms; in linguistics it refers to language forms and rules for their construction and combination.

Morphosyntax Study of how morphemes participate in the building of surface syntactic forms.

Motor apraxia See **Ideomotor apraxia**.

Motor cortex Part of the cerebral cortex anterior to the central sulcus, which is involved in motor behavior. It comprises the primary motor area and the associated cortical areas in the frontal lobes.

Motor neuron A neuron that receives stimuli from other neurons and relays stimuli from its soma in the spinal cord to the muscles and glands.

Motor theory of speech perception According to this theory speech perception is based on its production, i.e., speech is perceived by mimicking articulatory movements. Imitation does not necessarily have to be realized at the level of articulators.

MRI Magnetic Resonance Imaging. One of the neuroimaging methods used to study the brain. See also **fMRI**.

Multiple sclerosis Degenerative progressive disease of the central nervous system characterized by degeneration of the myelin sheath and the axons. It is manifested as weakness and incoordination.

Myelin sheath Fatty substance wrapped around the axon in several layers, which insulates it from the extracellular fluid. Most axons are myelinated, which contributes to faster propagation of the impulse along the axon. Breaks in the myelin sheath are called nodes of Ranvier.

Myelination The formation of myelin sheath around the axon. It begins in the fetal period and continues until after birth.

Neglect Disorder of directing attention caused most frequently by brain damage. Patients ignore the stimuli on the side of the body contralateral to the side of the lesion (e.g., they leave the food on one side of the plate, cannot describe one side of a scene, etc.). See also **Extinction**.

Neocortex From an evolution standpoint, the most recent part of the cortex, consisting of six layers. Ordinarily, the term cortex is typically used to refer to the neocortex.

Neologism A new word, coined for different reasons, some of which may be pathological (e.g., in Wernicke's aphasia).

Nerve cell See **Neuron**.

Neural groove A transitory phase in the nervous system development during which the neural plate turns into the neural tube. It is formed when the neural plate gradually elongates, with its sides rising and folding inward.

Neural networks Neural network models consist of three layers (units): the input layer, the hidden layer, and the output layer. The units (that represent neurons) are interconnected, and these connections increase and decrease the activation level of the particular receptive unit. Each unit receives stimuli from the preceding layer and stimulates the next. Each input is weighted, i.e., has a particular value. The activation level of each unit depends on the weighted sum of all inputs. Hidden units provide the model with the information necessary for correct matching of the input layer to the output layer by changing the strength of connections among units. In order to achieve this, the author of the model must set the rules, i.e., a quantitative description of the necessary processing changes depending on the final outcome. In the training phase, the neural networks learn to respond with a particular output to given inputs, by modifying the connections among units (by adapting the weights), and by comparing each output with the given, i.e., expected target output.

Neural plate The first phase of the development of the nervous system; forms by thickening of the dorsal ectoderm. See also **Neural groove** and **Neural tube**.

Neural tube A tube-like structure formed by the coming together of the edges of the neural groove. It eventually develops into the central nervous system.

Neurogenesis Development of the nervous system.

Neuroimaging Any method or technique of imaging the brain activity.

Neuron A cell specialized for receiving and transmitting stimuli by conducting electrical signals. A typical neuron consists of the cell body, dendrites, axon, and the presynaptic axon terminal. There are principal neurons and interneurons.

Neuron doctrine The view that brain functions are realized through coordinated activity of independent neurons. It is believed that it was first defined by Santiago Ramon y Cajal.

Neurotransmitters Chemical substances that mediate transmission of information from one neuron to the next at chemical synapses. They are produced in presynaptic neurons and stored in vesicles in presynaptic terminals. There are about a hundred different kinds of neurotransmitters, and different populations of neurons produce and respond to only one or to a limited number of them. They are released at the synapse, across which they act on the postsynaptic neurons by binding to appropriate receptors.

Nociferous cortex According to the theory of neural noise, this is the area of cerebral cortex that, due to anomalies of its own, inhibits normal functioning of neighboring areas and makes some other areas take over the function. It usually refers to epileptic foci in the brain.

Node of Ranvier (nodus Ranvieri) A break in the myelin sheath where the axon is in direct contact with the extracellular fluid, and action potential can be generated.

Nonassociative learning A type of learning during which the organism learns and memorizes the properties of a stimulus that it has been subjected to once or repeatedly. Principal subtypes are habituation and sensitization.

Nondeclarative (implicit, indirect) memory/knowledge Knowledge that has been acquired and stored without explicit memory of it. It is an unintentional, unconscious type of retaining knowledge. Opposite: declarative (explicit, direct).

Nonfluent Usually associated with speech that is effortful, difficult and includes numerous errors. Such speech is one of the characteristics of Broca's aphasia.

Nonlexical procedure (in reading) A type of reading that is based on general rules. Because of this procedure, it is possible to read nonsense words if they are spelled in accordance with the rules of the language. It is also referred to as indirect procedure, because it is believed that the path from grapheme to phoneme is indirect, i.e., that it involves the phonological loop. It is more characteristic of languages with a high degree of grapheme-to-phoneme correspondence (e.g., Croatian) than of those that have lower correspondence (e.g., English). Deficits in this procedure cause deep dyslexia. Opposite: lexical procedure.

Normalization Neglecting the linguistically irrelevant differences in the speech of different speakers. For example, absolute formant values vary among speakers of the same language, even in the same person at different occasions; however, in the process of speech acquisition we have learned to automatically and unconsciously extract from the acoustic signal the data that are relevant for comprehension and communication in our language, in addition to using other available information (e.g., whether it is a man or a woman, whether the speaker might have a cold, whether he is talking over the phone, etc.). Due to the process of normalization, we will recognize a vowel as /a/ even when acoustic analysis reveals that its first and second formant frequencies are 664 and 1183 Hz, respectively (if spoken by a male voice), or 884 and 1393 Hz, respectively (if spoken by a female voice; Bakran, 1996).

Nucleus (a) cell structure that contains DNA; (b) a group of cell bodies in the central nervous system.

Nucleus ruber A red nucleus located in midbrain.

Occipital lobe (lobus occipitalis) Part of the cerebrum posterior to the parieto-occipital notch, for the most part taken by the primary and secondary visual areas.

Ontogenetic development Development of an individual during life.

Operculum Lid. The frontal operculum (operculum frontale) is part of the frontal lobe immediately anterior to the face area in the primary motor area. Together with the fronto-parietal operculum (*operculum frontoparietale*) and the temporal operculum (operculum temporale) it hides the insula.

Optic chiasm (chiasma opticum) The point of contact of the visual nerves from the two eyes (on the ventral side of the diencephalon); axons from the nasal parts of the retina cross to the opposite side.

Optical ataxia Condition manifested as difficulties in moving limbs under visual control.

Oral apraxia Impaired ability to perform voluntary movements of the tongue, lips, larynx, and other oral musculature.

Orbit The bony cavity that protects the eye (eye socket).

Orbital frontal cortex Part of the prefrontal cortex that forms the base of the frontal lobe and makes contact with the superior orbital wall (above the eyes). Its principal role is to control our functioning in social and emotional situations and in rational decision making.

Organ of Corti Part of the inner ear positioned along the basilar membrane in the cochlea containing auditory receptors.

Orthography Rules for correct spelling.

Ossicles The three small bones in the middle ear. See anvil, hammer, and stirrup.

Otolith(ic) organ (Saccule and utricle); a type of the vestibular organ in the inner ear whose innervation is based on the movement of otoliths (tiny calcium carbonate crystals). See also **Cupular organ**.

Oval window A small opening in the osseous labyrinth, bordering between the middle and the inner ear, closed by the footplate of the stapes. At this point the sound vibrations are transferred to the fluids in the inner ear.

Paradigm The set of all grammatical forms derived from the same root.

Paradigmatic relation Items that can occupy the same place in a sentence are said to be paradigmatically related. For example, the words *cats* and *dogs* are paradigmatically related because they can be inserted in a sentence like I like … see syntagmatic relation.

Parallel models Models that propose that different functions are performed simultaneously, contrary to serial models.

Parallel processing Simultaneous (parallel) processing of different properties of a complex stimulus. For example, in the visual system, the data about form, color, or orientation of the object are transmitted and processed in parallel.

Paralysis Total loss of voluntary motor control. The synonym plegia is used in compound terms that indicate the part that is paralyzed (e.g., hemiplegia, quadriplegia).

Paraphasia Substitution of one word for another according to the criterion of similar pronunciation (phonemic paraphasia) or related meaning (semantic paraphasia).

Paresis Partial loss of voluntary motor control.

Parietal lobe (lobus parietalis) Part of the cerebrum posterior to the central sulcus (Rolandic fissure), anterior to the parieto-occipital notch, and superior to the lateral (Sylvian) fissure.

Parkinson's disease Neurodegenerative disorder in the basal ganglia. Primary symptoms include difficulties in initiating movements, slowness of movements, poorly articulated speech, and tremor at rest.

Parsing Assigning syntactic structure to each new word as the utterance progresses; analysis of sentence syntactic structure.

Percept Result of perception.

Perception Reception, acquisition, and interpretation of stimuli. In can be subdivided into exteroception (relating to external stimuli), interoception, and proprioception (relating to stimuli from one's one body). Phenomenal perception refers to information mediated by the senses; nonphenomenal perception is associated with thoughts and feelings. Active perception brings the desired elements into consciousness intentionally, and passive perception refers to stimuli that have entered our consciousness unintentionally. The result of perception is percept.

Periaqueductal gray matter Part of the brain stem gray matter that plays an important part in emotion-related vocalizations, e.g., crying, laughing, groaning, etc.

Perilymph Fluid in the internal ear that flows between the osseous and the membranous labyrinth.

Peripheral nervous system Part of the nervous system outside the spinal cord and the skull. It comprises somatic and autonomic nervous systems. It relays data from the periphery to the central nervous system and on the basis of motor commands from the central nervous system, it controls the muscles. Opposite: central nervous system.

Perseveration Continuing with some behavior in spite of changed circumstances. For example, in a card-sorting test the patient will continue to sort cards according to color even when the examiner has made it clear that the criterion has changed and that they are to be sorted according to shapes or their number. In speech, perseveration can be manifested as repetition of a word or phrase that has no relation to the context or situation. It can be found in patients with prefrontal brain lesions, and it is believed to reflect the loss of inhibitory control.

PET Positron Emission Tomography. A neuroimaging method used to visualize brain activity during various tasks.

Philogenetic development Development of the species.

Phoneme The smallest distinctive unit of speech on the basis of which words can be distinguished. For example, the words *heat, beet, pete,* differ only in the first phoneme. In some languages (e.g., Croatian), as a rule one symbol (grapheme) is used to write each phoneme. In others (e.g., English), one and the same phoneme may be spelled using two or more symbols that are not necessarily always the same (see ea, ee, and e in above examples, which may in addition to ie all be used to spell /i/). On the other hand, one and the same grapheme may be read as different phonemes. For example, in English, the grapheme may be used for phoneme /I/ (bit) or for /ai/ (bite).

Phonemic paraphasia Substitution of phonemes within words. Contrary to semantic paraphasias characteristic of Wernicke's aphasia, phonemic paraphasias may be found in patients who suffer from Broca's or conduction aphasia. See also **Semantic paraphasia**.

Phonetic word A prosodic unit consisting of all syllables under a common stress. It may comprise one or more linguistic words, and it is therefore by about 40% longer than the average linguistic word (Škarić, 1991, p. 318).

Phonetics In its widest sense it is the science of speech. It deals with the production and perception of speech, the voice, and nonverbal communication.

Phonological dysgraphia A condition in which familiar words may be written relatively well, but nonwords (meaningless words that are spelled in accordance with language rules) cannot.

Phonological dyslexia A condition in which the reading of familiar words is intact, but reading of unknown and meaningless words is impaired. See also **Deep dyslexia**.

Phonological loop One component of working memory (besides the central executive and the visuospatial sketchpad). Spoken information is held briefly and articulated subvocally—hence the alternative term: articulatory loop.

Phonology The study of phonemes of a particular language and their relations.

Photoreceptors Visual receptor cells in the retina. See also **Cones** and **Rods**.

Phrenology Pseudoscience according to which the skull configuration reflects personality traits and intellectual abilities.

Planum temporale Part of the temporal lobe extending along the posterior part of the lateral (Sylvian) fissure. In about 60% of people it is larger in the left hemisphere, in the area approximately corresponding to Wernicke's area.

Plasticity The ability of the nervous system to change, which underlies development, learning, and recovery from injury.

Polarized The nerve cell is said to be polarized when it has reached a negative electrical potential (approximately –70mV) that allows it to receive a stimulus. See also **Resting potential**.

Polymodal Capable of responding to more than one sensory modality.

Pons Part of the brain stem, located between the midbrain and the medulla.

Population code A neural code based on the general distribution of activity in a population of neurons. Stronger stimuli activate a greater number of receptors.

Postcentral gyrus A large gyrus in the parietal lobe, immediately posterior to the central sulcus. It seats the primary somatosensory area.

Posterior Used to describe the position or direction of various structures in vertebrates that is toward the back (the tail). See also caudal. Opposite: anterior, i.e., rostral.

Postsynaptic neuron A neuron that receives information across the synaptic cleft from the presynaptic neuron.

Pragmatics An area of linguistics that studies language use. Its primary subjects of interest are discourse and language conventions, e.g., analysis of the differences between formal and informal speech.

Precentral gyrus A large gyrus in the frontal lobe, immediately anterior to the central sulcus. It seats the primary motor area.

Precuneus Part of the multimodal association area located in the medial part of the parietal lobe.

Prefrontal cortex Cortical areas in the frontal lobe, anterior to the primary and association motor cortex; they participate in planning complex cognitive behaviors, socially acceptable behavior, and expressing personality traits.

Premotor cortex/area Part of the secondary and association motor area that corresponds to the dorsolateral part of Brodmann's area 6. It is located anterior to the primary motor area, between the supplementary motor area and the lateral fissure. It is involved in the planning and programming of voluntary movements.

Presynaptic neuron A neuron that releases neurotransmitters whose information is relayed across the synaptic cleft to the next neuron.

Primacy effect The effect refers to the influence of the order of presentation of stimuli or information on the success of memorizing and/or forming attitudes. The effect is manifested as better memory for stimuli/information that were presented first than for those that followed later. Opposite: recency effect.

Primary motor area Part of the cerebral cortex anterior to the central sulcus, in the precentral gyrus, which corresponds to Brodmann's area 4. Each individual location in the primary motor areas controls a corresponding muscle group on the opposite side of the body.

Primary progressive aphasia A neurodegenerative disorder that results in progressive and selective deterioration of language functions.

Primary sensory area Part of the sensory cortex that receives information from different sensory systems. For example, the primary visual area is in the occipital lobe, in Brodmann's area 17, and the primary auditory area is in the temporal lobe, corresponding to Brodmann's areas 41 and 42.

Primary somatosensory area Part of the brain immediately posterior to the central sulcus, in the postcentral gyrus, where the sensations arriving from the entire body are represented, following the somatotopic organization. It corresponds to Brodmann's areas 1, 2 and 3.

Primates The term originates from the Latin word *primus* (meaning the first, in the first place); it refers to one of the 14 lines of mammals that include humans as well. There are five families of primates: primitive primates, New World monkeys, Old World monkeys, apes, and hominids. The closest relatives of the humans are chimpanzees (that, together with gibbons, orangutans, and gorillas belong to the family of apes), with whom we share about 99% of genetic material. The only surviving species of hominids are humans.

Prime A preparative stimulus. Being exposed to this stimulus may affect later responses. See **priming**.

Priming Preparation; the phenomenon that being exposed to some stimulus unconsciously results in later improved performance. Semantic priming—word identification is facilitated by previous presentation of a semantically related word. Negative priming—inhibited processing of the target stimulus after it has appeared as a distractor in a preceding task.

Principal neurons They comprise about 70% of all cortical neurons. They have numerous dendritic spines that contribute to the richness of connections; their axons are long and make projection, association, and commissural fibers. They are also called pyramidal neurons, as opposed to extrapyramidal ones (interneurons).

Principle of equipotentiality One of the two principles defined by K. Lashley; according to this principle any part of the brain can take over functions of other parts, i.e., neurons in different cortical areas contribute almost equally to complex learned behaviors. See also **Principle of mass action**, another principle.

Principle of mass action One of the principles established by K. Lashley, according to which cortical neurons act together during learning; the more neurons involved, the better the performance. See also the **Principle of equipotentiality**, the other of Lashley's principles.

Procedural memory/knowledge Refers to the knowledge of how something is done and includes the ability to perform skilled movements. A kind of nondeclarative memory.

Projection fibers Myelinated axons of neurons that connect the cerebral cortex with the lower parts of the central nervous system. The connections between the cortex and the subcortical areas are very important for functioning of the brain, because lesions in these pathways may cause disorders identical to those of related functional areas. Projection fibers may be afferent or efferent.

Proliferation of neurons Rapid multiplication of nerve cells that starts immediately after the development of the neural tube. It is followed by the migration phase.

Proposition Propositional representations are explicit, direct, abstract entities, which represent the mental content of the mind. The form in which concepts and relations are represented is not language- or modality-specific.

Proprioception Perception of one's own body on the basis of sensation of internal forces within the body (e.g., in tendons and muscles).

Proprioceptors Receptors in muscles, joints, and tendons that enable receiving information about body posture, balance, and muscle tone.

Prosody Suprasegmental aspect of speech that includes relations between duration, intensity, and tone. It may be affective or linguistic. Affective prosody refers to expression of emotions, attitudes, and moods; linguistic prosody provides information about sentence type (interrogative, statement, etc.), sentence stress, and the place and type of word accents.

Prosopagnosia Inability to recognize faces; impaired holistic processing. It is frequently a result of lesions in the fusiform gyrus.

Proximal Closer to a referent point. Opposite: distal.

Pulvinar One of the thalamic nuclei.

Pure alexia The patient is incapable of reading words with otherwise intact language functioning.

Putamen One of the structures in the basal ganglia.

rCBF Regional Cerebral Blood Flow. Measuring regional cerebral blood flow indicates the activity of particular brain regions during certain tasks.

Recency effect The effect refers to the influence of the order of presentation of stimuli or information on the success of memorizing and/or forming attitudes. The effect is manifested as better memory for information presented at the end of a series than for information presented at the beginning. Opposite: primacy effect.

Receptors (a) Cell structures that receive stimuli and transform them into bioelectric impulses suitable for neural transfer to the brain; the organ of Corti in the inner ear, for example, is the sound receptor. (b) Proteins in the postsynaptic membrane that bind appropriate neurotransmitters.

Redundancy The term originally belonging to communication theory, which refers to the phenomenon that a message contains more information than is necessary for it to be successfully transmitted and received. It is believed that speech contains twice as much information as a minimum necessary for comprehension (in the acoustic signal, in grammar, etc.). Due to this it is possible to understand speech even in very difficult listening conditions, e.g., in noise, despite the impaired hearing or speech disorders.

Refractory period A brief period (several milliseconds) occurring immediately after generation of an action potential during which the cell is unable to respond to another stimulus. After the phase of absolute refraction (about 1 to 2 milliseconds) during which the action potential cannot occur regardless of stimulus intensity, follows the relative refractory period. During this phase, a stimulus of greater intensity is needed to produce an action potential than is the case when the cell was at rest.

Reinforcement That which influences the probability of responding in a certain way (usually reward → positive reinforcement or punishment → negative reinforcement).

Representation Mapping of various functions, body parts and sensory organs in the brain, which is typically manifested as increased brain activity. It may be revealed and measured by different electrical cortical stimulations or by neuroimaging and other methods (e.g., PET, fMRI, MEG).

Response time Time interval between the beginning of the stimulus and the subject's response.

Resting potential A stable electrical potential across the cell membrane when the neuron is at rest, i.e., without external stimulation. Its value is about –70mV. Such a negatively charged cell is ready to receive the stimulus (polarized). See also **Action potential**.

Reticular formation (formatio reticularis) Part of the brainstem through which run almost all sensory and motor pathways, connected with other nuclei of the brainstem, with the cerebellum, midbrain and the telencephalon. It plays an important role in the regulation of arousal and attention.

Retina Part of the eye where visual receptors are located. From here, the visual stimuli are relayed to the brain along the visual pathway.

Retinal eccentricity Distance of the stimulus from the fixation point in divided visual-field experiments.

Retinotopic organization (map) Topographic organization of the representations of visual stimuli in the brain that have retained spatial relations present at the periphery (in the retina). Multiple retinotopic maps have been found in the cortex as well as in subcortical areas.

Retrieval The third phase of learning during which the stored material is drawn from memory in the form of a conscious representation, recognition, or as a form of learned behavior. Sometimes the term *recall* may be used.

Retrograde amnesia Disordered recall of information acquired before onset of amnesia, i.e., before the injury that has caused it and/or the events that preceded it. It spans a limited time period before the injury (usually several years), i.e., before amnesia onset. Recovery from retrograde amnesia progresses from events that are farthest away from the moment of amnesia onset. Events closest to the time of injury remain unavailable the longest, sometimes permanently. Opposite: anterograde amnesia.

Rods Visual receptor cells (photoreceptors), specialized for vision in poor light. See cones.

ROI Region of Interest. An approach in brain research in which the region where increased activity during a task is expected is determined in advance, and during the test changes in metabolism or blood flow are looked for. See also **Subtraction methods**.

Rolandic fissure See central sulcus.

Rostral Toward the front; "toward the head." Opposite: caudal. See also **Anterior**.

Saccule (sacculus) One of the two otolithic organs in the inner ear, in the membranous portion of the vestibular organ. It is responsible for reception of linear accelerations and head movements in the vertical plane. See also **Utricle**.

Saltatory conduction Propagation of the nerve impulse along the myelinated axon so that the impulse jumps from one node of Ranvier (where the action potential is generated) to the next.

Schizophrenia A psychiatric disorder characterized by some or all of these symptoms: delusions, hallucinations, inappropriate emotional behavior, thought disorder, odd behavior, etc.

Secondary motor area Part of the frontal cortex that receives information from association areas and relays it to primary motor areas. The secondary motor area comprises the premotor cortex and supplementary motor area, Brodmann's areas 8, 44, and 45, as well as the posterior cingulate. Secondary motor areas are located anterior to the primary motor areas and they control several primary centers and enable complex movements and planned use of muscles.

Secondary sensory area Part of the sensory cortex that receives information from the primary areas. Recognition of wholes and patterns takes place here. Secondary sensory areas are also modality-specific (like the primary sensory areas). For example, the secondary visual area is located in occipital lobe (Brodmann's areas 18 and 19), and the secondary auditory area in the temporal lobe (Brodmann's area 22).

Secondary somatosensory area A small part of the cortex that is located between the central sulcus and the lateral fissure (Brodmann's area 43).

Selective attention The ability to focus on certain stimuli, thoughts, or actions, while at the same time neglecting others. It can be reflex (automatic) or intentional. An example of reflex selective attention is the situation where we detect when someone says our name in a conversation that we are not monitoring consciously. Intentional selective attention is conscious focusing of attention on one segment of a complex stimulus. An example of such selective attention is the ability of a symphony conductor who can auditorily single out each individual musician in the orchestra during a performance. See also **Cocktail-party effect**.

Semantic memory Knowledge of facts and general information about the world acquired by means of formal education (e.g., in school). The facts are learned independent of context (e.g., the capital of Germany or the equation for calculating the area of a square). This is one type of declarative memory/learning. Opposite: episodic memory.

Semantic paraphasia Substitution of one term with another that belongs to the same semantic category (e.g., dog for cat). It is a frequent symptom of Wernicke's aphasia. See also **Phonemic paraphasia**.

Semantics A field of linguistics that studies meaning in language.

Semicircular canals Part of the vestibular organ in the inner ear consisting of three semicircular canals (in each ear) perpendicular to each other. The canals respond to rotational accelerations of the head.

Sensation Detection of stimulus. It is caused by direct influence of the stimulus on the sensory organ. Frequently erroneously equated with perception. Although it is impossible to draw a clear line between sensation and perception, the convention that sensation is subcortical whereas perception is cortical has been generally accepted (Pinel, 2005). More precisely, sensation is the result of the activity of receptors and their afferent pathways to the corresponding sensory areas in the cortex, whereas perception is the result of neuronal activity after the first synapse in the sensory cortex (Kolb & Whishaw, 1996). Sensations differ with respect to modality, quality, intensity, duration, extensity, and local sign, i.e., with respect to the place of reception.

Sensitive period See **Critical period**.

Sensitization Increased sensitivity to milder stimuli that occur after exposure to a more intense stimulus, or in an area surrounding the injury. In addition to habituation, one of the types of nonassociative learning.

Sensory memory A store for sensory stimuli. In this store the stimuli are kept very briefly: from several tens of milliseconds to a maximum of two seconds. Depending on sensory modality, this memory can be echoic, haptic, or iconic. See also **Echoic store**, **Iconic store**, **Haptic store**.

Sensory neglect See **Neglect**.

Sensory/detection threshold See **Absolute limen**.

Serial models Models that posit that different activities or functions are carried out one after another (in sequence, series) as opposed to parallel models.

Serial processing Processing of data (stimuli) in which the stimulus or a function are processed one by one in sequence, i.e., the processing of one component cannot begin until the processing of a preceding one has been completed. See also **Serial models**.

Short-term memory See **Working memory**.

Sign language A system of symbols for communication within the deaf community. It is a language in its own right. It is based on movements and positions of hands and on facial expressions.

Soma See **Cell body**.

Somatic sensory system Part of the peripheral nervous system that interacts with the environment (afferent and efferent nerves).

Somatosensation A common term for sensations of touch, pain, temperature, and kinesthetic sensation.

Somatosensory (somatic sensory) cortex Part of the cortex, primarily in the postcentral gyrus, in which sensory data from body surface, subcutaneous tissue, muscles, and joints are processed.

Somatotopic organization (map) A type of topographic organization in which spatial relations from the surface of the body are preserved in the neural, primarily cerebral, representation of the body. Neighboring body parts are represented in neighboring areas (e.g., fingers, hand, arm). Severing of connections with a segment of body surface (e.g., limb amputation) will result in cerebral projections of neighboring peripheral parts expanding into the area that is no longer getting stimuli from the original peripheral location.

Spatial summation Summation of potentials that arrive simultaneously at different locations of the postsynaptic membrane.

Specialization The idea that one particular area of the brain is in charge of a particular cognitive function or behavior, i.e., specialized for it.

SPECT Single-Photon Emission Computed Tomography. One of the neuroimaging methods of visualizing brain activity; similar to PET.

Spinal cord (medulla spinalis) Part of the central nervous system that connects the brain with the body parts below the neck. Along the spinal cord, information from the cerebral cortex and other brain structures travels toward the muscles and all body organs (autonomic nervous system), and information about sensations, including proprioceptive ones, as well as information from some organs travels from the periphery toward the brain.

Spinal nerves (nervi spinales) Thirty-one pairs of peripheral nerves that exit the spinal cord and innervate the muscles with their motor parts—in the front (exiting from the ventral horns); or receive sensations with their sensory parts in the back (exiting from dorsal horns) to relay them along the spinal cord to the thalamus and the cortex.

Split-brain A condition when for some reason (usually to stop epileptic seizures from spreading to the other hemisphere) the connection(s) between the left and the right hemisphere have been severed surgically (see commissurotomy). It may also refer to a congenital condition in which the corpus callosum has not developed (acallosal persons).

SPS Syntactic Positive Shift. In ERP, a positive wave that occurs about 600 ms after the beginning of a syntactically incorrect or unexpected stimulus. Corresponds to the term *P600*.

Stapes See **Stirrup**.

Stereognosis Recognition of an object by touch.

Stirrup (stapes) One of the three ossicles in the middle ear. On its lateral end it is connected with the anvil and its medial end (the plate) closes the oval window that connects it with the inner ear.

Storage The second phase of learning, during which some of the available information is stored in memory.

Stroke A sudden brain disorder caused by hemorrhage (bleeding) or ischemia (suppression of blood flow). The most frequent consequences include amnesia, aphasia, paralysis, and coma.

Stroop effect The original Stroop test consisted of a task of naming colors presented in two ways: in the form of spots and in the form of words printed in incongruent color (e.g., the word *blue* printed in red). Naming colors in the latter task was slower due to the inconsistency in the data. More generally, Stroop effect may be produced by other incongruent stimuli combinations.

Subplate zone A layer of temporary neurons that is formed immediately below the layer of the developing cerebral cortex.

Subtraction method Interpretation of neuroimaging results in the way that the activity recorded during rest is subtracted from the activity recorded during some tested function. The obtained images reflect the location, shape, and extent of relevant areas and enable measurement of the size of change. In this way it is possible to compare areas activated by two different tasks. See also **ROI**.

Sulcus A deep valley in the cortex between gyri.

Superior Above something else; when used in describing positions of various brain structures in primates it refers to the position above or direction upward from another structure. Opposite: inferior. See also **Dorsal**.

Superior olive Part of the brain stem. Lateral superior olive is the part of the auditory pathway where intensity differences between the sounds arriving to the left and the right ear are processed. Sounds whose frequencies are higher than 3 kHz are localized here as well. The medial superior olive is part of the auditory pathway that is responsible for processing time differences between sounds arriving to the left and the right ear, on the basis of which sounds can be localized on the horizontal plane.

Supplementary motor area (SMA) Part of the secondary motor area that roughly corresponds to Brodmann's area 6. Located within and along the longitudinal fissure.

Supramarginal gyrus (gyrus supramarginalis) A gyrus in the inferior part of the parietal lobe. It is believed that in the language-dominant hemisphere it is involved in phonological and partly in semantic processing, and it is an important part of the phonological store; it corresponds to Brodmann's area 40.

Surface dysgraphia A condition in which writing of irregular words and non-words is impaired, with intact writing of regular words.

Surface dyslexia A condition in which reading of regular words is unimpaired, but the patients are incapable of reading irregular words, due to deficits in the lexical reading procedure (with spared nonlexical procedure). Opposite: deep dyslexia. See also **Phonological dyslexia**.

Syllabic script Each symbol represents a syllable. See *Hiragana*, *Katakana*.

Sylvian fissure See **Lateral fissure**.

Synapse The point of communication between neurons; it may be chemical or electric.

Synaptic cleft In chemical synapses, a tiny space between the presynaptic and the postsynaptic neuron.

Synaptic vesicles Little bubbles in the presynaptic axon terminals that contain neurotransmitters.

Synaptogenesis Development of synapses.

Syntagm A part of the language structure that contains more than one word.

Syntagmatic relation Items in an utterance are said to be syntagmatically related if they can be stringed together. For example, the words *dogs* and *bark* are syntagmatically related. See also **Paradigmatic relation**.

Syntax An area of linguistics that studies sentence structure.

Tachistoscope A device that enables presentation of visual stimuli in short time intervals, used in studies of lateralization of cerebral functions by means of the divided visual field tests.

Telegraphic speech Speech consisting only of lexical words (nouns and verbs), with no grammatical words (conjunctions, adverbs); characteristic of Broca's aphasia.

Telencephalon Part of the diencephalon that is transformed into cerebral hemispheres approximately in the seventh gestation week.

Temporal lobe (lobus temporalis) Part of the cerebrum located inferior to the lateral (Sylvian) fissure; extends posteriorly to the parieto-occipital notch that separates it from the occipital lobe; it also borders with the ventral portion of the parietal lobe.

Temporal summation Summation of potentials that reach the neuron in very short time intervals. Because of this process, several consecutive subliminal stimuli may elicit action potential, whereas each one of them on its own would not do so.

Teratogens Exogenous substances that cause birth defects.

Tertiary areas See **Association cortex**.

Thalamus A collection of subcortical nuclei located almost in the center of the brain (it is the major component of the diencephalon), where numerous neural fibers come together and cross. It receives visual and auditory signals, and it is involved in movement control. It is connected with the cerebellum and the basal ganglia. It also receives input from the limbic system. The thalamus integrates and interprets signals before relaying them to other parts of the brain. It also plays a role in memory processes. All information, with the exception of olfaction, are processed in the thalamic nuclei (seven groups) before they reach the cerebral cortex.

Theory of mind A theory about the internal mental state of others, i.e., the ability to think and interpret it, which enables us to understand and predict their behavior. The theory posits a set of assumptions and inferences about intentions, goals, feelings, beliefs, motivation, and knowledge of a person on the basis of his/her behavior, that is supposedly governed by that mental state. The theory works two ways: knowing someone's mental state we can predict their behavior, and on the basis of someone's overt behavior we can make assumptions about their mental state.

Threshold A level of membrane potential at which action potential can be elicited.

TMS Transcranial Magnetic Stimulation. One of the methods of studying brain activity.

Tone languages Languages in which patterns of pitch (tone) contribute to the lexical identification of words (e.g., Chinese). Partial tone languages have significant pitch on some syllables only (e.g., Croatian, Lithuanian).

Tonotopic organization (map) The spatial relations among receptors sensitive to particular sound frequencies (in the cochlea) are preserved along the auditory pathway and in the auditory cortex. Changes in relations in the peripheral organ are reflected in tonotopic maps at higher levels. For example, listening to a limited number of tones of specific frequencies will increase the cortical area in which these tones are projected. See also topographic organization.

Top-down processing Processing of stimuli under the influence of factors such as previous experience and expectations. The processing is initiated by the individual. It is also referred to as conceptually driven processing (as opposed to data-driven that is associated with bottom-up processing). Opposite: bottom-up processing.

Topographic organization (map) Representation of the peripheral receptors in the central nervous system in a way that preserves their spatial relations—neighboring (peripheral) receptors are represented in neighboring areas in the brain. Examples of such organization are retinotopic maps (for visual stimuli), tonotopic maps (for auditory stimuli), and somatosensory maps (in the motor and sensory cortices).

Trace model This model of word recognition assumes individual processing units (nodes) at three levels: features, phonemes, and words. The feature nodes are connected with the phoneme nodes, which are in turn connected with the word nodes. The connections between levels are reciprocal and facilitatory. Connections at the same level are inhibitory. The nodes affect one another proportional to their levels of activation and the strength of mutual connections. Spreading of excitation and inhibition among nodes develops an activation pattern or trace. The recognized word is determined by the activation level of possible candidate words.

Tract A bundle of axons (in the central nervous system).

Transcortical motor aphasia A consequence of the disconnection of Broca's area from the rest of the frontal lobe. The main characteristic of this type of aphasia is lack of the desire to speak, with preserved comprehension and repetition of the speech of others. In extreme cases it may lead to echolalia. The patients speak unwillingly and have great word-finding difficulties, but articulation is relatively good. Their sentences are simple, consisting primarily of nouns.

Transcortical sensory aphasia In this type of aphasia, speech comprehension is impaired (presumably because access to semantic data about words is disabled), but syntactic and phonological functions are preserved. The patients cannot read or write and have great word-finding difficulties. Most frequently, this type of aphasia is a consequence of lesions in the supramarginal and angular gyri.

Transition Part of the acoustic signal in which rapid changes are noticeable (e.g., in speech, they occur at the boundary between two sounds).

Traumatic brain injury Brain lesion caused by mechanical injury.

Universal grammar An innate predisposition to develop certain grammatical structures that are common to all languages. Languages differ in how these universal grammatical properties are implemented.

Utricle (utriculus) One of the two otolithic organs in the inner ear, in the membranous portion of the vestibular organ. It is responsible for reception of linear accelerations and head movements in the horizontal plane. See also **Sacculus**.

Ventral In descriptions of locations of structures in vertebrates, denoting direction or position toward the front (the belly) or away from the top of the head. In primates, due to their upright posture, the term *inferior* is also used to refer to the position or direction away from the top of the head. Opposite: dorsal, i.e., superior.

Ventral path See **What–where dichotomy**.

Ventricle A cavity in an organ. In the brain, there are four ventricles filled with cerebro-spinal fluid: two lateral ventricles, the third and the fourth ventricle.

Vestibular nucleus A group of neurons in the brain stem primarily responsible for motor reactions to vestibular stimuli.

Vestibular organ Part of the inner ear responsible for vestibular sensation, i.e., sense of balance. It consists of three semicircular canals (cupular organ) and the otolithic organs (utricle and saccule).

Visceral nervous system See **Autonomic nervous system**.

Visual (optic) agnosia Impaired recognition of objects on the basis of visual stimuli despite the fact that visual information reaches the visual cortex; holistic and analytic processing are impaired, but the patients are relatively better at recognizing object properties (e.g., color, form, movement) than the entire object or its use. See also **Prosopagnosia**.

Visual field advantage The phenomenon that the visual stimuli presented to one visual field are responded to faster or more accurately than those presented to the other visual field. It is taken as an indicator of superiority of the contralateral cerebral hemisphere for the particular task. It is usually measured by briefly presenting test stimuli to the left or the right of the fixation point. The conventional abbreviations are LVFA for left visual field advantage and RVFA for right visual field advantage.

Visuospatial sketchpad A component of working memory (besides the phonological loop and central executive) that is involved in the visual and spatial data processing.

VOT Voice Onset Time. Time (measured in milliseconds) between the moment of explosion to the onset of periodic phonation, which is an important element of acoustic description of stops. Voiced stops (e.g., /b/, /g/) have shorter VOTs than their voiceless counterparts (e.g., /p/, /k/).

Weber's law States that the difference in intensity (ΔI) necessary to distinguish a referent (I) and some other stimulus increases with the intensity of the referent ($\Delta I/I = k$). See also **JND**.

Weighting Attributing importance (weight) to one result or parameter compared with others.

Wernicke's aphasia Traditionally refers to the speech and language disorder caused by a lesion in part of the temporal lobe corresponding to Wernicke's area. The disorder is characterized by difficulties in speech comprehension with intact production, hence the alternative terms: sensory or receptive aphasia. The patients' speech is fluent, but their utterances are nonsensical, which is frequently described as word salad. Paraphasias, neologisms and logorrhea are also present.

Wernicke's area Part of the posterior temporal lobe of the language-dominant (typically left) hemisphere, traditionally considered to be the center of speech and language perception. It corresponds to the posterior part of Brodmann's area 22 and was named after 19th century physician Karl Wernicke who was among the first to describe deficits in speech perception and associate them with lesions in that part of the brain.

What–where dichotomy/analysis (In visual modality) the idea that object analysis (*what*) and their position in space (*where*) are processed along different pathways in the visual cortex. In the ventral pathway that runs from the primary visual cortex through the inferior temporal lobe the objects are recognized (the *what* pathway). In the dorsal pathway that runs from the primary visual cortex through the posterior temporal lobe proceeds spatial analysis, i.e., determining objects position in space (the *where* pathway).

Where–what See **What–where dichotomy**.

White matter Parts of the nervous system, consisting mostly of neuronal axons, whose myelin sheath is responsible for their white color, as opposed to gray matter.

Wisconsin Card Sorting Test (WCST) In this test, cards with different numbers of symbols varying in color and shape are used. The subject takes one card at a time and puts it on a pile of other cards. On the basis of the experimenter's feedback (by trial and error) the subject learns whether the sorting criterion is shape, color, or number of symbols. After 10 consecutive correctly sorted cards, the experimenter changes the sorting criterion without a warning, and the subject must work out the new criterion. Failure on the test is most frequently manifested as perseveration, and it reveals disorders in functions that are controlled by the frontal lobes.

Word salad Speech characteristic of Wernicke's aphasia. It is fluent and sounds normal, with good prosody, but it is nonsense.

Working memory A fundamental ability to monitor and update information rapidly at any given moment. According to Baddeley (2000) it is a system consisting of three components: the central executive, the phonological/articulatory loop, and the visuospatial sketchpad.

Appendix

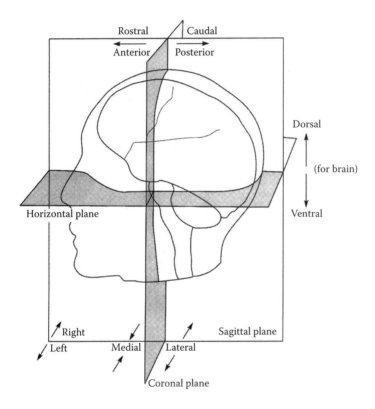

FIGURE A.1. Principal axes and sections of the brain.

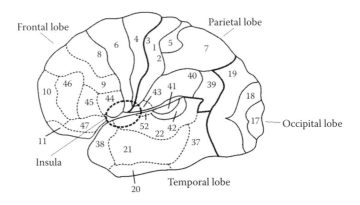

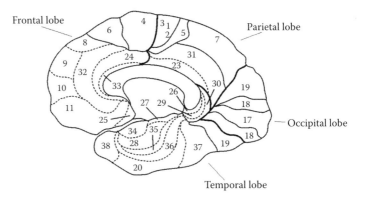

FIGURE A.2. Brodmann's areas in lateral and midsagittal view, including the four lobes.

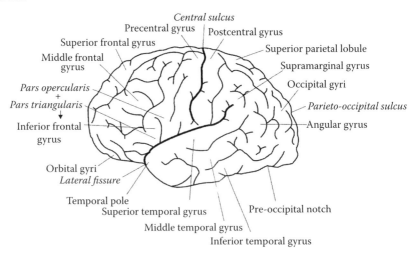

FIGURE A.3. Lateral view of the brain.

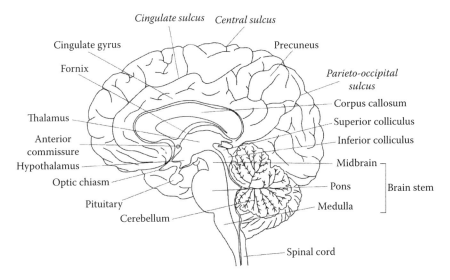

FIGURE A.4. Midsagittal view of the brain.

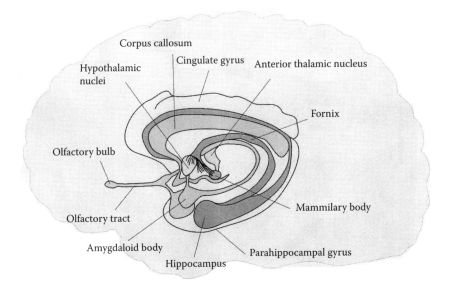

FIGURE A.5. The limbic system.

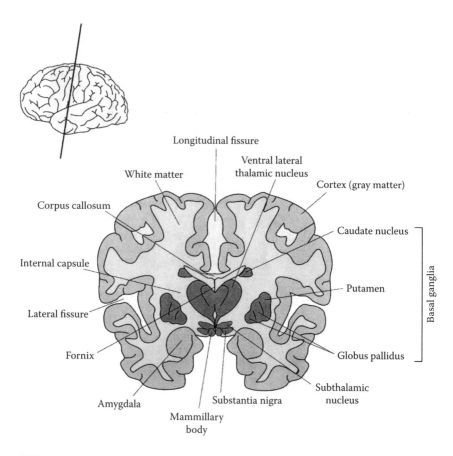

FIGURE A.6. Coronal (frontal) view of the brain with the basal ganglia.

References

Abrahams, S., Brammer, M., Simmons, A., Goldstein, L., Andrew, C., Curtis, V., Leigh, P. & Williams, S. (2000). Overt verbal fluency and confrontation naming in fMRI. Retrieved January 31, 2001, from http://www.apnet.com/www/journal/hbm2000/6657.html

Ackermann, H., Lutzenberger, W., & Hertrich, I. (1999). Hemispheric lateralization of the neural encoding of temporal speech features: A whole-head magnetencephalography study. *Cognitive Brain Research, 7*(4), 511–518.

Ahonniska, J., Cantell, M., Tolvanen, A., & Lyytinen, H. (1993). Speech perception and brain laterality: The effect of ear advantage on auditory event-related potentials. *Brain and Language 45,* 127–146.

Ainsworth, W. A. (1997). Some approaches to automatic speech recognition. In W. J. Hardcastle & J. Laver (Eds.), *The handbook of phonetic sciences* (pp. 720–743). Oxford: Blackwell.

Aitkin, L. (1990). *The auditory cortex.* London: Chapman and Hall.

Albert, M. L. & Obler, L. K. (1978). *The bilingual brain.* New York: Academic Press.

Alho, K., Medvedev, S. V., Pakhomov, S. V., Roudas, M. S., Tervaniemi, M., Reinikainen, K., Zeffiro, T., & Näätänen, R. (1999). Selective tuning of the left and right auditory cortices during spatially directed attention. *Cognitive Brain Research, 7*(3), 335–341.

Alonso-Bua, B., Diaz, F., & Ferraces, M. A. (2006). The contribution of AERPs (MMN and LDN) to studying temporal vs. linguistic processing deficits in children with reading difficulties. *International Journal of Psychophysiology, 59*(2), 159–167.

Amunts, K., Schleicher, A., Ditterich, A., & Zilles, K. (2000). Postnatal changes in cytoarchitectonic asymmetry of Broca's region. Retrieved January 31, 2001, from http://www.apnet.com/www/journal/hbm2000/6211.html

Andrilović, V., & Čudina, M. (1990). *Osnove opće i razvojne psihologije.* Zagreb: Školska knjiga.

Angrilli, A., Dobel, C., Rockstroh, B., Stegagno, L., & Ebert T. (2000). EEG brain mapping of phonological and semantic tasks in Italian and German languages. *Clinical Neurophysiology, 111*(4), 706–716.

Anneken, K., Lohmann, H., Floeel, A., Konrad, C., Buchinger, C., Deppe, M., & Knecht, S. (2000). Is language ability related to the extent of hemispheric language lateralization? Retrieved January 31, 2001, from http://www.apnet.com/www/journal/hbm2000/6721.html

Anourova, I., Artchakov, D., Korvenoja, A., Koivisto, J., Aronen, H., Ilmoniemi, R., & Carlson, S. (2002). Timing of "what" and "where" responses in the auditory system. Retrieved July 9, 2002, from http://fens2002.bordeaux.inserim.fr/pages/posters/R6/A184_1.html

Azari, N. P., Knorr, U., Arnold, S., Antke, C., Ebner, A., Niemann, H., et al. (1999). Reorganized cerebral metabolic interactions in temporal lobe epilepsy. *Neuropsychologia, 37*(6), 625–636.

Baciu, M., Kahane, P., David, D., Minotti, L., Le Bas, J.-F., & Segebarth, C. (2000). Hemispheric language dominance testing by fMRI in epileptic patients, using a rhyme detection task. Retrieved January 31, 2001, from http://www.apnet.com/www/journal/hbm2000/5963.html

Baddeley, A. (2000). Working memory: The interface between memory and cognition. In S. Gazzaniga (Ed.), *Cognitive Neuroscience: A Reader* (pp. 292–304). Oxford: Blackwell.

Bakran, J. (1996). *Zvučna slika hrvatskoga govora.* Zagreb: IBIS grafika.

Basili, A. G., Diggs, Ch. C., & Rao, P. R. (1980). Auditory processing of brain-damaged adults under competitive listening conditions. *Brain and Language, 9*, 362–371.

Bastiaansen, M. C. M., Van der Linden, M., Ter Keurs, M., Dijkstra, T., & Hagoort, P. (2005). Theta responses are involved in lexical-semantic retrieval during language processing. *Journal of Cognitive Neuroscience, 17*(3), 530–541.

Bates, E. (1994). Modularity, domain specificity and the development of language. *Discussions in Neuroscience, 10*(1–2), 136–149.

Baum, S., & Pell, M. (1999). The neural bases of prosody. Insights from lesion studies and neuroimaging. *Aphasiology, 8,* 581–608.

Beatse, E., Sunaert, S., Wilm, G., Van Hecke, P., & Marchal, G. (2000). The combined study of language and sensorimotor regions in patients with brain lesions using a mixed blocked and event related paradigm. Retrieved January 31, 2001, from http://www.apnet.com/www/journal/hbm2000/6576.html

Beauregard, M., Breault, C., & Bourgouin, P. (2000). Neural substrate of the episodic memory retrieval of emotionally-laden pictures: A gender comparative fMRI study. Retrieved January 31, 2001, from http://www.apnet.com/www/journal/hbm2000/7179.html

Becker, J. T., MacAndrew, D. K., & Fiez, J. A. (1999). A comment on the functional localization of the phonological storage subsystem of working memory. *Brain and Cognition, 41*(1), 27–38.

Bellmann Thiran, A., Adriani, M., Fornari, E., Maeder, P., Meuli, R., Bach, M., Thiran, J. P., & Clarke, S. (2002). Reorganisation of specialised auditory networks in a patient with progressive aphasia. Retrieved July 9, 2002, from http://fens2002.bordeaux.inserim.fr/pages/posters/R3/A074_2.html

Benefield, H., Crosson, B., Cato, M. A., Sadek, J. R., Gopinath, K., Soltysik, D., Bauer, R. M., Auerbach, E. J., Gokcay, D., & Briggs, R. W. (2000). Role of medial frontal cortex in word retrieval. Retrieved January 31, 2001, from http://www.apnet.com/www/journal/hbm2000/6157.html

Bennett, S., & Netsell, R. W. (1999). Possible roles of the insula in speech and language processing: Directions for research. *Journal of Medical Speech Language Pathology, 7*(4), 255–272.

Benraiss, A., Haveman, A., Liegeois-Chauvel, C., & Besson, M. (2000). The role of prosody to disambiguate an ambiguous sentence: An electrophysiologic approach. Retrieved January 31, 2001, from http://www.apnet.com/www/journal/hbm2000/

Bentin, S., Mouchetant-Rostaing, Y., Giard, M. H., Echallier, J. F., & Pernier, J. (1999). ERP manifestations of processing printed words at different psycholinguistic levels: Time course and scalp distribution. *Journal of Cognitive Neuroscience, 11*(3), 235–260.

Berlin, C. I. (1977). Hemispheric asymmetry in auditory tasks. In S. Harnad, R. W. Doty, L. Goldstein, J. Joyner, & G. Krauthmer (Eds.), *Lateralization in the nervous system* (pp. 303–323). New York: Academic Press.

Bernard, F., Desgranges, B., Eustache, F., & Baron, J. C. (2002). Functional neuro-anatomy of age-related episodic memory decline using PET subtraction and correlation methods. Retrieved July 9, 2002, from http://fens2002.bordeaux.inserim.fr/pages/posters/R1/A008_1.html

Berthoz, S., Artiges, E., Van DeMoortele, P. F., Poline, J. B., Rouquette, S., & Martinot, J. L. (2000). Personality trait and brain activity: Ability to identify and communicate emotions is reflected by differences in cerebral activations during emotion-inducing stimuli processing. Retrieved January 31, 2001, from http://www.apnet.com/www/journal/hbm2000/6303.html

Billingsley, R., McAndrews, M. P., Crawley, A., & Mikulis, D. (2000). Functional MRI analyses of phonological and semantic processing in adults with temporal-lobe epilepsy. Retrieved January 31, 2001, from http://www.apnet.com/www/journal/hbm2000/5912.html

Binder, J. R., Kaufman, J. N., Possing, E. T., Liebenthal, E., Tong, R., & Ward, B. D. (2000). Functional parcellation of human auditory cortex: Sensitivity to intensity and spectral pattern information. *Neuroimage, 11*, S296.

Blumstein, S. (1988). Neurolinguistics: An overview of language-brain relations in aphasia. In F. J. Newmeyer (Ed.), *Linguistics: The Cambridge survey: Vol. 3. Language: Psychological and Biological Aspects* (pp. 210–236). Cambridge: Cambridge University Press.

Blumstein, S. (1995). On the neurobiology of the sound structure of language: Evidence from aphasia. In K. Elenius & P. Branderud (Eds.), *Proceedings of the XIIIth International Congress of Phonetic Sciences, 2,* 180–185.

Blumstein, S., Goodglass, H., & Tartter, V. (1975). The reliability of ear advantage in dichotic listening. *Brain and Language, 2,* 226–236.

Blumstein, S., & Stevens, K. (1979). Acoustic invariance in speech production: Evidence from measurements of the spectral characteristics of stop consonants. *Journal of the Acoustical Society of America, 66*(4), 1001–1017.

Boatman, D. (2000). Speech perception after right hemispherectomy. *Govor, 17,* 129–140.

Boatman, D., Freeman, J., Vining, E., Pulsifer, M., Miglioretti, D., Minahan, R., Carson, B., Brandt, J., & McKhann, G. (1999). Language recovery after left hemispherectomy in children with late-onset seizures. *Annals of Neurology, 46,* 579–586.

Bocker, K. B. E., Bastiaansen, M. C. M., Vroomen, J., Brunia, C. H., & de Gelder, B. (1999). An ERP correlate of metrical stress in spoken word recognition. *Psychophysiology, 36*(6), 706–720.

Bokde, A. L. W., Tagamets, M.-A., Friedman, R. B., & Horwitz, B. (2000). fMRI functional connectivity of the inferior frontal gyrus. Retrieved January 31, 2001, from http://www.apnet.com/www/journal/hbm2000/6322.html

Bookheimer, S. Y., Zeffiro, T. A., Blaxton, T., Gaillard, W. D., & Theodore, W. H. (2000). Activation of language cortex with automatic speech tasks. *Neurology, 55*(8), 1151–1157.

Booth, J. R., Burman, D. D., Harasaki, Y., Van Santen, F., Gitelman, D. R., Parrish, T. B., & Mesulam, M. M. (2000). The development of orthographic, phonologic, semantic and syntactic representations in reading: Analytic versus automatic processing. Retrieved January 31, 2001, from http://www.apnet.com/www/journal/hbm2000/6318.html

Borković, Lj. (2004). *Neuropsiholingvistička osnova slušanja, mišljenja i govora (temelji verbotonalne teorije).* Zagreb: Hrvatska verbotonalna udruga.

Boulanouar, K., Cances, C., Gros, H., Viallard, G., Berry, I., Demonet, J. F., & Celsis, P. (2000). fMRI assessment of the differential response to syllables and tones in the auditory cortex of dyslexics and controls using an habituation-recovery paradigm with variable rate of deviant. Retrieved January 31, 2001, from http://www.apnet.com/www/journal/hbm2000/6638.html

Bradshaw, J. L., & Nettleton, N. C. (1983). *Human cerebral asymmetry.* Inglewood Cliffs, NJ: Prentice Hall.

Brechmann, A., & Scheich, H. (2000). The right human auditory cortex is predominantly involved in the discrimination and the direction of frequency modulated tones. Retrieved January 31, 2001, from http://www.apnet.com/www/journal/hbm2000/6715.html

Brinar, V., Brzović, Z., & Zurak, N. (1999). *Neurološka propedeutika.* Čakovec: Zrinski.

Brockway, J. P. (2000). fMRI may replace the Wada test for language lateralization/localization. Retrieved January 31, 2001, from http://www.apnet.com/www/journal/hbm2000/6142.html

Brown, G. D. A., Hulme, C., Hyland, P. D., & Mitchell, I. J. (1994). Cell suicide in the developing nervous system: A functional neural network model. *Cognitive Brain Research, 2*, 71–75.

Bruder, G., Kayser, J., Tenke, C., Amador, X., Friedman, M., Sharif, Z., & Gorman, J. (1999). Left temporal lobe dysfunction in schizophrenia: Event-related potential and behavioral evidence from phonetic and tonal dichotic listening tasks. *Archives of General Psychiatry, 56*(3), 267–276.

Buchinger, C., Floel, A., Lohmann, H., Deppe, M., Henningsen, H., & Knecht, S. (2000). Lateralization of expressive and receptive language functions in healthy volunteers. Retrieved January 31, 2001, from http://www.apnet.com/www/journal/hbm2000/6627.htm

Burton, M. W., Small, S. L., & Blumstein, S. E. (2000). The role of segmentation in phonological processing: An fMRI investigation. *Journal of Cognitive Neuroscience, 12*(4), 679–690.

Butler, A. J., Fink, G. R., Wunderlich, G., Dohle, C., Binkofski, F. C., Tellman, L., Seitz, R. J., Zilles, K., & Freund, H.-J. (2000). Reaching to remembered targets: Comparison of visual and kinesthetic cueing in left and right hemispace. Retrieved January 31, 2001, from http://www.apnet.com/www/journal/hbm2000/6311.html

Cahill, L. (2003). Sex- and hemisphere-related influences on the neurobiology of emotionally influenced memory. *Prog. Neuropsychopharmacol Biol Psychiatry, 27*(8), 1235–1241.

Capek, C. M., Bavelier, D., Corina, D., Newman, A. J., Jezzard, P., & Neville, H. J. (2004). The cortical organization of audio-visual sentence comprehension: an fMRI study at 4 Tesla. *Brain Research. Cognitive Brain research, 20*(2), 111–119.

Caplan, D. (1988). The biological basis for language. In F. J. Newmeyer (Ed.), *Linguistics: The Cambridge survey: Vol. 3. Language: Psychological and biological aspects* (pp. 237–255). Cambridge: Cambridge University Press.

Caplan, R., Dapretto, M., & Mazziotta, J. C. (2000). An fMRI study of discourse coherence. Retrieved January 31, 2001, from http://www.apnet.com/www/journal/hbm2000/6804.html

Carpentier, A., Pugh, K., Studholme, C., Spencer, D., & Constable, T. (2000a). Language processing for different input modalities. Retrieved January 31, 2001, from http://www.apnet.com/www/journal/hbm2000/

Carpentier, A., Westerveld, M., Pugh, K., Skrinjar, O., Studholme, C., MacCarthy, K., Thompson, J., Spencer, D., & Constable, T. (2000b). Evidence of language plasticity in epilepsy. Retrieved January 31, 2001, from http://www.apnet.com/www/journal/hbm2000/

Celsis, P., Doyon, B., Boulanowar, K., Pastor, J., Démonet, J.-F., & Nespoulous, J.-L. (1999). ERP correlates of phoneme perception in speech and sound contexts. *Neuroreport: For Rapid Communication of Neuroscience Research, 10*(7), 1523–1527.

Chambers, C. D., Stokes, M. G., & Mattingley, J. B. (2004). Modality-specific control of strategic spatial attention in parietal cortex. *Neuron, 44*(6), 925–930.

Chang, P. I., & Hammong, G. R. (1987). Mutual interactions between speech and finger movements. *Journal of Motor Behavior, 19*, 265–274.

Changeux, J.-P. (1983). *L'homme neuronal.* Paris: Fayard.

Chee, M., Sriram, N., Lee, K. M., & Soon, C. S. (2000). Modulation of prefrontal activity in congruent, neutral and incongruent word classification. Retrieved January 31, 2001, from http://www.apnet.com/www/journal/hbm2000/6530.htm

Chee, M. W. L., Tan, E. W. L., & Thiel, T. (1999). Mandarin and English single word processing studied with functional magnetic resonance imaging. *The Journal of Neuroscience, 19,* 3050–3056.

Chen, C., Halpern, A., Bly, B., Edelman, R., & Schlaug, G. (2000). Planum temporale asymmetry and absolute pitch. Retrieved January 31, 2001, from http://www.apnet.com/www/journal/hbm2000/7233.html

Cherry, B., & Kee, D. W. (1991). Dual-task interference in left-handed subjects: Hemispheric specialization vs. manual dominance. *Neuropsychologia, 29,* 1251–1255.

Chistovich, L. A. (1984). Relation between speech production and speech perception. In Van den Broecke & A. Cohen (Eds.), *Proceedings of the Xth International Congress of Phonetic Sciences* (pp. 55–58). Dordrecht: Foris Publications.

Chomsky, N. (2000). *New horizons in the study of language and mind.* Cambridge: Cambridge University Press.

Chomsky, N., & Halle, M. (1968). *The sound pattern of English.* New York: Harper and Row.

Chugani, H. T., Phelps, M. E., & Mazziotta, J. C. (1987). Positron emission tomography study of human brain functional development. *Annals of Neurology, 22,* 487–497.

Churchland, P. M. (1988). *Matter and consciousness.* Cambridge, MA: MIT Press.

Clarke, S., Adriani, M., Bellmann Thiran, A., Meuli, R., Fornari, E., Frischknecht, R., Bindschaedler, C., Rivier, F., Thiran, J. P., & Maeder, P. (2002). Contralateral effects of right hemispheric lesions on cortical activation patterns to auditory tasks: fMRI study. Retrieved July 9, 2002, from http://fens2002.bordeaux.inserim.fr/pages/posters/R7/A220_6.html

Cohen, H., & Forget, H. (1995). Auditory cerebral lateralization following cross gender hormone therapy. *Cortex, 31,* 565–573.

Cohen, H., Gelinas, C., Lassonde, M., & Geoggroy, G. (1991). Auditory lateralization for speech in language-impaired children. *Brain and Language, 41,* 395–401.

Cohen, H., & Segalowitz, N. (1990). Cerebral hemispheric involvement in the acquisition of new phonetic categories. *Brain and Language, 38,* 398–409.

Colier, W. N. J. M., Jaquet, I., van der Hoeven, M. M., Hagoort, P., & Oeseburg, B. (2000). Lateral left frontal oxygenation changes upon picture naming task by functional near infrared spectroscopy. Retrieved January 31, 2001, from http://www.apnet.com/www/journal/hbm2000/6671.html

Colombo, J. (1982). The critical-period concept: Research, methodology and theoretical issues. *Psychological Bulletin, 91*(2), 260.

Committeri, G., Galati, G., Paradis, A. L., Poline, J. B., Berthoz, A., Pizzamiglio, L., & Le Bihan, D. (2002). Egocentric and allocentric coding of relative distance in a 3D environment: Lingual/parahippocampal activation during environmental judgements. Retrieved July 9, 2002, from http://fens2002.bordeaux.inserim.fr/pages/posters/R3/A074_8.html

Constable, R. T., Pugh, K. R., Berroya, E., Mencl, W. E., Westerweld, M., Ni, W., & Shankweiler, D. (2004). Sentence complexity and input modality effects in sentence comprehension: an fMRI study. *Neuroimage, 22*(1), 11–21.

Cooper, C. E., & Delpy, D. T. (1995). Taking the lid off the brain. *The Biochemist.* October/November, 13–16.

Coren, S., & Ward, L. M. (1989). *Sensation and perception.* San Diego: Harcourt Brace Jovanovich.

Corina, D. P., Poliakov, A., Keith, S., Martin, R., Mulligan, K., Maravilla, K., Brinkley, J. F., & Ojemann, G. A. (2000). Correspondences between language cortex identified by cortical stimulation mapping and f MRI. Retrieved January 31, 2001, from http://www.apnet.com/www/journal/hbm2000/6335.html

Coslett, H. B., & Monsul, N. (1994). Reading with the right hemisphere: Evidence from transcranial magnetic stimulation. *Brain and Language, 46,* 198–211.

Costa, A., Miozzo, M., & Caramazza, A. (1999). Lexical selection in bilinguals: Do words in the bilingual's two lexicons compete for selection? *Journal of Memory and Language, 41*(3), 365–397.

Coulson, S., & Wu, Y. C. (2005). Right hemisphere activation of joke-related information: An event-related brain potential study. *Journal of Cognitive Neuroscience, 17*(3), 494–506.

Coutin-Churchman, P., & Pietrosemoli, L. G. (2002). Right hemisphere involvement in the processing of a second language. www.neuro-linguistica.org/publicaciones/

Cowell, P. E., Allen, L. S., Zalatimo, N. S., & Denenberg, V. H. (1992). A developmental study of sex and age interactions in the human corpus callosum. *Developmental Brain Research, 66,* 187–192.

Creutzfeldt, O., Ojemann, G., & Lettich, E. (1989a). Neuronal activity in human lateral temporal lobe. I. Responses to speech. *Experimental Brain Research, 77,* 451–475.

Creutzfeldt, O., Ojemann, G., & Lettich, E. (1989b). Neuronal activity in human lateral temporal lobe. II. Responses to the subject's own voice. *Experimental Brain Research, 77,* 476–489.

Crinion, J., & Price, C. J. (2005). Right anterior superior temporal activation predicts auditory sentence comprehension following aphasic stroke. *Brain, 128*(12), 2858–2871.

Crosson, B., Rao, S. M., Woodley, S. J., Rosen, A. C., Hammeke, T. A., Bobholz, J. A., Mayer, A., Cunningham, J. M., Fuller, S. A., Binder, J. R., Cox, R. W., & Stein, E. A. (1999). Mapping of semantic, phonological, and orthographic verbal working memory in normal adults with functional magnetic resonance imaging. *Neuropsychology, 13*(2), 171–187.

Crosson, B., Bacon Moore, A., Gopinath, K., White, K. D., Wikerenga, C. E., Gaiefsky, M. E., Fabrizio, K. S., Peck, K. K., Soltysik, D., Milsted, C., Briggs, R. W., Conway, T. W., & Rothi, L. J. (2005). Role of the right and left hemispheres in recovery of function during treatment of intention in aphasia. *Journal of Cognitive Neuroscience, 17*(3), 392–406.

Crozier, S., Sirigu, A., Lehericy, S., De Moortele, P. F. van, Pillon, B., Grafman, J., Agid, Y., Dubois, B., & Lebihan, D. (2000). Distinct prefrontal activations in processing sequence at the sentence and script level: An fMRI study. *Neuropsychologia, 38*(13), 1469–1476.

Cybulska-Klosowicz, A., & Kossut, M. (2002). Patterns of brain activation during sensory discrimination. Retrieved July 9, 2002, from http://fens2002.bordeaux.inserim. fr/pages/posters/R2/A041_13.html

Dabić-Jevtić, M., & Mikula, I. (1994). *Evocirani potencijali kore mozga.* Zagreb: Školska knjiga.

Damasio, A. R., & Damasio, H. (1992). Brain and language. *Scientific American, 267*(3), 89–95.

Daniels, S. K., Corey, D. M., Fraychinaud, A., Depolo, A., & Foundas, A. L. (2006). Swallowing lateralization: The effects of modified dual-task interference. *Dysphagia.* Mar 17; [Epub ahead of print] . Retrieved March 19, 2006, from http://www.kfinder.com

D'Arcy, R. C., Ryner, L., Richter, W., Service, W., & Connolly, J. F. (2004). The fan effect in fMRI: Left hemisphere specialization in verbal working memory. *Neuroreport, 15*(12), 1851–1855.

Deane, P. D. (1992). *Grammar in mind and brain.* Berlin: Mouton de Gruyter.

De Bot, K. (1992). A bilingual production model: Levelt's "speaking" model adapted. *Applied Linguistics, 13,* 1–24.

Dehaene, S., Dupoux, E., Mehler, J., Cohen, L., Paulesu, R., Perani, D., van de Moortele, P.-F., Lehericy, S., & Le Bihan, D. (1997). Anatomical variability in the cortical representation of first and second language. *NeuroReport, 8,* 3809–3815.

Dehaene-Lambertz, G., & Baillet, S. (1998). A phonological representation in the infant brain. *NeuroReport, 9,* 1885–1888.

Demestre, J., Meltzer, S., Garcia-Albea, J. E., & Vigil, A. (1999). Identifying the null subject: Evidence from event-related brain potentials. *Journal of Psycholinguistic Research, 28*(3), 293–312.

Demonet, J.-F. (1998). Tomographic brain imaging of language functions (Prospects for a new brain/language model). In B. Stemmer & H. Whitaker (Eds.), *Handbook of neurolinguistics* (pp. 131–142). San Diego: Academic Press.

De Nil, L. F., Kroll, R. M., Kapur, S., & Houle, S. (2000). A positron emission tomography study of silent and oral single word reading in stuttering and nonstuttering adults. *Journal of Speech Language and Hearing Research, 43*(4), 1038–1053.

Devlin, J., Russell, R., Davis, M., Price, C., Wilson, J., Matthews, P. M., & Tyler, L. (2000). Susceptibility and semantics: comparing PET and fMRI on a language task. Retrieved January 31, 2001, from http://www.apnet.com/www/journal/hbm2000/5950.html

Dien, J., Frishkoff, G. A., & Tucker, D. M. (2000). Differentiating the n3 and n4 electrophysiological semantic incongruity effects. *Brain and Cognition, 43*(1–3), 148–152.

Dimond, S. J. (1980). *Neuropsychology: A textbook of systems and psychological functions of the human brain.* London: Butterworths.

Dingwall, W. O. (1988). The evolution of human communicative behavior. In F. J. Newmeyer (Ed.), *Linguistics: The Cambridge survey: Vol. 3. Language: Psychological and biological aspects* (pp. 274–313). Cambridge: Cambridge University Press.

Dronkers, N. F. (1996). A new brain region for coordinating speech articulation. *Nature, 384,* 159–161.

Dronkers, N. F. (2000). The pursuit of brain-language relationships. *Brain and Language, 71,* 59–61.

Dronkers, N. F. (2004). Lesion analysis of the brain areas involved in language comprehension. *Cognition, 92,* 145–177.

Dronkers, N. F., & Ludy, C. A. (1998). Brain lesion analysis in clinical research. In B. Stemmer & H. Whitaker (Eds.), *Handbook of neurolinguistics* (pp. 173–187). San Diego: Academic Press.

Drubach, D. (2000). *The brain explained.* Upper Saddle River, NJ: Prentice Hall Health.

Dubost, V., Beauchet, O., Najafi, B., Aminian, K., & Mourey, F. (2002). Gait and attention in young subjects: Performances in relation to different cognitive tasks while walking. Retrieved July 9, 2002, from http://fens2002.bordeaux.inserim.fr/pages/posters/R4/A108_3.html

Ducommun, C., Thut, G., Clarke, S., Spinelli, L., Bellmann, A., & Michel, C. M. (2000). When and where are sound location and sound motion processed? An auditory EP mapping study. Retrieved January 31, 2001, from http://www.apnet.com/www/journal/hbm2000/6479.html

Dudaš, G. (1989). Lateralizacija slušanja raznovrsnih govornih znakova. *Govor VI, 1,* 65–74.

Duffau, H., & Capelle, L. (2000). May surgery in eloquent areas induce brain plasticity? Retrieved January 31, 2001, from http://www.apnet.com/www/journal/hbm2000/6020.html

Duffau, H., Capelle, L., Lopes, M., Faillot, T., & Bitar, A. (2000). The insula in the dominant hemisphere: The essential area of speech? A study using intraoperative brain stimulations. Retrieved January 31, 2001, from http://www.apnet.com/www/journal/hbm2000/6021.html

Durif, C., Jouffrais, C., & Rouiller, E. M. (2002). Single unit activity in auditory cortical areas of monkeys performing an acoustico-motor conditional task. Retrieved July 9, 2002, from http://fens2002.bordeaux.inserim.fr/pages/posters/R2/A040_5.html

Dutia, M. B. (2002). Stress and cerebellar plasticity in the vestibulo-oculomotor system. Retrieved July 9, 2002, from http://fens2002.bordeaux.inserim.fr/pages/posters/R11000/R11375.html

Eden, G., Brown, C., Jones, K., Given, B., & Zeffiro, T. (2000). Phonological and visual motion processing in reading impaired children. Retrieved January 31, 2001, from http://www.apnet.com/www/journal/hbm2000/7138.html

Efron, R. (1990). *The decline and fall of hemispheric specialization.* Hillsdale, NJ: Lawrence Erlbaum Associates.

Ely, P. W., Graves, R. E., & Potter, S. M. (1989). Dichotic listening indices of right hemisphere semantic processing. *Neuropsychologia 27*(7), 1007–1015.

Emmorey, K. D., & Fromkin, V. A. (1988). The mental lexicon. In F. J. Newmeyer (Ed.), *Linguistics: The Cambridge survey. Vol. 3. Language: Psychological and biological aspects* (pp. 124–149). Cambridge: Cambridge University Press.

Epstein, H. (1980). Brain growth and cognitive functioning. In D. Steer (Ed.) *The emerging adolescent: Characteristics and implications.* Fairborn, Ohio: National Middle-School Association.

Erdeljac, V., & Mildner, V. (1999). Temporal structure of spoken-word recognition in Croatian in light of the cohort theory. *Brain and Language, 68,* 95–103.

Escera, C., Alho, K., Schröger, E., & Winkler, I. (2000). Involuntary attention and distractibility as evaluated with event-related brain potentials. *Audiology and Neuro Otology. Special Issue: Mismatch Negativity, 5*(3–4), 151–166.

Eulitz, C., Eulitz, H., & Elbert, T. (1999). Magneto- und elektroenzephalographische Korrelate der Verarbeitung von visuellen verbalen und nicht-verbalen Reizen. *Zeitschrift für klinische Neurophysiologie, 30,* 44–53.

Eysenck, M. W., & Keane, M. T. (2000). *Cognitive Psychology.* (4th ed.). Hove: Taylor and Francis.

Fabbro, F. (1999). *The neurolinguistics of bilingualism: An introduction.* Hove: Psychology Press.

Fabbro, F. (2001a). The bilingual brain: Bilingual aphasia. *Brain and Language, 79,* 201–210.

Fabbro, F. (2001b). The bilingual brain: Cerebral representation of languages. *Brain and Language, 79,* 211–222.

Fabri, M., Polonara, G., Salvolini, U., & Manzoni, T. (2002). Cortical representation of the trunk midline in the first somatic sensory area of the human brain. Retrieved July 9, 2002, from http://fens2002.bordeaux.inserim.fr/pages/posters/R5/A158_4.html

Fant, G. (1967). Auditory patterns of speech. In W. Wathen-Dunn (Ed.), *Models for the perception of speech and visual form* (pp. 111–125). Cambridge, MA: MIT Press.

Faust, M., Barak, O., & Chiarello, C. (2005). The effects of multiple script priming on word recognition by the two cerebral hemispheres: Implications for discourse processing. *Brain and Language,* aug. doi:10.1016/j.bandl.2005.07.002

Faust, M., & Lavidor, M. (2003). Semantically convergent and semantically divergent priming in the cerebral hemispheres: Lexical decision and semantic judgement. *Brain Research. Cognitive Brain Research, 17*(3), 585–597.

Feindel, W. (1994). Cortical localization of speech: Evidence from stimulation and excision. *Discussions in Neuroscience 10*(1–2), 34–45.

Ferster, D., & Spruston, N. (1995). Cracking the neuronal code. *Science, 270,* 756–757.

Fischbach, G. D. (1992). Mind and brain. *Scientific American, 267*(3), 48–57.

Flores d'Arcais, G. B. (1988). Language perception. In F. J. Newmeyer (Ed.), *Linguistics: The Cambridge survey. Vol. 3. Language: Psychological and biological aspects* (pp. 97–123). Cambridge: Cambridge University Press.

Flynn, F. G., Benson, D. F., & Ardila, A. (1999). Anatomy of the insula—functional and clinical correlates. *Aphasiology, 13*(1), 55–78.

Fodor, J. A. (1983). *The modularity of mind.* Cambridge, MA: MIT Press.

Fowler, C. A., & Galantucci, B. (2005). The relation of speech perception and speech production. In D. B. Pisoni & R. E. Remez (Eds.), *The handbook of speech perception* (pp. 633–652). Oxford: Blackwell Publishing.

Fox, P. T., Ingham, R., Ingham, J., Zamarripa, F., Xiong, J. H., & Lancaster, J. L. (2000). Brain correlates of stuttering and syllable production—a PET performance-correlation analysis. *Brain, 123,* 1985–2004.

Frackowiak, R. (1994). Functional mapping of verbal memory and language. *Trends in Neurosciences, 17*(3), 109–115.

Friederici, A.D., Pfeifer, E., & Hahne, A. (1993). Event-related brain potentials during natural speech processing: Effects of semantic, morphological and syntactic violations. *Cognitive Brain Research, 1,* 183–192.

Friederici, A. D., Steinhauer, K., & Frisch, S. (1999). Lexical integration: Sequential effects of syntactic and semantic information. *Memory and Cognition, 27*(3), 438–453.

Friederici, A. D., Wang, Y. H., Hermann, C. S., Maess, B., & Oertel, U. (2000). Localization of early syntactic processes in frontal and temporal cortical areas: A magneto-encephalographic study. *Human Brain Mapping, 11*(1), 1–11.

Friedman, A., & Polson, M. C. (1981). Hemispheres as independent resource systems: Limited-capacity processing and cerebral specialization. *Journal of Experimental Psychology: Human Perception and Performance, 7,* 1031–1058.

Frishkoff, G. A., Tucker, D. M., Davey, C., & Scherg, M. (2004). Frontal and posterior sources of event-related potentials in semantic comprehension. *Brain Research. Cognitive Brain Research, 20*(3), 329–354.

Fromkin, V. A. (1995). Neurobiology of language and speech. In K. Elenius & P. Branderud (Eds.), *Proceedings of the XIIIth International Congress of Phonetic Sciences 2,* 156–163.

Fujimoto, R., Miyatani, M., Oka, N., & Kiriki, K. (2000). Effects of relatedness proportion on semantic priming: An event-related potential analysis/1. *Japanese Journal of Psychonomic Science, 18*(2), 139–148.

Gage, F. (2002). Regulation of functional neurogenesis in the adult brain. Retrieved July 9, 2002, from http://fens2002.bordeaux.inserim.fr/pages/posters/R10000/R110049. html

Galaburda, A. M. (1994). Language areas, lateralization and the innateness of language. *Discussions in Neuroscience, 10*(1–2), 118–124.

Galaburda, A. (2002). Thalamic and cortical plasticity after early cortical injury: A model for sound processing abnormalities in dyslexia. Retrieved July 9, 2002, from http://fens2002.bordeaux.inserim.fr/pages/posters//R10000/R10148.html

Galić, S. (2002). *Neuropsihologijska procjena.* Jastrebarsko: Slap.

Galloway, L. M. (1982). Bilingualism: Neuropsychological considerations. *Journal of Research and Development in Education, 15*(3), 12–28.

Galuske, R. A. W., Schmidt, K. E., Goebel, R., Lomber, S. G., & Payne, B. R. (2002). The role of feedback in the shaping of representations in primary visual cortex. Retrieved July 9, 2002, from http://fens2002.bordeaux.inserim.fr/pages/posters/R10000/R10342.html

Gandour, J., Wong, D., Dzemidzic, M., Lowe, M., Tong, Y., & Li, X. (2003). A cross-linguistic fMRI study of perception of intonation and emotion in Chinese. *Human Brain Mapping, 18*(3), 149–157.

Gandour, J., Wong, D., Lowe, M., Dzemidzic, M., Satthamnuwong, N., Tong, Y., & Li, X. (2002). A cross-linguistic fMRI study of spectral and temporal cues underlying phonological processing. *Journal of Cognitive Neuroscience, 14*(7), 1076–1087.

Garavan, H., Murphy, K., Kaufman, J., Mooney, E., Stein, E. A., & Kübler, A. (2002). Brain activation during attention switching within and between verbal and visuo-spatial working memory. Retrieved July 9, 2002, from http://fens2002.bordeaux. inserim.fr/pages/posters/R1/A009_4.html

Gazzaniga, M. S. (1994). Language and the cerebral hemispheres. *Discussions in Neuro-science 10*(1–2), 106–109.

Gazzaniga, M. S. (2000). Right hemisphere language following brain bisection: A 20-year perspective. In M. S. Gazzaniga (Ed.), *Cognitive neuroscience: A reader* (pp. 411–430). Oxford: Blackwell.

Gazzaniga, M. S., Ivry, R. B., & Mangun, G. R. (2002). *Cognitive science: The biology of the mind*. New York: W. W. Norton.

Gentner, T. Q., & Ball, G. F. (2005). A neuroethological perspective on the perception of vocal communication signals. In D. B. Pisoni & R. E. Remez (Eds.), *The handbook of speech perception* (pp. 653–675). Oxford: Blackwell.

Ghazanfar, A. A., & Hauser, M. D. (1999). The neurethology of primate vocal communi-cation: Substrates for the evolution of speech. *Trends in Cognitive Sciences, 10*(31), 377–384.

Gilbert, Ch. D., Das, A., Ito, M., Kapadia, M., & Westheimer, G. (2000). Spatial Integra-tion and Cortical Dynamics. In M. S. Gazzaniga (Ed.), *Cognitive neuroscience: A reader* (pp. 224–240). Oxford: Blackwell.

Giraud, A. L., Lorenzi, C., Ashburner, J., Wable, J., Johnsrude, I., Frackowiak, R. & Kleinschmidt, A. (2000). Representation of the temporal envelope of sounds in the human brain. *Journal of Neurophysiology, 84*(3), 1588–1598.

Gitelman, D., Nobre, A., Sonty, S., Thompson, C., Johnson, N., Weintraub, S., Parrish, T., & Mesulam, M. M. (2000). Phonological and semantic activations in primary progressive aphasia. Retrieved January 31, 2001, from http://www.apnet.com/www/ journal/hbm2000/6817.html

Gitterman, M. R., & Sies, L. F. (1990). Aphasia in bilinguals and ASL signers: Implica-tions for a theoretical model of neurolinguistic processing based on a review and synthesis of the literature. *Aphasiology, 4*(3), 233–239.

Gitterman, M. R., & Sies, L. F. (1992). Nonbiological determinants of the organization of language in the brain: A comment on Hu, Qiou, and Zhong. *Brain and Language, 43*, 162–165.

Goldman-Rakic, P. S. (2000). Architecture of the prefrontal cortex and the central execu-tive. In M. S. Gazzaniga (Ed.), *Cognitive neuroscience: A reader* (pp. 391–402). Oxford: Blackwell.

Goodglass, H., & Kaplan, E. (1983). *The assessment of aphasia and related disorders*. Philadelphia: Lea and Febinger.

Gootjes, L., Raiji, T., Salmelin, R., & Hari, R. (1999). Left-hemisphere dominance for processing of vowels: A whole-scalp neuromagnetic study. *Neuroreport, 10*(14), 2987–2991.

Gordon, B., Hart, J., Boatman, J., Crone, N., Nathan, S., Uematsu, S., Holcomb, H., Krauss, G., Selnes, O. A., & Lesser, R. P. (1994). Language and brain organization from the perspectives of cortical electrical recording, PET scanning, and acute lesions studies. *Discussions in Neuroscience, 10*(1–2), 46–51.

Gordon, H. W. (1980). Cerebral organization in bilinguals: I. Lateralization. *Brain and Language, 9,* 255–268.

Gorno-Tempini, M. L., Cipolotti, L., & Price, C. J. (2000). Levels of processing that influence object category differences in brain activation studies. Retrieved January 31, 2001, from http://www.apnet.com/www/journal/hbm2000/6422.htm

Gould, E. (2002). Adult neurogenesis in the mammalian brain. Retrieved July 9, 2002, from http://fens2002.bordeaux.inserim.fr/pages/posters/R13000/R13190.html

Grabowski, T. J., Damasio, H., & Tranel, D. (2000). Retrieving names of unique entities engages the left temporal pole. Retrieved January 31, 2001, from http://www.apnet.com/www/journal/hbm2000/6834.html

Grachev, I. D., & Apkarian, A. V. (2000). Chemical network of the human brain: Evidence of reorganization with aging. Retrieved January 31, 2001, from http://www.apnet.com/www/journal/hbm2000/6469.html

Grainger, J., & Dijkstra, T. (1992). On the representation and use of language information in bilinguals. In R. J. Harris (Ed.), *Cognitive processing in bilinguals* (pp. 207–220). Amsterdam: North-Holland.

Grbavac, Ž. (1992). *Neurologija.* Zagreb: Sveučilište u Zagrebu (Sagena).

Green, A., Nicholson, N. S., Vaid, J., & White, N. (1990). Hemispheric involvement in shadowing vs. interpretation: A time-sharing study of simultaneous interpreters with matched bilingual and monolingual controls. *Brain and Language, 39*(1), 107–133.

Greenough, W. T., Black, J. E., & Wallace, C. S. (1987). Experience and brain development. *Child Development, 58,* 539–559.

Griffiths, T. D., Johnsrude, I., Dean, J. L., & Green, G. G. (1999). A common neural substrate for the analysis of pitch and duration pattern in segmented sound? *Neuroreport: For Rapid Communication of Neuroscience Research, 10*(18), 3825–3830.

Grindrod, C. M., & Baum, S. R. (2003). Sensitivity to local sentence context information in lexical ambiguity resolution: evidence from left- and right-hemisphere-damaged individuals. *Brain and Language, 85*(3), 503–523.

Gros, H., Boulanouar, K., Viallard, G., Thorpe, S., Ranjeva, J.-P., Nespoulous, J.-L., & Celsis, P. (2000). Context dependent asymmetry of the event-related fMRI response in the extra-striate cortex following visual presentation of an ambiguous grapheme. Retrieved January 31, 2001, from http://www.apnet.com/www/journal/hbm2000/6433.html

Grosjean, F. (1980). Spoken word recognition processes and the gating paradigm. *Perception and Psychophysics, 28*(4), 267–283.

Grosjean, F. (1992). Another view of bilingualism. In R. J. Harris (Ed.), *Cognitive processing in bilinguals* (pp. 51–52). Amsterdam: North-Holland.

Grosjean, F. (1997). Individual bilingualism. In Z. Lengyel, J. Navracsics, & O. Simon (Eds.), *Applied Linguistic Studies in Central Europe, 1,* 103–113.

Grube, M., Ruebsamen, R., & Von Cramon, D. Y. (2002). Spatial hearing in patients with acquired brain lesions affecting primary auditory cortex. Retrieved July 9, 2002, from http://fens2002.bordeaux.inserim.fr/pages/posters/R7/A220_10.html

Guberina, P. (1992–1993). Psiholingvističke strukture i perceptivne strukture u svjetlu verbotonalne teorije. *Filologija, 20–21,* 139–151.

Guillem, F., Rougier, A., & Claverie, B. (1999). Short- and long-delay intracranial ERP repetition effects dissociate memory systems in the human brain. *Journal of Cognitive Neuroscience, 11*(4), 437–458.

Gur, R. C., Alsop, D., Glahn, D., Petty, R., Swanson, C. L., Maldjian, J. A., Turetsky, B. I., Detre, J. A., Gee, J., & Gur, R. E. (2000). An fMRI study of sex differences in regional activation to a verbal and a spatial task. *Brain and Language, 74*(2), 157–170.

Gutbrod, D., Nirkko, A., Ozdoba, Ch., Buerki, M., Degonda, N., Heinemann, D., Loevblad, K. O., Schroth, G., & Schnider, A. (2000). Segregation of orthographic, phonological, semantic, and syntactic language areas in functional magnetic resonance imaging. Retrieved January 31, 2001, from http://www.apnet.com/www/journal/hbm2000/6555.html

Habib, M., Robichon, F., Levrier, O., Khalil, R., & Salamon, G. (1995). Diverging asymmetries of temporo-parietal cortical areas: A reappraisal of Geschwind/Galaburda theory. *Brain and Language, 48,* 238–258.

Hagberg, G. E., Franzen, O., Lingstrom, B., Madison, G., Martland, D., & Merker, B. (2000). Activation patterns during passive listening to regular and irregular pulse trains. Retrieved January 31, 2001, from http://www.apnet.com/www/journal/hbm2000/7149.html

Hagoort, P., & Brown, C. M. (1995). Electrophysiological insights into language and speech processing. In K. Elenius & P. Branderud (Eds.), *Proceedings of the XIIIth International Congress of Phonetic Sciences, 2,* 172–178.

Hagoort, P., & Brown, C. M. (2000a). ERP effects of listening to speech compared to reading: The p600/sps to syntactic violations in spoken sentences and rapid serial visual presentation. *Neuropsychologia, 38*(11), 1531–1549.

Hagoort, P., & Brown, C. M. (2000b). ERP effects of listening to speech: Semantic ERP effects. *Neuropsychologia, 38*(11), 1518–1530.

Hagoort, P., & Kutas, M. (1995). Electrophysiological insights into language deficits. In F. Boller & J. Grafman (Eds.), *Handbook of neuropsychology* (pp. 105–134). Amsterdam: Elsevier.

Hagoort, P., Wassenaar, M., & Brown, C. (2003). Real-time semantic compensation in patients with agrammatic comprehension: Electrophysiological evidence from multiple-route plasticity. *Proceedings of the National Academy of Sciences of the USA, 100*(7), 4340–4345.

Hahne, A., & Friederici, A. D. (1999). Electrophysiological evidence for two steps in syntactic analysis: Early automatic and late controlled processes. *Journal of Cognitive Neuroscience, 11*(2), 194–205.

Hall, D., Johnsrude, I., Goncalves, M., Haggard, M., Palmer, A., Summerfield, Q., Akeroyd, M., & Frackowiak, R. (2000). Auditory cortical representations of spectral and temporal complexity measured using fMRI. Retrieved January 31, 2001, from http://www.apnet.com/www/journal/hbm2000/6126.html

Halle, M., & Stevens, K. N. (1959). Analysis by synthesis. In W. Wathen-Dunn & L. E. Woods (Eds.), *Proceedings of the seminar on speech comprehension and processing* (Vol. 2, paper D7). AFCRC-TR-59-198.

Haller, S., Radue, E., W., Erb, M., Grodd, W., & Kircher, T. (2005). Overt sentence production in event-related fMRI. *Neuropsychologia, 43*(5), 807–814.

Hampson, R. E., & Deadwyler, S. A. (2002). Spatial and nonspatial processing by hippocampal neurons: Are they the same? Retrieved July 9, 2002, from http://fens2002.bordeaux.inserim.fr/pages/posters/R13000/R13499.html

Harris, R. J. (Ed.). (1992). *Cognitive processing in bilinguals.* Amsterdam: North-Holland.

Harrison, R. V., Smith, D. W., Nagasawa, A., Stanton, S., & Mound, R. J. (1992). Developmental plasticity of auditory cortex in cochlear hearing loss: Physiological and psychophysical findings. *Advances in the Biosciences, 83,* 625–632.

Hart, J., Jr., Sloan Berndt, R., & Caramazza, A. (2000). Category-specific naming deficit following cerebral infarction. In M. S. Gazzaniga (Ed.), *Cognitive neuroscience: A reader* (pp. 406–410). Oxford: Blackwell.

Hauk, O., & Pulvermüller, F. (2004). Neurophysiological distinction of action words in the fronto-central cortex. *Human Brain Mapping, 21* (3), 191-201.

Hauser, M. D., Chomsky, N., & Fitch, W. T. (2002). The faculty of language: What is it, who has it, and how did it evolve? *Science, 298,* 1569–1579.

Heining, M., Young, A. W., Williams, S. R. C., Andrew, C., Brammer, M. J., Gray, J. A., & Phillips, M. L. (2000). Neural responses to auditory and visual presentations of anger, disgust, fear and sadness. Retrieved January 31, 2001, from http://www.apnt.com/www/journal/hbm2000/6275.html

Helenius, P., Salmelin, R., Service, E., & Connolly, J. F. (1999). Semantic cortical activation in dyslexic readers. *Journal of Cognitive Neuroscience, 11*(5), 535–550.

Helenius, P., Salmelin, R., Service, E., Conolly, J. F., Leinonen, S., & Lyytinen, H. (2000). Time course of auditory word comprehension in dyslexia. Retrieved January 31, 2001, from http://www.apnet.com/www/journal/hbm2000/5979.html

Hellige, J. B. (1990). Hemispheric asymmetry. *Annual Review of Psychology, 41,* 55–80.

Hellige, J. B. (1993). *Hemispheric asymmetry.* Cambridge: Cambridge University Press.

Hernandez, A. E., Martinez, A., Wong, E. C., Frank, L. R., & Buxton, R. B. (2000). In search of the language switch: An fMRI study of picture naming in Spanish–English bilinguals. *Brain and Language, 73,* 421–431.

Herrmann, C. S., Friederici, A. D., Oertel, U., Maess, B., Hahne, A., & Alter, K. (2003). The brain generates its own sentence melody: A Gestalt phenomenon in speech perception. *Brain and Language, 85*(3), 396–401.

Hicks, R. E. (1975). Intrahemispheric response competition between vocal and unimanual performance in normal adult human males. *Journal of Comparative and Physiological Psychology, 89,* 50–60.

Hier, D. B., Yoon, W. B., Mohr, J. P., Price, T. R., & Wolf, P. (1994). Gender and aphasia in the stroke data bank. *Brain and Language, 47,* 155–167.

Hill, R. S., & Walsh, C. A. (2005). Molecular insights into human brain evolution. *Nature, 437,* 64–67.

Hiltunen, J., Rinne, J., Laine, M., Kaasinen, V., & Sipila, H. (2000). Production of animals vs. artefacts: A PET activation study on category-specific processing. Retrieved January 31, 2001, from http://www.apnet.com/www/journal/hbm2000/6289.html

Hinton, G. E. (1992). How neural networks learn from experience. *Scientific American, 267*(3), 145–151.

Holcomb, P. J., & Anderson, J. E. (1993). Cross-modal semantic priming: A time-course analysis using event-related brain potentials. *Language and Cognitive Processes, 8,* 379–411.

Holloway, V., Liegeois, F., Baldeweg, T., Gadian, D. G., Vargha-Khadem, F., & Connelly, A. (2000). Language lateralisation using fMRI in children undergoing Wada testing. Retrieved January 31, 2001, from http://www.apnet.com/www/journal/hbm2000/6272.html

Homae, F., Hashimoto, R., Nakajima, K., Miyashita, Y., & Sakai, K. L. (2000). Contextual decision vs. lexical decision: An fMRI study of language processing. Retrieved January 31, 2001, from http://www.apnet.com/www/journal/hbm2000/6269.html

Hoosain, R. (1991). Cerebral lateralization of bilingual functions after handedness switch in childhood. *Journal of Genetic Psychology, 152*(2), 263–268.

Hoosain, R. (1992). Differential cerebral lateralization of Chinese–English bilingual functions? In R. J. Harris (Ed.), *Cognitive processing in bilinguals* (pp. 561–571). Amsterdam: North-Holland.

Hoosain, R., & Shiu, L.-P. (1989). Cerebral lateralization of Chinese–English bilingual functions. *Neuropsychologia, 27,* 705–712.

Horga, D. (1996). *Obrada fonetskih obavijesti.* Zagreb: Hrvatsko filološko društvo.

Horga, D. (1998). Reorganizacija izgovora pri fiksiranom zagrizu. *Govor, 15,* 35–57.

Horga, D. (2002a). The influence of bite-blocks on continuous speech production. In A. Braun and H. R. Masthoff (Eds.), *Phonetics and its applications. Festschrift for Jens-Peter Köster on the occasion of his 60th birthday* (pp. 143–152). Stuttgart: Franz Steiner Verlag.

Horga, D. (2002b). Moždana lateralizacija u jezičnom prevođenju. In D. Stolac, N. Ivanetić & B. Pritchard (Eds.), Zbornik savjetovanja Hrvatskoga društva za primijenjenu lingvistiku (pp. 193–201). Zagreb-Rijeka: HDPL & Grafotrade.

Horwitz, B., Jeffries, K. J., & Braun, A. R. (2000). Functional connectivity among language areas during speech production. Retrieved January 31, 2001, from http://www.apnet.com/www/journal/hbm2000/6206.html

Howard, P. (2000). *The owner's manual for the brain.* Atlanta: Bard Press.

Howard, D., Patterson, K., Wise, R., Brown, W. D., Friston, K., Weiller, C., & Frackowiak, R. (1992). The cortical localization of the lexicons. *Brain, 115,* 1769–1782.

Hsieh, L., Gandour, J., Wong, D., & Hutchins, G. D. (2000). A PET study of the perception of Chinese tones. Retrieved January 31, 2001, from http://www.apnet.com/www/journal/hbm2000/6596.html

Hugdahl, K., & Anderson, L. (1986). The forced-attention paradigm in dichotic listening to CV-syllables: A comparison between adults and children. *Cortex, 22,* 417–432.

Hugdahl, K., Anderson, L., Asbjornsen, A., & Dalen, K. (1990). Dichotic listening, forced attention, and brain asymmetry in righthanded and lefthanded children. *Journal of Clinical and Experimental Neuropsychology, 12*(4) 539–548.

Hugdahl, K., Law, I., Kyllingsbaek, S., Bronnick, K., Gade, A., & Poulson, O. B. (2000). Effects of attention on dichotic listening: An o-15-PET study. *Human Brain Mapping, 10*(2), 87–97.

Hulit, L. M., & Howard, M. R. (2002). *Born to talk: An introduction to speech and language development.* (3rd ed.). Boston, MA: Allyn & Bacon.

Hurford, J. R. (1991). The evolution of the critical period for language acquisition. *Cognition, 40,* 159–201.

Hurford, J. R. (1994a). Evolutionary modelling of language. *Discussions in Neuroscience, 10*(1–2), 158–168.

Hurford, J. R. (1994b). Linguistics and evolution: A background briefing for non-linguistics. *Discussions in Neuroscience, 10*(1–2), 149–157.

Huttenlocher, P. R. (1990). Morphometric study of human cerebral cortex development. *Neuropsychologia, 28,* 517–527.

Huttenlocher, P. R. & Dabholkar, A. S. (1997). Regional differences in synaptogenesis in human cerebral cortex. *Journal of Comparative Neurology, 387,* 167–178.

Hyltenstam, K. (1992). Non-native features of near-native speakers: On the ultimate attainment of childhood L2 learners. In R. J. Harris (Ed.), *Cognitive processing in bilinguals* (pp. 351–368). Amsterdam: North-Holland.

Hynd, G. W., Obrzut, J. E., Weed, W., & Hynd, C. R. (1979). Development of cerebral dominance: Dichotic listening asymmetry in normal and learning-disabled children. *Journal of Experimental Child Psychology, 28,* 445–454.

Iidaka, T., Murata, T., Omori, M., Kosaka, H., Okada, T., Sadato, N., & Yonekura, Y. (2000). Functional MRI study of neural network involved in emotional face processing. Retrieved January 31, 2001, from http://www.apnet.com/www/journal/hbm2000/5975.html

Indefrey, P., Brown, C., Hellwig, F., Herzog, H., Seitz, R., & Hagoort, P. (2000). Two ways to meaning—a combined PET/ERP study. Retrieved January 31, 2001, from http://www.apnet.com/www/journal/hbm2000/6065.html

Isahai, N., Takeuchi, F., & Kuriki, S. (2000). MEG responses during word composition task. Retrieved January 31, 2001, from http://www.apnet.com/www/journal/hbm2000/6019.html

Ivry, R. B., & Robertson, L. C. (1999). *The two sides of perception.* Cambridge, MA: MIT Press.

Jakobson, R., Fant, G., & Halle, M. (1976). *Preliminaries to speech analysis.* Cambridge, MA: MIT Press.

Jäncke, L., & Shah, N. J. (2000). Individual differences in auditory cortex activation are related to the performance in a verbal auditory discrimination task. Retrieved January 31, 2001, from http://www.apnet.com/www/journal/hbm2000/6682.html

Jaramillo, M., Alku, P., & Paavilainen, P. (1999). An event-related potential (ERP) study of duration changes in speech and nonspeech sounds. *Neuroreport: For Rapid Communication of Neuroscience Research, 10*(16), 3301–3305.

Jenkins, L. (2000). *Biolinguistics: Exploring the biology of language.* Cambridge: Cambridge University Press.

Joanette, Y., Goulet, P., & Le Dorze, G. (1988). Impaired word naming in right-brain-damaged right-handers: Error types and time-course analysis. *Brain and Language, 34,* 54–64.

Johnson, J. S., & Newport, E. L. (1989). Critical period effects in second language learning: The influence of maturational state on the acquisition of English as a second language. *Cognitive Psychology, 21,* 60–99.

Johnson, M. H. (2000). Cortical mechanisms of cognitive development. In M. S. Gazzaniga (Ed.), *Cognitive neuroscience: A reader* (pp. 241–258). Oxford: Blackwell.

Judaš, M., & Kostović, I. (1997). *Temelji neuroznanosti.* Zagreb: MD.

Juncos-Rabadán, O. (1994). The assessment of bilingualism in normal aging with the bilingual aphasia test. *Journal of Neurolinguistics, 8*(1), 67–73.

Just, M. A., Newman, S. C., Keller, T. A., McEleney, A., & Carpenter, P. A. (2004). Imagery in sentence comprehension: An fMRI study. *Neuroimage, 21*(1), 112–124.

Kalat, J. W. (1995). *Biological psychology.* Pacific Grove, CA: Brooks/Cole.

Kali, S., & Dayan, P. (2002). The contributions of hippocampus and neocortex to the formation of long-term episodic and semantic memories. Retrieved July 9, 2002, from http://fens2002.bordeaux.inserim.fr/pages/posters/R5/A141_16.html

Kandel, E. (2002). Genes, local protein synthesis at synapses and long-term memory. Retrieved July 9, 2002, from http://fens2002.bordeaux.inserim.fr/pages/posters/R11000/R11181.html

Kandel, E. R., & Hawkins, R. D. (1992). The biological basis of learning and individuality. *Scientific American, 267*(3), 79–86.

Kansaku, K., Yamaura, A., & Kitazawa, S. (2000). Sex differences in lateralization revealed in the posterior language areas. *Cerebral Cortex, 10*(9), 866–872.

Kasher, A., Batori, G., Soroker, N., Graves, D., & Zaidel, E. (1999). Effects of right- and left-hemisphere damage on understanding conversational implicatures. *Brain and Language, 68*(3), 566–590.

Kean, M.-L. (1995). Phonological structure and the analysis of phonemic paraphrasias. In K. Elenius & P. Branderud (Eds.), *Proceedings of the XIIIth International Congress of Phonetic Sciences, 2,* 186–192.

Keatley, C. W. (1992). History of bilingualism research in cognitive psychology. In R. J. Harris (Ed.), *Cognitive processing in bilinguals* (pp. 15–50). Amsterdam: North-Holland.

Kemmerer, D. (2005). The spatial and temporal meanings of English prepositions can be independently impaired. *Neuropsychologia, 43,* 797–806.

Kent, R. D. (2004). The uniqueness of speech among motor systems. *Clinical Linguistics and Phonetics, 18*(6–8), 495–505.

Kent, R. D., & Tjaden, K. (1997). Brain functions underlying speech. In W. J. Hardcastle & J. Laver (Eds.), *The handbook of phonetic sciences* (pp. 220–255). Oxford: Blackwell.

Kertesz, A., & McCabe, P. (1977). Recovery patterns and prognosis in aphasia. *Brain, 100,* 1–18.

Kess, J. F. (1992). *Psycholinguistics: Psychology, linguistics and the study of natural language.* Amsterdam: John Benjamins.

Khan, S. C., Frisk, V., & Taylor, M. J. (1999). Neurophysiological measures of reading difficulty in very-low-birthweight children. *Psychophysiology, 36*(1), 76–85.

Khateb, A., Annoni, J. M., Landis, T., Pegna, A. J., Custodi, M. C., Fonteneau, E., Morand, S. M., & Michel, C. M. (1999). Spatio-temporal analysis of electric brain activity during semantic and phonological word processing. *International Journal of Psychophysiology, 32*(3), 215–231.

Kiefer, M., & Spitzer, M. (2000). Time course of conscious and unconscious semantic brain activation. *Neuroreport, 11*(11), 2401–2407.

Kim, K. H. S., Relkin, N. R., Lee, K. M., & Hirsch, J. (1997). Distinct cortical areas associated with native and second languages. *Nature, 388,* 171–174.

Kim, Y.-H., Kim, S.-Y., Hong, I.-K., Parrish, T. B., & Kim, H.-I. (2000a). Reorganization of language areas in the patients recovered from aphasia after stroke or surgical resection. Retrieved January 31, 2001, from http://www.apnet.com/www/journal/hbm2000/

Kim, Y.-H., Kim, S.-Y., Hong, I.-K., Parrish, T. B., Kim, H.-G., & Kim, H.-I. (2000b). Activation of intraparietal sulcus in the processing of written Korean words representing visuospatial components of language. Retrieved January 31, 2001, from http://www.apnet.com/www/journal/hbm2000/6075.html

Kimura, D. (1961a). Some effects of temporal-lobe damage on auditory perception. *Canadian Journal of Psychology, 15,* 156–165.

Kimura, D. (1961b). Cerebral dominance and the perception of verbal stimuli. *Canadian Journal of Psychology, 15,* 166–171.

Kimura, D. (1967). Functional asymmetry of the brain in dichotic listening. *Cortex, 3,* 163–178.

Kimura, D. (1973a). The asymmetry of the human brain. *Scientific American, 228,* 70–78.

Kimura, D. (1973b). Manual activity during speaking: I. Right-handers. *Neuropsychologia, 11,* 45–50.

Kimura, D. (1973c). Manual activity during speaking: II. Left-handers. *Neuropsychologia, 11,* 51–55.

Kimura, D. (1975). Cerebral dominance for speech. In D. B. Tower (Ed.), *The nervous system: Vol. 3. Human communication and its disorders* (pp. 365–371). New York: Raven.

Kimura, D. (1979). Neuromotor mechanisms in the evolution of human communication. In H. E. Steklis & M. J. Raleigh (Eds.), *Neurobiology of social communication in primates* (pp. 197–219). New York: Academic Press.

Kimura, D. (1983). Sex differences in cerebral organization for speech and praxic functions. *Canadian Journal of Psychology, 37*(1), 19–35.

Kimura, D. (1992). Sex differences in the brain. *Scientific American, 267*(3), 119–125.

Kinsbourne, M. (1976). The ontogeny of cerebral dominance. In R. W. Rieber (Ed.), *The neuropsychology of language*. New York: Plenum.

Kinsbourne, M., & Cook, J. (1971). Generalized and lateralized effects of concurrent verbalization on a unimanual skill. *Quarterly Journal of Experimental Psychology, 23*, 341–345.

Kircher, T. T. J., Liddle, P., Brammer, M., Williams, S. R. C., Simmons, A., Bartels, A., Murray, R. M., & McGuire, P. K. (2000). Right temporal activation during the production of neologisms in thought-disordered schizophrenic patients. An ER fMRI study. Retrieved January 31, 2001, from http://www.apnet.com/www/journal/hbm2000/6579.html

Kitazawa, S., & Kansaku, K. (2005). Sex difference in language lateralization may be task-dependent. *Brain, 128,* E30.

Kiviniemi, K., Laine, M., Tarkiainen, A., Jaervensivu, T., Martin, N., & Salmelin, R. (2000). Neurocognitive effects of anomia treatment: An MEG study. Retrieved January 31, 2001, from http://www.apnet.com/www/journal/hbm2000/6186.html

Klein, D., Milner, B., Zatorre, R. J., Zhao, V., & Nikelski, J. (1999). Cerebral organization in bilinguals: A PET study of Chinese–English verb generation. *NeuroReport, 10,* 2841–2846.

Klinke, R., Hartmann, R., Heid, S., & Kral, A. (2002). Responses of the auditory cortex to cochlear implantation in congenitally deaf cat. Retrieved July 9, 2002, from http://fens2002.bordeaux.inserim.fr/pages/posters/R10000/R10463.html

Klopp, J., Halgren, E., Marinkovic, K., & Nenov, V. (1999). Face-selective spectral changes in the human fusiform gyrus. *Clinical Neurophysiology, 110*(4), 676–682.

Knoesche, T. R., Maess, B., & Friederici, A. D. (1999). Processing of syntactic information monitored by brain surface current density mapping based on MEG. *Brain Topography, 12*(2), 75–87.

Kohn, B. (1980). Right-hemisphere speech representation and comprehension of syntax after left cerebral injury. *Brain and Language, 9,* 350–361.

Kolb, B., & Whishaw, I. (1996). *Fundamentals of human neuropsychology*. San Francisco: Freeman.

Kölsch, S., Schroger, E., & Tervaniemi, M. (1999). Superior pre-attentive auditory processing in musicians. *Neuroreport, 10*(6), 1309–1313.

Kopp, F., Schroger, E., & Lipka, S. (2006). Synchronized brain activity during rehearsal and short-term memory disruption by irrelevant speech is affected by recall mode. *International Journal of Psychophysiology, 61*(2), 188–203.

Kosslyn, S. M. (1987). Seeing and imagining in the cerebral hemispheres: A computational approach. *Psychological Review, 94,* 148–175.

Kosslyn, S. M., Thompson, W. L., Kim, I. J., & Alpert, N. M. (2000). Topographical representations of mental images in primary visual cortex. In M. S. Gazzaniga (Ed.), *Cognitive neuroscience: A reader* (pp. 202–207). Oxford: Blackwell.

Kostović, I. (1979). *Razvitak i građa moždane kore*. Zagreb: Jugoslavenska medicinska naklada.

Kraemer, M., & Zenhausern, R. (1993). Dichotic listening and the cerebral organization of the phonetic and semantic components of language. *International Journal of Neuroscience, 71*(1–4), 45–50.

Krashen, S. D. (1973). Lateralization, language learning, in the critical period: Some new evidence. *Language Learning, 23*(1), 63.

Krause, B. J., Schmidt, D., Mottaghy, F. M., Taylor, J., Halsband, U., Herzog, H., Tellmann, L., & Muller-Gartner, H. W. (1999). Episodic retrieval activates the precuneus irrespective of the imagery content of word pair associates. *Brain, 122*(2), 255–263.

Kroll, J. F., & Sholl, A. (1992). Lexical and conceptual memory in fluent and nonfluent bilinguals. In R. J. Harris (Ed.), *Cognitive processing in bilinguals* (pp. 191–204). Amsterdam: North-Holland.

Kuhl, P. K. (2004). Early language acquisition: Cracking the speech code. *Nature reviews: Neuroscience, 5,* 831–843.

Kuhl, P. K., Williams, K. A., Lacerda, F., Stevens, K. N., & Lindblom, B. (1992). Linguistic experience alters phonetic perception in infants by 6 months of age. *Science, 255,* 606–608.

Kujala, T., Alho, K., Kekoni, J., Hamalainen, H., Reinikainen, K., Salonen, O., Standertskjold-Nordenstam, C.-G., & Näätänen, R. (1995). Auditory and somatosensory event-related brain potentials in early blind humans. *Experimental Brain Research, 104,* 519–526.

Kuperberg, G., Halgren, E. Greve, D., Fischl, B., Desikan, R., Waters, G., Vijayan, S., Rauch, S., West, C., Holcomb, P., & Caplan, D. (2000). Event-related fMRI reveals distinct patterns of neural modulation during semantic and syntactic processing of sentences. Retrieved January 31, 2001, from http://www.apnet.com/www/journal/hbm2000/6957.html

Kuperberg, G. R., McGuire, P. K., Bullmore, E. T., Brammer, J. J., Rabe-Hesketh, S., Wright, I. C., Lythgoe, D. J., Williams, S. C. R., & David, A. S. (2000). Common and distinct neural substrates for pragmatic, semantic, and syntactic processing of spoken sentences: An fMRI study. *Journal of Cognitive Neuroscience, 12*(2), 321–341.

Kusmierek, P., Laszcz, A., Sadowska, J., & Kowalska, D. M. (2002). Effects of partial lesion to the dorsal auditory cortical stream on auditory recognition, discrimination and localization. Retrieved July 9, 2002, from http://fens2002.bordeaux.inserim.fr/pages/posters/R5/A141_18.html

Ladefoged, P. (2004). Phonetics and phonology in the last 50 years. Retrieved March 16, 2006, from http://www.linguistics.ucla.edu/faciliti/workpapph/103/1-Ladefoged-MITSoundToSense.pdf

Laine, B., Salmelin, R., Helenius, P., & Martilla, R. (2000). Brain activation during reading in deep dyslexia: An MEG study. *Journal of Cognitive Neuroscience, 12*(4), 622–634.

Lange, G., Steffener, J., Christodoulou, Ch., Liu, W.-Ch., Bly, B., DeLuca, J., & Natelson, B. (2000). fMRI of auditory verbal working memory in severe fatiguing illness. Retrieved January 31, 2001, from http://www.apnet.com/www/journal/hbm2000/6800.html

Lassonde, M., Sauerwein, H., Chicoine, A-J., & Geoffroy, G. (1991). Absence of disconnexion syndrome in callosal agenesis and early callosotomy: Brain reorganization or lack of structural specificity during ontogeny? *Neuropsychologia, 29*(6), 481–495.

Laver, J. (1994). *Principles of phonetics.* Cambridge: Cambridge University Press.

Le Carret, N., Petrescu, A., Amieva, H., Fabrigoule, C., & Allard, M. (2002). Age-related shift in cerebral activation pattern during selective attention task: And fMRI study. Retrieved July 9, 2002, from http://fens2002.bordeaux.inserim.fr/pages/posters/R4/A108_8.html

Le Clec, H. G., Dehaene, S., Cohen, L., Melher, J., Dupoux, E., Poline, J.-B., Lehéricy, S., Van de Moortele, P.-F., & LeBihan, D. (2000). Distinct cortical areas for names of numbers and body parts independent of language and input modality. *Neuroimage, 12*(4), 381–391.

Legg, C. R. (1989). *Issues in psychobiology.* London: Routledge.

Lenneberg, E. H. (1967). *Biological foundations of language*. New York: Wiley.

Leppaenen, P. H. T., Pihko, E., Eklund, K. M., & Lyytinen, H. (1999). Cortical responses of infants with and without a genetic risk for dyslexia: II. Group effects. *Neurore-port: For Rapid Communication of Neuroscience Research, 10*(5), 969–973.

Levelt, W. J. M. (1989). *Speaking: From intention to articulation*. Cambridge, MA: MIT Press.

Levelt, W. J. M., Roelofs, A., & Meyer, A. S. (1999). A theory of lexical access in speech production. *Behavioral and Brain Sciences, 22,* 1–75.

Levinson, S. C. (1983). *Pragmatics*. Cambridge: Cambridge University Press.

Levinthal, Ch., & Hornung, M. (1992). Orthographic and phonological coding during visual word matching as related to reading and spelling abilities in college students. *Reading and Writing, 4*(3), 231–243.

Levy, J. (1969). Possible basis for the evolution of lateral specialization of the human brain. *Nature, 224,* 614–615.

Levy, J., & Reid, M. (1976). Variations in writing posture and cerebral organization. *Science, 194,* 337–339.

Levy, M. N., Koeppen, B. M., & Stanton, B. A. (Eds.). (2005). *Berne & Levy principles of physiology* (4th ed.). Mosby Elsevier.

Liberman, A., & Mattingly, I. (1985). The motor theory of speech perception revised. *Cognition, 21,* 1–36.

Liberman, A., Cooper, F., Shankweiler, D., & Studdert-Kennedy, M. (1967). Perception of the speech code. *Psychological Review, 74,* 431–461.

Lieberman, P. (1991). *Uniquely human*. Cambridge, MA: Harvard University Press.

Lieberman, P., & Blumstein, S. E. (1988). *Speech physiology, speech perception, and acoustic phonetics*. Cambridge: Cambridge University Press.

Liotti, M., Woldorff, M. G., Perez, R., & Mayberg, H. S. (2000). An ERP study of the temporal course of the stroop color-word interference effect. *Neuropsychologia, 38*(5), 701–711.

Liu, H.-L., Pu, L., Feng, Ch.-M., Tan, L. H., Spinks, J. A., Perfetti, Ch. A., Xiong, J., Fox, P. T., & Gao, J.-H. (2000). Brain activation in the processing of single Chinese character: An event-related fMRI study. Retrieved January 31, 2001, from http://www. apnet.com/www/journal/hbm2000/5901.html

Lobaugh, N. J., McIntosh, A. R., Roy, P., Caldwell, C. B., & Black, S. E. (2000). Regional SPECT perfusion correlates with regional measures of corpus callosum in Alzheimer's disease and in healthy aging. Retrieved January 31, 2001, from http://www. apnet.com/www/journal/hbm2000/7127.html

Locke, J. L. (1994). Phases in the development of linguistic capacity. *Discussions in Neuroscience, 10*(1–2), 26–34.

Löfqvist, A. (1997). Theories and models of speech production. In W. J. Hardcastle & J. Laver (Eds.), *The handbook of phonetic sciences* (pp. 405–426). Oxford: Blackwell.

Lohmann, H., Floel, A., Knecht, S., Deppe, M., Konrad, C., & Henningsen, H. (2000). Language and spatial attention can lateralize to the same hemisphere in healthy humans. Retrieved January 31, 2001, from http://www.apnet.com/www/journal/hbm2000/6118.html

Lomber, S. G., & Payne, B. R. (2002). Contributions of converging visual signals to receptive field representations. Retrieved July 9, 2002, from http://fens2002.bordeaux.inserim.fr/pages/posters/R13000/R13033.html

Lončarić, S. (2002). Neuronske mrež: Uvod. http://ipg.zesoi.fer.hr

Lubow, R.E., Tsal, Y., Mirkin, A., & Mazliah, G. (1994). English and Hebrew letter report by English- and Hebrew-reading subjects: Evidence for stimulus control, not hemispheric asymmetry. *Brain and Cognition, 25*(1), 34–51.

Luce, P. A., Goldinger, S. D., Auer, E. T., & Vitevitch, M. S. (2000). Phonetic priming, neighborhood activation, and PARSYN. *Perception & Psychophysics, 62,* 615–625.

Luce, P. A., & McLennan, C. T. (2005). Spoken word recognition: The challenge of variation. In D. B. Pisoni & R. E. Remez (Eds.), *The handbook of speech perception* (pp. 591–609). Oxford: Blackwell.

Luce, P. A., & Pisoni, D. B. (1998). Recognizing spoken words: The neighborhood activation model. *Ear & Hearing, 19*(1), 1–36.

Luria, A. R. (1973). *The working brain*. Harmonds-Worth: Penguin.

Luria, A. R. (1976). *Osnovi neuropsihologije*. Beograd: Nolit.

Luria, A. R. (1982). *Osnovi neurolingvistike*. Beograd: Nolit.

Lurito, J. T., Kareken, D. A., Dzemidzic, M., Lowe, M. J., Radnovich, A., Staser, J., et al. (2000). Functional MRI of covert object naming. Retrieved January 31, 2001, from http://www.apnet.com/www/journal/hbm2000/6231.html

Macnamara, J., & Kushnir, S. L. (1971). Linguistic independence of bilinguals: The input switch. *Journal of Verbal Learning and Verbal Behavior, 10,* 480–487.

MacNeilage, P. F. (1997). Acquisition of Speech. In W. J. Hardcastle & J. Laver (Eds.), *The handbook of phonetic sciences* (pp. 302–332). Oxford: Blackwell.

MacSweeney, M., Campbell, R., Calvert, G., McGuire, Ph., David, A., Suckling, J., Woll, B. L., & Brammer, M. J. (2000). Activation of lateral temporal cortex during speechreading in deaf people. Retrieved January 31, 2001, from http://www.apnet.com/www/journal/hbm2000/6649.html

Magiste, E. (1987). Changes in the lateralization pattern of two immigrant groups in Sweden. *International and intercultural communication annual: Vol. 11. Cross cultural adaptation: Current theory and research* (pp. 233–251). Beverly Hills: Sage.

Magiste, E. (1992). Leaning to the right: hemispheric involvement in bilinguals. In R. J. Harris (Ed.), *Cognitive processing in bilinguals* (pp. 549–560). Amsterdam: North-Holland.

Malagoli, M., Murray, A. D., Vennery, A., Welch, A., Currie, D. G., Kaar, G., & Staff, R. T. (2000). Language mapping in a left-handed patient with glioma using H2O15 Positron Emission Tomography. Retrieved January 31, 2001, from http://www.apnet.com/www/journal/hbm2000/6655.html

Malakoff, M. E. (1992). Translation ability: A natural bilingual and metalinguistic skill. In R. J. Harris (Ed.), *Cognitive processing in bilinguals* (pp. 515–530). Amsterdam: North-Holland.

Malamed, F., & Zaidel, E. (1993). Language and task effects on lateralized word recognition. *Brain and Language, 45,* 70–85.

Marsh, L. G., & Maki, R. H. (1976). Efficiency of arithmetic operations in bilinguals as a function of language. *Memory and Cognition, 4,* 459–464.

Marslen-Wilson, W. D. (1980). Speech understanding as a psychological process. In J. C. Simon (Ed.), *Spoken language generation and understanding* (pp. 39–67). Dordrecht: Reidel.

Marslen-Wilson, W. D., & Tyler, L. K. (1980). The temporal structure of spoken language comprehension. *Cognition, 6,* 1–71.

Marslen-Wilson, W. D., & Warren, P. (1994). Levels of perceptual representation and process in lexical access: Words, phonemes, and features. *Psychological Review, 101,* 653–675.

Martin, F. H., Kaine, A., & Kirby, M. (2006). Event-related brain potentials elicited during word recognition by adult good and poor phonological decoders. *Brain and Language, 96*(1), 1–13.

Mathiak, K., Hertrich, I., Lutzenberger, W., & Ackermann, H. (2000). Encoding of temporal speech features (formant transients) during binaural and dichotic stimulus application: A whole-head magnetencephalography study. *Cognitive Brain Research, 10*(1–2), 125–131.

Maunsell, J. H. R. (1995). The brain's visual world: Representation of visual targets in cerebral cortex. *Science, 270,* 764–769.

Mayer, J., Haider, H., Dogil, G., Ackermann, H., Erb, M., Riecker, A., Wildgruber, D., & Grodd, W. (2000). Cognitive substrate of syntactic operations—evidence from fMRI. Retrieved January 31, 2001, from http://www.apnet.com/www/journal/hbm2000/6432.html

Mayer, J., Wildgruber, D., Riecker, A., & Dogil, G. (2002). Prosody production and perception: Converging evidence from fMRI studies. Retrieved February 5, 2003, from http://www.lpl.univ-aix.fr/sp2002/pdf/mayer.pdf

McCarthy, G., Blamire, A. M., Rothman, D. L., Gruetter, R., & Shulman, R. G. (1993). Echoplanar magnetic resonance imaging studies of frontal cortex activation during word generation in humans. *Proceedings of the National Academy of Sciences, U.S.A., 90,* 4952–4956.

McClelland, J. L. (1991). Stochastic interactive processes and the effect of context on perception. *Cognitive Psychology, 23,* 1–44.

McClelland, J. L., & Elman, J. L. (1986). The TRACE model of speech perception. *Cognitive Psychology, 18,* 1–86.

McClelland, J., & Rumelhart, D. (Eds.). (1986). *Parallel distributed processing: Vol. 2. Psychological and biological models.* Cambridge, MA: MIT Press.

McColl, R., & Moncrieff, D. (2000). Language lateralization in normal and dyslexic children: An fMRI study. Retrieved January 31, 2001, from http://www.apnet.com/www/journal/hbm2000/6675.html

McCrory, E., Frith, U., Brunswick, N., & Price C. (2000). Abnormal functional activation during a simple word repetition task: A PET study of adult dyslexics. *Journal of Cognitive Neuroscience, 12*(5), 753–762.

McKhann, G. M. (1994). Summary remarks for the FESN study group: Evolution and neurology of language. *Discussions in Neuroscience, 10*(1–2), 16–20.

McQueen, J. M., & Cutler, A. (1997). Cognitive processes in speech perception. In W. J. Hardcastle & J. Laver (Eds.), *The handbook of phonetic sciences* (pp. 566–585). Oxford: Blackwell.

McRoberts, G. W., & Sanders, B. (1992). Sex differences in performance and hemispheric organization for a nonverbal auditory task. *Perception and Psychophysics, 51*(2), 118–122.

Mechelli, A., Humphreys, G. W., Mayall, K., Olson, A., & Price, C. J. (2000). Contrasting effects of word length and visual contrast in fusiform and lingual gyri during reading. Retrieved January 31, 2001, from http://www.apnet.com/www/journal/hbm2000/6410.html

Meyer, M., Alter, K., Friederici, A. D., & von Cramon, D. Y. (2000). Different hemodynamic response to sentence-level syntactic and prosodic processing. Retrieved January 31, 2001, from http://www.apnet.com/www/journal/hbm2000/6181.html

Meyer, M., Steinhauer, K., Alter, K., Friederici, A. D., & von Cramon, D. Y. (2004). Brain activity varies with modulation of dynamic pitch variance in sentence melody. *Brain and Language, 89*(2), 277–289.

Mildner, V. (1993). Neurolingvistički pristup prepoznavanju okluziva. *Suvremena lingvistika, 19*(1–2), 159–169.

Mildner, V. (1996). *Funkcionalna moždana asimetrija u bilingvalnih osoba: Razlike u percepciji engleskog i hrvatskog jezika.* Unpublished dissertation, Filozofski fakultet Sveučilišta u Zagrebu.

Mildner, V. (1999). Functional cerebral asymmetry for verbal stimuli in a foreign language. *Brain and Cognition, 40,* 197–201.

Mildner, V. (2000). Is the hand to speech what speech is to the hand? *Brain and Cognition, 43,* 345–349.

Mildner, V. (2001). Some quick arithmetic. *Brain and Cognition, 46,* 205–209.

Mildner, V. (2002). Languages in space. *Brain and Cognition, 48,* 463–369.

Mildner, V. (2004). Hemispheric asymmetry for linguistic prosody: A study of stress perception in Croatian. *Brain and Cognition, 55,* 358–361.

Mildner, V., & Golubić, A. (2003). Funkcionalna mozgovna asimetrija pri obradi jezicnih podataka na materinskom i stranom jeziku. *Govor 20*(1–2), 277–288.

Mildner, V., & Ratković, Z. (1997). Aktivnost moždanih hemisfera pri obradi fonoloških zadataka na materinskom i stranom jeziku. *Strani jezici, 26,* 405–415.

Mildner, V., & Rukavina, Z. (1994). Prepoznavanje rime kao mjera fonemskog procesiranja. *Govor, 11,* 51–62.

Mildner, V., & Rukavina, Z. (1996a). Moždana lateralizacija jezićnih funkcja. In M. Andrijašević & L. Zergollern-Miletić (Eds.), Zbornik savjetovanja Hrvatskog društva za primijenjenu lingvistiku "Jezik i komunikacija" (pp. 248–256). Zagreb.

Mildner, V., & Rukavina, Z. (1996b). Hemispheric specialization for phonological processing. In P. McCormack & A. Russell (Eds.), *Proceedings of the Sixth Australian International Conference on Speech Science and Technology* (pp. 385–389). Canberra: Australian Speech Science and Technology Association.

Mildner, V., Stanković, D., & Petković, M. (2005). The relationship between active hand and ear advantage in the native and foreign language. *Brain and Cognition, 57,* 158–161.

Milner, B. (1974). Hemispheric specialization: Scope and limits. In F. O. Schmitt & F. G. Worden (Eds.), *The neurosciences: Third study program* (pp. 75–89). Cambridge, MA: MIT Press.

Milner, B. (1994). Carotid-amytal studies of speech representation and gesture control. *Discussions in Neuroscience, 10*(1–2), 109–118.

Milner, B., Taylor, L., & Sperry, R. W. (1968). Lateralized suppression of dichotically presented digits after commissural section in man. *Science, 161,* 184–186.

Moeller, M., Ganslandt, O., Kober, H., Nimsky, C., Buchfelder, M., Pauli, E., Stefan, H., & Fahlbusch, R. (2000). Presurgical noninvasive localization of speech-related brain areas by magnetoencephalography confirmed by direct electrocorticography. Retrieved January 31, 2001, from http://www.apnet.com/www/journal/hbm2000/6623.html

Moen, I. (1993). Functional lateralization of the perception of Norwegian word tones— evidence from a dichotic listening experiment. *Brain and Language, 44,* 400–413.

Molfese, D. L. (1978). Neuroelectric Correlates of Categorical Speech Perception in Adults. *Brain and Language, 5,* 25–35.

Molfese, D. L. (1980). The phoneme and the engram: Electrophysiological evidence for the acoustic invariant in stop consonants. *Brain and Language, 9,* 372–376.

Molfese, D. L., & Molfese, V. J. (1979). VOT distinctions in infants: Learned or innate? In H. Whitaker & H. Whitaker (Eds.), *Studies in neurolinguistics* (Vol. 4.). New York: Academic Press.

Molfese, D. L., Fonaryova Key, A. P., Maquire, M. J., Dove, G. O., & Molfese, V. J. (2005). Event-related evoked potentials (ERPs) in speech perception. In D. B. Pisoni & R. E. Remez (Eds.), *The handbook of speech perception* (pp. 99–121). Oxford: Blackwell.

Mondor, T. A., & Bryden, M. P. (1992). On the relation between auditory spatial attention and auditory perceptual asymmetries. *Perception and Psychophysics, 52,* 393–402.

Moore, B. C. (1997). *An introduction to the psychology of hearing.* San Diego: Academic Press.

Morton, J. (1979). Word recognition. In J. Morton & J. D. Marshall (Eds.), *Psycholinguistics 2: Structures and processes* (pp. 109–156). Cambridge, MA: MIT Press.

Müller, H. M., & Kutas, M. (1996). What's in a name? Electrophysiological differences between spoken nouns, proper names and one's own name. *NeuroReport, 8,* 221–225.

Müller, R. A. (2000). Big "housing" problem and a trace of neuroimaging: Broca's area is more than a transformation center. *The Behavioral and Brain Sciences, 23*(1), 42.

Myers, P. S. (1999). *Right hemisphere damage: Disorders of communication and cognition.* San Diego: Singular.

Nakai, T., Matsuo, K., Kato, C., Tanaka, S., Glover, G., Moriya, T., & Okada, T. (2000). The auditory attention system during dual listening task performance. Retrieved January 31, 2001, from http://www.apnet.com/www/journal/hbm2000/6169.html

Neville, H. (1991). Neurobiology of cognitive and language processing. Effects of early experience. In K. R. Gibson & A. C. Peterson (Eds.), *Brain maturation and cognitive development* (pp. 335–380). Hawthorne, NY: Aldine de Gruyter.

Neville, H. J., Mills, D. L., & Lawson, D. S. (1992). Fractionating language: Different neural subsystems with different sensitive periods. *Cerebral Cortex, 2,* 244–258.

Newman, A. J., Crina, D., Tomann, A., Bavelier, D., Jezzard, P., Braun, A., Clark, V., Mitchell, T., & Neville, H. J. (1998). Effects of age of acquisition on cortical organization for American sign language: An fMRI study. *NeuroImage, 7*(4, pt. 2), S194.

Nirkko, A. C., Baader, A. P., Loevblad, K.-O., Milani, P., & Wiesendanger, M. (2000). Cortical representation of music production in violin players: Behavioral assessment and functional imaging of finer sequencing, bimanual coordination and music specific brain activation. Retrieved January 31, 2001, from http://www.apnet.com/www/journal/hbm2000/6994.html

Nottebohm, F. (1994). The song circuits of the avian brain as a model system in which to study vocal learning, communication and manipulation. *Discussions in Neuroscience 10*(1–2), 72–81.

Nowicka, A., & Szatkowska, I. (2002). Sex-related differences in the modulation of event-related potentials by word repetition. Retrieved July 9, 2002, from http://fens2002.bordeaux.inserim.fr/pages/posters/R1/A008_16.html

Oberecker, R., Friedrich, M., & Friederici, A. D. (2005). Neural correlates of syntactic processing in two-year-olds. *Journal of Cognitive Neuroscience, 17*(10), 1667–1678.

Obler, K. L., & Gjerlow, K. (1999). *Language and the brain.* Cambridge: Cambridge University Press.

Obler, L. K., Zatorre, R. J., Galloway, L., & Vaid., J. (1982). Cerebral lateralization in bilinguals: Methodological issues. *Brain and Language, 15,* 40–54.

Obrzut, J. E., Boliek, C. A., & Obrzut, A. (1986). The effect of stimulus type and directed attention on dichotic listening with children. *Journal of Experimental Child Psychology, 41,* 198–209.

Ojemann, G. A. (1983). Brain organization for language from the perspective of electrical stimulation mapping. *Behavioral and Brain Sciences, 6,* 189–230.

Ojemann, G. A. (1994). Intraoperative investigations of the neurobiology of language. *Discussions in Neuroscience, 10*(1–2), 51–57.

Ojemann, G. A., & Whitaker, H. A. (1978). The bilingual brain. *Archives of Neurology, 35,* 409–412.

Oller, D. K. (2000). *The emergence of the speech capacity.* Mahwah, NJ: Lawrence Erlbaum Associates.

Ortigue, S., Michel, C. M., Murray, M. M., Mohr, C., Carbonnel, S., & Landis, T. (2004). Electrical neuroimaging reveals early generator modulation to emotional words. *Neuroimage, 21*(4), 1242–1251.

Palolahti, M., Leino, S., Jokela, M., Kopra, K., & Paavilainen, P. (2005). Event-related potential suggest early interaction between syntax and semantics during on-line sentence comprehension. *Neuroscience Letters, 384*(3), 222–227.

Pansini, M. (1988). Koncept gramatike prostora. *Govor, 5*(2), 117–128.

Pansini, M. (1995). Univerzalnost verbotonalnih zasada. *Govor, 12*(2), 125–134.

Pansini, M. (2002). http://www.suvag.hr/~mpansini

Papke, K., Hillebrand, E., Knecht, St., Deppe, M., & Heindel, W. (2000). Retest reliability of language lateralization using functional MRI. Retrieved January 31, 2001, from http://www.apnet.com/www/journal/hbm2000/6389.htm

Papps, B. P., Best, J. J. K., & O'Carroll, R. E. (2000). Semantic memory functioning and the left temporal lobe. *Neurocase, 6*(3), 179–192.

Paradis, M. (1994). Neurolinguistic aspects of implicit and explicit memory: Implications for bilingualism and second language acquisition. In N. Ellis (Ed.), *Implicit and explicit language learning* (pp. 393–419). London: Academic Press.

Paradis, M. (Ed.). (1995). *Aspects of bilingual aphasia.* New York: Pergamon.

Paradis, M. (2004). A neurolinguistic theory of bilingualism. Amsterdam: John Benjamins.

Parsons, L., Brown, S., Martinez, M., Hodges, D., Krumhansl, C., & Fox, P. (2002). Mapping musical invention in the brain. Retrieved July 9, 2002, from http://fens2002. bordeaux.inserim.fr/pages/posters/R3/A074_16.html

Payne, J. D., Jacobs, W. J., Hardt, O., Lopez, C., & Nadel, L. (2002). Stress and binding: A role for the hippocampus in contextual and episodic memory. Retrieved July 9, 2002, from http://fens2002.bordeaux.inserim.fr/pages/posters/R1/A008_17.html

Penfield, W., & Rasmussen, T. (1950). The cerebral cortex of man: A clinical study of the localization of function. New York: Macmillan.

Penfield, W., & Roberts, L. (1959). *Speech and brain mechanisms.* Princeton, NJ: Princeton University Press.

Perani, D., Dehaene, S., Grassi, F., Cohen, L., Cappa, S. F., & Dupoux, E. (1996). Brain processing of native and foreign languages. *NeuroReport, 7,* 2439–2444.

Perani, D., Paulesu, E., Galles, N. S., Dupoux, E., Dehaene, S., Bettinardi, V., Cappa, S. F., Fazio, F., & Mehler, J. (1998). The bilingual brain: Proficiency and age of acquisition of the second language. *Brain, 121,* 1841–1852.

Perlstein, W. M., Bradley, M. M., & Lang, P. J. (2000). fMRI evidence of affective influence on prefrontal cortex activity during working memory. Retrieved January 31, 2001, from http://www.apnet.com/www/journal/hbm2000/6192.html

Peters, M. (1992). Cerebral asymmetry for speech and the asymmetry in the path lengths for the right and left recurrent nerves. *Brain and Language, 43,* 349–352.

Petz, B. (Ed.). (1992). *Psihologijski rječnik.* Zagreb: Prosvjeta.

Pihan, H., Altenmüller, E., Hertrich, I., & Ackermann, H. (2000). Lateralization of affective speech processing depends on activation of the subvocal rehearsal system: A DC-potential study. Retrieved January 31, 2001, from http://www.apnet.com/www/journal/hbm2000/6534.html

Pinel, J. P. J. (2005). *Biopsychology* (4th ed.). Boston: Allyn & Bacon.

Plumet, J., Gil, R., & Gaonac, H. D. (2002). Neuropsychological assessment of possible change in memory and executive functions with advancing age. Retrieved July 9, 2002, from http://fens2002.bordeaux.inserim.fr/pages/posters/R1/A008_20.html

Porter, R. J., & Berlin, C. I. (1975). On interpreting developmental changes in the dichotic right-ear advantage. *Brain and Language, 2,* 186–200.

Posner, M. (1993). Seeing the mind. *Science, 262,* 673–674.

Posner, M. (1995). Modulation by instruction. *Nature, 373,* 198–199.

Posner, M., & Dehaene, S. (1994). Attentional networks. *Trends in Neurosciences, 17*(2), 75–79.

Posner, M. I., & Raichle, M. E. (1997). *Images of mind.* New York: Scientific American Library.

Pouratian, N., Bookheimer, S., O'Farrell, A., Sicotte, N., Cannestra, A., Becker, D., & Toga, A. (2000). Optical imaging of bilingual cortical representations. Retrieved January 31, 2001, from http://www.apnet.com/www/journal/hbm2000/6251.html

Pozojević-Trivanović, M. (1984). *Slušanje i govor.* Zagreb: Sveučilišna naklada Liber.

Praamstra, P., & Stegeman, D. F. (1993). Phonological effects on the auditory N400 event-related brain potential. *Cognitive Brain Research, 1,* 73–86.

Premack, D., & Premack, A. J. (1994). How "Theory of Mind" constrains language and communication. *Discussions in Neuroscience, 10*(1–2), 93–105.

Preston, M. S., & Lambert, W. E. (1969). Interlingual interference in a bilingual version of the Stroop colour-word task. *Journal of Verbal Learning and Verbal Behavior, 8,* 295–301.

Proverbio, A. M., Leoni, G., & Zani, A. (2004). Language switching mechanisms in simultaneous interpreters: an ERP study. *Neuropsychologia, 42*(12), 1636–1656.

Pu, Y., Lu, H.-L., Feng, C.-M., Tan, L. H., Xiong, J., Spinks, J. A., Perfetti, Ch. A., Fox, P. T., & Gao, J.-H. (2000). Comparison of brain response in the processing of Chinese and English languages: An event-related fMRI study. Retrieved January 31, 2001, from http://www.apnet.com/www/journal/hbm2000/5942.html

Pulvermüller, F. (1992). Constituents of a neurological theory of language. *Concepts in Neuroscience, 3*(2), 157–200.

Purves, D., Augustine, G. J., Fitzpatrick, D., Katz, L. C., LaMantia, A.-S., McNamara, J., & Williams, M. S. (Eds.). (2001). *Neuroscience* (2nd ed.). Sunderland, MA: Sinauer Associates.

Raichle, M. E. (1994). Positron emission tomographic studies of verbal response selection. *Discussions in Neuroscience 10*(1–2), 130–136.

Rajah, M. N., & Mcintosh, A. R. (2005). Overlap in the functional neural systems involved in semantic and episodic memory retrieval. *Journal of Cognitive Neuroscience, 17*(3), 470–482.

Ramsey, N., Sommer, I., & Kahn, R. (2000). Combining language tasks in fMRI analysis improves reliability of the derived laterality index. Retrieved January 31, 2001, from http://www.apnet.com/www/journal/hbm2000/6643.html

Rapp, A. M., Leube, D. T., Erb, M., Grodd, W., & Kircher, T. T. (2004). Neural correlates of metaphor processing. *Brain Research. Cognitive Brain Research, 20*(3), 395–402.

Rasmussen, T., & Milner, B. (1977). The role of early left-brain injury in determining lateralization of cerebral speech functions. *Annals of the New York Academy of Sciences, 299,* 355–369.

Rauschecker, J. P. (1995). Compensatory plasticity and sensory substitution in the cerebral cortex. *Trends in Neuroscience, 18*(1), 36–43.

Remez, R. E. (2005). Perceptual organization of speech. In D. B. Pisoni & R. E. Remez (Eds.), *The handbook of speech perception* (pp. 28–50). Oxford: Blackwell.

Repp, B. H (1977). Measuring laterality effects in dichotic listening. *Journal of the Acoustical Society of America, 62*(3), 720–737.

Riecker, A., Ackermann, H., Wildgruber, D., & Grodd, W. (2000). Lateralized fMRI activation at the level of the anterior insula during speaking and singing. Retrieved January 31, 2001, from http://www.apnet.com/www/journal/hbm2000/6621.htm

Ringo, J. L., Doty, R. W., Demeter, S., & Simard, P. Y. (1994). Time is of the essence: A conjecture that the hemispheric specialization arises from interhemispheric conduction delay. *Cerebral Cortex, 4,* 331–343.

Rivera-Gaxiola, M., Csibra, G., Johnson, M. H., & Karmiloff-Smith, A. (2000). Electrophysiological correlates of cross-linguistic speech perception in native English speakers. *Behavioural Brain Research, 111*(1–2), 13–23.

Rizzolatti, G., & Arbib, M. A. (1998). Language within our grasp. *Trends in Neuroscience, 21,* 188–194.

Rizzolatti, G., & Craighero, L. (2004). The mirror-neuron system. *Annual Review of Neuroscience, 27,* 169–192.

Rodriguez-Fornells, A., van der Lugt, A., Rotte, M., Britti, B., Heinze, H-J., & Münte, T. F. (2005). Second language interferes with word production in fluent bilinguals: Brain potential and functional magnetic imaging evidence. *Journal of Cognitive Neuroscience, 17*(3), 422–433.

Romaine, S. (1989). *Bilingualism*. London: Blackwell.

Rose, S. P. R. (1995). Molecular mechanisms in memory formation. *The Biochemist,* October/November, 9–12.

Rosenblum, L. D. (2005). Primacy of multimodal speech perception. In D. B. Pisoni & R. E. Remez (Eds.), *The handbook of speech perception* (pp. 51–78). Oxford: Blackwell Publishing.

Rossell, S. L., Bullmore, E. T., Williams, S. C. R., & David, A. S. (2002). Sex differences in functional brain activation during a lexical visual field task. *Brain and Language, 80,* 97–105.

Rossini, P. (2002). Sensorimotor cortical reorganization: Clinical perspectives. Retrieved July 9, 2002, from http://fens2002.bordeaux.inserim.fr/pages/posters/R12500/R12876.html

Rossion, B., Bodart, J. M., Pourtois, G., Thioux, M., Bol, A., Cosnard, G., Benoit, G., Michel, C., & De Volder, A. (2000). Functional imaging of visual semantic processing in the human brain. *Cortex, 36*(4), 579–591.

Runjić, D. (1996). Prikaz rada "Oporavak motoričkih funkcija nakon moždane kapi: Pozitronska emisijska tomografija." *Cerebrovascular diseases,* 1995, 5, 282–291). *Verbotonalni razgovori, 12,* 4–7.

Rupp, A., Hack, S., Schneider, P., Stippich, C., & Scherg, M. (2000). Auditory-evoked fields reflect psychoacoustic thresholds of temporal gap detection. Retrieved January 31, 2001, from http://www.apnet.com/www/journal/hbm2000/6299.html

Rutten, G.-J., van Rijen, P., van Veelen, C., & Ramsey, N. (2000). Test-retest reliability of fMRI measurement of language lateralization is improved by combined task analysis. Retrieved January 31, 2001, from http://www.apnet.com/www/journal/hbm2000/6676.html

Salmelin, R., Schnitzler, A., Schmitz, F., & Freund, H.-J. (2000). Single word reading in developmental stutterers and fluent speakers. *Brain, 123*(6), 1184–1202.

Satz, P., Bakker, D. J., Teunissen, J., Goebel, R., & Van der Vlugt, H. (1975). Developmental parameters of the ear asymmetry: A multivariate approach. *Brain and Language, 2,* 171–185.

Saur, R., Erb, M., Grodd, W., & Kammer, T. (2002). Is there domain specificity in prefrontal working memory areas? An event-related fMRI study. Retrieved July 9, 2002, from http://fens2002.bordeaux.inserim.fr/pages/posters/R1/A009_13.html

Saygin, A. P., Wilson, S. M., Dronkers, N. F., & Bates, E. (2004). Action comprehension in aphasia: Linguistic and nonlinguistic deficits and their lesion correlates. *Neuropsychologia, 42*(13), 1788–1804.

Saykin, A., Flashman, L., Johnson, S., Santulli, R., Wishart, H., Baxter, L., Guerin, St., Weaver, J., & Mamourian, A. (2000). Frontal and hippocampal memory circuitry in early Alzheimer's disease: Relation of structural and functional MRI changes. Retrieved January 31, 2001, from http://www.apnet.com/www/journal/hbm2000/6910.html

Schacter, D. L. (2000). Understanding implicit memory: A cognitive neuroscience approach. In M. S. Gazzaniga (Ed.), *Cognitive neuroscience: A reader* (pp. 305–323). Oxford: Blackwell.

Scheef, L., Kuhl, C. K., Neugebauer, U., Schoeb, Y., & Schild, H. H. (2000). Is the new selective Wernicke paradigm really selective for Wernicke's area? Retrieved January 31, 2001, from http://www.apnet.com/www/journal/hbm2000/6526.html

Scheich, H., Ohl, W., & Brechmann, A. (2002). Pattern analysis, discrimination learning and categorization of frequency modulations in rodent and human auditory cortex. Retrieved July 9, 2002, from http://fens2002.bordeaux.inserim.fr/pages/posters/R10500/R10620.html

Schmidt, D., Weiss, P. H., Amorim, M. A., Shah, J., Fink, G., Berthoz, A., Krause, B. J., & Müller-Gärtner, H. W. (2002). Cerebral representation of visuospatial working memory introducing 3D. Retrieved July 9, 2002, from http://fens2002.bordeaux.inserim.fr/pages/posters/R1/A009_14.html

Schmitt, B. M., Muente, T. F., & Kutas, M. (2000). Electrophysiological estimates of the time course of semantic and phonological encoding during implicit picture naming *Psychophysiology, 37*(4), 473–484.

Schönwiesner, M., Von Cramon, D. Y., & Rübsamen, R. (2002). Is it tonotopy after all? Retrieved July 9, 2002, from http://fens2002.bordeaux.inserim.fr/pages/posters/R6/A184_16.html

Scoville, W. B., & Milner, B. (2000). Loss of recent memory after bilateral hippocampal lesions. In M. S. Gazzaniga (Ed.), *Cognitive neuroscience: A reader* (pp. 262–279). Oxford: Blackwell.

Searleman, A. (1980). Subject variables and cerebral organization for language. *Cortex, 16*(2), 239–254.

Seidenberg, M. S., & McClelland, J. L. (1989). A distributed, developmental model of word recognition and naming. *Psychological Review, 96,* 523–568.

Seikel, J. A., King, D. W., & Drumright, D. G. (1997). *Anatomy and physiology for speech, language and hearing.* San Diego: Singular.

Shankweiler, D., & Studdert-Kennedy, M. (1975). A continuum of lateralization for speech perception? *Brain and Language, 2,* 212–225.

Shatz, C.J. (1992). The developing brain. *Scientific American,* September, 61–67.

Shaywitz, B. A., Shaywitz, S. E., Pugh, K. R., Constable, R. T., Skudlarski, P., Fulbright, R. K., Bronen, R. A., Fletcher, J. M., Shankweiler, D. P., Katz, L., & Gore, J. C. (1995). Sex differences in the functional organization of the brain for language. *Nature, 373,* 607–609.

Shaywitz, B., Shaywitz, S., Pugh, K., Mencl, E., Fulbright, R., Constable, R., Skudlarski, P., Jenner, A., Letcher, J., Marchione, K., Shankweiler, D., Katz, L., Lacadie, C., & Gore, J. (2000). Disruption of posterior brain systems for reading in children with developmental dyslexia. Retrieved January 31, 2001, from http://www.apnet.com/www/journal/hbm2000/5923.html

Shergill, S. S., Brammer, M. J., Williams, S., Murray, R., & McGuire, P. (2000). Mapping auditory hallucinations in schizophrenia using functional magnetic resonance imaging. *Archives of General Psychiatry, 57*(11), 1033–1038.

Sherwin, B. B. (2003). Estrogen and cognitive functioning in women. *Endocrine Reviews, 24,* 133–151.

Shtyrov, Y., Kujala, T., Lyytinen, H., Ilmoniemi, R. J., & Naatanen, R. (2000a). Auditory cortex evoked magnetic fields and lateralization of speech processing. *Neuroreport, 11*(13), 2893–2896.

Shtyrov, Y., Kujala, T., Palva, S., Ilmoniemi, R. J., & Naatanen, R. (2000b). Left hemisphere's dominance in speech processing is not entirely based on acoustic structure of speech sounds. Retrieved January 31, 2001, from http://www.apnet.com/www/journal/hbm2000/6405.html

Simon, G., Bernard, C., Lalonde, R., & Rebai, M. (2002). Electrophysiological and behavioral study in the processing of visual word recognition. Retrieved July 9, 2002, from http://fens2002.bordeaux.inserim.fr/pages/posters/R3/A074_21.html

Simon-Thomas, E., Role, K. O., & Knight, R. T. (2005). Behavioral and electrophysiological evidence of a right hemisphere bias for the influence of negative emotion on higher cognition. *Journal of Cognitive Neuroscience 17*(3), 518–529.

Singer, W. (1995). Development and plasticity of cortical processing architectures. *Science, 270,* 758–764.

Singh, M. (1990). Lateralized interference in concurrent manual activity: Influence of age in children. *International Journal of Neuroscience, 50*(1–2), 55–58.

Škarić, I. (1991). Fonetika hrvatskoga književnog jezika. In S. Babić, D. Brozović, M. Moguš, S. Pavešić, I. Šakrić, & S. Težak (Eds.), *Povijesni pregled, glasovi i oblici hrvatskoga književnog jezika* (pp. 61–377). Zagreb: HAZU, Globus.

Sommer, I. E. C., Aleman, A., Bouma, A., & Kahn, R. S. (2004). Do women really have more bilateral language representation than men? A meta-analysis of functional imaging studies. *Brain, 127,* 8, 1845–1852.

Sommer, I. E. C., Aleman, A. & Kahn, R. S. (2005). Reply to "Time-resolved sex differences in language lateralization." *Brain, 128,* E29.

Sparks, R., & Geschwind, N. (1968). Dichotic listening in man after section of neocortical commissures. *Cortex, 4,* 3–16.

Specht, K., Holterl, C., Schnitker, R., Weis, S., Herzog, H., Krause, B. J., & Huber, W. (2000a). Right hemisphere activations after stroke: A PET study. Retrieved January 31, 2001, from http://www.apnet.com/www/journal/hbm2000/

Specht, K., Shah, N. J., & Jäncke, L. (2000b). Bilateral inferior frontal networks are involved in speech perception processes. Retrieved January 31, 2001, from http://www.apnet.com/www/journal/hbm2000/6298.html

Sperry, R. W. (1981). Some effects of disconnecting the cerebral hemispheres (Nobel lecture). Retrieved February 28, 2006, from http://nobelprize.org/medicine/laureates/1981/sperry-lecture.html

Spreen, O., Tupper, D., Risser, A., Tuokko, H., & Edgell, D. (1984). *Human developmental neuropsychology.* New York: Oxford University Press.

Springer, S. P., & Deutsch, G. (1997). *Left brain, right brain.* (5th ed.). New York: W. H. Freeman.

Squire, L. R., & Zola, S. M. (2000). Episodic memory, semantic memory, and amnesia. In M. S. Gazzaniga (Ed.), *Cognitive neuroscience: A reader* (pp. 280–291). Oxford: Blackwell.

Starreveld, P. A. (2000). On the interpretation of onsets of auditory context effects in word production. *Journal of Memory and Language, 42*(4), 497–525.

Staudt, M., Niemann, G., Erb, M., Wildgruber, D., Kraegeloh-Mann, I., & Grodd, W. (2000). Bilateral language organization in congenital right hemiparesis—different contributions from left and right hemisphere. Retrieved January 31, 2001, from http://www.apnet.com/www/journal/hbm2000/6143.html

Stenberg, G., Lindgren, M., Johansson, M., Olsson, A., & Rosen, I. (2000). Semantic processing without conscious identification: Evidence from event-related potentials. *Journal of Experimental Psychology: Learning, Memory, and Cognition, 26*(4), 973–1004.

Sternberg, R. J. (2003). *Cognitive psychology* (3rd ed.). Belmont, CA: Wadsworth.

Stickler, D., Gilmore, R., Rosenbek, J. C., & Donovan, N. J. (2003). Dysphagia with bilateral lesions of the insular cortex. *Dysphagia, 18*(3), 179–181.

Stowe, L. A. (2000). Sentence comprehension and the left inferior frontal gyrus: Storage, not computation (Commentary). *The Behavioral and Brain Sciences, 23*(1), 51.

Strange, P. (1995). What is so special about the brain, anyway? *The Biochemist,* October/November, 4–8.

Stryker, M. P. (1995). Growth through learning. *Nature, 375,* 277–278.

Studdert-Kennedy, M., & Shankweiler, D. (1970). Hemispheric specialization for speech perception. *Journal of the Acoustical Society of America, 48,* 579–594.

Suchan, B., Gayk, A. E., & Daum, I. (2002). Topographic ERP correlates of visuospatial working memory. Retrieved July 9, 2002, from http://fens2002.bordeaux.inserim.fr/pages/posters/R1/A009_15.html

Sussman, H. (1994). Let's get down to the "wetware" and look at evolutionarily motivated mechanisms. *Behavioral and Brain Sciences, 17*(1), 182–183.

Sussman, H., Franklin, P., & Simon, T. (1982). Bilingual speech: Bilateral control? *Brain and Language, 15,* 125–142.

Suzuki, M., Asada, Y., Ito, J., Hayashi, K., Inoue, H., & Kitano, H. (2003). Activation of cerebellum and basal ganglia on volitional swallowing detected by functional magnetic resonance imaging. *Dysphagia, 18*(2), 71–77.

Swaab, D. F., & Hofman, M. A. (1995). Sexual differentiation of the human hypothalamus in relation to gender and sexual orientation. *Trends in Neuroscience, 18,* 264–270.

Syka, J., Popelar, J., Nwabueze-Ogbo, F. C., Kvasnak, E., & Suta, D. (2002). Processing of acoustical signals in the inferior colliculus and the effects of functional ablation of the auditory cortex. Retrieved July 9, 2002, from http://fens2002.bordeaux.inserim.fr/pages/posters/R12000/R12392.html

Tadinac-Babić, M. (1994). *Ispitivanje lateralizacije funkcija mozgovnih hemisfera tehnikom podijeljenog vidnog polja.* Unpublished dissertation, Filozofski fakultet Sveučilišta u Zagrebu.

Tadinac-Babić, M. (1999). Ispitivanje lateralizacije funkcija mozgovnih hemisfera tehnikom pvp uz korištenje verbalnog materijala. *Govor, 16,* 57–68.

Takahashi, H., Ejiri, T., Nakao, M., Nakamura, N., Kaga, K., & Herve, T. (2002). Auditory evoked-potential mappings unravel functional organizations of rat auditory cortex; both the primary auditory field (A1) and anterior auditory field (AAF) show tonotopic organization and the latter has extreme loudness-dependence. Retrieved July 9, 2002, from http://fens2002.bordeaux.inserim.fr/pages/posters/R6/A184_18.html

Tamamaki, K. (1993). Language dominance in bilinguals' arithmetic operations according to their language use. *Language Learning, 43,* (2), 239–262.

Tan, L. H., Spinks, J. A., Gao, J.-H., Liu, H.-L., Perfetti, C. A., Xiong, J., Stofer, K. A., Pu, Y., Liu, Y., & Fox, P. T. (2000). Hemispheric asymmetry in reading Chinese characters and words: Functional MRI findings. Retrieved January 31, 2001, from http://www.apnet.com/www/journal/hbm2000/5941.html

Tandon, N., Fox, P., Ingham, R., Ingham, J., Collins, J., Pridgen, S., & Lancaster, J. (2000). TMS induced modulation of cerebral blood flow in stutterers. Retrieved January 31, 2001, from http://www.apnet.com/www/journal/hbm2000/6161.html

Tarkka, I. M. (2000). Difficulties in semantic category formation in aphasia are reflected in event-related potentials. Retrieved January 31, 2001, from http://www.apnet.com/www/journal/hbm2000/

Tasko, S. M., Kent, R. D., & Westbury, J. R. (2002). Variability in tongue movement kinematics during normal liquid swallowing. *Dysphagia, 17*(2), 126–138.

Taylor, K. I., Meier, E., Brugger, P., & Weniger, D. (2002). Right hemispheric competency for idiomatic and metaphoric language. Retrieved July 9, 2002, from http://fens2002.bordeaux.inserim.fr/pages/posters/R3/A074_23.html

Thach, W. T., Mink, J. W., Goodkin, H. P., & Keating, J. G. (2000). Combining versus Gating Motor Programs: Different Roles for Cerebellum and Basal Ganglia? In M. S. Gazzaniga (Ed.), *Cognitive neuroscience: A reader* (pp. 366–375). Oxford: Blackwell.

Thierry, G., Cardebat, D., & Demonet, J.-F. (2000). Semantics versus syntax race: semantics first at start up and second at finish. Retrieved January 31, 2001, from http://www.apnet.com/www/journal/hbm2000/6652.html

Thompson, R. F. (1993). *The brain: A neuroscience primer.* (2nd ed.). New York: W. H. Freeman.

Toepel, U., & Alter, K. (2002). Cerebral strategies in the segmentation and interpretation of speech. ISCA Archive, http://www.isca-speech.org/archive/sp2002/sp02_071.pdf

Tompkins, C. A., Lehman, M. T., Baumgaertner, A., Fossett, T. R. D., & Vance, J. E. (1996). Suppression and discourse comprehension in right brain-damaged adults: Inferential ambiguity processing. *Brain and Language, 55,* 172–175.

Tong, Y., Gandour, J., Talavage, T., Wong, D., Dzemidzic, M., Xu, Y., et al. (2005). Neural circuitry underlying sentence-level linguistic prosody. *Neuroimage, 28*(2), 417–428.

Tsunoda, T. (1975). Functional differences between right- and left-cerebral hemispheres detected by the key-tapping method. *Brain and Language, 2,* 152–170.

Turdiu, J. (1990). *Klinička neuropsihologija.* Zagreb: Školska knjiga.

Turner, R., & Frackowiak, R. (1995). Functional brain mapping. *The Biochemist,* 25–29.

Ungerleider, L. G. (1995). Functional brain imaging studies of cortical mechanisms of memory. *Science, 270,* 769–775.

Vaid, J. (1983). Bilingualism and brain lateralization. In S. Segalowitz (Ed.), *Language functions and brain organization* (pp. 315–339). New York: Academic Press.

Van Boven, R. W., Ingeholm, J. E., Beauchamp, M. S., Bikle, Ph. C., & Ungerleider, L. G. (2005). Tactile form and location processing in the human brain [Electronic version]. *Proceedings of the National Academy of Sciences of the USA, 102*(35), 12601–12605.

van der Veen, F. M., Jennings, J. R., Meltzer, C. C., Muldoon, M. F., Ryan, C. M., Townsend, D. W., & Price, J. C. (2000). Hypertension and cerebral blood flow during cognitive tasks: A PET investigation. Retrieved January 31, 2001, from http://www.apnet.com/www/journal/hbm2000/6136.html

Van Lieshout, P., Renier, W., Eling, P., & de Bot, K. (1990). Bilingual language processing after a lesion in the left thalamic and temporal region: A case report with early childhood onset. *Brain and Language, 38*(2), 173–194.

Vargha-Khadem, F., Gadian, D. G., Copp, A., & Mishkin, M. (2005). FoxP2 and the neuroanatomy of speech and language. *Nature reviews (Neuroscience) 6,* 131–138.

Varley, R. A., Klessinger, N. J. C., Romanowski, C. A. J., & Siegal, M. (2005). *Proceedings of the National Academy of Sciences of the USA, 102,* 3519–3524.

Verchinski, B., Meyer-Lindenberg, A., Japee, Sh., Kohn, Ph., Egan, M., Bigelow, L., Callicott, J., Bertolino, A., Mattay, V., Bergman, K., & Weinberger, D. (2000). Gender differences in gray matter density: A study of structural MRI images using voxel-based morphometry. Retrieved January 31, 2001, from http://www.apnet.com/www/journal/hbm2000/7206.html

Vlachos, F., & Karapetsas, A. (2002). Electrophysiological and psychological study in children with dysgraphia. Retrieved July 9, 2002, from http://fens2002.bordeaux.inserim.fr/pages/posters//R1/A008_26.html

Volberg, G., & Hubner, R. (2004). On the role of response conflicts and stimulus position for hemispheric differences in global/local processing: An ERP study. *Neuropsychologia, 42*(13), 1805–1813.

von Koss Torkildsen, J. (2002). Functional lateralization of the processing of intonation in Norwegian—a dichotic listening experiment. Retrieved February 5, 2003, from http://folk.uio.no/janneto/300kopi/300kopi.html

Votaw, M. (1992). A functional view of bilingual lexicosemantic organization. In R. J. Harris (Ed.), *Cognitive processing in bilinguals* (pp. 299–321). Amsterdam: North-Holland.

Vuletić, D. (1987). *Govorni poremećaji: Izgovor.* Zagreb: Školska knjiga.

Vuletić, D. (1993). Lingvističke značajke afazija. *Govor, 10*(1), 89–100.

Walter, H., Blankenhorn, M., Groen, G., Schaefer, S., Wunderlich, A., Tomczak, R., & Spitzer, M. (2000). Altered neural activation patterns in schizophrenic patients during a verbal and a visuospatial working memory task: An fMRI study. Retrieved January 31, 2001, from http://www.apnet.com/www/journal/hbm2000/6710.html

Wang, Y., Oertel, U., Mayer, M., Herrmann, C. S., Maess, B., & Friederici, A. D. (2000a). MEG source localization of early syntactic processes. Retrieved January 31, 2001, from http://www.apnet.com/www/journal/hbm2000/

Wang, Y. P., Sakuma, K., & Kakigi, R. (2000b). The dynamic processes for word and picture encoding in the human brain as revealed by magnetoencephalography. *Neuroscience Letters, 289*(2), 135–138.

Warren, J. D., Smith, H. B., Denson, L. A., & Waddy, H. M. (2000). Expressive language disorder after infarction of left lentiform nucleus. *Journal of Clinical Neuroscience, 7*(5), 456–458.

Watamori, T. S., & Sasanuma, S. (1978). The recovery process of two English–Japanese bilingual aphasics. *Brain and Language, 6,* 127–140.

Watanabe, Y., Abe, S., Ishikawa, T., Yamada, Y., & Yamane, G. Y. (2004). Cortical regulation during the early stage of initiation of voluntary swallowing in humans. *Dysphagia, 19*(2), 100–108.

Weber-Fox, C., Davis, L. J., & Cuadrado, E. (2003). Event-related brain potential markers of high-language proficiency in adults. *Brain and Language, 85*(2), 231–244.

Webster, D. B. (1995). *Neuroscience of communication.* San Diego: Singular.

Weinberger, N. M. (2004). Specific long-term memory traces in primary auditory cortex. *Nature reviews (Neuroscience), 5,* 279–290.

Weismer, G. (1997). Motor speech disorders. In W. J. Hardcastle & J. Laver (Eds.), *The handbook of phonetic sciences* (pp. 191–219). Oxford: Blackwell.

Weniger, D., Crelier, G. R., Alkadhi, H., & Kollias, S. S. (2000). Picture-word matching as a paradigm in determining regions of language processing: An fMRI study. Retrieved January 31, 2001, from http://www.apnet.com/www/journal/hbm2000/6599.html

Westbury, C. (1998). Research strategies (psychological and psycholinguistic methods in neurolinguistics). In B. Stemmer & H. Whitaker (Eds.), *Handbook of neurolinguistics* (pp. 83–93). San Diego, CA: Academic Press.

Whitaker, H. A. (1995). Roots: Five notes on the history of neurolinguistics. In K. Elenius & P. Branderud (Eds.), *Proceedings of the XIIIth International Congress of Phonetic Sciences, 2,* 164–171.

Whitaker, H. A. (1998a). Neurolinguistics from the Middle Ages to the Pre-Modern Era: Historical vignettes. In B. Stemmer & H. Whitaker (Eds.), *Handbook of neurolinguistics* (pp. 27–54). San Diego, CA: Academic Press.

Whitaker, H. A. (1998b). Electrical stimulation mapping of language cortex. In B. Stemmer & H. Whitaker (Eds.), *Handbook of neurolinguistics* (pp. 125–130). San Diego, CA: Academic Press.

Willmes, K. (1998). Methodological and statistical considerations in cognitive neurolinguistics. In B. Stemmer & H. Whitaker (Eds.), *Handbook of neurolinguistics* (pp. 57–70). San Diego, CA: Academic Press.

Wuillemin, D., Richardson, B., & Lynch, J. (1994). Right hemisphere involvement in processing later-learned languages in multilinguals. *Brain and Language, 46,* 620–636.

Xiong, J., Stofer, K. A., Pu, Y., Liu, H.-L., Tan, L. H., Gao, J.-H., & Fox, P. T. (2000). Different language processing strategy and neural pathways for Chinese speakers. Retrieved January 31, 2001, from http://www.apnet.com/www/journal/hbm2000/6500.html

Xu, J., Kemeny, S., Park, G., Frattali, C., & Braun, A. (2005). Language in context: emergent features of word, sentence, and narrative comprehension. *Neuroimage, 25*(3), 1002–1015.

Xu, J., Yamaguchi, S., Kobayashi, S., Yamashita, K., & Takahashi, K. (2000). Cerebral activation during numerical calculation—A functional MRI study. Retrieved January 31, 2001, from http://www.apnet.com/www/journal/hbm2000/

Yamamoto, S., Kashikura, K., Kershaw, J., & Kanno, I. (2000). Visual mental imagery of a letter of alphabet: A functional magnetic resonance imaging study. Retrieved January 31, 2001, from http://www.apnet.com/www/journal/hbm2000/6559.html

Yokoyama, S., Okamoto, H., Miyamoto, T., Yoshimoto, K., Kim, J., Iwata, K., Jeong, H., Uchida, S., Ikuta, N., Sassa, Y., Nakamura, W., Horie, K., Sato, S., & Kawashima, R. (2006). Cortical activation in the processing of passive sentences in L1 and L2: An fMRI study. *Neuroimage, 30*(2), 570–579.

Yovel, G., Levy, J., Grabowecky, M., & Paller, K. A. (2003). Neural correlates of the left-visual-field superiority in face perception appear at multiple stages of face processing. *Journal of Cognitive Neuroscience, 15*(3), 462–474.

Zaidel, E. (1983). Disconnection syndrome as a model for laterality effects in the normal brain. In J. B. Hellige (Ed.), *Cerebral hemisphere asymmetry: Method, theory and application* (pp. 95–115). New York: Praeger Press.

Zaidel, E. (1985). Introduction. In F. D. Benson & E. Zaidel (Eds.), *The dual brain: Hemispheric specialization in humans* (pp. 47–63). London: Guilford Press.

Zaidel, E., Zaidel, D. W., & Bogen, J. E. (2005). The split brain. Retrieved July 18, 2005, from http://www.its.caltech.edu/~jbogen/text/ref130.htm

Zarevski, P. (1994). *Psihologija pamćenja i učenja.* Jastrebarsko: Naklada Slap.

Zatorre, R. J. (1989). On the representation of multiple languages in the brain: Old problems and new directions. *Brain and Language, 36,* 127–147.

Zavoreo, I., & Demarin, V. (2004). Breath holding index in the evaluation of cerebral vasoreactivity. *Acta Clinica Croatica, 43,* 15–19.

Zeffiro, T., Eden, G., Jones, K., & Brown, C. (2000). Evidence for involvement of an articulatory motor loop in phonological processing. Retrieved January 31, 2001, from http://www.apnet.com/www/journal/hbm2000/7230.html

Zeki, S. (1992). The visual image in mind and brain. *Scientific American, 267*(3), 69–76.

Zhang, W., Ma, L., Li, D., & Weng, X. (2000). Brain mapping of reading Chinese character and number. Retrieved January 31, 2001, from http://www.apnet.com/www/journal/hbm2000/7184.html

Author Index

Subject Index

C

U